THE TRANSFORMATION OF SOUTHEAST ASIAN ECONOMIES

The Transformation of Southeast Asian Economies

Teofilo C. Daquila

Nova Science Publishers, Inc.
New York

For permission to use material from this book please contact us:
Telephone 631-231-7269; Fax 631-231-8175
Web Site: http://www.novapublishers.com

LIBRARY OF CONGRESS CATALOGING-IN-PUBLICATION DATA

Daquila, Teofilo C.
Economic transition of Southeast Asia / Teofilo C. Daquila.
p. cm.
Includes bibliographical references and index.
ISBN 13 978-1-60021-108-9
ISBN 10 1-60021-108-9
1. Southeast Asia--Economic policy. 2. Southeast Asia--Economic conditions. I. Title.
HC441.D357 2006
338.959--dc22 2006007860

Published by Nova Science Publishers, Inc. ✦ New York

For Grace and Debbie
My critics and best friends

CONTENTS

PREFACE

This is a book on the economics and economic relations of Southeast Asia. It analyzes the growth, development and crisis experiences of the Southeast Asian economies, in particular, Indonesia, Malaysia, the Philippines, Singapore and Thailand. It also deals with the external relations of Southeast Asia: within the ASEAN regional grouping and ASEAN's external trade and investment relations. It is written by an insider - a Southeast Asian specialist from within the region - based on his teaching, research and consulting activities.

The book has the following features. First, it is developed based on the proposition that the robust economic performance of the Southeast Asian economies during the past four decades has been attributed to the various factors, developments and independent national policies which have been pursued by the individual member countries rather than to any regional economic framework. The Association of Southeast Asian Nations (ASEAN) was formed in 1967 by the five founding members, namely, Indonesia, Malaysia, the Philippines, Singapore and Thailand (also known as ASEAN-5). Brunei joined in 1984 and Vietnam, in 1995. Laos and Myanmar were admitted in 1997 and Cambodia, in 1999. Until 1992, the ASEAN economic cooperation, however, was generally viewed as weak since regional cooperative schemes on trade, industry, banking and agriculture, to name a few, were ineffective and underutilized. However, following the ASEAN Summit in Singapore in 1992, the regional initiatives have been strengthened including the adoption of trade liberalization measures which will result in the ASEAN Free Trade Area (AFTA).

Second, the book covers eleven topics which is suitable for a one-semester course on the economics and economic relations of Southeast Asia. Third, it has a narrow area coverage as it focuses only on the five economies in Southeast Asia such as Indonesia, Malaysia, the Philippines, Singapore, and Thailand. Thus, based on these two points, the book has an advantage of being focused and condensed in terms of topic coverage, and narrow in terms of area coverage.

Fourth, the composition of the book and the approach followed in writing it provide additional plus points. A macro picture of growth and development is presented in the first part, followed by a micro or sectoral approach in the second part (the domestic sector) and in the third part (the external sector). The fourth part provides a comprehensive account of the causes and impact of the 1997/98 economic crisis on the four sectors in the economy such as the production, financial, external and labor sectors. The sectoral treatment of the crisis impact and the analytical treatment of policy responses to the crisis differentiate this book from other publications on the same topic.

Finally, this book provides an analysis of national developments, policies and factors which have contributed to the economic transformation of the respective Southeast Asian economies. Those are the five features which this book provides to the students and readers. It is recommended as a textbook for courses on Southeast Asian economics and other development economics courses with Southeast Asian orientation. It is certainly useful to other readers interested in Southeast Asia.

Teofilo C. DAQUILA
Southeast Asian Studies Programme, National University of Singapore
May 2006

ACKNOWLEDGEMENTS

This book would have not been possible without the support and assistance extended to me by the many individuals and institutions in various parts of the world for my academic, teaching and research activities. I would like to thank the students and participants at various universities and institutions where materials in this book have been utilized including the National University of Singapore, the Institute of Asian Studies (USA), the University of Melbourne (Australia), the Institute of Southeast Asian Studies (Singapore), George Washington University (GWU), and Chulalongkorn University (Thailand).

I would like to thank the following people at the National University of Singapore for their help in one way or another: Professors Brenda Yeoh, Reynaldo Ileto, Lily Kong, Tan Tai Yong, Ernest Chew, Yong Mun Cheong, Victor Savage, Dodo Thampapillai, Tilak Abeysinghe, Goh Beng Lan, John Miksic, Anne Pakir, Lysa Hong, Alan Chan, Hui Weng Tat, Albert Lau, John Richardson, Paulin Straughan and Chua Beng Huat..

I also acknowledge the research grant extended to me by the National University of Singapore (Faculty Research Grant # R-117-000-006-112) and the Lee Foundation Singapore. I am also thankful for the visiting fellowship awards and other forms of assistance from the various institutions which have enabled me to conduct my research activities related to the book. These include the Nordic Institute of Asian Studies (NIAS), Australian National University (Economics Division, Research School of Pacific and Asian Studies), El Colegio de Mexico's (Center for Africa and Asian Studies), Ludwig-Maximilians Universität München (Center for Economic Studies), the Malaysian Institute of Economic Research, Thai Development Research Institute, Philippine Institute for Development Studies, University of the Philippines School of Economics, Yuchengco Center, Rizal Commercial Banking Corporation, Bank of the Philippine Islands, Institute of Southeast Asian Studies, the ASEAN Secretariat, ASEAN University Network, Korea Association of Southeast Asian Studies, Korea University's Graduate School of International Studies, and Korea Institute of International Economic Policy.

In order to present and discuss the various parts of this book, I was able to solicit the generous assistance of the various institutions for hosting my seminar presentations in various parts of the world including: Geschwister-Scholl-Institut fur Politische Wissenschaft (Munich), Stiftung Wissenschfat Und Politik (Ebenhausen), Sciences-Po Asia-Europe Program at the University of Paris, International Institute for Asian Studies (Leiden), the Center for Pacific and Asian Studies (Stockholm), University of Malaya's Department of Applied Economics, Vienna Institute for International Economic Studies, Center for the

Study of International Institutions (Austria), and Samsung Economic Research Institute (Korea).

I have also benefited from the many authors and publications cited in this book. Thanks are also due to Akhmad Bayhaqi and Ang Chin Hong for their excellent research assistance in terms of updating the data.

I am also grateful to my past and present colleagues and friends in the Southeast Asian Studies Programme at the National University of Singapore, particularly Rohani binte Jantan, Lucy Tan and Rohani binte Sungib for their kind help in their own ways.

Finally, my warmest thanks and appreciation to my loving wife and daughter for their love, support, encouragement and prayers without which this book would have not been completed. Thanks also to Tatay, Ina po, Papa, Mama, Inay, my brothers and sisters, and my friends particularly Nic and Lina Cabaneiro, Merlyne and Oca Paunlagui, Mahen and Punita Mahendrarajah, and Myrna Austria.

I am also extremely grateful to Nova Science Publishers, in particular, Mr. Frank Columbus, Ms Nadya Columbus, and the management, editorial, production and distribution teams, for their great help and resources in having this book published.

Above all, to God be the glory!

Teofilo C. DAQUILA
Southeast Asian Studies Programme
National University of Singapore
May 2006

PART I: AN OVERVIEW OF SOUTHEAST ASIA'S ECONOMIC PERFORMANCE

Chapter 1

THE PICTURE

ABSTRACT

This chapter presents a macro picture of Southeast Asia's economic performance, in particular, Indonesia, Malaysia, the Philippines, Singapore and Thailand. It provides an analysis of economic trends and patterns during the post-1960 period based on economic indicators such as the real GDP, per capita income, structural change in output and trade, and social development.

INTRODUCTION

Countries with high rates of economic growth do not necessarily have high levels of economic development. Even if the economy grows strongly, there is no economic development if people are poor, unemployed, and/or the gap between the rich and the poor widens. Economic growth is necessary but not sufficient for economic development. Thus, the terms 'economic growth' and 'economic development' have different meanings. While economic growth essentially involves rate of changes in output or income per capita, economic development is a much broader concept as it includes economic growth plus changes in the economic, social and institutional structures of the economy as well as improvement in the standards of living of the majority of the population.

With reference to the five Southeast Asian economies, namely, Indonesia, Malaysia, the Philippines, Singapore and Thailand, these countries had remarkable economic growth and development during the past three decades and a half prior to the economic crisis which began in July 1997. Excluding the Philippines, the four Southeast Asian economies belonged to a group called by the World Bank as High Performing Asian Economies (HPAEs).[1]

The Southeast Asian economies have been transformed from low-income to middle- and high-income levels. They have experienced rapid structural change in output in which the contribution of agriculture to total output has declined while that of the non-agricultural

1 In addition, the HPAEs include Japan, Hong Kong, the Republic of Korea, and Taiwan. These eight HPAEs were the subject of the World Bank's study which was completed in 1993 titled "The East Asian Miracle: Economic Growth and Public Policy." See also John Page, "The East Asian Miracle: Four Lessons for Development Policy," in Stanley Fischer and Julio Rotemberg (eds.), *NBER Macroeconomics Annual*, Cambridge: MIT Press, 1995, pp.219-269.

sector has increased. These economies are also characterized with a rapid expansion of exports and foreign direct investments (FDI) as well as a change in the structure of exports away from primary products and into manufactured goods. There have been significant inflows of FDI particularly on export-oriented industries. Moreover, these economies have achieved a higher level of social development in terms of the improvement in the well-being of their population. The rest of the chapter provides an overview of the trends and patterns of the economic performance of Southeast Asian economies during the post 1960 period in terms of the rates of growth of output and per capita income, the structural changes in output and trade, and social development.

Economic Growth

Two commonly used measures of economic growth are the rate of growth of real GDP and the level or rate of growth of per capita income. These measures are shown in Tables 1.1 and 1.2.

Real GDP Growth

In terms of real GDP growth, the Southeast Asian region had shown an impressive economic performance during the past three decades and a half prior to the 1997/98 economic crisis as it expanded by a weighted-average growth rate of about 7.0 percent during the 1961-96 period.

The region grew strongly in the 1960s for an average growth rate of 6.0 percent per annum. The bouyant economic performance continued in the 1970s with an average growth rate of 7.3 percent per annum as Southeast Asian economies benefited from enormous foreign exchange earnings due to the sharp increase in the world price of primary commodities particularly in the early 1970s. As a consequence of strong fundamental demand and of changes in agricultural policies in the former Soviet Union (leading to large imports of grain), world commodity prices more than doubled between early 1972 and early 1974, before receding in the 1974-75 recession.[2] The growth rate in the 1970s would have been higher had the oil shocks not taken place – first in 1973/74 and again in 1978/79. The world price of oil rose almost fourfold from US$3.70 to US$11.65 per barrel in December 1973, which was probably the largest one-quarter economic shock the global economy has ever experienced since more than 10 percent of the world payments for trade were redirected in a single quarter. The price of oil rose again from an average price of US$13.39 per barrel in 1978 to about US$30.21 per barrel in 1979.[3] The oil shocks hit the Southeast Asian region in both ways. Oil producers like Indonesia, Malaysia and Brunei received a foreign exchange bonanza while oil importers like Singapore, Philippines and Thailand suffered severe inflationary pressures and higher costs of production.

---

2 Ian Little, Richard Cooper, Max Corden and Sarath Rajapatirana, *Boom, Crisis Adjustment: The Macroeconomic Experience of Developing Ccountries,* New York: Oxford University Press for the World Bank, 1992, p.17.

3 For basic data, see IMF, *International Financial Statistics Yearbook,* Washington D.C.:International Monetary Fund, 1998, p.172.

Table 1.1. Real GDP Growth Rate in Southeast Asia, in percent

	INDO	MSIA	PHILS.	SPORE	THAI	ASEAN-5 weighted average
1961-1970	4.2	6.5	4.9	10.0	8.2	6.0
1971-1979	7.8	8.0	6.0	9.0	7.1	7.3
1980-1990	6.6	6.2	2.1	7.6	7.7	6.1
1991-1996	7.8	9.6	2.8	8.9	8.2	7.7
1997	4.7	7.3	5.2	8.7	1.4	4.1
1998	-13.1	-7.4	-0.6	-0.1	-10.8	-8.0
1997-1998	-4.2	-0.02	2.3	4.4	-6.1	-1.9
1999	0.9	6.1	3.4	5.9	4.2	3.6
2000	4.8	8.3	4.0	9.9	4.3	6.0
2001	3.4	0.4	3.2	-2.3	1.9	1.7
2002	3.7	4.2	4.6	2.2	5.3	4.0
1999-2002	3.2	4.8	3.8	3.9	3.9	3.8
1991-2002	4.3	6.4	3.1	6.5	4.4	4.8
2003 estimate	3.3	4.2	4.0	1.7	4.5	3.5
1961-1996	6.4	7.3	4.0	8.8	7.7	6.6
1961-1998	5.9	6.9	3.9	8.6	7.0	6.2
1961-2002	5.6	6.7	3.9	8.1	6.7	6.0

Note: *Throughout this book, ASEAN-5 includes Indonesia (INDO), Malaysia (MSIA), Philippines (PHILS), Singapore (SPORE) and Thailand (THAI). Source: World Development Index CD ROM (2003), ASEAN Secretariat website (*www.aseansec.org*), and *Looking Beyond Short-term Shocks:* Regional Overview, Washington DC: The World Bank, East Asia Update, April 2003.

During the 1980s, the Southeast Asian region slowed down to an average growth rate of 6.1 percent largely due to the weak growth record of the Philippine economy. As Booth stated:

> The five ASEAN countries (excluding Brunei) all experienced a marked deceleration in growth in the mid-1980s with 1985 being the trough of the slow-down for all five economies. Malaysia, Singapore and the Philippines all experienced an absolute decline in GDP in 1985, and while the rate of growth was still positive in Indonesia and Thailand, it was much lower than had been achieved in the early 1980s. However, all the ASEAN countries have seen a recovery in growth in the 1986-90 period with Thailand and Singapore achieving double digit growth rates in some years, Malaysia averaging growth of around 9 percent per annum in 1988-90, and Indonesia over 6 percent. Thus, in the three years from the end of 1987 to the end of 1990, real GDP is estimated to have increased by almost 40 percent in Thailand, around 30 percent in Malaysia and Singapore, and 21 percent in Indonesia. Even in the Philippines, real GDP is estimated to have grown by 15 percent over these years.[4]

[4] Anne Booth, "An Economic Overview of Southeast Asia," *Southeast Asian Affairs.* Singapore: Institute of Southeast Asian Studies, 1992, p.22.

There were opposing forces which took place during the 1980s. On the negative front, there were three factors. First, the Southeast Asian economies experienced recessionary conditions in the early 1980s due to the higher world interest rates which stemmed from a tight monetary policy of the Federal Reserve Bank of the United States which was aimed at containing the inflationary pressures generated by the oil shocks. A decrease in money supply led to higher interest rates which were then transmitted to the rest of the world including the Southeast Asian region. Higher interest rates reduced the demand for interest-sensitive consumer durables and the demand for private investment. Both consumption and investment fell and consequently, aggregate demand and hence output of the Southeast Asian economies declined. The increase in interest rates also led to the severe external indebtedness of the Southeast Asian economies, except Singapore. Among these economies, the Philippine economy did very poorly as it registered a very severe contraction of 0.6 percent in 1984. In addition to the recessionary impact of the higher interest rates, the weak performance of the Philippine economy was also attributed to the severe consequences of the assassination of former Senator Benigno Aquino in 1983 when he came back to the Philippines from exile in the United States. This triggered a loss of confidence and massive capital flight. The Philippines also declared a debt moratorium in 1984 as having been unable to repay its foreign borrowings.

Second, the major trading partners of Southeast Asian economies like the United States, Japan and Europe also experienced recession. As in 1974, a combination of the suddenly higher oil prices and the contractionary policies in leading industrial countries (Britain, Germany, Japan and the United States) induced a second world recession in 1981-82, more severe (in relation to potential output) than the 1975 recession. The US recession of 1982 was at first not foreseen, and then its magnitude was greatly underestimated.[5]

Third, the world prices of Southeast Asia's primary exports fell during the 1980s including Thai rice and maize, Malaysian rubber, hardwood, tin, and palm oil, and Philippine coconut oil. Relative to 1980-84 period, the average prices of these commodities dropped during the 1985-89 period as follows: from 347.8 to 240.9 for rice (in US$ per metric ton); from 3.62 to 2.75 for maize (in US$ per bushel); from 49.2 to 42.68 for rubber (in US cents per pound); from 272.85 to 247.50 for hardwood (in US$ per cubic meter); from 626.91 to 365.41 for tin (in US cents per pound); from 505.07 to 369.44 for palm oil (in US$ per metric ton); and from 28.01 to 19.75 for coconut oil (in US cents per pound).[6] Moreover, the export revenues of Indonesia and Malaysia were severely affected as the average price of crude petroleum also dropped markedly from US$32.51 in 1980-84 to US$18.48 in 1985-89. The declining prices of oil and other primary product exports prompted Malaysia and Indonesia to develop manufactured exports.[7] On the positive front, the Southeast Asian economies received massive inflows of export-oriented foreign direct investments from Japan following a strong appreciation of the yen in 1985. Japanese investments in Southeast Asia rose from US$855 million in 1986 to US$4,484 million in 1989.[8]

---

5 Ian Little, et.al. (1993), pp.20-21.

6 For basic data, see IMF (1998), p.172.

7 Gerald Tan, "Comparative Economic Development," in Gerald Tan, *ASEAN Economic Development and Cooperation*, Singapore: Times Academic Press, 1996, p.34.

8 For basic data, see OECD, *International Direct Investment Statistics Yearbook,* Paris: OECD, 1998, p.200.

Following the slowdown in the 1980s, the Southeast Asian region recovered in the 1991-96 period with an annual average growth rate of 7.7 percent. But, the 1997/98 economic crisis resulted in a real output contraction by about 2 percent during this period. The crisis devastated the Southeast Asian economies that their average growth fell to 6.2 percent during the 1961-98 period compared to 6.6 percent during the 1961-96 period. As the Asian Development Bank stated, "Asia's once vibrant economies, used to decades of rapid growth, were plunged into deep recession (because of the 1997/98 crisis)."[9] Even poverty indicators revealed the deterioration in Southeast Asian economies. According to the World Bank, poverty rates surged after the 1997 financial crisis in Indonesia and Thailand, reaching 65 percent and 33 percent, respectively, by 1999 at the US$2 a day level.[10]

In 1999-2000, the Southeast Asian economies staged a dramatic recovery with Singapore and Malaysia registering the most gains. Things turned sour once again in the year 2001 when their economies significantly slowed down following the Sept 11 bombing and the lackluster performance of the export sector. However, the contraction in 2001 was much less devastating than the 1997/98 economic debacle. This is clearly seen in Fig.1.1. The 1997/98 crisis was a full-blown one as it transformed itself from currency to financial to economic and to political crisis. In Indonesia, it had even become a social crisis which led to the resignation of former President Suharto.

However, from the late 2001 until 2002, the prices of agricultural products like rice, rubber, palm oil, coconut products and lumber rose significantly. Consequently, the year 2002 posted a modest recovery for all economies with Thailand and Malaysia recording the largest gains. The year 2003, however, registered an overall slowing down of economic activities because of deep concerns about the impact of SARS, the Iraq crisis and terrorist-related attacks, the slump in the electronics sector and the collapse of the WTO talks in Cancun.

Per Capita Income

Table 1.2 shows the gross national income (GNI) per capita of Southeast Asian economies. It increased from a weighted average of US$158 in 1970 to US$1,717 in 1990 and to US$1,906 in 1997. However, the July 1997/98 economic crisis reduced their per capita income to US$1,429 in 1998. In 2002, average per capita income further dropped to US$1,378 because of the weaker economic performance during the 2001-02 period.

---

[9] See Asian Development Bank, *Asian Development Outlook 1999,* New York: Oxford University Press, p.21.

[10] World Bank, East Asia Update: Looking Beyond Short-term Shocks - Regional Overview with special focus on *East Asia's Urban Transformation,* April 2003, p.7.

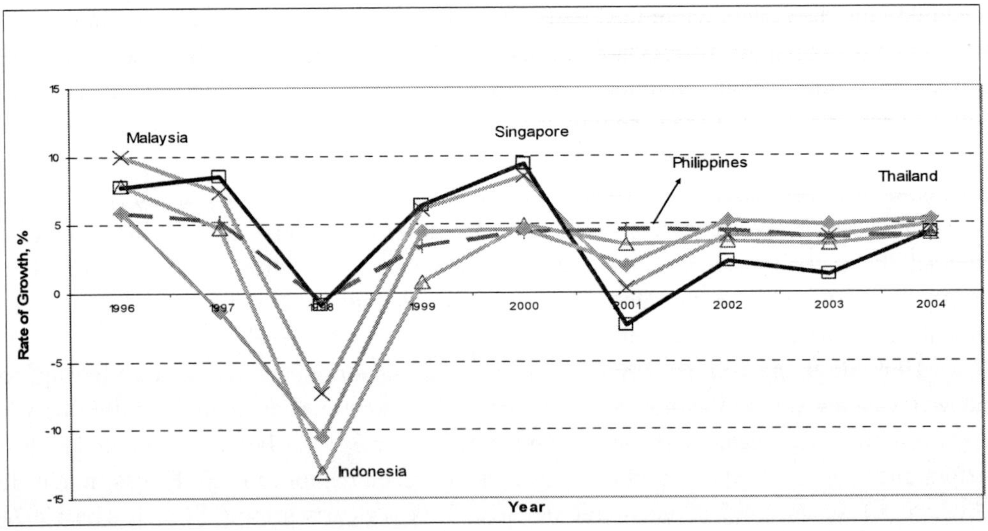

Fig.1.1 – Growth Rate of Real GDP in ASEAN-5 (1996-2004). Source of basic data: Asean Surveillance Coordinating Unit database, ASEAN Secretariat

Table 1.2. GNI Per capita in Southeast Asia, Atlas Method

	INDO	MSIA	PHILS.	SPORE	THAI	ASEAN-5 weighted average
	In US dollars					
1970	80	400	230	950	210	158
1980	500	1830	690	4830	720	686
1990	620	2380	740	11740	1520	1011
1995	1000	4030	1040	23010	2770	1717
1997	1110	4600	1240	27440	2780	1906
1998	660	3640	1090	24580	2110	1429
1999	580	3450	1060	24190	2000	1340
2000	570	3380	1040	24740	2000	1333
2002	710	3540	1020	20690	1980	1378
	Growth rates, in percent					
1971-79	20.7	16.2	11.5	17.9	13.0	15.8
1980-90	3.9	4.5	2.5	10.3	8.7	5.4
1991-96	10.2	11.1	8.3	13.7	12.1	11.1
1997-98	-20.3	-9.1	-4.0	-1.0	-15.9	-12.3
1999-02	2.5	-0.6	-1.6	-4.0	-1.6	-0.9
1970-96	11.2	9.9	6.4	13.7	10.8	10.1
1970-02	8.3	7.5	4.8	10.7	7.7	7.4

Source: World Bank, *World Development Indicators*, Washington DC: World Bank, Various Issues.

During the 1970-2002 period, per capita income among Southeast Asian economies increased by a weighted average of about 8 percent. From low-income levels, these economies have been transformed to middle- and high-income levels. However, we observed that within the Southeast Asian region, there is considerable variation in their per capita incomes which reflects the disparities in their levels of economic development and in the living standards enjoyed by the people of Southeast Asia.[11] Singapore displayed the most rapid improvement in its income per capita from US$950 in 1970 to US$23,010 in 1995 and to US$27,440 in 1997. However, its per capita income decreased to US$24,580 in 1998 and to US$20,690 in 2002. Singapore was classified as the most advanced developing economy by the World Bank in 1996. As Saw stated, the marked improvement in Singapore's per capita income has been attributed to its consistently high economic growth rate and the low rate of population increase.[12]

The incomes per capita of Indonesia, Malaysia and Thailand also improved by an average growth rate of about 10-11 percent during the 1970-96 period. The Philippines, however, registered the lowest increase of 6.4 percent during the same period. During the 1997/98 period, their per capita income fell by about 16 percent for Thailand, 9 percent for Malaysia, 20.3 percent for Indonesia, and 4 percent for the Philippines. During the 1999-2002 period, the per capita income improved by an average growth of about 1 percent for the ASEAN-5 economies.

Change in Output Structure

The Southeast Asian economies have experienced rapid change in the output structure, whereby the agricultural sector's contribution to GDP has declined while the contribution of the non-agricultural sector (industrial and services sectors) has risen. The contribution to GDP of the different sectors are shown in Table 1.3. Among the agricultural-based economies, Indonesia registered the largest decrease in the contribution of agriculture to GDP from 46 percent in 1970 to about 18 percent in 2002 for Indonesia, with the smallest decrease registered in Singapore from 2.3 percent to 0.1 percent in the same period.

Despite the declining share of the agricultural sector, it continues to be an important sector due to the following reasons. First, in terms of land utilization, the proportion of land area devoted to agriculture is still very substantial. For example in Indonesia, the land use allocation in 1992 was as follows: 12.4 percent of 181,157,000 hectares was for arable and permanent crops, 6.5 percent for permanent pasture, and 60 percent for forest and woodland, for a combined proportion of about 79 percent of the total land area. The balance of 21 percent was allocated to residential, commercial, industrial and recreational uses. In 2001, about 18 percent of its total land area was classified as agricultural (cropped) land and 85.6 percent classified as non-cropped land.

---

11 Based on their per capita incomes, some of the East Asian economies are classified into four groups as follows. The first group of economies are those which had very low per capita incomes in 1960 and have experienced very modest growth rates since then; these include Cambodia, Burma, Laos and Vietnam. A second group of low achievers include Brunei and the Philippines, as these economies had relatively high per capita GDP in 1960 but have grown very slowly since then. A third group comprises what perhaps are the true 'Asian miracles', those economies which had low per capita GDP in 1960 but which have grown rapidly since then: these include Indonesia, South Korea and Thailand. The fourth group includes high achievers in the growth stakes who started from rather higher per capita GDP levels, but have grown fast since the 1960s: these include Taiwan, Malaysia and Singapore. See Anne Booth, "Initial Conditions and Miraculous Growth: Why is Southeast Asia Different from Taiwan and South Korea?" *World Development,* Vol.27, No.2, 1999, pp.301-302.

12 Swee Hock Saw, "The ASEAN Region in Perspective," in Swee Hock Saw (ed.), *ASEAN Economies in Transition,* Singapore: Singapore University Press, 1980, p32.

Second, the agricultural sector is a potent engine of growth particularly when prices of agricultural commodities rose as in the early 1970s which resulted in a significant increase in the foreign exchange earnings of Southeast Asian exporters. Third, the agricultural sector continues to employ a large though declining share of the labor force. For Indonesia, the Philippines and Thailand, employment in the agricultural sector remained high at 43 percent, 37 percent, and 35 percent of total employment, respectively in 2002.

Table 1.3. Sectoral Distribution of GDP in Southeast Asia (in %)

	Agriculture	Industry (All sectors)	Manufacturing	Services
Indonesia				
1970	46.0	21.0	11.0	33.0
2002	17.5	44.5	26.6	38.1
Malaysia				
1970	32.0	25.0	16.0	43.0
2002	8.0	48.2	30.1	43.8
Philippines				
1970	28.8	29.4	23.1	41.8
2002	14.9	31.6	24.1	53.5
Singapore				
1970	2.3	29.8	20.5	67.9
2002	0.1	33.6	24.3	60.4
Thailand				
1970	27.8	26.2	17.7	45.9
2002	8.5	42.0	35.0	49.5
Weighted average				
1970	28.2	21.7	14.3	35.8
2002	8.5	32.2	22.3	37.0

Source: World Bank, *World Development Indicators*, Washington DC: World Bank, Various issues; and Asian Development Bank, *Key Indicators of Developing Asian and Pacific Countries*, Manila: Asian Development Bank, Various issues.

Among the Southeast Asian economies, Indonesia and Malaysia registered the largest increase in the contribution of the industrial sector from 21 percent to about 45 percent for the former and from 25 percent to 48.2 percent for the latter during the 1970 to 2002 period. This is followed by Thailand and Singapore. The Philippines registered the smallest increase from 29.4 percent to 31.6 percent. In the industrial sector, manufacturing is the largest sub-sector accounting for a share ranging from a low of about 24.1 percent in the Philippines to a high of 35 percent in Thailand in 2002. The manufacturing sector has been considered as the prime mover of Southeast Asian economies. The dominance of this sector has been largely due to the impact of the industrialization policy which has continuously depended on foreign direct investments. The manufacturing output during the import-substitution industrialization (ISI) phase which was adopted in the 1950s and the 1960s was targeted at the domestic market while, during the export-oriented industrialization (EOI) phase since the 1970s, output was directed towards the foreign markets. During these phases of industrialization, the bulk of FDI in Southeast Asia has been in the manufacturing sector.

As the economy grows and as per capita income rises, the Southeast Asian people tend to increase their demand for goods and services. Thus, more services and institutions have been created to provide for their rising demand for goods and services. This is reflected in the growing importance of the services sector, particularly, financial and business sector as well as transport and communications sector. The services sector in Singapore has the largest contribution ranging from 60-70 percent of the total output during the 1970-2002 period. This is consistent with Singapore's long-term plan of becoming a financial and business hub in the region.

From the above analysis, the Southeast Asian economies experienced a structural transformation away from agriculture towards non-agricultural sector, with the manufacturing sector providing substantial stimulus to economic growth. This is in line with the "patterns-of-development analysis of structural change which focuses on the sequential process through which the economic, industrial and institutional structure of an underdeveloped economy is transformed over time to permit new industries to replace traditional agriculture as the engine of economic growth."[13]

Change in Trade Structure

Consistent with the change in output structure, the Southeast Asian trade has also undergone transformation. The shares of primary and manufactured goods to exports and imports are shown in Table 1.4. The ASEAN5 weighted average shares of primary exports fell drastically from 82 percent in 1970 to 21 percent in 2001. Exports of manufactured goods rose markedly from 18 percent to 79 percent during the same period which indicates the faster pace of diversification that has taken place in ASEAN-5 economies. For imports, the share of primary commodities fell from 35 percent to 22 percent while the share of manufactured goods increased from 65 percent to 78 percent during the 1970-2002 period. Thus, the structure of Southeast Asian trade has changed away from the exports of primary commodities towards manufactured goods mainly electrical and electronics and transport equipment and machinery, and towards rising proportion of manufactured imports.

Social Development

As countries become richer, on average the incidence of income poverty falls.[14] Improvement could also be observed in the commonly used measures of the society's well-being which include the state of current health, nutritional status, literacy rates, educational attainments, housing conditions, crime rates, divorce rates, as well as other aspects of social and cultural development.[15] Economic growth and its relatively equitable distribution in the

13 Michael Todaro, "Chapter 2 - Diverse Structures and Common Characteristics of Developing Nations", in Michael Todaro, *Economic Development in the Third World,* New York: Longman, 1994, p.67.

14 See World Bank, "Growth, Inequality and Poverty," *World Development Report,* Washington DC: World Bank, 2000/01, p.45.

15 Chong Yah Lim, *Development and Underdevelopment*, Singapore: Longman Publications, 1991, p.36.

form of improved living standards, has assisted in the maintenance of political stability which has enhanced prospects for further growth.[16]

Table 1.4. Structure of Exports and Imports in Southeast Asia

	Exports (% of total)		Imports (% of total)		Value (US$ mil.)	
	Primary	Manufactured	Primary	Manufactured	Exports	Imports
Indonesia						
1970	98	2	25	63	1108	1002
2001	43	56	39	61	56317	30962
Malaysia						
1970	72	26	41	58	1687	1401
2001	19	80	15	82	88004	73079
Philippines						
1970	92	8	29	71	1041	1236
2001	19	80	24	76	32150	31358
Singapore						
1970	69	28	41	57	1554	2461
2001	11	85	18	80	121754	116002
Thailand						
1970	81	16	19	77	710	1299
2001	22	74	23	75	65113	65113
Weighted Average						
1970	82	18	35	65		
2001	21	79	22	78		
Total value (US$ mil.)						
1970	4905	1093	2042	3848		
2001	75656	278442	79878	277723		

Source: United Nations Conference on Trade and Development (www.unctad.org)

The Southeast Asian countries have succeeded in improving the welfare of the general populace and have made dramatic improvements in social development[17] as shown in Table 1.5 in terms of (a) higher primary enrolment ratio (percentage of school age population), (b) lower infant mortality rates (per 1000 livebirths), (c) longer life expectancy (in years), (d) reduced fertility rates (number of births per woman), (e) better access to health care (percentage of population), (f) better access to safewater (percentage of population), and (g) higher expenditures on social security (percentage of total government expenditures). As expected, Singapore scores the most significant gains in all social indicators, and Indonesia,

---

16 Department of Foreign Affairs and Trade, *ASEAN Free Trade Area: Trading Bloc Or Building Block?*, Canberra: Australian Government Publishing Service, 1994, p.55.

17 Seiji Naya and Pearl Imada, "Economic Success of the NIEs and ASEAN: Some Lessons for Latin America?", *Southeast Asian Affairs,* Singapore: Institute of Southeast Asian Studies, 1992, p.44.

the least improvement. For all countries, the fertility and mortality rates have dropped markedly in 2001 relative to 1970-75.

Table 1.5. Indicators of Social Development

		Indo	Msia	Phils	Spore	Thai	Weighted Average
Primary enrolment ratio (%)	1970-75	86	91	107	110	83	90
	1980-85	117	101	107	115	96	110
	1989-94	114	93	111	107	98	109
	2000-01	92	98	93	...	85	92
Infant Mortality (per 1000 livebirths)	1970-75	104	46	60	22	74	87
	1980-85	80	28	51	9	44	65
	1989-94	53	12	40	5	36	45
	2001	33	8	29	3	24	29
Life Expectancy at birth (in years)	1970-75	49	63	58	70	61	54
	1980-85	56	68	62	72	65	60
	1989-94	63	71	65	75	69	65
	2001	66	73	70	78	69	68
Fertility Rates	1970-75	5.4	5.2	6.1	2.1	5.0	5
	1980-85	4.1	4.2	4.7	1.6	3.0	4
	1989-94	2.7	3.4	3.8	1.8	2.0	3
	2001	2.4	3.0	3.4	1.5	2.0	3
Population with access to sanitation, in %	1990-U	66	94	85	100	95	77
	1990-R	38	98	63	...	75	...
	2000-U	69	100	93	100	96	80
	2000-R	46	98	69	...	96	...
Population with access to safe water, in %	1970-75	11	34	50	100	25	23
	1980-85	38	80	54	100	67	49
	1989-94	42	78	81	100	...	45
	1990-U	92	96	93	100	87	92
	1990-R	62	94	82	...	78	...
	2000-U	90	97	91	100	95	92
	2000-R	69	94	79	...	81	...
Expenditure on social Security	1970-75	...	3.3	2.2	5.7	3.3	1
	1980-85	...	6.4	2.8	3.7	3.8	2
	1989-94	...	8.0	3.7	5.3	5.5	2
% of central government expenditure allocated to: 1992-2001*	Health	2	6	5	5	8	4
	Education	6	23	19	21	22	12
	Defence	4	11	2	26	8	5

Notes: (a) The symbols U and R denote urban and rural, respectively.

Sources: UNDP Human Development Indicators 2002 (www.hdr.undp.org); ADB, Key Indicators of Developing Member Countries 2003 (www.adb.org); World Bank, *Social Indicators of Development*, (www.worldbank.org); UNICEF (www.unicef.org).

As the World Bank cited, many studies have documented that as countries become richer, both fertility and mortality rates decline, on average, with reductions in mortality typically preceding reductions in fertility.[18] Life expectancy rose from a weighted average of 54 years during the 1970-75 period to 68 years in 2001. However, with the increase in life expectancy, many countries are now experiencing demographic ageing (defined as an increase in the percentage of a population aged 65 years old or over)[19] which will certainly impact on social security expenditures including pensions and health services and on population policies. As Saw stated, each country adopted a national population policy aimed at checking the rapid rate of population growth to alleviate the population pressures on employment, education and housing and to raise the general standard of living of the masses.[20] The first two countries to introduce this policy in 1966 were Singapore and Malaysia, followed by Indonesia in 1968, and by the Philippines and Thailand in 1970. In each country, there is now an extensive family planning programme which has been an integral part of the national development plan.

As for expenditures on education, except for Indonesia, about 20-25 percent of the government budget has been allocated to education which reflects the emphasis of their respective governments on human development. As ESCAP (2001) stated, *"education is one of the key components of human development, as it is a basic condition for human beings to develop their full capabilities."*[21] As Sudipto Mundle stated, *"few would disagree that the rapid development of human resources is a necessary, if not a sufficient, condition for sustaining high rates of economic growth."*[22] However, as Table 1.5 shows, while the primary enrolment ratio broadly improved during the 1970-1994 period, we observed a declining ratio in 2000-01 which could be due to the fact that a significant number of children were not in school and/or dropped out before completing their primary education. A study by Oxfam International revealed that there was uneven progress in providing access to education which has resulted in deep regional disparities within the countries of Asia and the Pacific.[23]

CONCLUSION

This chapter provides an overview of the trends and patterns depicting the robust economic performance of the five Southeast Asian economies (Indonesia, Malaysia, the Philippines, Singapore and Thailand) during the past three decades and a half prior to the 1997/98 crisis as reflected not only in terms of the high rates of output growth, but also in terms of the increase in the per capita income. These economies also experienced changes in

---

18 See World Bank, "Growth, Inequality and Poverty," ..., p.49.

19 For an excellent discussion of this problem, see Peter Lloyd-Sherlock, "Old Age and Poverty in Developing Countries: New Policy Challenges," *World Development,* Vol.28, No.12, 2000, pp.2157-2168.

20 Swee Hock Saw, 1980, p.21.

21 ESCAP defines human development as the "process of enabling people to develop their full capabilities, thereby enlarging their choices as to what they can do in their lives and how they can participate in the development of their society." See ESCAP, *Reducing Disparities: Balanced Development of Urban and Rural Areas and Regions within the Countries of Asia and the Pacific*. Bangkok: Economic and Social Commission for Asia and the Pacific, 2001, p.4.

22 Sudipto Mundle, "Financing Human Development: Some Lessons from Advanced Asian Countries," *World Development,* Vol.26, No.4, 1998, pp.659-672.

23 See ESCAP, *Reducing Disparities ...",* 2001, p.27.

the structures of their output (away from agriculture towards non-agricultural sectors) and trade (away from primary goods towards manufactured products). These economies have also experienced better standards of living for their people as reflected in the improvement in their state of health, nutritional status, literacy rates, educational attainments, and housing conditions, to name a few.

QUESTION FOR DISCUSSION

1. The Southeast Asian economies have been transformed from low- to middle- and high-income levels, and from agricultural- to non-agricultural societies. Discuss the benefits and costs of their economic transformation.

SUGGESTED MATERIAL FOR CASE STUDY

World Bank, 2000/01, "Growth, Inequality and Poverty," *World Development Report,* Washington DC: World Bank, pp.45-59.

REFERENCES FOR CHAPTER 1

Asian Development Bank, 1999, *Asian Development Outlook 1999,* New York: Oxford University Press.

Booth, Anne, 1992, "An Economic Overview of Southeast Asia," *Southeast Asian Affairs,* Singapore: Institute of Southeast Asian Studies, pp.21-43.

Booth, Anne, 1999, "Initial Conditions and Miraculous Growth: Why is Southeast Asia Different from Taiwan and South Korea?" *World Development,* Vol.27, No.2, pp.301-321.

Department of Foreign Affairs and Trade (DFAT), 1994, *ASEAN Free Trade Area: Trading Bloc Or Building Block?,* Canberra: Australian Government Publishing Service.

ESCAP, 2001, *Reducing Disparities: Balanced Development of Urban and Rural Areas and Regions within the Countries of Asia and the Pacific*. Bangkok: Economic and Social Commission for Asia and the Pacific.

IMF, 1998, *International Financial Statistics Yearbook,* Washington D.C.:International Monetary Fund.

Lim, Chong Yah, 1991, *Development and Underdevelopment*, Singapore: Longman Publications.

Little, Ian, Richard Cooper, Max Corden and Sarath Rajapatirana, 1992, *Boom, Crisis Adjustment: The Macroeconomic Experience of Developing Ccountries,* New York: Oxford University Press for the World Bank.

Lloyd-Sherlock, Peter, 2000, "Old Age and Poverty in Developing Countries: New Policy Challenges," *World Development,* Vol.28, No.12, pp.2157-2168.

Mundle, Sudipto, 1998, "Financing Human Development: Some Lessons from Advanced Asian Countries," *World Development,* Vol.26, No.4, 1998, pp.659-672.

Naya, Seiji and Pearl Imada, 1992, "Economic Success of the NIEs and ASEAN: Some Lessons for Latin America?", *Southeast Asian Affairs,* Singapore: Institute of Southeast Asian Studies.

OECD, 1998, *International Direct Investment Statistics Yearbook,* Paris: OECD.

Page, John, 1995, "The East Asian Miracle: Four Lessons for Development Policy," in Stanley Fischer and Julio Rotemberg (eds.), *NBER Macroeconomics Annual*, Cambridge: MIT Press, pp.219-269.

Saw, Swee Hock, 1980, "The ASEAN Region in Perspective," in Swee Hock Saw (ed.), *ASEAN Economies in Transition,* Singapore: Singapore University Press, pp.1-42.

Tan, Gerald, 1996, "Comparative Economic Development," in Gerald Tan, *ASEAN Economic Development and Cooperation*, Singapore: Times Academic Press, pp.26-50.

Todaro, Michael, 1994, "Chapter 2 - Diverse Structures and Common Characteristics of Developing Nations", in Michael Todaro, *Economic Development in the Third World,* New York: Longman, pp.27-66.

World Bank, 1993, *The East Asian Miracle: Economic Growth and Public Policy*, Washington DC: USA

World Bank, 2000/01, "Growth, Inequality and Poverty," *World Development Report,* Washington DC: World Bank.

World Bank, 2003, *East Asia Update: Looking Beyond Short-term Shocks - Regional Overview with special focus on East Asia's Urban Transformation,* Washington DC: World Bank.

Chapter 2

EXPLAINING THE PICTURE

ABSTRACT

This chapter identifies and analyzes the determinants of Southeast Asia's economic performance using a supply-side framework based on the role of capital accumulation, labor accumulation and total factor productivity growth. Empirical studies have argued that factor accumulation (capital and labor) is a more significant determinant of economic growth than productivity growth. Discussion focuses on capital formation, labor accumulation and productivity growth as well as policies that have promoted or hindered these determinants. The second set of determinants include structural policies such as industrial and trade policies. The third set of determinants includes "other factors" such as political stability and credibility bonus.

INTRODUCTION

As Todaro pointed out, the post-World War II literature on economic development has been dominated by five major and sometimes competing strands of thought which include (i) the linear-stages of growth model, (ii) theories and patterns of structural change, (iii) the international dependence revolution, (iv) the neoclassical, free market counterrevolution, and (v) the endogenous growth model.[1]

According to the linear-stages approach which was developed in the 1950s and the early 1960s, development was viewed as a series of successive stages of economic growth which, according to Rostow, include the traditional society, the pre-conditions stage, the takeoff, the drive to maturity and the age of high mass consumption. The Harrod-Domar model prescribes that the right quantity and mixture of saving, investment and foreign aid were required for developing nations to replicate the growth path followed by the more developed countries

In the 1970s, two competing schools of thought were developed. The first, which dealt with the theories and patterns of structural change, utilized modern economic theory and statistical approach to analyse the internal process of structural change of a developing country. The second model, known as the international dependence revolution, viewed underdevelopment in the context of the "international and domestic power relationships,

---

1 For a full discussion of these models, see Michael Todaro, "Theories of Development: A Comparative Analysis," *Economic Development in the Third World,* New York: Longman, 1994, pp.67-98.

institutional and structural rigidities, and the resulting proliferation of dual economies and dual societies both within and among the nations of the world."[2]

The neoclassical counterrevolution model prevailed throughout the 1980s which focused on the benefits provided by free markets, open economies and privatization of inefficient and wasteful government agencies, and which emphasized the idea that underdevelopment results primarily from heavy government intervention and regulation of the economy.

Since the late 1980s and early 1990s, the endogenous growth theory has emerged which attempts to explain why some countries develop faster than other countries, and why government may still play a significant role in the development process.

SUPPLY-SIDE ANALYSIS

The impressive economic performance of the five Southeast Asian (ASEAN-5) economies during the past four decades was attributed more to the impact of each member's policies, factors and developments affecting individual member countries rather than that of any regional economic arrangements. As Garnaut put it,

> The five member countries of the Association of Southeast Asian Nations (ASEAN) have recently received increased international notice for their relatively strong economic growth performance and for their assertion of a collective approach to a range of foreign economic policy issues. The five countries have experienced strong growth in industrial output and foreign trade since then, but this has owed little to the regional organization. Decisions taken since 1976 may increase the importance of the ASEAN arrangements to economic growth and development within the region.[3]

But even after 1976, there was very little economic cooperation among the ASEAN-5 economies. Naya supported Garnaut's view as follows:The growth in the economies, trade, and investment potential of member countries has been due not to the combined market or any cooperative efforts, but rather to the good economic performance of individual countries. It is important, therefore, to look at the five countries as separate entities.[4]Thus, the growth and development experiences of the Southeast Asian economies cannot be explained by the ASEAN regional economic cooperation and integration schemes. The ASEAN regional economic cooperation was very weak and that regional cooperative measures were broadly ineffective, despite ASEAN's existence since 1967. It was only since 1992, following the ASEAN Summit meeting in Singapore, that regional schemes have been strengthened including the adoption of trade liberalization measures that will pave the way for the formation of the ASEAN Free Trade Area (also known as AFTA).

This chapter analyzes the Southeast Asian economic performance in the context of a supply-side framework in which its proximate determinants include changes in the various production factors - the high rates of capital formation, increases in the labor force, and

---

2 Michael Todaro, "Theories of Development…", p.68.

3 Ross Garnaut (ed.), *ASEAN in a Changing Pacific and World Economy,* Canberra: Australian National University Press, 1980, p.1.

4 Seiji Naya, "Economic Performance and Growth Factors of the ASEAN Countries," in Linda G. Martin (ed.), *The ASEAN Success Story: Social, Economic and Political Dimensions,* Hawaii: East-West Center, 1987, p.48

improvement in technology. The ultimate determinants are those developments, factors and economic policies which affect capital, labor and technology. The 'other supply-side determinants' include structural adjustment policies and reforms in the industrial and trade sectors. There are also a host of 'other factors' which have contributed to Southeast Asia's economic success such as a generally stable political environment in the region and a credibility-bonus factor (which are discussed later). However, the impact of all these types of determinants or "ingredients" cannot be disaggregated as one ingredient influences another. These policies or "ingredients are interactive ... and ... were introduced in conjunction with other policies"[5].

In explaining the remarkable performance of ASEAN-5 economies during the past four decades, many studies have attributed it to the role of neoclassical economic policies espoused by multilateral bodies such as the IMF, the World Bank and the WTO.[6] These include free markets, and dismantling of public ownership, statist planning and government regulation of economic activitities. However, this free market, minimal government intervention and market-friendly approach has been criticized as having been responsible for the 1997/98 economic crisis. This will be explained later in section 5 of this chapter.

Most of the studies investigated in the analysis were concerned mainly with the issue of factor (capital and labor) accumulation versus productivity growth as the sources of economic growth, and argued that factor accumulation rather than productivity growth is a more important determinant of economic growth.[7] These studies employed a conventional aggregate production function which states that the level of aggregate output (Q) in an

---

5 Joseph Stiglitz, "Some Lessons from the East Asian Miracle," *The World Bank Research Observer,* Vol.11, No.2, 1996, p.151

6 These studies include the World Bank's own publication titled "The East Asian Miracle: Economic Growth and Public Policy, 1993, and John Page's article titled "The East Asian Miracle: Four Lessons for Development Policy," in Stanley Fischer and Julio Rotemberg (eds.), *NBER Macroeconomics Annual*: Vol. 9, 1994, Cambridge: MIT Press, pp.219-269. Other studies include Seiji Naya, "Economic Performance and Growth Factors of the ASEAN Countries," in Linda.G. Martin (ed.), *The ASEAN Success Story: Social, Economic and Political Dimensions,* Hawaii: East-West Center, 1987, 47-87; David Lim, "Explaining the Growth Performance of Asian Developing Economies," *Economic Development and Cultural Change,* Vol. 42, No.4. 1994, pp.829-844; Alvyn Young, "The Tyranny of Numbers: Confronting the Statistical Realities of the East Asian Growth Experience," *Quarterly Journal of Economics*, Vol. 110, No.3-4, 1994, pp.641-680; Alvyn Young, "Lessons from the East Asian NICS: a Contrarian View," *European Economic Review,* Vol.38, No.3, 1995, pp.964-973; Jong-Il Kim and Lawrence Lau, "The Source of Economic Growth of the East Asian Newly Industrializing Countries," *Journal of the Japanese and International Economies*, Vol.8, No.3, 1994, pp.235-271; Paul Krugman, "The Myth of Asia's Miracle," *Foreign Affairs*, Vol.73, No.6, 1994, pp.62-78; Peter Drysdale and Yiping Huang, "Technological Catch-up and Economic Growth in East Asia and the Pacific," *The Economic Record*, Vol.73, No.222, 1995, pp.201-211, Susan Collins and Stephen Bosworth, "Economic Growth in East Asia: Accumulation versus Assimilation", in William Bainard and George Perry, (eds.), *Brookings Papers on Economic Activity,* Washington DC: Brookings Institution, 1997, pp.135-203; Stanley Fischer, "Lessons from East Asia and the Pacific Rim," in William Bainard and George Perry, (eds.). *Brookings Papers on Economic Activity*, Vol.1997, No.2, Washington DC: Brookings Institution, 1997, pp.345-350; Stephen Haggard and Euysung Kim, "The Sources of East Asia's Economic Growth," *Access Asia Review,* Vol.1, No.1, Summer 1996, pp.31-63; and Nicholas Crafts, "East Asian Growth before and after the Crisis," *IMF Staff Papers,* Vol.46, No.2, 1999, pp.139-166.

7 The economists who analyzed the East Asian 'miracle' can be classified into two camps – fundamentalists and mystics. Growth fundamentalists stress the dominant role of factor accumulation in explaining the HPAEs' high-income growth rates. Mystics, on the other hand, while acknowledging the importance of accumulation, tend to place greater emphasis on the role of the acquisition and mastery of technology. See John Page (1995), pp.223-224, for detailed discussion.

economy depends on the various production factors available in the economy which include the aggregate supply of labor (L) and capital (K), and the level of technology (T). Symbolically, it can be expressed as follows:

$$Q = f(L, K, T) \tag{1}$$

Equation (1) has been specified in the form of Cobb-Douglas production function as follows:

$$Q = T\, K^{\alpha}\, L^{\beta} \tag{2}$$

Equation (2) can be re-expressed in terms of growth rates as follows:

$$\omega_Q = \omega_T + \alpha\, \omega_K + \beta\, \omega_L \tag{3}$$

Thus, according to equation (3), the proximate sources of output growth ω_Q are the growth rate of total factor productivity ω_T, the growth rate of capital ω_K weighted by α and the growth rate of labor ω_L weighted by β, where α = output share of capital and β = output share of labor. When the sum of α and β exceeds unity, the production function exhibits increasing returns to scale whereby output increases more than proportionately to the increase in labor and capital. The growth rate of total factor productivity ω_T is defined as the growth in output which is not attributed to increases in capital and labor. This term is treated as a residual after calculating all the other components of the equation and it represents the contribution of the TFP growth.

Capital Accumulation

The study by the World Bank estimated that, during the 1960-87 period, the share of output growth attributed to capital accumulation was 65 percent for developing countries and 57 percent for East Asia. It is therefore important to determine the factors and policies which have been responsible for rapid accumulation of capital in Southeast Asia.[8]

Policies that Affect Capital Formation

These factors include a stable macroeconomic management and high savings rate. A sound macroeconomic management provides a more secure environment for private sector investment decisions and eventually a certain return on their investments. An increase in the savings rate will provide more financial resources which can be mobilized to finance the nation's investment requirements. Financial liberalization, including the lifting of interest rate ceilings on deposits and loans, would contribute to stimulating savings and investment. Favorable foreign investment policies, including an increase in foreign equity participation

---

8 World Bank, *World Development Report*, New York: Oxford University Press, 1991, p.45.

will encourage the inflow of foreign direct investment which in turn will stimulate capital formation.

i. Stable Macroeconomic Environment

Good macroeconomic management is associated with faster growth for a given rate of investment.[9] It involves sound fiscal, monetary and exchange rate policies as well as good external debt management.

In terms of fiscal policy, the Southeast Asian governments had exercised fiscal prudence as reflected in a significant improvement of their government budget balances. Table 2.1 shows that, overall budget deficits as a proportion of GDP rose during the 1971-85 period. Subsequently, however, we observed a marked improvement in the government budget balances as reflected in the reduction of the deficits as well as the generation of budget surpluses. In 1998, the governments of Indonesia, Malaysia, the Philippines and Thailand once again incurred deficits which was part of their expansionist fiscal policy stance in response to the 1997 economic crisis. Among the five economies, the Singapore government is an exception as it has been consistently in the black during the 1971-2002 period, except in 1981-85. However, as a proportion of GDP, Singapore's government budget surplus fell to 7.6 percent in 1997-98 and picked up slightly to 8 percent in 1999-2002 period.

Table 2.1. Fiscal Balance in Southeast Asia (Average in each sub-period, % of GDP)

	INDO	MSIA	PHILS	SPORE	THAI	ASEAN5 weighted average
1971-75	-3.1	-6.7 (a)	-1.1 (b)	0.6	-2.9	-2.6
1976-80	-4.2	-9.1	-1.3	1.0	-3.0	-3.4
1981-85	-3.8	-11.4	-2.8	-2.0	-3.7	-4.3
1986-90	-2.2	-5.6	-3.4	5.2	1.3	-1.8
1991-96	0.3	0.2	-0.5	13.0	2.6	1.3
1997	0.5	2.4	0.1	11.7	-1.5	0.7
1998	-1.7	-1.8	-1.9	3.4	-2.8	-2.3
1997-98 crisis period	-0.6	0.3	-0.9	7.6	-2.2	0.03
1999-02	-1.2	-2.7	-2.7	8.0	-1.8	-1.3

Note: (a) excludes 1971-72, (b) excludes 1971. Source: ADB, *Key Indicators of Asian and Pacific Member Countries*, Manila: Asian Development Bank, 1984, 1990, 2000 and 2003 issues, and IMF, *International Financial Statistics Yearbook*, Washington DC: IMF, 2000.

To finance their budget deficits, the government fiscal authorities have utilized external and domestic financing. The second half of the 1970s was characterized with low and even negative real interest rates. In the case of the United States, the real interest rates (the difference between nominal interest rate, proxied by the treasury bill rate, and the rate of inflation, which was based on the annual changes in the CPI index) reached an average of –

9 Michael Bleaney, "Macroeconomic Stability, Investment and Growth in Developing Countries," *Journal of Development Economics,* Vol.48, No.2, 1996, pp.461-477.

1.04 percent during the 1976-80 period.[10] With lower real costs of financing, many developing countries including those in Southeast Asia (with the exception of Singapore) borrowed heavily in the international markets to avail of the enormous surplus funds made available by the OPEC countries as a result of the quadrupling of the crude oil prices. During the 1975-79 period, Thailand, the Philippines and Malaysia's external debt expanded by an average growth rate of 46 percent, 42 percent, and 30 percent from 13 percent, 11 percent and 27 percent, respectively, in the 1970-74 period.[11]

In the early 1980s, the tight monetary policy of the US Federal Reserve Bank to contain inflation caused both nominal and real interest rates to rise. From an average of 7.8 percent during the 1976-80 period, nominal interest rates in the US rose to an average of 10.7 percent during the 1980-84 period. Real interest rates also increased from an average of –1.04 percent to 4.74 percent during the same comparative period. However, some countries continued to borrow heavily despite the higher borrowing costs. The external debt of Malaysia, the Philippines and Thailand increased by an average growth rate of about 50 percent, 28 percent and 23 percent, respectively, during the 1980-82 period.

In terms of monetary policy, Southeast Asian central banks have been successful in controlling inflation from their high levels in the 1970s (as shown in Table 2.2) to lower levels in the 1980s, except in the Philippines due to the inflationary pressures of the peso devaluation against the US dollar from 7.10 pesos during the 1971-80 period to 17.10 pesos during the 1981-90 period (Table 2.3). The generally low and stable inflation rates in Southeast Asia have stimulated economic growth. As Corden puts it:

> The hypothesis is that low or moderate inflation over long periods provides a favorable environment for growth. He further stated that all the seven economies (Indonesia, Malaysia, Singapore, Thailand, Korea, Taiwan and Hong Kong) have been exceptional high-growth economies by world standards, and all, but Korea and Indonesia have also been long-period, low inflation countries, while Korea and Indonesia fall into the moderately-low inflation category. Taiwan and Singapore stand out for their low inflation and high growth stories.[12]

The stability of prices in Southeast Asia has been attributed to the effectiveness of government policies to control inflation. The Southeast Asian economies, except Singapore, have employed the orthodox means of controlling inflation through restrictive monetary policies. A cut in the growth rate of money supply increases interest rates and this dampens investment and interest-sensitive consumer durables. As total demand declines, holding supply constant, the prices of goods and services, and hence inflation rate falls. To control money supply, the conventional instruments used by central bank authorities are open market operations (OMO), changes in the discount rate, and changes in the reserve requirements.

---

10 For basic data, see IMF, *International Financial Statistics Yearbook*, Washington DC: IMF, 2000.

11 Bhanoji Rao, Teofilo Daquila, and Yean Pau Woo, *ASEAN External Debt Perspectives.* Singapore: Times Academic Press, 1994.

12 Max Corden, *Pragmatic Orthodoxy: Macroeconomic Policies in Seven East Asian Economies,* Occasional Papers No.61, California: International Center for Economic Growth, 1996, p.38.

Table 2.2. Inflation Rates in Southeast Asia, (Average in each sub-period, in percent)

	INDO	MSIA	PHILS.	SPORE	THAI	ASEAN5 weighted average
1971-75	20.3	7.4	17.4	9.7	10.1	15.8
1976-80	15.4	4.5	11.7	3.7	10.5	11.5
1981-85	8.7	4.7	21.1	3.3	5.1	10.5
1986-90	7.1	5.0	7.6	1.3	3.9	5.9
1991-96	8.7	3.9	9.9	2.4	5.0	7.2
1997-98 crisis period	32.2	4.0	7.8	0.9	6.8	16.1
1999-02	11.9	1.9	5.1	0.5	1.0	6.1
1971-80	19.4	6.5	13.8	7.3	9.7	13.7
1981-90	7.9	3.3	14.4	2.3	4.5	8.2
1991-02	13.7	3.2	7.9	1.5	4.0	8.3

Source: ADB, *Key Indicators of Developing Asian and Pacific Countries*, Manila: Asian Development Bank, 1984, 1990, 2000 and 2003 issues, and IMF, *International Financial Statistics Yearbook*, Washington DC: IMF, 2000

Among the five Southeast Asian economies, the Central Bank of the Philippines has relied more on OMO as it has a relatively well-developed and active secondary market in government securities. The use of OMO by the Bank of Indonesia began seriously with the implementation of financial sector reforms in the 1980s. Due to small size and narrowness of government securities market in Malaysia, the use of OMO is severely limited. Bank Negara Malaysia has relied more on the statutory reserve requirement. In Singapore, the money supply is largely endogenous as it is determined by its balance of payments position due to highly open nature of its economy.[13] Instead of relying on traditional instruments, the Monetary Authority of Singapore (MAS) uses exchange-rate targetting in which the appreciation of the Singapore dollar is managed against a basket of foreign currencies. Since 1975, the MAS has operated a managed float by relating the Singapore dollar to an undisclosed trade-weighted basket of currencies (and occasionally varying the weights). The MAS intervenes in the foreign exchange market whenever market forces threatened to force the exchange rate out of an undisclosed target band which is set by the MAS and that may well be changed from time to time. Thus, the volatility of the Singapore dollar is managed which in turn results in low and stable prices, and hence low and stable rates of inflation.

In terms of exchange rate policy, the Southeast Asian central banks have relied on changes in the value of their domestic currencies vis-à-vis foreign currencies. Table 2.3 shows the ASEAN exchange rates from 1971-2002.

[13] Chong Yah Lim and Associates, *Policy Options for the Singapore Economy*, Singapore: McGraw Hill, 1988, p. 323.

Table 2.3. Exchange Rates in SE Asia (Domestic currency per US dollar)

	INDO	MSIA	PHILS	SPORE	THAI
	Rupiah	Ringgit	Peso	Dollar	Baht
1971-75	410.7	2.6	6.8	2.60	20.6
1976-80	504.4	2.3	7.4	2.30	20.4
1981-85	867.8	2.4	12.6	2.10	23.7
1986-90	1645.0	2.6	21.6	2.00	25.7
1991-96	2136.5	2.6	26.4	1.55	25.3
1997-98 crisis period	6461.5	3.4	35.2	1.58	36.36
1999-02	8962.3	3.8	46.5	1.75	41.33
1971-80	457.3	2.5	7.1	2.50	20.50
1981-90	1256.4	2.5	17.1	2.10	24.70
1991-02	5132.6	3.1	34.5	1.62	32.47

Source: ADB, *Key Indicators of Developing Asian and Pacific Countries,* Manila: Asian Development Bank, 1984, 1990, 2000 and 2003 and IMF, *International Financial Statistics Yearbook,* Washington D.C.:IMF, 2000.

The Singapore dollar has appreciated against the US dollar from an average of S$2.50 in the 1970s to an average of S$1.62 in 1991-2002. While the Malaysian ringgit was relatively at par with the Singapore dollar in the 1970s at around RM2.5 per US dollar, its value depreciated slightly to an average of RM3.1 during the 1991-2002 period. The Thai baht remained relatively constant in the 1970s for an average of Bt20.5 per US dollar, but rose to an average of Bt32.5 in the 1991-2002 period. The Philippine peso has weakened from an average of Pp7.1 in the 1970s to an average of Pp34.5 in the 1991-2002 period. The value of the Indonesian rupiah against the US dollar also fell from an average of Rp457.3 in the 1970s to about Rp5,132 in the 1991-2002 period. Thus, the Singapore dollar, the Malaysian ringgit and the Thai baht are broadly the more stable currencies in Southeast Asia while the Indonesian rupiah and the Philippine peso showed relatively wider variations particularly during and after the 1997/98 crisis. This is reflected in Figure 2.1.

The overall stable exchange rates of Southeast Asia's currencies occurred despite higher current account deficits, except in Singapore, where its current account balance has improved significantly during the entire period. This is shown in Table 2.4. The need to correct the deficits through deeper devaluations did not take place because of significant inflows of foreign capital. Net direct and portfolio investments expanded almost fivefold from US$2,435 million in 1980 to US$9,854 million in 1995 for the five Southeast Asian economies.[14] However, during the 1997/98 crisis and beyond, the Southeast Asian economies have shown marked improvement in their current account balance.

14 World Bank, *World Development Indicators*, New York: Oxford University Press, 1997, pp.215-216.

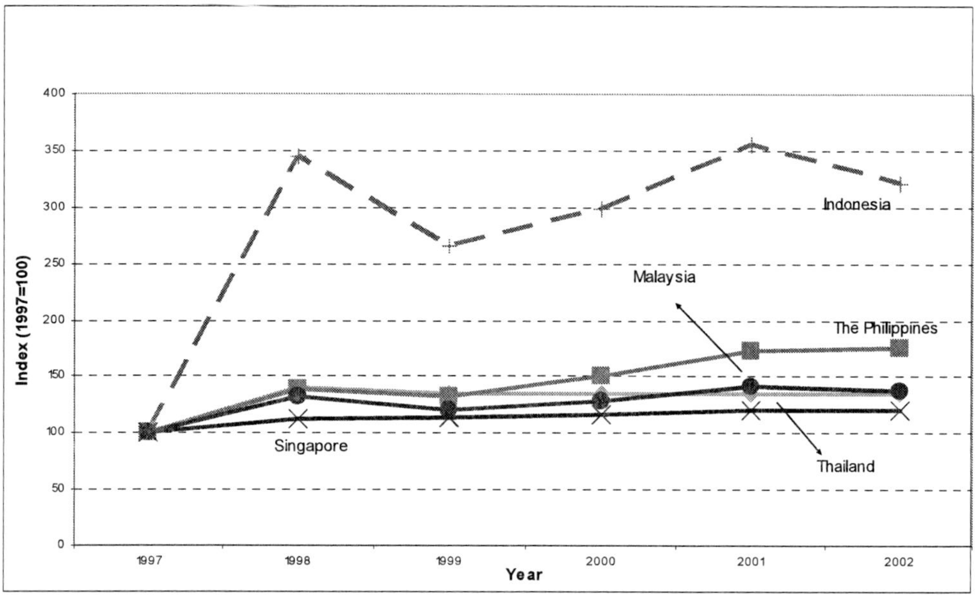

Fig.2.1. – ASEAN-5 Exchange Rates, 1997-2002 (1997=100).Source of basic data: ASEAN Surveillance Coordinating Unit database, ASEAN Secretariat.

Table 2.4. Current Account Balance in Southeast Asia (% of GDP)

	INDO	MSIA	PHILS	SPORE	THAI	ASEAN5 weighted average
1970-75	-2.5	-3.2 (a)	-0.5	-10.3 (b)	-2.0	-0.6
1976-80	1.1	2.6	-0.8	-8.3	-5.4	-2.4
1981-85	-3.7	-8.2	-5.3	-4.8	-5.2	-5.0
1986-90	-2.6	2.1	-1.7	5.5	-1.5	-1.6
1991-96	-2.5	-6.2	-3.6	13.2	-6.7	-3.5
1997-98	1.0	3.6	1.5	20.8	5.4	3.0
1999-02	4.6	10.3	6.3	18.4	7.3	7.1

Note: (a) excludes 1970-72, (b) excludes 1970-74. Sources: ADB, *Key Indicators of Developing Asian and Pacific Countries,* Manila: Asian Development Bank, 1984, 1990, 2000 and 2003, and IMF International Financial Statistics Yearbook, Washington D.C.:IMF, 2000.

ii. High Savings Rates

A more common view of the relationship between savings and economic growth is that a higher level of savings will be able to finance investments and hence accelerate economic growth. The relationship between savings, investment and economic growth is developed in the context of a simplified version of the famous Harrod-Domar model which states that the rate of growth of GNP is determined jointly by the national savings ratio (positive effect) and the national capital-output ratio (negative effect). The economic logic is that in order to grow, economies must save and invest a certain proportion of their GNP. The more they can save and invest, the faster they can grow.

Domestic savings rates of some ASEAN economies have seen a marked improvement, except in the Philippines. This is shown in Table 2.5. In 1975, Singapore and Indonesia had the highest savings rate of 29.4 percent and 26.7 percent, respectively. Singapore's savings rate improved significantly to 40.6 percent in 1985 and to 50 percent in 1995. In 1999, it remained high at about 52 percent of GDP, but fell to about 45 percent in 2002. The savings rates for Malaysia, Thailand and Indonesia also grew markedly and reached about 47 percent, 33 percent and 32 percent, respectively in 1999. However, in 2002, their savings rates dropped to 42 percent, 23 percent and 21 percent, respectively. In the Philippines, the savings rate fell significantly to about 17 percent in 1985 and to about 15 percent in 1995, and subsequently improved to about 27 percent in 2002.

Table 2.5 also shows that the higher savings rate in Southeast Asia is accompanied by rising investment ratios from an average of about 27 percent in 1975 to about 35 percent in 1995, but was reduced significantly to 20 percent in 2002. In terms of the domestic resource gaps (the difference between gross domestic saving and gross domestic investment), Singapore, Indonesia and Malaysia were broadly in better domestic resource balance position than Thailand and the Philippines. Singapore has shown a remarkable improvement from very high deficits in the 1970s to high levels of surpluses during the 1990-2002 period.

Several factors have contributed to the broadly high savings rate in Southeast Asia.[15] First, rapid income growth boosts savings rates as households acquire resources faster than they increase consumption. This is contrary to a more common view that a higher level of savings will be able to finance investments and hence accelerate economic growth. The evidence is not really consistent with the view that growth produces saving.[16] In Singapore, for example, various institutions have contributed to the increase in savings, namely, the government-mandated Central Provident Fund (CPF) saving scheme, the substantial government budget surpluses, and postal savings banks.

Second, with rapid changes in the size and age composition of households, societies with a high proportion of prime-age workers will save more than those with high proportion of young or old. Third, real interest rates in Southeast Asia were positive which stimulated financial savings. From a low of 0.26 percent in Indonesia during the 1970-90 period, real interest rates rose to a high of 4.41 percent in Thailand in 1977-90. Fourth, with prudent fiscal spending, some Southeast Asian economies have relatively higher level of public savings than other developing economies. For example, public savings increased from 5.5 percent of GDP in 1974-80 to 18.5 percent in 1981-90 in Singapore and from an average of 3.2 percent of GDP in 1961-80 to 10.3 percent in 1981-90 in Malaysia. Finally, Singapore and Malaysia have efficient compulsory savings scheme known as the CPF and the Employees Provident Fund, respectively, which have significantly contributed to overall savings.

---

15 World Bank, The East Asian Miracle: Economic Growth and Public Policy, New York: Oxford University Press, 1993.

16 Stanley Fischer, "Lessons from East Asia and the Pacific Rim," in William Bainard and George Perry (eds.), *Brookings Papers on Economic Activity*: Vol, 1997, No.2, Washington DC: Brookings Institution, 1997, p.346.

Table 2.5. Gross Domestic Saving and Investment (% of GDP)

	INDO	MSIA	PHILS	SPORE	THAI	ASEAN-5 weighted average
GDS (S)						
1970	14.3	26.4	21.9	18.4	21.2	19.5
1975	26.7	25.7	24.8	29.4	22.1	25.2
1980	38.0	32.7	24.2	38.1	22.9	30.1
1985	30.3	32.5	17.4	40.6	25.5	26.7
1990	32.3	34.5	18.4	43.6	33.8	30.3
1995	30.6	39.7	14.6	50.0	34.7	30.9
1999	31.7	47.3	19.6	51.7	33.4	32.9
2002	21.1	41.8	26.8	44.7	23.3	26.7
GDI (I)						
1970	15.8	22.4	21.3	38.7	25.6	21.0
1975	23.7	25.3	30.9	40.0	26.7	27.4
1980	24.1	30.4	29.1	46.3	29.1	28.1
1985	28.1	27.6	14.3	42.5	28.2	25.2
1990	30.7	32.4	24.2	36.4	41.4	33.0
1995	30.7	41.5	24.0	35.8	41.8	34.5
1999	11.4	22.4	18.8	32.4	20.5	19.7
2002	14.3	24.4	19.3	20.6	23.8	20.4
Resource Gap (S-I)						
1970	-1.5	4.0	0.5	-20.3	-4.4	-1.5
1975	3.0	0.4	-6.1	-10.5	-4.6	-2.2
1980	14.0	2.3	-4.9	-8.3	-6.3	2.0
1985	2.2	4.9	3.1	-1.9	-2.7	1.5
1990	1.5	2.1	-5.8	7.2	-7.5	-2.7
1995	-0.1	-1.8	-9.4	14.3	-7.1	-3.6
1999	20.3	24.9	0.9	19.3	12.9	13.2
2002	6.8	17.4	7.5	24.1	-0.5	6.3

Note: GDS = Gross Domestic Saving (S), GDI = Gross Domestic Investment. Source: ADB, *Key Indicators of Developing Asian and Pacific Countries*, Manila: Asian Development Bank, 1984, 2000 and 2003.

iii. Financial Liberalization Policies

From a simple financial sector during the post-independence period characterized with one or few commercial banks and simple financial instruments (e.g. savings deposits), Southeast Asian economies have now attained a higher level of financial development. The financial structure has widened and deepened as more banks and non-bank financial institutions have been set up and as more and diverse financial instruments have been created and are now widely available, including interest-bearing instruments.

Singapore and Malaysia were more open economies and had fairly well- developed financial systems in the 1960s and 1970s. Liberalization measures have continued and their financial systems have matured. In Indonesia, Thailand, and the Philippines, financial liberalization began in the 1980s. The Philippines has far-reaching financial reforms. Liberalization efforts of the financial system in Southeast Asia have certainly contributed to the rising trade and investment between Southeast Asian economies and their major trading partners; namely, Japan, US and the European Union. These reforms include, among others, interest rate reforms, entry of foreign banks, changes in foreign equity rules, and others.

iv. Favorable Foreign Investment Policies

There is evidence to support the hypothesis that FDI has been an important stimulus to overall investment.[17] In each of the Southeast Asian countries studied, except the Philippines, overall investments have been associated with the higher growth of FDI.

The Southeast Asian governments have relied on FDIs to a different extent with Singapore being the most dependent, as it has no natural resources and has very limited domestic market size. During the 1960s, it had massive economic problems including high rates of unemployment at about 8-9 percent. Domestic savings and entrepreneurship were practically lacking. Thus, since the 1960s, the Singapore government has explicitly and deliberately depended on export-oriented FDI. The Philippines, Indonesia, Malaysia and Thailand have natural resources and much larger domestic markets. Indonesia and Malaysia are oil and gas producers and have benefited substantially from the oil price hikes in the 1970s. However, as oil prices have been declining and given that oil is a non-renewable resource, both Indonesia and Malaysia have diversified their economies and increased their dependence on FDI.

Over the years, foreign investment policies have been further liberalized. The Southeast Asian host governments have relaxed investment laws and regulations in order to attract investors in a way that only Singapore had done earlier in the 1960s and 1970s. A significant change in the host government policy has been the relaxation of regulations on foreign equity ownership in the case of export firms. Most Southeast Asian governments now allow 100% foreign ownership as long as they produce mainly for exports. Southeast Asia's leading investors are Japan, the United States (US) and the European Union (EU). FDI reached a cumulative total of US$140 billion at the end of 1993, with about 24 percent coming from Japan, 17 percent from the EU and 13 percent from the US, with the triad accounting for a total of 54 percent of the total FDI in ASEAN.[18] Bulk of the investments has been in the manufacturing sector due to their export-orientation. The services sector has also received a large amount of FDI particularly financial and business sector as well as transport and communications sector.

Japanese investments have come into Southeast Asia with the end-in-view of relocating her production processes as domestic industries in Japan began to lose their competitiveness following the strong appreciation of the yen in 1985. Following the behavior of Japanese investors and with the strengthening of their own domestic currencies, the newly-industrialized countries (NIC) had also increased their FDI into the Southeast Asia. Lee states that

> NIC investment in ASEAN is one aspect of the economic linkages which are becoming increasingly important in the Asia-Pacific region. As the NICs become more developed, with human resources embodying higher skills and utilising more sophisticated technology, one

---

17 Florian Alburo, Carlos Bautista, and Maria Socorro Gochoco, "Pacific Direct Investment Flows into ASEAN," *ASEAN Economic Bulletin,* Vol.8, No.3, 1992, p.306.

18 UNCTAD, *Investing in Asia's Dynamism,* Switzerland: UNCTAD Division on Transnational Corporations and Investment and Services of the European Commission, 1996.

> can envisage continued and increased flows of foreign investment to those countries which use more labor-intensive technologies and are more cost-competitive. The ASEAN countries should therefore endeavor to attract not only developed country multinationals, but also NIC investments as well.[19]

Labor Accumulation

During the 1960-87 period, increases in labor accounted for 23 percent of the output growth for the developing countries and 28 percent for East Asia.[20] The Southeast Asian economies in the 1960s had severe unemployment problems arising from enormous labor surplus. Over the years, Singapore and Malaysia have experienced tight labor market conditions particularly on the skilled-labor level.

Policies that Affect Labor Force

In order to cope with the rising demand for labor, the Singapore and Malaysian governments influences and regulates the supply of labor through population control and immigration policies. In Singapore, basically there are two reasons for allowing foreign workers into the labor market. First, is to alleviate the domestic labor shortages or imbalances (particularly in the construction and manufacturing sector). Secondly, it is the government's desire to upgrade the quality of skills of the population by granting permanent residence and citizenship to skilled workers who can be assimilated without difficulty into the local scenario.[21] Moreover, according to BG George Yeo, former Minister for Information and the Arts, the policy of attracting foreign talent in Singapore is part of a much larger undertaking to keep Singapore's growth and regionalization drive on track.[22]

Other policies that increase the labor force include increasing the retirement age and even encouraging retirees to continue working. Incentives are also given to increase population in the form of tax rebates. Housewives are also encouraged to work with the government giving incentives by way of tax rebates for hiring maids and setting up more childcare facilities. The Philippines, Thailand and Indonesia have always had an abundant labor supply and therefore the policies which are adopted in Singapore and Malaysia are considered to a much lesser extent.

Total Factor Productivity Growth

TFP growth accounted for a significant share in the economic growth of developed countries ranging from a low of 50 percent in the US and a high of 87 percent in Germany during the 1960-85 period. As Krugman cited, MIT Professor Robert Solow estimated that

---

19 Tsao Yuan Lee, "NIC Investments in ASEAN: The Pattern in the Eighties," in Lee Ying Soon (ed.), *Foreign Direct Investment in ASEAN,* Kuala Lumpur: Malaysian Economic Association, 1990, pp.132-133.

20 World Bank, *World Development Report,* New York: Oxford University Press, 1991, p.45.

21 Chong Yah Lim, *Development and Underdevelopment*, Singapore: Longman Publications, 1991, p.213.

22 *The Straits Times,* July 31, 1997, p.33.

technological progress had accounted for 80 percent of the long-term rise in US per capita income, with increased investment in capital explaining only the remaining 20 percent.[23] However, for developing countries, the share of TFP growth was estimated at 12 percent and at 15 percent for East Asia.[24] Krugman questioned the long-term growth potential of the East Asian economies as he growth pointed out that their rapid economic growth had depended more on increased factor inputs than on productivity. As he stated:

> Asia's growth is mainly the result of the same things that drive growth everywhere: high investment rates, mainly though not entirely financed by high domestic saving, a rapidly improving level of education, and the transfer of large numbers of underemployed peasants into the modern sector...(T)he fish-and-rice character of Asian growth implies that this growth is bound to slow down: investment cannot continually rise as a share of GDP, people can spend only so many years in school and a rapidly developing country eventually runs out of peasants."[25]

Thus, for Krugman, Asia's rapid growth was "mainly a matter of perspiration rather than inspiration." Jeffrey Sachs, however, responded that many countries perspire, but few achieve sustained high rates of growth, and that Asia's success had been built on substantial foundations.[26] As he put it:

> Asia has been able to encourage saving, and to attract capital and technology to the region, because the underlying economic conditions have been sound, including a private-sector orientation, export competitiveness and prudent economic management.[27]

For Southeast Asia, there are very few published studies on total factor productivity (TFP) estimates. Some earlier estimates are summarized in Table 2.6. Indonesia and Thailand might be classified as productivity-driven economies since TFP accounts for about 25 percent of output growth in these economies. The Philippines is an investment-driven economy with little or no productivity growth at all. In Malaysia and Singapore, TFP has not been a major source of output growth. In fact as Krugman pointed out, all of Singapore's growth can be explained by increases in measured inputs, and that there is no sign at all of increased efficiency.[28] TFP growth has been very low for the majority of Singapore's manufacturing industries during 1970-1979 period due to the predominance of foreign capital in *Singapore* manufacturing, the government's low wage policy combined with the influx of low-skilled foreign labor and the relatively low level of industrial competence in Singapore.[29] However, it was not correct to equate low TFP growth to slow technological change as low TFP growth indicates only slow disembodied technological change and that embodied technological

---

23 Paul Krugman, "The Myth of Asia's Miracle," *Foreign Affairs*, Vol.73, No.4, 1994, p.68.

24 World Bank, *World Development Report*, 1991, p.145.

25 Paul Krugman, "Wrong, It Never Existed," *Time,* September 29, 1997, p.37.

26 Jeffrey Sachs, "Asia's Miracle is Alive and Well," *Time,* September 29, 1997.

27 Jeffrey Sachs, "Asia's Miracle ..."

28 Paul Krugman, "The Myth ...," 1994, p.71.

29 Yuan Tsao, "Growth without Productivity: Singapore Manufacturing in the 1970s," *Journal of Development Economics*, Vol.19, No.1-2, 1985, pp.25-38.

change was significant in Singapore during the 1970s.[30] For most recent period (1987-94), TFP has contributed significantly at 30 percent of GDP growth.[31]

Table 2.6. Total Factor Productivity Estimates in Southeast Asia (a)

Country	Drysdale and Huang (1995) 1950-88	Kawai (1995) 1970-90	World Bank (1993) 1960-89	Collins and Bosworth (1996) 1960-1994
Indonesia	2.1 (31.3) (b)	1.5 (23.8)	1.2 (23.1)	0.8 (14.3)
Malaysian	-0.5 (-7.5)	1.6 (23.8)	1.1 (17.5)	0.9 (13.2)
Philippines	0.2 (4.1)	-0.7 (-19.6)	-	- 0.4 (-10.5)
Thailand	1.7 (29.3)	1.9 (27.1)	2.5 (36.8)	1.8 (24.0)
Singapore	0.8 (10.4)	1.1 (14.9)	1.2 (15)	1.5 (18.1)

(a) In percentage points with percentage contribution to output growth in parentheses. (b) refers to 1962-88. Source: Data for Indonesia, Malaysia, Philippines and Thailand were obtained from Edward Chen K.Y., "The Total Factor Productivity Debate: Determinants of Economic Growth in East Asia", Asian-Pacific Economic Literature, Vol.11, No.1, 1997, p.31. For Singapore, data were taken from the studies cited above: Peter Drysdale and Yiping Huang, "Technological Catch-up and Economic Growth in East Asia and the Pacific," *The Economic Record*, Vol.73, No.222, 1995, pp.201-211; Hiroki Kawai, "International Comparison of Economic Growth," in: Shujiro Urata (ed.), *Trade Liberalization and Economic Development*, Tokyo: Institute of Developing Economies, 1994; World Bank, *The East Asian Miracle: Economic Growth and Public Policy* New York: Oxford University Press, 1993; and Nicholas Crafts, "East Asian Growth Before and After the Crisis," *IMF Staff Papers,* Vol.46, No.2, 1999, pp.139-166 (for Collins and Bosworth, 1996 data).

Policies that Affect Technology

Total factor productivity is also commonly referred to as technical progress or improvement in technology. Technology consists of a software component which is knowledge and a hardware component which includes machinery and equipment. Improvement of technology therefore entails upgrading of people's knowledge (skills and know-hows), and development and acquisition of better quality machinery and equipment. The upgrading of the skills and know-hows has been achieved through education, training and re-training programs in both government and private sectors. The improvement in the quality of human resources through education and training is a key element in explaining growth in the Southeast Asian region by achieving high levels of educational attainment which provided a skilled workforce capable of handling the requirements of industrialization.[32] Kuruvilla and Erickson highlighted the significant role of a national skills development efforts in Singapore and pointed out the strong relationship between investments in human capital and economic

---

30 Edward Chen, "The Total Factor Productivity Debate: Determinants of Economic Growth in East Asia," *Asian-Pacific Economic Literature,* Vol.11, No.1, May 1997, p.30.

31 Bhanoji Rao and Christopher Lee, "Sources of Growth in the Singapore Economy and its Manufacturing and Services Sectors," *Singapore Economic Review,* Vol.40, No.1, 1995, pp.83-115.

32 Seiji Naya and Pearl Imada, "Economic Success of the NIEs and ASEAN: Some Lessons for Latin America?" *Southeast Asian Affairs,* Singapore: Institute of Southeast Asian Studies, 1992, p.50.

growth.[33] Additionally, preventive health care, increasing nutritional levels, and population policies have contributed to increased productivity, savings and upgrading of the quality of the labor force.

The difference among the Southeast Asian countries lies in the extent of upgrading with Singapore and Malaysia having certainly provided more opportunities for both civil servants and private sector workers to upgrade themselves than in other Southeast Asian economies. This differential has been due to various factors which characterized other Southeast Asian economies; namely, the lack of financial resources, the larger size of the labor force, lower skill requirements in the industrial sector, and out-dated educational curricula. Singapore and Malaysia are also in a better position to develop and acquire better quality machinery and equipment as they have been both hosts to a larger number of multinational corporations which bring in technology through foreign direct investments. Southeast Asian governments have also relied on various ways to improve technology including the promotion of research and development (R&D) activities through (a) financial assistance schemes, (b) exchange and joint international programs in science and technology and (c) granting of innovation grants. However, the extent with which these measures have been implemented in Southeast Asian countries depend on the financial resources available. Singapore, unlike other Southeast Asian governments, have more resources to invest in R & D. For example, the Economic Development Board (EDB) awarded over S$130 million in the form of innovation development grants to 90 local and foreign companies as part of a drive to develop Singapore into an innovation development hub.[34]

Structural Adjustment Policies and Reforms

Industrial Policies

In terms of industrialization policy, Southeast Asian economies followed import-substitution policy (ISI) in the 1950s and 1960s. The manufacturing industry received massive inflows of FDI in which industries produced simple and low-priced consumer goods for their respective domestic markets. The Philippines has the longest ISI policy which has brought two effects; namely, an inward-looking manufacturing sector which heavily depended on industrial imports from the developed countries, and an urban-biased development policy. On the other hand, Singapore had the shortest ISI policy experience due to the smallness of her domestic market and limited economies of scale.[35] However, the import substitution in Singapore was quite unlike that in the neighboring countries as it was characterized by very mild protection.[36] In promoting an inward-oriented manufacturing sector, five critical policy instruments were used; namely, exchange controls which were

---

33 See Sarosh Kuruvilla and Christopher Erickson, "An Assessment of the Singapore Skills Development System: Does it Constitute a Viable Model for other Developing Countries?" *World Development,* Vol.30, No.8, 2002, pp.1461-1476.

34 *The Straits Times*, February 19, 1997, p.38.

35 Hank Lim, "Pattern of ASEAN Industrialization," in Swee Hock Saw (ed), *ASEAN Economies in Transition*, Singapore: Singapore University Press, 1980, pp.169-242.

36 Mohamed Ariff, "Industrial Restructuring and Regional Development in the ASEAN Countries: an Overview," Japan: United Nations Center for Regional Development, 1989.

administered by the central banks, the use of import controls, tax and fiscal incentives, the use of various social and ameliorative policy instruments (for example, minimum wage and soft credit terms policy through relatively low interest rates), and tariff policy.

During the late 1960s, Singapore switched to export-oriented industrialization (EOI) which has relied heavily on FDI particularly in labor- intensive industries. Government intervention in the domestic economy was pervasive and extensive and took two forms: first, involving infrastructural activities, and second, direct establishment of wholly-owned or partly-owned industrial and commercial ventures including the national shipping line, the airlines, the Development Bank of Singapore, the Singapore Petroleum Company, the National Iron and Steel Mills, a large trading and investment company. Since 1979, however, Singapore's EOI policy has shifted away from labor-intensive manufacturing towards more skill-oriented, high-technology and high-value-added industries. The shift in emphasis stemmed from the tight labor market conditions and rising domestic costs of production which would hurt the competitiveness of domestically-produced goods.

During the 1970s and 1980s, other Southeast Asian economies relied less on ISI policy and began to follow Singapore's EOI policy cum FDI. Some factors which accounted for this change in industrialization policy include the limited success of ISI, declining and fluctuating prices of primary commodities, and the consequent pursuit of export-diversification policy. The need to diversify is reflected in the changing structure of trade - away from primary toward manufactured goods on the export side and the rising proportion of manufactured goods on the import side.

In order to promote an outward-oriented industrialization policy, the Southeast Asian governments have provided strong support through a package of incentives including tax exemptions, improvement of the investment climate, and provision of industrial infrastructure including the establishment of industrial parks and export-processing zones (EPZs). These EPZs have offered a variety of fiscal and financial incentives to investors, the main ones being the "five freedoms" – from corporate income tax, import duties, import quotas, property taxes and excise taxes. In 1984, the major fiscal incentives offered in ASEAN consisted of the following: (a) 3-5 years tax holiday and duty free import of raw materials and capital goods for Indonesia, (b) tax holiday up to 8 years and duty free imports of all goods pertaining to manufacturing in Malaysia with some exceptions, (c) exemption from municipal and provincial taxes and duty free imports of all capital goods in the Philippines, and (d) 3-8 years tax holiday and exemption of import duties and business tax on imported machinery, equipment, raw materials, components and construction materials in Thailand.[37]

Trade Liberalization Policies

Trade policies essentially take two forms: one set of policies affects prices and the other, affects quantity. The price-oriented measures include tariffs, export taxes or subsidies, retention schemes, duty exemptions, and import deposits. Quantity-oriented measures include import-quotas, import bans, licensing of imports, and export quotas, or price measures related to export targets. Little, et.al stated that

---

37 United Nations, An Evaluation of Export Processing Zones in Selected Asian Countries, Bangkok: UN/ESCAP, 1985, pp. 21-23.

> From 1965 to 1990 our countries [including Indonesia and Thailand among the 18 countries studied] experienced twenty-six tightening and thirty three liberalising episodes, identified on the basis of changes in import quotas, tariffs, export taxes, and subsidies in each... import quotas were the most common tool. Tariffs, export subsidies, and taxes played a minor role in these episodes. In most instances, tariffs were imposed mainly for revenue purposes. At times, export taxes were raised with a devaluation so as to siphon off the higher export revenues in domestic currency resulting from a devaluation. Sometimes, export subsidies were used to offset the bias against exports arising from an increase in the items subject to quotas or an accompanying increase in tariffs.[38]

The Southeast Asian economies have different tariff structure. Singapore has the lowest tariff rates being a highly open export-oriented economy. As a result of trade liberalization measures, the trade-weighted tariff rates fell in 1992 relative to 1986 as follows (in percent): from 0.8 to 0.7 for Singapore, from 10.8 to 10 for Malaysia, from 18 to 10.4 for Indonesia, from 21.4 to 19.8 for the Philippines, and from 31.7 to 27.6 for Thailand.[39] Thus, Thailand has the highest tariff rates due to the import-substitution policy which has given protection to domestic manufacturing industries. Indonesia, Malaysia and the Philippines have a tariff structure somewhere between Singapore and Thailand. The differences in tariff structures helped to explain their differences in designing and implementing trade liberalization measures involving tariff cuts and lessening of non-tariff barriers.

Over the years, tariff cuts have been implemented with the mean tariff for manufactured goods during the 1990-93 period was 20.3 percent for Indonesia; 15.2 percent for Malaysia; 19.5 percent for the Philippines; 0.6 percent for Singapore; and 21.6 percent for Thailand.[40] Trade liberalization measures have boosted Southeast Asian trade and investments which in turn have stimulated economic growth and development in these economies.[41] The precise relationship between exports and GNP growth is more clearly demonstrated by the generally large export elasticities for the Southeast Asian economies, fully indicative of the high level of trade dependence.[42] The outward-looking trade strategies and pragmatic exchange rate policies, combined with rapid expansion in exports is a replication of the path taken by the newly industrialized countries in the 1960s and early 1970s.[43] From inward-looking toward

---

38 Ian Little, Richard Cooper, Max Corden, and Sarath Rajapatirana, *Boom, Crisis Adjustment: The Macroeconomic Experience of Developing Countries,* New York: Oxford University Press for the World Bank, 1993, p.265.

39 Department of Foreign Affairs and Trade, *ASEAN Free Trade Area: Trading Bloc Or Building Block?,* Canberra: Australian Government Publishing Service, 1994, p.65.

40 World Bank, *World Development Indicators*, Washington DC: World Bank, 1997, pp.252-254.

41 See, for example, Bela Balassa, "The Lessons of East Asian Development: An Overview". *Economic Development and Cultural Change*, Vol.36, No.3, 1988, pp.273-289; David Dollar, "Outward-oriented Developing Economies Really Do Grow More Rapidly: Evidence from 95 LDCs, 1976-1985," *Economic Development and Cultural Change,* Vol.40, No.3, 1992, pp.523-544; Moshan Bahmane-Oskooee and Janardhanan Alse, "Export Growth and Economic Growth: An Application of Cointegration and Error-correction Modeling," *Journal of Developing Areas* Vol.27, July 1993, pp.535-542; Santo Dodaro, "Exports and Growth: A Reconsideration of Causality," *Journal of Developing Areas,* Vol.27, No.2, 1993, pp.227-244; Ann Harrison, "Openness and Growth: A Time-series, Cross-country Analysis for Developing Countries," *Journal of Development Economics,* Vol.48, No.2, 1996, pp. 419-447; and Jaleel Ahmad, "Exports and Economic Growth in the ASEAN Countries: Cointegration and Causality Tests," *Rivista Internazionale di Scienze Economiche e Commerciale* Vol.44, 1997, pp.419-430.

42 John Wong, *ASEAN Economies in Perspective*, Singapore: Macmillan Press, 1979, p.13.

43 Colin Kirkpatrick, "The ASEAN Countries: the Next NICs?" *EIU Regional Reference Series*, 1989, p.7.

outward-oriented trade policies, the Southeast Asian trade has undergone transformation away from primary goods towards manufactured products as discussed in the first chapter.

Several factors accounted for the change in the structure of output and trade in the Southeast Asian economies. The first factor is openness to foreign trade as commonly measured by the proportion of total trade (exports plus imports) to output. This is shown in Table 2.7. The openness of all Southeast Asian economies has increased significantly. This is particularly so for Singapore and Malaysia, being the most open economies in Southeast Asia given their high total trade (exports + imports) to GDP ratios which were estimated in 2002 at about 320 percent and 210 percent, respectively.

The second factor is openness to capital flows including foreign direct investments. The Southeast Asian economies have received massive amount of FDI since the appreciation of the yen in 1985, which have been mostly in the manufacturing industry which produces largely manufactured goods for exports. The third factor is the impact of external disturbances such as falling and volatile prices of primary commodities. Foreign exchange earnings declined which was detrimental to the balance of payments and overall economic growth. Finally, the industrialization policy in Southeast Asia has shifted away from import-substitution in the 1950s and 1960s towards export-orientation since the 1970s. All of these factors have promoted the production of and trade in manufactured goods. Another factor is the success of export growth promotion in four activities, namely, the provision of infrastructure; preferential access to capital and foreign exchange; the development of export markets; and other regulations designed to enhance the reputation of the country's exports.[44]

Table 2.7. ASEAN Trade Ratios

	INDO	MSIA	PHILS	SPORE	THAI	ASEAN-5 weighted average
X to GDP						
-1970	13.4	41.4	21.6	105.6	15.0	22.4
-1980	34.2	56.7	23.6	215.4	24.1	37.8
-1990	25.3	74.5	27.5	201.8	34.1	40.5
-2002	35.4	113.8	48.9	173.6	64.8	65.6
M to GDP						
-1970	15.0	37.3	21.1	126.0	19.4	23.9
-1980	20.2	54.3	28.5	223.7	30.4	35.7
-1990	23.7	72.4	33.3	194.9	41.7	42.0
-2002	28.6	96.4	47.8	146.1	57.5	57.0
(X+M) to GDP						
-1970	28.4	78.7	42.6	231.6	34.4	46.3
-1980	54.4	111.0	52.0	439.0	54.5	73.5
-1990	49.1	147.0	60.8	396.7	75.8	82.4
-2002	64.0	210.1	96.8	319.7	122.3	122.6

Note: X = exports, M= imports, GDP = gross domestic product. Source: ADB, *Key Indicators of Developing Asian and Pacific Countries*, Manila: Asian Development Bank, Various Issues.

44 Joseph Stiglitz, "Some Lessons from the East Asian Miracle," *The World Bank Research Observer*, Vol.11, No.2, 1996, pp.170-171.

OTHER FACTORS

Political Stability

The above factors and policies have worked effectively because of a relatively stable political environment. Singapore has been led by former Prime Ministers Lee Kuan Yew and Goh Chok Tong followed by PM Lee Hsien Loong for more than three decades now. Under their leadership, Singapore has been very stable and has been transformed into the most developed country among the developing nations.

Indonesia, led by former President Suharto since 1965, has had some episodes of political unrest as in the East Timor episode and some pockets of demonstrations in various parts of Indonesia. At the height of the 1997/98 economic crisis, former President Suharto was forced to resign because of the strong pressures from the different sectors of the economy particularly the student populace. He was succeeded by former presidents: Habibie, Gus Dur Wahid, Megawati Sukarnoputri, and currently, President Susilo Bambang Yudhoyono.

The Philippines has had five Presidents since 1965; namely, Ferdinand Marcos, Corazon Aquino, Fidel Ramos, Joseph Estrada and Gloria Macapagal Arroyo. There was a number of military rebellions during the Marcos regime. A people power uprising in February 1986 led to the overthrow of Marcos rule and installation of Mrs. Aquino as president until 1992. This event, known as People Power I, was replicated in People Power II which ended President Estrada's term and launched Mrs. Arroyo into presidency, who herself had faced a military mutiny in September 2003. There were also episodes of armed battles between the Communists and the government as well as between Christians and Muslims in the southern Philippines. Moreover, there were kidnapping activities not only in the cities, but also in other parts of the Philippines. There were also some disputes over Sabah and Spratly Islands involving some Southeast Asian countries. Except for some episodes of internal instabilities, the Southeast Asian region could be characterized as broadly stable.

Moreover, the Southeast Asian region has also consistently followed what is commonly known as the "ASEAN way" of doing things, that is, by consensus. The display of Southeast Asian solidarity and the resulting regional stability enhance the group's dealings with other countries. This certainly provides an incentive for foreign investors. In a survey conducted by the Japanese External Trade Organization (JETRO), the relatively stable political climate in the Southeast Asian region was found to be the most important determinant of Japanese direct investments in the region.[45]

Credibility Bonus

In addition to political stability, the above factors and policies have worked effectively because the Southeast Asian people have confidence in their respective governments and policies. For policies to be effective, there should be a credibility bonus in which people strongly believe that their government is seriously committed to implement policies and reforms to achieve the targeted objectives. Furthermore, people believe that they would share in the fruits of these policies. With people being confident in the leadership and policies and

---

45 *The Straits Times,* September 13, 1996.

being satisfied with the effects of those policies, social unrest can be avoided. As Campos and Root stated:

> Among the few countries that have overcome underdevelopment, eight East Asian economies - Japan, the Republic of Korea, Taiwan, Hong Kong, [and four of the five ASEAN countries] Singapore, Thailand, Malaysia, and Indonesia - stand out because of their unusually rapid growth. Their dramatic success is frequently attributed to the adoption of appropriate economic policies. But their policies would have not worked unless each country's populace believed that the policies could be sustained and by implication that some of the benefits would be available to all.[46]

Singaporeans have supported the policies undertaken by their government as they have witnessed and experienced better and high standards of living, rising income per capita and higher savings. In other countries, although income per capita has risen, some people are dissatisfied as the effects of the policies have not filtered through them. The presence of strikes and demonstrations in some countries attest to the lack of confidence and support in their governments and their policies. Moreover, the frequent change in leadership will also cause social unrest. During the 1997/98 economic crisis, however, the lack of confidence of both domestic and foreign investors contributed to the weakening of some Southeast Asian currencies against the US dollar. The Thai government had firmly committed to implement the IMF reforms which had sent positive signals to various economic agents, both domestic and external. The Thai economy has become stable and had shown a modest economic recovery during the immediate post-crisis period.

Is the IMF/WB Model Still Relevant ?

The IMF/World Bank's "free market, minimal government intervention, and market-friendly approach" has been generally accepted as a useful model to explain the East Asian "economic miracle" during the pre-crisis period. Known as the East Asian Economic Model (EAEM), it is characterized by high dependence on the external economy through foreign direct investment and trade, with the government acting to mobilize these resources. Because of its success in East Asia, it has been lauded by the IMF and the World Bank and has even made it a model for other developing countries. However, the 1997/98 crisis has exposed the dangers of being highly dependent on foreign investment and exports, and institutional problems like crony capitalism in which the allocation of funds has been based on political connections.

Southeast Asia and even Northeast Asian economies, particularly the badly hit economies of Thailand, Indonesia, Malaysia and South Korea, are still feeling the impact of the 1997/98 crisis so that the EAEM is seen as no longer relevant during the post-crisis period, and even considered this model as "defunct" and the time has come for an "end of the EAEM."[47] Among Southeast Asia, Thailand and Malaysia have re-examined the validity of this model. In Thailand's case, PM Thaksin has considered an alternative two-track model in which the

---

46 Jose Edgardo Campos and Hilton Root, *The Key to the Asian Miracle: Making Shared Growth Credible*, Washington, D.C.: Brookings Institution, 1996, p.1.

47 The Straits Times, "Will East Asia buy World Bank's economic model?" Oct 12, 2002, p.28.

role of FDI is lessened and SMEs are given more emphasis to stimulate economic growth. Under the leadership of Dr Mahathir and presumably even under his successor Mr Badawi, the Malaysian economy will be leaning more towards the domestic economy. Malaysia's domestic orientation is due to its new "Look East" policy arising from the successful economic recovery of South Korea following its "self-reliant" model which emphasizes the agribusiness sector as an engine of growth.

In the case of the Philippines, the previous and current administrations have been supportive of the IMF/WB policies and reforms. However, there has been resistance coming from various groups since inspite of the reforms the Philippines has had a disapppointing economic growth performance. According to the 1996 World Bank report, the Philippines has not been able to sustain the required growth long enough to reduce the poverty incidence to the levels of neighboring Southeast Asian countries. In fact, the Philippines has been excluded in the 1993 study by the World Bank because of its lackluster performance! Even the quality of life in the Philippines according to surveys has deteriorated. The Pulse Asia's survey, across all socio-economic classes, reported that the material quality of life has indeed worsened rather than improved, with the poorer Filipinos suffering more than the better-off or well-to-do in life. Those who are rated "poor or very poor" were the ones most severely affected by a deteriorating quality of life in the past 12 months (2001). For the year 2002, Pulse Asia conducted another survey and reported that most Filipinos (52 percent) of the 1200 adults surveyed believe that their lives have gotten worse in 2002 (Inquirer, 23 Aug 2003) compared to only 17 percent who believe things had improved. At the national level, the situation was even bleaker as 65 percent of respondents said that conditions had worsened since a year ago. Thus the reported deterioration of the QOL in the Philippines is indeed a puzzle for economic development experiences. Despite the skilled and educational labor force and abundant natural resources, the Philippines has lagged behind other countries in Asia. It seems that the EAEM does not really work for the Philippines.

Indonesia is unlikely to follow the successes of Korea and Thailand with the former having been able to regain market confidence in April 1998 while in the latter investor sentiment recovered more slowly and returned to pre-crisis level in 2002.[48] Both Korea and Thailand have followed a "self-reliance" model as discussed above. However, in the case of Indonesia, it was pointed out in an opinion-editorial that:

> Self reliance is a noble idea. Yet we need to acknowledge our strengths and weaknesses, and work on our weaknesses by any means – including the use of foreign instruments like the IMF, if necessary. True, we should not let the IMF overstay its welcome; yet sending it home when we can still make use of it is, well, wasteful.[49]

However, there has been so much dissatisfaction with the intervention by the IMF and the World Bank. As legislator Syamsul Balda stated: "We have been working with the IMF for years, and it has caused us a lot of disadvantages and few benefits."[50] As such, in the spirit of increasing nationalism, there were calls by some legislators in the National Assembly to cut Indonesia's ties with the IMF arguing that its policy prescriptions are not suitable for

---

48 Asia Times, "Indonesia faces up to post-IMF reality," August 15, 2003.

49 Opinion and editorial, "IMF", Centre for Strategic and International Studies, March 7, 2003.

50 The Straits Times, "Mega pressured to cut IMF ties," August 9, 2002, p.A6.

Indonesia. There was also a coalition of economists who reportedly stated that Indonesia's economic growth would return to the pre-crisis level, if only Indonesia would part with the IMF immediately.[51] Leading a concerted campaign to free Indonesia from foreign control, Indonesia's own National Development Planning Minister Kwik Kian Gie, former coordinating minister for economy and finance, had criticized Jakarta's dependence on the IMF. He stated that: "The IMF says the development of the macroeconomty will bring happiness. I said to them I hope it is so. But I have a different opinion."[52] Some legislators had recommended that Indonesia should prepare the best possible exit plan from the IMF. Thus, after five years of being under IMF's control, Indonesia will break free from the IMF's bailout program and loan lifeline at the end of the year 2003 when its US$5 billion line of credit expires.[53] The IMF will act as auditors and advisors in the monitoring of Indonesia's post-IMF economic reform program twice a year. This has been viewed as a nationalist triumph. As Asia Times stated:

> This is a political victory for the nationalists, who have long argued that the IMF program was a violation of Indonesia's sovereignty. They cited Indonesia's apparent shame and anger when seeing then-IMF managing director Michel Camdessus, standing over ex-president Suharto, arms folded across his chest like a reproving schoolmaster, as Suharto signed the first-ever Letter of Intent on Jan 15, 1998.[54]

However, some have argued that there was a lack of seriousness on the part of the political leadership to undertake economic reforms.[55] Many policies stated in the Letters of Intent were not performed and as such the IMF delayed its loan disbursement for a year. For example, there were delays in the the removal of tariff control hiding behind protectionist barriers and in the privatization of state assets and enterprises, so that the process of reforms is being reverted to protectionism.[56] Thus, the lack of commitment on the part of the Indonesian government combined with the delay in the IMF's financial assistance resulted in the ineffectiveness of Indonesia's recovery program.

As for Singapore, the EAEM is still very much relevant. Singapore has continued to depend on FDI and trade as these are Singapore's main engines of growth given a small economy and lack of natural resources. As a free trader and a vocal champion of global free trade, Singapore has placed its highest priority on and support for a strong-rule based multilateral trading system embodied in the WTO. Singapore has also supported regional initiatives such as ASEAN, APEC and ASEM – which Singapore believes are all complementary to the WTO process. However, the Singapore government has recently forged bilateral Free Trade Agreements (FTAs) with New Zealand, Japan, EFTA, Australia and the United States and has on-going negotiations with Mexico, Canada, South Korea and India.

---

51 Opinion and editorial, "IMF," Centre for Strategic and International Studies, March 7, 2003. (CSIS website: www.csis.or.id/imf1.htm)

52 The Straits Times, "Mega pressured ..."

53 Asia Times, "Indonesia faces up to post-IMF reality," August 15, 2003.

54 Asia Times, "Indonesia faces up to ...".

55 CSIS, "IMF Strategy," CSIS website.

56 CSIS, "Speed up reform, avoid return to protectionism," opinion-editorial in the Jakarta Post, December 27, 2002, CSIS website.

The Singapore government has always emphasized that her FTAs are intended to complement both multilateral and regional initiatives, and not to substitute them.

Because of the questions raised against the continued relevance of the EAEM in the developing world, the World Bank launched a new book titled "Can East Asia Compete? Innovation for Global Markets" which provides an optimistic scenario for East Asia's future. The book argues that East Asia can regain its competitive advantage through (i) innovations with research and development, financial and business services, and information and communication technology as the three engines, and (ii) through opening up their markets.

CONCLUSION

In this chapter, we identified the determinants of Southeast Asia's economic performance based on a supply-side framework following the neoclassical model espoused by the IMF and the World Bank, also known as the East Asian Economic Model, which has been empirically supported by many studies.

In terms of the proximate sources of output growth, the rapid growth of capital accumulation was observed to be a more significant determinant than the growth in labor accumulation and in total factor productivity. The rapid pace of capital accumulation has been made possible due to various factors and policies which include a stable macroeconomic environment, high savings rate, liberalized financial sector, and favorable foreign investment policies. Labor accumulation policies include natural population growth. However, Singapore and Malaysia, having experienced tight labor market conditions, have relied more on foreign workers. Policies that improve productivity include education, training and re-training programs, and research and development activities. Other significant contributory factors are structural adjustment policies and reforms in the industrial and trade sectors, as well as political stability and credibility bonus.

While the East Asian Economic Model has been generally accepted to explain Southeast Asia's robust performance prior to 1997/98 crisis, it is seen as no longer relevant because of the dangers exposed by its free market, minimal government intervention and market-friendly approach particularly with regard to the costs of being heavily dependent on foreign investments and trade. As such, some countries in Southeast Asia have begun to re-orient themselves towards their domestic economies, place more emphasis on the SMEs as engine of growth, and rely less on foreign capital.

QUESTIONS FOR DISCUSSION

1. Southeast Asian economies have similar and different characteristics. What are these? Discuss how their similarities and differences have contributed to their economic growth and development?
2. The governments in Southeast Asia have some common economic objectives of achieving higher economic growth and development, relatively equal income distribution, lower unemployment and providing more social and economic opportunities for their people. Thus, the government leaders and policy makers have implemented economic policies towards the achievement of some, if not all, of these

objectives. However, in most cases, the government has often done more harm than good. Based on some examples in Southeast Asia, discuss this viewpoint.

SUGGESTED MATERIALS FOR CASE STUDIES

Asia

Mundle, Sudipto, 1998, "Financing Human Development: Some Lessons from Advanced Asian Countries," *World Development,* Vol.26, No.4, pp.659-672.

Singapore

Kuruvilla, Sarosh and Christopher Erickson, 2002, "An Assessment of the Singapore Skills Development System: Does it Constitute a Viable Model for other Developing Countries?" *World Development,* Vol.30, No.8, pp.1461-1476.

Thailand

Parnwell, Michael and Daniel Arghiros, 1996, "Introduction: Uneven Development in Thailand," in Michael Parnwell (ed.), *Uneven Development in Thailand,* Aldershot, UK: Avebury, 1996, pp.1-27.

REFERENCES FOR CHAPTER 2

Ahmad, Jaleel and Somchai Harnhirun, 1997, Exports and Economic Growth in the ASEAN Countries: Cointegration and Causality Tests, *Rivista Internazionale di Scienze Economiche e Commerciale,* Vol.44, pp.419-430.

Alburo, Florian, Carlos Bautista, and Maria Socorro Gochoco, 1992, "Pacific Direct Investment flows into ASEAN," *ASEAN Economic Bulletin,* Vol.8, No.3, pp.284-308.

Ariff, Mohamed, 1989, "Industrial Restructuring and Regional Development in the ASEAN Countries: an Overview," Paper presented at the International Conference on Industrial Transformation and Regional Development in an age of Global Interdependence, Japan: United Nations Center for Regional Development.

Asian Development Bank, Various Issues, *Asian Development Outlook,* New York: Oxford University Press.

Asian Development Bank, 1997, *Emerging Asia: Changes and Challenges,* Manila: Asian Development Bank.

Asian Development Bank, Various Issues, *Key Indicators of Asian and Pacific Member Countries,* Manila: Asian Development Bank.

Asiaweek, February 14 and 21, 1997.

Bahmani-Oskooee, Mohsen and Alse, Janardhanan, 1993, "Export Growth and Economic Growth: An Application of Cointegration and Error-Correction Modeling," *Journal of Developing Areas,* Vol.27, No.4, pp.535-542.

Balassa, Bela, 1988, "The Lessons of East Asian Development: An Overview". *Economic Development and Cultural Change*, Vol.36, No.3, pp.273-289.

Bleaney, Michael, 1996, "Macroeconomic Stability, Investment and Growth in Developing Countries," *Journal of Development Economics,* Vol.48, No.2, pp.461-477.

Booth, Anne, 1992, "An Economic Overview of Southeast Asia," *Southeast Asian Affairs,* Singapore: Institute of Southeast Asian Studies, pp.21-43.

Jose Edgardo Campos and Hilton Root, 1996, *The Key to the Asian Miracle: Making Shared Growth Credible,* Washington, D.C.: Brookings Institution.

Carroll, C., D. Weil, and Lawrence Summers, 1993, "Savings and Growth: A Re-interpretation," Paper presented at the Carnegie-Rochester Public Policy Conference, Bradley Policy Research Centre, April 23-24.

Chen, Edward, 1997, "The Total Factor Productivity Debate: Determinants of Economic Growth in East Asia," *Asian-Pacific Economic Literature,* Vol.11, No.1, pp.18-38.

Chia, Siow Yue, 1996, "The Deepening and Widening of ASEAN," *Journal of Asia Pacific Economy,* Vol.1, pp.59-78.

Collins, Susan and Barry Bosworth, 1997, "Economic Growth in East Asia: Accumulation versus Assimilation," in W. Bainard and G. Perry, eds, *Brookings Papers on Economic Activity,* Washington DC: Brookings Institution, pp.135-203.

Corden, Max, 1996, *Pragmatic Orthodoxy: Macroeconomic Policies in Seven East Asian Economies,* Occasional Papers No.61, California: International Centre for Economic Growth.

Crafts, Nicholas, 1999, "East Asian Growth Before and After the crisis," *IMF Staff Papers,* Vol. 46, No.2, pp.139-166.

Department of Foreign Affairs and Trade (DFAT), 1994, *ASEAN Free Trade Area: Trading Bloc Or Building Block?* Canberra: Australian Government Publishing Service.

Dodaro, Santo, 1993, "Exports and Growth: A Reconsideration of Causality," *Journal of Developing Areas,* Vol.27, No.2, pp.227-244.

Dollar, David, 1992, "Outward-oriented Developing Economies Really do Grow More Rapidly: Evidence from 95 LDCs, 1976-1985," *Economic Development and Cultural Change,* Vol.40, No.3, pp.523-544.

Drysdale, Peter and Huang, Yiping, 1995, "Technological Catch-up and Economic Growth in East Asia and the Pacific," *The Economic Record*, Vol.73, No.222, pp.201-211.

Fischer, Stanley, 1997, "Lessons from East Asia and the Pacific Rim," in W. Bainard and G. Perry (eds.), *Brookings Papers on Economic Activity*, Washington DC: Brookings Institution, pp.345-350.

Garnaut, Ross (ed.), 1980, *ASEAN in a Changing Pacific and World Economy.* Canberra: Australian National University Press.

Haggard, Stephen and Kim, Euysung, 1996, "The Sources of East Asia's Economic Growth," *Access Asia Review,* Vol.1, No.1, pp.31-63.

Harrison, Ann, 1996, "Openness and Growth: A Time-Series, Cross-Country Analysis for Developing Countries," *Journal of Development Economics,* Vol.48, No.2, pp.419-447.

Hill, Hal, 1996, "Indonesia's Industrial Policy and Performance: Orthodoxy Vindicated," *Economic Development and Cultural Change,* Vol.45, No.1, pp.147-174.

International Monetary Fund, 1998, *International Financial Statistics,* Washington DC.: International Monetary Fund.

Kawai, Hiroki, 1994, "International Comparison of Economic Growth," in H. Urata, (ed.), *Trade Liberalization and Economic Development*, Tokyo: Institute of Developing Economies.

Kim, Jong-Il. and Lawrence Lau, 1994, "The Source of Economic Growth of the East Asian Newly Industrializing Countries," *Journal of the Japanese and International Economies*, Vol.8, No.3, pp.235-271.

Kirkpatrick, Colin, 1989, "The ASEAN Countries: The Next NICs?" *EIU Regional Reference Series*, pp.5-14.

Krugman, Paul, 1994, "The Myth of Asia's Miracle," *Foreign Affairs*, Vol.73, No.6, pp. 62-78.

Lee Tsao Yuan, 1990, "NIC Investments in ASEAN: The Pattern in the Eighties", in Soon Lee Ying (ed.), *Foreign Direct Investment in ASEAN,* Kuala Lumpur: Malaysian Economic Association, pp.112-135.

Lim Chong Yah, 1991, *Development and Underdevelopment*, Singapore: Longman Publications.

Lim Chong Yah and Associates, 1988, *Policy Options for the Singapore Economy,* Singapore: McGraw Hill, pp. 301-320.

Lim, David, 1994, "Explaining The Growth Performance of Asian Developing Economies," *Economic Development and Cultural Change,* Vol.42, No.4, pp.829-844.

Lim, Hank, 1980, "Pattern of ASEAN Industrialization," Saw Swee Hock (ed.), *ASEAN Economies in Transition*, Singapore: Singapore University Press, pp.169-242.

Little, Ian, Richard Cooper, Max Corden, and Sarath Rajapatirana, 1992, *Boom, Crisis Adjustment: The Macroeconomic Experience of Developing Ccountries,* New York: Oxford University Press for the World Bank.

Naya, Seiji, 1987, "Economic Performance and Growth Factors of the ASEAN Countries," Martin, L.G. (ed.), *The ASEAN Success Story: Social, Economic and Political Dimensions,* Hawaii: East-West Center, pp. 47-87.

Naya, Seiji and Pearl Imada, 1992, "Economic Success of the NIEs and ASEAN: Some Lessons for Latin America?" *Southeast Asian Affairs,* pp.44-57.

OECD, 1998, *International Direct Investment Statistics Yearbook,* Paris: OECD.

Page, John, 1994, "The East Asian Miracle: Four Lessons for Development Policy," Stanley Fischer, and J. Rotenberg (eds.), *NBER Macroeconomics Annual*, Cambridge: MIT Press, pp.219-269.

Rana, Pradumna, 1987, "Foreign Direct Investment and Economic Growth in the Asian and Pacific Region," *Asian Development Review*, Vol.5, pp.100-115.

Rao, Bhanoji, Teofilo Daquila, and Woo Yuen Pau, 1994, *ASEAN External Debt Perspectives,* Singapore: Times Academic Press.

Rao, Bhanoji and Christopher Lee, 1995, "Sources of Growth in the Singapore Economy and its Manufacturing and Services Sectors," *Singapore Economic Review,* Vol.40, No.1, pp.83-115.

Stiglitz, Joseph, 1996, "Some Lessons from the East Asian Miracle," *The World Bank Research Observer,* Vol.11, No.2, pp.151-177.

The Straits Times, September 13, 1996; February, 19, 1997, p.38; and July 31, 1997, p.33.

Todaro, Michael, 1994, *Economic Development in the Third World,* New York: Longman.

Tsao Yuan, 1985, "Growth without Productivity: Singapore Manufacturing in the 1970s," *Journal of Development Economics,* Vol.18, No.1-2, pp.25-38.

United Nations, 1985, *An Evaluation of Export Processing Zones in Selected Asian Countries,* Bangkok: UN/ESCAP, pp. 21-23.

UNCTAD, 1996, *Investing in Asia's Dynamism,* Switzerland: UNCTAD Division on Transnational Corporations and Investment and Services of the European Commission.

Vyas, V.S., 1983, "Asian Agriculture: Achievements and Challenges," *Asian Development Review*, Vol.1, No.2, pp.27-44.

Wong, John, 1979, *ASEAN Economies in Perspective,* Singapore: Macmillan Press.

World Bank, 1993, *The East Asian Miracle: Economic Growth and Public Policy,* New York: Oxford University Press.

World Bank, 1997, *World Development Indicators,* New York: Oxford University Press.

World Bank, 1991, *World Development Report,* New York: Oxford University Press.

Young, Alwyn, 1995, "Lessons from the East Asian NICS: a contrarian view," *European Economic Review,* Vol.38, No.3-4, pp.964-973.

Young, Alwyn, 1994, "The Tyranny of Numbers: Confronting the Statistical Realities of the East Asian Growth Experience," *Quarterly Journal of Economics,* Vol.110, No.3, pp.641-680.

Part II: The Domestic Economy of Southeast Asia

Chapter 3

THE AGRICULTURAL SECTOR IN SOUTHEAST ASIA: PRODUCTION, PROBLEMS AND POLICIES

ABSTRACT

This chapter provides an analysis of the significance of the agricultural sector in terms of land use, as a potent engine of growth, labor employment, providing food and raw materials, generating foreign exchange, contributing to capital formation, and providing a market for manufactured goods. It also discusses the Green Revolution: definition, components, and benefits and costs. It also identifies and analyzes the various problems besetting the agricultural sector such as the urban-biased industrialization policy, institutional problems, problems related to green revolution, rural-urban migration, external factors and the lack of regional cooperation in agriculture. The final section discusses the three areas of policy actions which are necessary for agricultural and rural development including (a) institutional transformation, (b) balanced development strategies, and (c) integration of production with overall rural development. On top of these policy areas, a regional ASEAN policy on agricultural cooperation should be promoted and developed.

INTRODUCTION

This chapter discusses the agricultural sector in Southeast Asia: its importance, production trends and patterns, the Green Revolution, problems and policies. The agricultural sector consists of agriculture, fishery and forestry. Table 3.1 shows the contribution of the agricultural sector to total GDP. The share of the agricultural sector to output has been decreasing for all countries. Owing to the limited land area, agriculture is not so important to Singapore, but because of its nodal position and historical development it continues to function as an important trading, processing, and financial center for the region's agricultural commodities.[1]

---

1 Siok-Hwa Cheng, "Development of ASEAN Agriculture," in Swee Hock Saw (ed.), *ASEAN Economies in Transition,* Singapore: Singapore University Press, 1980, p.70.

Production

There are two productions sub-sectors in Southeast Asia; namely, the subsistence sector and the commercial sector. The subsistence sector produces rice and maize. It is directly concerned with the livelihood of 80 percent or more of the rural population. In Southeast Asia, the most important food crop is rice. Most rice farmers are subsistence farmers who have received subsidies from the government in the form of price supports, fertilizer subsidies, provision of irrigation, infrastructure and credit facilities.

Table 3.1. Share of Agriculture to GDP, (%)

	1970	1975	1980	1985	1990	1995	2002
INDO	47.0	36.8	30.7	22.7	19.6	17.2	17.5
MSIA	32.0	27.7	23.8	20.8	18.7	12.9	8.0
PHILS	28.8	26.6	25.6	24.6	22.5	21.7	14.9
SPORE	2.3	1.6	1.2	0.8	0.3	0.2	0.1
THAI	30.2	30.5	24.8	19.9	14.4	10.9	9.0
ASEAN5 weighted average	33.1	28.5	23.2	20.6	17.4	15.1	12.9

Source: ADB, *Key Indicators of Developing Asian and Pacific Countries*, Manila: Asian Development Bank, 1984, 2000 and 2003 issues; Food and Agriculture Organization of the United Nations – FAOSTAT: http://apps.fao.org/default.htm

The commercial crop sector is also known as the export or cash crops sector. Indonesia produces and exports rubber, coffee, tea, tobacco, pepper and palm oil. In Malaysia, the main cash crops are rubber, palm oil, sawlogs and sawn-timber. The cultivation of rubber began during the colonial times and was pursued strongly by the British colonial government. In the mid-1980s, however, palm oil gradually replaced rubber as the most important export crop. There were about 2.4 million hectares of land which were planted with palm oil and about 1.7 million hectares were planted with rubber. Malaysia has become the world's largest producer and exporter of palm oil. In the Philippines, the main agricultural exports include sugar, coconut and lumber. Thailand's export crops include rice, corn, cassava or tapioca, and sugar molasses.

Importance of Agriculture

The agricultural sector has become important because of its contributions to Southeast Asian economies in terms of land use, being an engine of growth, employment creation, foreign exchange receipts, capital formation, and providing a market for manufactured goods.

Land Use

Table 3.2 shows that Indonesia has the largest total land area of about 2 million square kilometers of which about 20 percent has been allocated to agricultural purposes (arable land

and permanent crops). Thailand ranks next in terms of land area, but the proportion of land area directed to agricultural-cropped land was about 35 percent of the total land area. This indicates the significance of agricultural activities in Thailand. In Malaysia, the proportion of land planted to agricultural crops even rose from about 15 percent in 1980 to about 23 percent in 2001. But in Singapore, the share of land allocated to agricultural production decreased significantly and instead the proportion of land directed to other purposes increased from 87 percent to 98 percent including land for industrial, commercial and residential purposes.

Table 3.2. Land Area and Its Uses

	Total Area (1000 sq.km.)	Share of Total Area, %		
		Agriculture (cropped land)		Others
		Arable Land	Permanent Crops	
Indonesia				
1980	1904.6	9.9	4.4	85.6
2001	1904.6	11.0	7.0	82.0
Malaysia				
1980	329.8	3.0	11.6	85.4
2001	329.8	5.5	17.5	77.0
Philippines				
1980	300	17.5	14.8	67.7
2001	300	18.8	16.7	64.5
Singapore				
1980	0.6	3.3	9.8	86.9
2001	0.6	1.6	0.0	98.4
Thailand				
1980	513.1	32.3	3.5	64.2
2001	513.1	29.2	6.4	64.3
ASEAN-5				
1980	3048.1	0.1	0.1	99.8
2001	3048.1	0.1	0.1	99.8

Source: ADB, *Key Indicators of Developing Asian and Pacific Countries*, Manila: Asian Development Bank, 1984, 2000 and 2003 issues; Food and Agriculture Organization of the United Nations – FAOSTAT: http://apps.fao.org/default.htm

Potent Engine of Growth

The agricultural sector can serve as an engine of growth. For example, during the Philippine economic crisis in the 1980s, agriculture posted positive growth rates when all other sectors experienced negative growth. During the immediate post-1997 crisis, the agricultural sector grew while the manufacturing and finance sectors were hit severely.

Employment

Except in Singapore and Malaysia, the agricultural sector has continued to provide a major source of employment in Southeast Asia. This is shown in Table 3.3. The vast majority of the world's poorest people are located in rural areas and engaged primarily in subsistence agriculture as their basic concern is survival.[2]

Table 3.3. Employment in the Agricultural Sector (share of total employment, %)

	1970	1975	1980	1985	1990	1995	2002
INDONESIA	64	60.1	56.0	54.7	55.9	44	42.6
MALAYSIA	49	47.6	37.2	31.3	26.0	18.1	15.8
PHILIPPINES	54	53.5	51.4	48.9	45.2	44.1	37.4
SINGAPORE	3.4	2.2	1.6	0.7	0.4	0.2	0.2
THAILAND	79	72.7	70.8	65.2	63.9	52	35.4
ASEAN-5 weighted average	30	36.0	40.7	48.6	48.4	40.4	36.6

Source: ADB, *Key Indicators of Developing Asian and Pacific Countries*, Manila: Asian Development Bank, 1995, 1996, 2000 and 2003 issues; LABORSTA, an International Labor Office database on labor statistics operated by ILO Bureau of Statistics – http://laborsta.ilo.org

Source of Food and Raw Materials

The agricultural sector provides food and raw materials to the expanding industrial sector. Rubber, wood and palm products are utilized as inputs in the manufacture of final products. Table 3.4 shows the production of three major crops, namely, paddy rice, maize and coconut rose during the 1980-2002 period. Southeast Asia has been a major producer of coconuts, as it accounts for an average share of about 60 percent of total world production. As for rice, Southeast Asia shared an average of about 15 percent. In terms of maize, only 3 percent has been produced in the region. In Southeast Asia, as industrialization proceeds at a relatively fast pace and as population increases, massive amount of food supplies and raw materials are consumed. Domestic production has been insufficient particularly for rice and maize so that some countries have supplemented them with imported products from other parts of the world.

Generates Foreign Exchange

Southeast Asian economies, except for Singapore and Brunei, are major world producers and exporters of rice, rubber, timber, palm oil, coconut and sugar.[3] Indonesia, Malaysia, Philippines and Thailand are major net exporters of food, agriculture, fishery and forestry products and as such have earned foreign exchange from them. For example, rice exports by Thailand formed a valuable source of foreign exchange which generated about 3 percent of

---

2 Michael Todaro, "Chapter 10 – Agricultural Transformation and Rural Development," in Michael Todaro, *Economic Development in the Third World,* New York: Longman, 1994, p.286.

3 Siok-Hwa Cheng, "Development of ASEAN Agriculture…," 1980, p.72.

GNP annually during the good years.[4] The importance of rice to Thailand is captured in the following statements by Flaherty, Vandergeest and Miller (1999):

> Rice has been at the center of Thai life for centuries. It is not only the mainstay of the Thai diet, but was the country's largest single foreign exchange earner for over a century. Rice exports provided the foundation for Thailand's economic development and were the vanguard for the country's integration into the global economy. The Chao Phraya River plain, which is the richest and most extensive rice-growing area in the country, has often been described as the "Rice Bowl of Asia." ... Thailand continues to reign as the world's largest rice exporter, earning US$1.72 billion in 1996. [5]

Table 3.4. Production of Major Agricultural Crops ('000 Metric Tons)

		INDO	MSIA	PHILS	THAI	ASEAN-4	WORLD
Paddy rice	1980	29625 (7)	2070 (1)	7723 (2)	17368 (4)	56786 (14)	399360 (100)
	1990	45179 (9)	1960 (...)	9885 (2)	17193 (3)	74217 (14)	519995 (100)
	2002	51604 (9)	2091 (...)	13271 (2)	25945 (5)	92910 (16)	576280 (100)
Maize	1980	3991 (1)	8 (...)	3123 (1)	3000 (1)	10122 (3)	396770 (100)
	1990	6734 (1)	35 (...)	4854 (1)	3722 (3)	15345 (3)	482283 (100)
	2002	9277 (2)	70 (...)	4319 (1)	4170 (1)	17837 (3)	602589 (100)
Coconut	1980	10900 (32)	1219 (3)	8552 (25)	735 (2)	21406 (63)	33955 (100)
	1990	12120 (29)	1135 (3)	11023 (26)	1426 (3)	25704 (61)	42483 (100)
	2002	13000 (26)	700 (1)	13683 (28)	1396 (3)	28779 (58)	49634 (100)

Note: Figures in parentheses refer to shares of total world production. Source: ADB, Key Indicators of Developing Asian and Pacific Countries, Manila: Asian Development Bank, 1984, 2000 and 2003 issues; Food and Agriculture Organization of the United Nations – FAOSTAT: http://apps.fao.org/default.htm

However, foreign exchange earnings from agricultural exports depend heavily on their world prices. The commodity boom in the early 1970s generated a foreign exchange bonanza for Indonesia, Malaysia, the Philippines and Thailand. This is clearly evident in Table 3.5.

---

4 John Wong, "Chapter 4 – Agricultural and Rural Development: Legacy of the Urban Bias," in John Wong, *ASEAN Economies in Perspective*, Singapore: The Macmillan Press Ltd., 1979, p.94.

5 See Mark Flaherty, Peter Vandergeest and Paul Miller, 1999, "Rice Paddy or Shrimp Pond: Tough Decisions on Rural Thailand," *World Development*, Vol.27, No.12, 1999, pp.2045-2046.

Table 3.5. Major Agricultural Exports from Southeast Asia (in US$ Million)

	1970		1980		1990		2002	
	Value	**Share**	**Value**	**Share**	**Value**	**Share**	**Value**	**Share**
Indonesia								
-wood	104	9.4	56	0.2	2726	10.6	1838	3
-rubber	253	22.8	1165	4.9	891	3.5	1208	2
-coffee	69	6.2	658	2.7	369	1.4	232	0
-shrimp	n.a.	...	181	0.8	671	2.6	940	2
-Subtotal	426	38.4	2060	8.6	4657	18.1	4218	7
-Total exports	1108	100.0	23951	100.0	25675	100.0	57006	100
Malaysia								
-rubber	563	33.4	2121	16.4	1119	3.8	656	1
-sawlogs,timber	278	16.5	1820	14.0	2627	8.9	1057	1
-palm oil	86	5.1	1196	9.2	1631	5.5	3962	4
-Subtotal	928	55.0	5137	39.7	5377	18.3	5675	6
-Total exports	1686	100.0	12941	100.0	29445	100.0	93283	100
Philippines								
-coconut oil	96	8.4	567	9.8	361	4.4	353	1
-copper concen.	185	16.2	545	9.4	207	2.5	13	0
-logs&lumber	250	21.9	624	10.8	111	1.4	11	0
-sugar	188	16.5	273	4.7	20	0.2	36	0
-copra	80	7.0	47	0.8	20	0.2	1	0
-Subtotal	799	70.0	2056	35.5	719	8.8	413	1
-Total exports	1142	100.0	5788	100.0	8186	100.0	35208	100
Thailand								
-rice	121	17.0	952	14.6	1085	4.7	1630	2
-tapioca	59	8.3	727	11.2	904	3.9	5	0
-rubber	107	15.1	603	9.3	920	4.0	2464	4
-shrimp	n.a.	...	98	1.5	799	3.4	2221	3
-Subtotal	287	40.4	2380	36.6	3708	16.1	6319	9
-Total Exports	710	100.0	6504	100.0	23049	100.0	68801	100
ASEAN-4:								
Total of export Crops	2440	53	11633	24	14461	17	16626	7
Total Exports	4646	100	49184	100	86355	100	254299	100

Note: Share refers to share of each commodity to the country's total exports. Source: ADB, *Key Indicators of Developing Asian and Pacific Countries*, Manila: Asian Development Bank, 1984, 2000 and 2003 issues; UN Statistics Division – UN Commodity Trade Statistics (UN Comtrade).

The shares of the major agricultural exports to total exports in 1970 were high from a low share of 38 percent for Indonesia to a high share of 70 percent for the Philippines. Subsequently, however, the prices of agricultural commodities had been very volatile and on the whole have indicated a downward trend. Table 3.5 also shows that the shares of agricultural exports to total exports fell for all countries from 53 percent in 1970 to 24 percent in 1980 and to 7 percent in 2002.

Capital Formation

The agricultural sector contributes to capital formation by providing an 'investible surplus' in the form of savings and taxes collected from this sector which helps to finance the investment requirements of the expanding industrial sector.[6] In particular, the foreign exchange generated from the agricultural sector are essential in importing capital equipment and intermediate goods to support the manufacturing sector.

Market for Manufactured Goods

Since a sizeable proportion of the population still live and work in the agricultural and rural areas, this sector provides a market for manufactured goods including consumer and industrial goods. This is shown in Table 3.6. The proportion of people living in the rural areas has fallen, but it has remained significant ranging from about 40 percent of the total population in the Philippines to about 80 percent in Thailand in 2001. While Malaysia, Indonesia and the Philippines registered a faster decline in the proportion of people living in the rural areas, Thailand's decline was relatively slower.

GREEN REVOLUTION

Definition

In order to provide for food security, many Asian and Pacific governments have undertaken Green Revolution which refers to many different combinations of agricultural techniques and technological innovations including the introduction of high yielding varieties (HYVs) of basic crops.[7] The hybrid seeds have been produced by cross-breeding plants and crops of different varieties through scientific research. Its rationale was to close the gaps in rice productivity between Southeast Asia and East Asia. In the 1960s, Japan had a rice yield equivalent to twice that of Malaysia, three times that of Indonesia and Thailand, and four times that of the Philippines.[8]

---

6 Gerald Meier, *Leading Issues in Economic Development*. New York: Oxford University Press, 1989, p.328.

7 ESCAP, *Reducing Disparities: Balanced Development of Urban and Rural Areas and Regions within the Countries of Asia and the Pacific*, New York: Economic and Social Commission for Asia and the Pacific, 2001, p.77.

8 By 1975, sixty-two percent of the rice area in the Philippines was planted with the modern varieties, 41 percent in Indonesia, 36 percent in Malaysia, but only 7 percent in Thailand because of its slow response to Green Revolution. See John Wong, "Agricultural and Rural Development...," 1979, p.95.

Table 3.6. Rural versus Urban Population in Southeast Asia

	Indonesia	Malaysia	Philippines	Singapore	Thailand
Rural	Proportion of Total Population				
1970	82.9	73.0	68.2	0	86.8
1975	80.6	62.3	64.4	0	84.9
1980	77.8	58.0	62.5	0	83.0
1985	73.9	54.1	57.0	0	82.1
1990	69.4	50.3	51.2	0	81.3
1995	64.6	46.3	45.8	0	80.0
1999	60.8	43.5	42.4	0	78.7
2001	56.9	41.2	39.8	0	79.8
Urban	Proportion of Total Population				
1970	17.1	27.0	31.8	100	13.2
1975	19.4	37.7	35.6	100	15.1
1980	22.2	42.0	37.5	100	17.0
1985	26.1	45.9	43.0	100	17.9
1990	30.6	49.7	48.8	100	18.7
1995	35.4	53.7	54.2	100	20.0
1999	39.2	56.5	57.6	100	21.3
2001	43.1	58.8	60.2	100	20.2
Total	Million				
1970	116.2	8.8	36.9	2.0	36.4
1975	132.0	12.3	42.1	2.3	41.4
1980	147.3	13.8	48.3	2.4	46.7
1985	164.6	15.7	54.7	2.5	51.7
1990	179.3	17.8	62.0	3.0	55.8
1995	194.8	20.7	70.3	3.5	59.4
1999	207.4	22.7	76.8	3.9	61.8
2001	217.5	23.0	78.6	4.2	64.3

Source: ADB, *Key Indicators of Developing Asian and Pacific Countries*, Manila: Asian Development Bank, 1984, 1990, 1996, 2000 and 2003 issues; UN Statistical Yearbook for Asia and the Pacific, Various Issues; and United Nations Population Fund at http://www.unfpa.org.

Components

The Green revolution has various components. First, biological innovations involve innovations in seeds and fertilizer. Some of the characteristics of the HYV seeds are as follows: high yielding, disease resistant, fertilizer responsive, drought resistant, short maturity, short in stalk and high nutrient content. The International Rice Research Institute (IRRI) was set up in the Philippines in 1962 and has developed new high yielding varieties (HYVs) of rice including the first variety known as IR-8. The most recent rice hybrid known as 'super rice' was estimated to produce 12.5 tons of rice per hectare which is more than twice the Asian average of five to six tons a hectare. There can be two to three crops a year as it has a shorter growing period of about 110 days which is much less than 160 days for other varieties. It is expected that this new and more nutritious variety could help meet the rising demand for rice in the Southeast Asian region.

Second, mechanical innovations involve the introduction of mechanized farming. There was, however, a relatively slow progress since mechanization requires heavy capital investment, new pattern of farm management and requires large-size farms. However, many Southeast Asian farms are small-sized and fragmented.

Third, the usage of fertilizers particularly chemical fertilizers has helped to speed up the absorption of nutrients from the soil. Fourth, the Green Revolution relies on insecticides, pesticides, rodenticides, herbicides and fungicides – aimed at fighting diseases and pests. Fifth, Green Revolution involves cultivation technology and water control. Farmers need to have technical knowledge of planting crops. They also have to rely on the availability of irrigation facilities and agricultural extension services. In East Asia, for example, irrigated land in use rose significantly from 59 million hectares in 1979/81 to 69 million hectares in 1995/97 and is predicted to rise further to 78 million hectares in 2015.[9] Sixth, GR involves land reform which usually centers on the expropriation of lands in private ownership to be redistributed to tenants and landless workers. Seventh, farmers need to depend on agricultural credit. Eighth, farmers should also rely on support infrastructure.

Benefits and Costs

The Green Revolution generates some benefits including increase in rice production towards self-sufficiency and increase in productivity. Table 3.7 shows the level of rice paddy production in four rice growing countries in Southeast Asia. Indonesia is the largest producer of rice as it accounted for about 50 percent of the total production of the four countries during the 1970-2002 period. However, Indonesia's production was not sufficient for its population of about 140 million in the 1970s, which had turned it into the biggest rice importer in the world.[10] This trend has presumably continued given that its population has grown rapidly and reached 200 million in the year 2000. Thailand comes next in terms of production as it accounted for about one-third of the total production. Table 3.7 also shows the increase in productivity with Indonesia registering the largest gains between 1970 and 2002.

Other benefits include diversification of agricultural commodities including multiple cropping, additional rural employment, increases in family income, foreign exchange earnings, and spin-offs to other sectors in the form of forward and backward linkages. As the application of the new HYVs requires good irrigation, finance, storage and milling facilities, to name a few, the benefits have been spread unevenly even within and among the countries in Southeast Asia. Only the large farmers and landowners have gained from the Green Revolution given that they have direct access to the resources including finance. These farmers can introduce basic mechanization and buy out smaller lands to achieve economies of scale. But with strong and committed support from the government, even the small farmers and tenants could also benefit from the Green Revolution. Among Southeast Asian economies, Malaysia has had some success in implementing the Green Revolution in rice cultivation due to the Muda irrigation scheme in Kedah, the provision of bank credit, and Mardi's assistance to farmers.

---

9 ESCAP, *Reducing Disparities ....*, 2001, p.82.

10 Siok-Hwa Cheng, "Development of ASEAN Agriculture...," 1980, p.74

Table 3.7. Production and Productivity of Rice Paddy in Southeast Asia

	Indonesia	Malaysia	Philippines	Thailand	ASEAN4
	Production ('000 Metric Tons)				
1970	19324 (48.8)	1080 (2.7)	5322 (13.5)	13850 (35.0)	39577
1975	22340 (48.8)	1997 (4.3)	6159 (13.4)	15300 (33.4)	45796
1980	29652 (52.4)	1798 (3.2)	7723 (13.7)	17368 (30.7)	56541
1985	39033 (55.8)	1849 (2.6)	8806 (12.6)	20264 (29.0)	69952
1990	45180 (58.4)	1960 (2.5)	9885 (12.8)	20264 (26.2)	77289
1995	49744 (58.4)	2126 (2.5)	11284 (13.2)	22016 (25.8)	85170
1999	49534 (57.5)	1934 (2.2)	11388 (13.2)	23272 (27.0)	86128
2002	51604 (51.50	2091 (2.3)	13271 (14.3)	25945 (27.9)	92910
	Productivity (kilograms/hectare)				
1970	2040	2380	1780	1870	1947
1975	2630	2662	1664	1831	2150
1980	3293	2883	2155	1909	2534
1985	3942	2780	2588	2061	2939
1990	4302	2591	2808	3527	3766
1995	4349	3160	2856	3674	3862
1999	4261	2869	2863	2357	3294
2002	4433	3090	3280	2597	3525

Note: In production data, figures in the parentheses refer to share of each country's production to total ASEAN4 production. Source: FAO, *Production Yearbook*, Rome: Food and Agriculture Organization, and ADB, *Key Indicators of Developing Asian and Pacific Countries*, Manila: Asian Development Bank, 1984, 1996, 2000 and 2003 issues; Food and Agriculture Organization of the United Nations – http://apps.fao.org/default.htm.

On the other hand, the Green Revolution involves some costs including heavy dependence on expensive package of modern inputs to which a considerable proportion of the small-scale farmers in Asia do not have the means to acquire them,[11] environmental costs in the form of rapid depletion of soil nutrients, dependence on imported equipment and fertilizers to as much as 70 kilograms per hectare, the use of inappropriate technology, massive infrastructure costs, enormous government price subsidies, research and development costs, and unequal income distribution in favor of the big farmers and rich landowners.

Of particular interest is the heavy dependence on fertilizer usage which was about 15 kilograms before the introduction of the Green Revolution to about 140 kilograms per hectare because of a 'two-cropping pattern' and heavy usage of pesticide. It is to be noted that the oil shocks in the 1970s had caused a sharp increase in fertilizer prices which affected agricultural production severely. Thailand even banned rice exports following a reduction in rice productivity in 1973. The negative consequences of the Green Revolution on the environment is fully captured in the following statements by ESCAP (2001: 81):

> In Central Luzon (Philippines) the rice yield increased by 13 percent during the 1980s, but this came at the cost of a 21 percent increase in fertilizer use. In the Central Plains, yields went up only 6.5 percent, but fertilizer use rose 24 percent and the use of pesticides jumped by 53 percent. West Java (Indonesia) saw a 23 percent increase in yields, but an increase in the use

[11] Consequently, the Green Revolution benefited the small-scale farmers appreciably less than the large-scale farmers. For full discussion, see ESCAP, *Reducing Disparities ...,* 2001, p.78.

of fertilizers and pesticides of 65 and 69 percent respectively. The increase in the use of insecticides, pesticides and chemical fertilizers has led to contamination and degradation of the soil. Pesticide use also resulted in the development of stronger pests which in turn had to be exterminated by harsher and more powerful chemicals. Where yields are not declining, the rate of growth is slowing or leveling off in the following countries: China, Republic of Korea, Indonesia, Myanmar, Pakistan, the Philippines, Sri Lanka and Thailand.[12]

PROBLEMS

The agricultural sector in Southeast Asia has become backward and remained stagnant while other sectors are growing or becoming rapidly modernized. This situation has aggravated the growing structural dualism that has occurred in these economies. The slower pace of development in the agricultural sector has been attributed to various factors which can be classified into five groups; namely, (a) urban-biased industrialization policy, (b) institutional problems, (c) problems related to Green Revolution, (d) external factors, (e) rural-urban migration, (f) other factors, and (g) lack of regional cooperation in agriculture.

First, various governments in Southeast Asia have given their emphasis and support toward urban-biased industrial development modelled after the western industrialized nations. With wide-ranging experience and in-depth research in Asia, Scarlett Epstein and Jezeph (2001) stated that:

> Third World development began to loom largely on the world horizon only after the last world war when many of the pre-war colonies gained their independence. The governments of many new established nation states were understandly eager to take their rightful place among Western nations and took Western industrialized societies as their economic models. Many of the first lot of Third World politicians and Chief Secretaries of Planning Commissions were either Western macroeconomists or had studied at Western universities such as Harvard, London School of Economics, etc. This was reflected in a Western urban bias that was built into the development paradigms used in Third World Countries.[13]

It was commonly assumed that there exists a strong correlation between economic wealth and industrialization. As such the growth of the industrial sector particularly the manufacturing sector has been equated to economic growth and development. Consequently, Southeast Asian governments have been focusing on the urban-biased manufacturing sector by providing benefits and subsidies to promote this sector. As ESCAP (2001) put it:

> There was an unequal exchange of industrial and agricultural goods: industrial goods were being sold at "artificially" high prices to support an often inefficient industry and agricultural goods were sold at "artificially" low prices to keep the cost of living in urban areas down. The relative prices or terms of trade were turned against agriculture and this led to a transfer of resources from agriculture and the rural areas to industry and the urban areas. The state played a role by imposing price controls to keep agricultural prices down.[14]

---

12 ESCAP, *Reducing Disparities* ..., 2001, p.81.

13 See T. Scarlett Epstein and David Jezeph, "Development – There is Another Way: A Rural-Urban Partnership Development Paradigm," *World Development,* Vol.29, No.8, 2001, p.1443.

14 ESCAP, *Reducing Disparities* ..., 2001, p.31.

An example is in the case of Thai government's policy of subsidizing the industrial sector at the expense of the agricultural sector. The domestic price of rice was deliberately depressed up to 35 percent below the international level to hold down the cost of living in the urban areas, reduce pressure for wage increases, encouraged exports and enabled industry to compete with imports.[15]

The "urban-biased" policies in many developing countries has been the subject of intense criticism. Lipton (1977), one of the most influential critics who studied the rural-urban relations in developing countries, blamed many governments for having an "urban bias" in their development policies as the actual policies, instead of improving conditions in the rural areas and controlling rural-urban migration, had resulted in improved conditions in the urban areas and were aimed at placating the urban population and at promoting the development of the city.[16] Schiff and Valdes (1995) called this problem the "plundering of agriculture" as the net effect of direct interventions (agricultural sector policies) and indirect interventions (industrial protection and macroeconomic policies) was an enormous income transfer out of agriculture that depressed private investment in agriculture.[17]

Second, a set of institutional problems include the uneconomic size of landholdings, tenancy and land tenure arrangements, farmers' adherence to traditional values and practices, and restrictive land and labor laws. Southeast Asian agricultural farms are generally small and fragmented so that mechanization becomes unsuitable, costly and inefficient. Land tenure and distribution systems are inefficient and unequal as large tracts of land are owned by a few rich families particularly in the Philippines. Such a concentrated distribution of land ownership is typically accompanied in Latin America, as it is in many parts of Asia, by a feudal-type social system in which masses of small producers are dependent on the benevolence and goodwill of the large landowner.[18] Consequently, land reform measures have been faced with strong resistance and implemented unsuccessfully.[19] Lack of government revenues and land conversion usage from agricultural to residential and commercial lands have further compounded the problem of implementing land reforms. In terms of their behavior toward technological innovations which includes high cost of inputs, farmers in general are less receptive and would therefore adhere to traditional cultivation techniques.

Third, problems related to the Green Revolution include inadequate infrastructure particularly on irrigation and transport facilities, poor credit and marketing facilities, and heavy dependence on imported fertilizers and pesticides. These problems were more evident among smallholdings than among estates (with an area of more than a hundred acres). This is so since estates are large, modern, highly capitalized forms of organization for production with access to the latest technology and managerial expertise and skills while smallholdings

---

15 Chris Dixon, *Southeast Asia in the World Economy,* Cambridge: Cambridge University Press, 1991, p.150.

16 ESCAP, *Reducing Disparities ...*, 2001, p.34.

17 ESCAP, *Reducing Disparities ...*, 2001, p.33.

18 Michael Todaro, "Agricultural Transformation and Rural Development…," 1994, p.296.

19 As Dorner and Thiesenhusen explain, land reform usually involves the expropriation of lands in privte ownership for redistribution to previous tenants and landless workers. Prior to such reforms, land may be held in very large estates or in more modest units. It may be organized and operated as large firms with hired management and labor, or it may be subdivided into small tenancies or sub-tenancies. For a discussion of land reform in East Asia (China and Taiwan) and Southeast Asia (Philippines), see Peter Dorner and William Thiesenhusen, "Selected Land Reforms in East and Southeast Asia: Their Origins and Impacts," *Asian Pacific Economic Literature,* Vol.4, No.1, 1990, pp.65-95.

are small, tradition-bound, less capitalized units.[20] The implementation of irrigation-dependent new HYVs has been hampered to a large extent by the largely non-irrigated or under-irrigated rice farms in Southeast Asia as the construction of irrigation facilities require huge overhead costs. Moreover, the small poor farmers lack credit financing as they cannot provide collateral requirements and as banks usually prefer large farmers and landowners in order to minimize transaction costs. As ESCAP (2001) stated:

> Compared with other population groups, the poor are almost by definition in a disadvantaged position to benefit from government programmes, even if these are specially intended for them. They lack information about and documentation for such programmes and, since there is always competition for access to programmes, additional informal payments often need to be made which the poor cannot afford. At best, subsidies tend to reach population groups that are slightly better off than the target groups.[21]

Because of these problems related to the Green Revolution, many high-yielding varieties of rice cannot be grown successfully in many parts of the Southeast Asian region.

Fourth, external factors include growing protectionism in the developed countries, declining trend in agricultural commodity prices, and development of commodity substitutes. Developed countries like the European Union, Japan and the United States have relied on protectionist measures by relying increasingly on non-tariff barriers (NTBs). The EU has set quotas on its imports of agricultural products from Southeast Asian countries. Japan has used 22 categories of quotas in order to restrict rice imports.[22]

The Southeast Asian countries experienced a primary commodity boom during the 1970s when prices increased significantly. However, during the first half of the 1980s, the prices of agricultural commodities declined as shown in Table 3.8 (see, for example 1985 prices relative to 1980 prices). The prices in current dollar terms of non-fuel commodities fell sharply in 1981: food prices fell on the average by 15.7 percent, non-food agriculture raw material prices by 15.4 percent and mineral-metal prices by 9.6 percent.[23] In the aggregate, non-fuel primary commodity prices had declined by 14.8 percent with respect to their 1980 prices. In constant dollar terms, non-fuel primary commodity prices fell by about 11.6 percent in 1981. This trend has continued and further reduced the attractiveness of the agricultural sector for businessmen and investors, both foreign and domestic. The declining prices of agricultural commodities can be explained as follows. On the demand side, the proportion of consumer spending on food tends to decrease in the long-run as per capita income rises. On the supply side, the discovery of commodity substitutes has also contributed to price reduction of natural commodities. Synthetic rubber has been used in lieu of natural rubber in the production of tires. Artificial sweeteners have been in the market as an alternative commodity for natural sugar.

20 Siok-Hwa Cheng, "Development of ASEAN Agriculture...," 1980, pp.71-72.

21 See ESCAP, *Reducing Disparities...*, 2001, p.13.

22 Jan Hogendorn, *Economic Development*, New York: Harper-Collins Publishers, 1992, p561.

23 World Bank, *The Outlook for Primary Commodities*, Washington D.C.: World Bank, 1983, p.1.

Table 3.8. Commodity Prices of Major Southeast Asian Agricultural Products

	1970	1975	1980	1985	1990	1995	2002
Palm oil (US$/metric ton)	259.5	420.3	583.1	500.9	289.8	628.6	390.1
Maize (US$/metric ton)	58.3	119.5	125.7	112.3	109.3	123.4	99.3
Copra (US$/metric ton)	223.1	256.0	453.0	386.4	229.9	438.5	265.9
Plywood (US¢/sheet)	103.1	121.8	273.8	210.9	354.9	584.4	402.8
Rice (US$/m.ton)	113.8	301.9	340.3	204.2	270.2	314.8	222.4
Rubber (US¢/pound)	18.5	25.4	64.6	34.4	39.2	71.7	34.9
Coconut oil (US/metric ton)	282.1	374.8	618.7	533.1	318.0	616.3	373.3
Sugar (US¢/pound)	6.6	27.0	16.2	14.9	20.3	19.7	18.1

Note: These prices were quoted for Malaysian palm oil, Thai maize, Philippine plywood, Thai rice, Malaysian rubber, Philippine coconut oil, and Philippine sugar. Source: IMF International Financial Statistics, Washington DC: International Monetary Fund, 1994, 2000 and 2003 issues; also IFS website: http://ifs.apdi.net/imf/logon.aspx

Fifth, there is the problem of rural-urban migration as workers from the rural and agricultural areas move to the urban areas with expectations of better economic and social opportunities after some considerations. As ESCAP (2001) stated:

> Much of the migration research supports the idea that rural migrants move to the city because there are more and better opportunities for social and economic mobility for themselves and for their children. Migration is not a blind move by desperate people into the unknown. Most migrants take a rational decision after careful deliberation of the costs and benefits of the move based on available information about the place of origin and the place of destination (Breman 1996: 88, 223). Over the past decades, the rural population in most countries has acquired much more information about the situation in the urban areas, even if that information is not always reliable. This has been the consequence of an increase in travel between urban and rural areas, the presence of numerous relatives, friends and former neighbors in the urban areas, and the penetration of the mass media in the rural areas (Breman 1996:34).[24]

As discussed earlier with reference to Table 3.3, from 1970 to 2002, the proportion of labor in the agricultural sector to total labor employed fell from 49 percent to about 16 percent in Malaysia, from 54 percent to 37 percent in the Philippines, from 3 percent to 0.2 percent in Singapore, from 64 percent to 43 percent in Indonesia, and from 79 percent to 35 percent in Thailand. Consequently, the loss of workers in the agricultural sector had contributed to slower pace of agricultural development. In their paper, Scarlett Epstein and Jezeph (2001), emphasize the possibility and cost effectiveness of stemming the tide of

[24] ESCAP, *Reducing Disparities* ..., 2001, p.51.

migration to larger cities and increased urbanization of rural life by improving income-earning opportunities in rural areas such as the establishment of agro-based industries, and making them again more attractive in terms of economy and infrastructure.

Sixth, other factors include weather conditions, lack of trained manpower, rapid depletion of forest resources due to logging, soil erosion and watershed destruction, lack of research and development, and low level of intra-ASEAN agricultural production. The agricultural sector provides a relatively unstable source of income than the manufacturing sector given that the former is dependent heavily on the external environment including weather and climatic conditions. The presence of persistent drought in many areas of Southeast Asia is an unfavorable factor. Other calamities like storms, floods and volcano eruptions have contributed to the reduction in agricultural output.

Another problem is related to the land conversion process in the context of diversification. As cited in a study by Flaherty, Vandergeest and Miller (1999), Thai agriculturalists have recently discovered that rice paddies have been converted to inland shrimp farming which now represents 40 to 50 percent of Thailand's total cultured shrimp production.[25] This process has taken place unnoticed until early 1998 when high international prices for shrimp, coupled with the dramatic devaluation of the baht, resulted in a rapid expansion of shrimp farming in Thailand, particularly in the central region. As this has brought about so much environmental and social concerns in Thailand, the government, since June 3, 1998, has banned inland shrimp farming in the freshwater areas of the central region and designated rice bowl provinces as a pollution control zone. The ban has been extended to include all provinces on July 22, 1998.[26] Another example of the land conversion problem is the intensification of commercial logging and the introduction of commercial crops (UNEP/Earthscan 1999:75-76) which has induced some hill tribes to convert unsuitable upland areas for intensive commercial cropping and which has forced movement to marginal lands of rural people who relied on traditional shifting cultivation in Indonesia and Malaysia.[27]

Finally, the lack of regional cooperation in agriculture is also a contributory factor due to two issues. First, these economies are basically competitive rather than complementary as they produce and export relatively similar agricultural tropical products. Second is the lack of political commitment toward regional cooperation as benefits are distributed unevenly between countries in Southeast Asia.

POLICIES

Since the 1970s, there has been a remarkable transition in development thinking – one in which agricultural and rural development has been considered by many as the *sine qua non* of national development. As Todaro emphasized,

> Without such agricultural and rural development, industrial growth either would be stultified or, if it succeeded, would create such severe internal imbalances in the economy that the

---

[25] Mark Flaherty, Peter Vandergeest and Paul Miller, "Rice Paddy or Shrimp Pond ...", 1999, p.2046.

[26] Mark Flaherty, Peter Vandergeest and Paul Miller, "Rice Paddy or Shrimp Pond ...", 1999, p.2053-56.

[27] ESCAP, *Reducing Disparities ...*, 2001, p.81.

problems of widespread poverty, inequality, and unemployment would become even more pronounced.[28]

There are three policy areas of action which are necessary for agricultural and rural development.[29] The first area is institutional transformation including effective agricultural modernization by appropriate institutional re-organization, land reform institutional change, agricultural extension services, and creation of environment for mass participation in local decision making. Emphasis should be given to land reforms as it is an important instrument of agricultural development. A successful land reform program would include an extensive transfer of land from the landlords to the landless tenants and hence would recognize the crucial role that has been played by the small farmers. A successful implementation, however, would require strong political commitment and massive financial resources. Privatization of government-owned enterprises particularly those which are not profitable, and the issue of government bonds could provide some of the funds required to implement land reforms. Aside from land re-distribution from landlords to tenants, the government could develop new agricultural areas as in the case of the Jengka Triangle Project in Pahang, Malaysia where a large portion of equatorial rainforests was cleared to accommodate many landless farmers who were then residing in the western coast. They were given land of decent size to raise crops and undertake other agricultural activities.

The second policy area of action is the balanced development strategies for agriculture by way of upgrading agricultural production techniques, increasing rural infrastructure investment, improving marketing and credit systems, modernizing rural institutions and expanding rural education and health facilities. An important consideration is the creation of appropriate rural institutions and services directed specifically to the needs of the rural population in order to rectify the intra-sectoral imbalances between the large and small farmers. Small farmers should be encouraged to organize themselves for effective representation of their interests. In their study, Scarlett Epstein and Jezeph (2001) suggested that a Rural-Urban Partnership Development Paradigm which links urban centers with rural growth areas and growth centers will ensure an overall balanced development process. This partnership intends to create mutually beneficial network relations not only between farmers, agro-based processing enterprises and domestic industrial units in rural growth areas, but also between rural growth areas/centers and urban industrial centers.[30]

The third policy area of action is the integration of production with overall rural development by promoting a close link between agricultural production and distribution, rural capital formation, rural industrialization and other non-farm economic operations. Emphasis should be given to promoting and developing inter-sectoral linkages between agriculture and other sectors including fertilizer, banking and crop processing. The Thai government, for example, has actively promoted the mechanism of coordinating agricultural production and marketing since the 1980s particularly with the implementation of contract farming which has been practiced widely and intensively in Thailand.[31] Though the government has helped

---

28 Michael Todaro, "Agricultural Transformation and Rural Development...," 1994, p.286.

29 John Wong, "Agricultural and Rural Development...," 1979.

30 See T. Scarlett Epstein and David Jezeph, "Development – There is Another Way ..., p.1451.

31 Singh (2003) defines contract farming as an "arrangement between the primary producers and the agribusiness firm in order for the firm to produce certain pre-agreed, quantity and quality of produce at a particular price and time from the primary producers. For full discussion of contract farming in

contracting to take roots in Thailand, it now works between farmers and companies by way of market mechanism through brokers. The Thai government has also helped the farm sector and its farmers through the promotion of competition which has been beneficial for growers, and has also resulted in the pumping of more capital in the farm sector through the loans given to the contract growers by the Bank for Agriculture and Agricultural Cooperatives (BAAC).

In terms of the future consumption requirements, ESCAP (2001:79) made the following statements. First, by 2025, Asia will be the home of about 4 billion people and rice production will have to increase considerably for each person to have enough food. Second, expected economic growth will not only increase total food demand, but also alter the eating habits of the predominantly urban population. Third, food consumption in the industrialized world today is around 3,400 kilocalories per head per day, and this will increase by 2 percent to 3,470 kilocalories over the next 25 years. Fourth, over the same period, calorie consumption in Asia (including China) will rise from 2,400 kilocalories per head per day to 2,840 kilocalories, an increase of 18.3 percent. In other words, about 50 percent of the population of the world is moving from low calorie consumption to a more nutritious dietary level (Kern 2000). Fifth, farmers will have to react by diversifying towards high-value and high income-elastic crops and products. Consequently, the agricultural development strategy as concluded by Sawant and Mhatre (2000:114) should have three core components: (a) the promotion of diversification of agriculture, (b) a proactive emphasis on technological development for non-food grain crops and livestock products beside food-grain crops, and (c) the provision of efficient infrastructure covering credit and market related services to rural areas.

On top of these policy areas, a regional ASEAN policy on agricultural cooperation should be promoted and developed, in particular, in the area of agricultural research and training whereby trained and skilled personnel in the ASEAN region can undertake research and training activities financed jointly and with assistance from international development agencies. Also of interest is for countries experiencing labor shortage in the agricultural sector to hire workers from other Southeast Asian countries. This will lead to a win-win situation. Moreover, the formation of an ASEAN seed reserve facility would ensure the availability of seeds for member countries particularly those which are prone to natural calamities. There is a need to continue the implementation of the ASEAN Emergency Rice Reserve which would provide rice during times of unfavorable harvest and emergency cases. Finally, the ASEAN regional members should continue promoting its agricultural products to their external trading partners.

CONCLUSION

Despite its declining share to GDP, the agricultural sector has remained important in various ways. First, a significant proportion of the total land area remains allocated to agricultural crop production. Second, it serves as a potent engine of growth. Third, a large proportion of people are engage in agricultural activities. Fourth, it provides food and raw materials as inputs to the industrial sector. Fifth, it generates foreign exchange through the

Thailand, see Sukhpal Singh, "State, Agribusiness Firms and Farmers in Thailand: A Study of the Contract Farming System," Paper presented at the 3rd Asian Studies Foundation Conference, Thailand, Aug 2003.

exports of major cash crops. Sixth, it contributes to capital formation. Seventh, it provides a market for manufactured goods since a substantial proportion of the population continues to live in the agricultural and rural areas.

While it provides benefits on the one hand, the Green Revolution also has some costs. The benefits include an increase in rice production towards self-sufficiency and increase in productivity, diversification of agricultural commodities, additional rural employment, increases in family income, increase in foreign exchange, and forward and backward linkages. The costs include heavy reliance on expensive package of inputs like fertilizer and irrigation, environmental costs, massive infrastructure costs, heavy government subsidies, and unequal distribution of income and benefits favoring land-owners and big farmers.

The agricultural sector in Southeast Asia has faced a number of problems or constraints which can be classified into five groups; namely, (a) urban-biased industrialization policy, (b) institutional problems, (c) problems related to Green Revolution, (d) external factors, (e) rural-urban migration, (f) other factors, and (g) lack of regional cooperation in agriculture.

As for policies, there are three policy areas of action which are necessary for agricultural and rural development to take place. These include institutional transformation, balanced development strategies, and integration of production with overall rural development.

QUESTIONS FOR DISCUSSION

1. Despite its declining contribution to total output (gross domestic product), the agricultural sector has remained very important to Southeast Asian economies. Discuss.
2. The backwardness of the agricultural sector in the Southeast Asian economies is due mainly to the neglect of their respective governments. Do you agree or disagree with this statement? Explain.
3. Explain clearly some of the problems faced by the agricultural sector in Southeast Asia. What policies have been adopted in response to these problems?

SUGGESTED MATERIALS FOR CASE STUDIES

Thailand

Flaherty, Mark and Peter Vandergeest, 1999, "Rice Paddy or Shrimp Pond: Tough Decisions on Rural Thailand," *World Development,* Vol.27, No.12, pp.2045-2060.

Epstein, T. Scarlett and David Jezeph, 2001, "Development – There is Another Way: A Rural-Urban Partnership Development Paradigm," *World Development,* Vol.29, No.8, pp.1443-1454.

Michael Parnwell and Suranart Khamanarong, 1996, "Rural Industrialization in Thailand: Village Industries as a Potential Basis for Rural Development in the North-East," in Michael Parnwell, *Uneven Development in Thailand,* Aldershot, UK: Avebury, pp.161-185.

REFERENCES FOR CHAPTER 3

Cheng, Siok-Hwa, 1980, "Development of ASEAN Agriculture," in Swee Hock Saw (ed.), *ASEAN Economies in Transition,* Singapore: Singapore University Press, pp.70-100.

Dixon, Chris, 1991, *Southeast Asia in the World Economy,* Cambridge: Cambridge University Press.

Dorner, Peter and William Thiesenhusen, 1990, "Selected Land Reforms in East and Southeast Asia: Their Origins and Impacts," *Asian Pacific Economic Literature,* Vol.4, No.1, pp.65-95.

ESCAP, 2001, Reducing Disparities: Balanced Development of Urban and Rural Areas and Regions within the Countries of Asia and the Pacific, New York: Economic and Social Commission for Asia and the Pacific.

Flaherty, Mark, Peter Vandergeest and Paul Miller, 1999, "Rice Paddy or Shrimp Pond: Tough Decisions on Rural Thailand," *World Development,* Vol.27, No.12, 2045-2060.

Gerald Meier, 1989, *Leading Issues in Economic Development*, New York: Oxford University Press.

Hogendorn, Jan, 1992, *Economic Development,* New York: Harper-Collins Publishers.

Parnwell, Michael and Suranart Khamanarong, 1996, "Rural Industrialization in Thailand: Village Industries as a Potential Basis for Rural Development in the North-East," in Michael Parnwell, *Uneven Development in Thailand,* Aldershot, UK: Avebury, pp.161-185.

Scarlett Epstein, T. and David Jezeph, 2001, "Development – There is Another Way: A Rural-Urban Partnership Development Paradigm," *World Development,* Vol.29, No.8, pp.1443-1454.

Singh, Sukhpal, 2003, "State, Agribusiness Firms and Farmers in Thailand: A Study of the Contract Farming System," Paper presented at the 3rd Asian Studies Foundation Conference, Thailand.

Todaro, Michael, 1994, "Chapter 10 – Agricultural Transformation and Rural Development," in Michael Todaro, *Economic Development in the Third World,* New York: Longman, pp.285-324.

Wong, John, 1979, "Chapter 4 – Agricultural and Rural Development: Legacy of the Urban Bias," in John Wong, *ASEAN Economies in Perspective*, Singapore: The Macmillan Press Ltd, pp.93-119.

World Bank, 1983, *The Outlook for Primary Commodities,* Washington D.C.: World Bank.

Chapter 4

THE INDUSTRIAL SECTOR IN SOUTHEAST ASIA: DEVELOPMENT EXPERIENCES AND POLICIES

ABSTRACT

This chapter analyzes the industrial sector and its significance in the transformation process of Southeast Asian economies. These economies have different industrial patterns and development experiences. They have different modes of industrial development including import-substitution, export-promotion and export-substitution policies. The Philippines had the longest import-substitution policy while Singapore, the shortest. Malaysia, Thailand and Indonesia are in between. Country experiences, problems and policies are discussed.

INTRODUCTION

Industrialization is a process which involves the promotion and expansion of the industrial sector which broadly consists of manufacturing, mining and quarrying, and other secondary industries. This process has the following essential characteristics. First, the share of the industrial sector to gross domestic product increases except for cyclical fluctuations. Second, the share of industrial employment to total employment also broadly shows an increasing trend. However as Bagchi (1989) pointed out:

> While these two ratios are increasing, the income per head of the population goes up, except for temporary interruptions ...There are cases in which the per capita income goes up, income derived from secondary industry per head of the population also goes up, but there may be little growth either in the proportion of income derived from the secondary sector or in the ratio of the working force engaged in that sector. Such cases, except when they are observed for a highly developed country, not only make the unambiguous labelling of the process of development as industrialization difficult; they also pose questions regarding the sustainability of the process that has been observed.[1]

---

1 Amiya Kumar Bagchi, "Industrialization," in John Eatwell, Murray Milgate and Peter Newman (eds), *Economic Development,* London and Basingstoke, UK: The Macmillan Press, 1989, pp.160-173.

Developing countries, including Southeast Asia, have relied on industrial development in order to solve its major problems which include poverty, overpopulation and economic backwardness. It is hoped that by promoting and expanding the industrial sector, people will find employment particularly in labor-intensive manufacturing industries, receive their wages, and increase their income. Moreover, consumption demand and investment demand will be stimulated, and hence increase production. It is assumed that as the industrial sector grows and develops, the economy and the society becomes wealthier. Industrialization and the growth of that part of the working population that is engaged in industry, is therefore a means of raising national income per capita.[2]

However, rather than discuss the entire industrial sector, this chapter focuses on the manufacturing sector as it is the most dominant sub-sector in Southeast Asia. Indonesia, Malaysia, the Philippines, Singapore and Thailand are at different stages of industrialization with Singapore being the most industrially advanced, Indonesia being relatively a new comer, and Malaysia, Thailand and the Philippines lying in between. This chapter discusses the various modes of industrial development in Southeast Asia, and individual country experiences.

Modes Of Industrial Development

In Southeast Asia, there were three various modes of industrial development; namely, import substitution, export promotion, and export substitution.[3] Some of the salient characteristics of these approaches are discussed below.

Import-Substitution Approach

The import-substitution industrialization (ISI) approach is one in which the output of the industrial sector is geared towards the domestic market. Domestic industries are created to produce simple and inexpensive consumer goods. The objective is to protect the domestic industries by way of prohibiting imports of the traditional consumer goods. The government imposes a host of protectionist measures like higher tariffs, exchange controls, subsidies and direct government intervention. Thus, ISI approach is very costly as it is implemented by the government without regard for cost or efficiency. Its economic viability and sustainability depends to a large extent on the size of the consumer market – the bigger the market, the more viable and sustainable this approach becomes.

The ISI policy can be illustrated with experiences of the Philippines and Indonesia. The ISI approach evolved because of economic nationalism which was expected to create a local entrepreneurial class with the government's significant support and protection. In order to do this, the government utilized the agricultural profits from the exports of primary products to subsidize the local industrialists who were expected to replace the foreign industrialists who controlled the economy during the colonial period. The ISI approach was followed in the

2 Gunnar Myrdal, *An International Economy*, Harper & Bros., New York, 1956.

3 For a detailed discussion of these approaches, see Hank Lim, "Pattern of ASEAN Industrialization," in Swee Hock Saw (ed.), *ASEAN Economies in Transition*, Singapore: Singapore University Press, 1980, pp.169-242.

Philippines as government heavily favored industrial interests. In Indonesia, ISI signified an act of economic nationalism to break away from the Dutch colonial industrialists.

Export-Promotion Approach

The industrial sector is also geared towards the domestic market. However, the industrial output consists of goods and services which are necessary to stimulate the expansion of primary exports. Its economic viability and sustainability depends on the continued availability of the country's natural resources to produce primary exports.

This approach can be illustrated by the industrialization experiences of Malaysia and Thailand in the early 1960s. Their industrial development relied heavily on the promotion and expansion of primary product exports. Both these countries operated under a relatively free market system in contrast to the Philippines and Indonesia's ISI policy which involved heavy government intervention. However, Malaysia's experiences differed from those in Thailand in terms of the extent of local and foreign participation. In Malaysia, the utilization of natural resources was based upon foreign technology and capital to produce those primary products like rubber, tin and palm oil. However, Thailand's production of rice has not involved foreign participation, and hence described as an indigenous export product.

In Malaysia and Thailand, the production of primary exports was supported by commercial and processing activities supplied by the industrial sector. In Malaysia, there was a flow of modern inputs from industry to export agriculture. In Thailand, the servicing function contributed a smaller role given the slow expansion of supply of domestic raw materials from primary sector to domestic industries.

Export-Substitution Approach

This approach is applicable to an economy which does not export primary products because it simply does not have them. What it has is abundant supply of labor. As such, it can manufacture labor-intensive consumer goods. Given the limited size of the internal consumer market, the viability and sustainability of this approach depends on the economy's ability to direct its output to the external market, that is, to find overseas buyers for its industrial goods. This approach is commonly referred to as export-oriented industrialization (EOI) policy.

Among Southeast Asian economies, Singapore has adopted this approach following a short implementation of ISI policy. During the early 1960s, Singapore had a very bleak future given the diminishing importance of entrepot trade, massive unemployment, rising population, lack of natural resources, and most importantly, its separation from Malaysia in 1965. Singapore recognized the limitation of ISI policy as it could not reap economies of scale. Thus, the Singapore government shifted its industrial policy away from ISI and towards EOI policy.

Industrial Policy Experiences in Southeast Asia

The Philippines

Several studies have analyzed the industrialization process in the Philippines.[4] The Philippines has the longest history of import substitution among the five Southeast Asian countries. The adoption of this inward-looking industrialization policy during the 1950s to the mid-1960s was based on what Antonio (1997) termed as biases, namely, the resentment of foreign domination as the country started its break from its colonial past, and a belief in the effectiveness of government intervention which was drawn from the prevailing economic model of Keynesianism. First, to replace imports by domestically-produced goods was an indication of economic liberation from the Philippine's former colonial masters. Second, the Philippine government intervened heavily by maintaining an overvalued currency and through its liberal use of tariff walls in order to protect the domestic infant industries from foreign competition.

The adoption of ISI approach has generated both benefits and costs to the Philippine economy. On the positive front, an import-dependent import-substituting policy provided a less demanding entry point for stabilization, reduced significantly the risks of failure for local entrepreneurs, and did not require high levels of technology. On the negative front, the ISI policy led to the following effects. First, it created an industrial structure which was dominated by import-dependent, import-substituting industries directed mainly to the domestic market and which was made profitable by government protection from foreign competition. Second, the import-dependent nature of industries resulted in an economy susceptible to foreign exchange crises including the existence of a black market for foreign exchange. Third, it brought about corruption and smuggling activities. Fourth, it led to heavy concentration of industries around the Metro Manila area as international shipping ports and airports were located in Manila, which in addition, provided a large domestic market for manufactured products. Fifth, it penalized exporters as they had to pay more for their inputs because of the overvalued exchange rate and because highly protectionist policies raised the costs of both imports and local production.[5]

In the late 1960s, the Philippine government adopted policies aimed at encouraging exports and foreign investment. For example, the Investment Incentives Act of 1967, the Foreign Business Regulations Act of 1968, and the Export Incentives Act of 1970 were adopted to streamline and rationalize foreign investment policy in the Philippines. The Board of Investment was created in 1970 to set up an investment priorities plan in order to identify the industries which would be given government incentives. With the declaration of martial law in 1972, Presidential Decree 66 was promulgated for the creation of export processing

---

4 Some of these studies include World Bank, *The Philippines: Priorities and Prospects for Development*. Washington DC: The World Bank, 1976; Romeo Bautista, John Power and Associates, *Industrial Promotion Policies in the Philippines*, Manila: Philippine Institute for Development Studies, 1979; Erlinda Medalla, Gwendolyn Tecson, Romeo Bautista and John Power, *Catching Up with Asia's Tigers,* Vol.1, Main Report, Manila: Philippine Institute for Development Studies, 1995; and Emilio Antonio Jr., "Industrial Policies in the Philippines: Growing Reliance on Market Mechanisms," in Seiichi Masuyama, Donna Vandenbrink, and Siow Yue Chia (eds), *Industrial Policies in East Asia*, Japan: Nomura Research Institute and Singapore: Institute of Southeast Asian Studies, 1997, pp.233-252.

5 World Bank, The Philippines: Priorities and Prospects for Development, 1976.

zones. Moreover, the government had taken over or had strong presence in several industries including electricity generation and distribution, petroleum refining industry, coconut and sugar industries, the development of the energy sector and the selection of eleven strategic industries. Thus, the period from the late 1960s to the 1970s was characterized mainly as the rise of crony capitalism since economic incentives were given to businessmen who were friends or close to the seat of political power. Heavy protection of domestic consumer goods industries by the government reflected the continuation of the old import-substitution bias, with effective rates of protection on industrial consumer goods being four times higher than those on capital goods in both 1965 and 1974, and with the number of quantitative restrictions on imports doubling from 1970 to 1980.

During the 1980s, the Philippine economy experienced severe political and economic crises including the external debt crisis in the early 1980s, the Aquino assassination in 1983, the overthrow of the Marcos government in 1986, and the military uprisings during Corazon Aquino's regime (1986-1992) - all these contributed to the economic and political instabilities in the Philippines during this period.

Ironically, however, the 1980s also witnessed significant market-oriented policy reforms. First, tariffs were gradually reduced and quantitative restrictions on imports were relaxed. The average tariff rate was reduced from 43 percent in 1980 to 28 percent in 1985. Moreover, from 1981 to 1988, the share of import items that were restricted decreased from 47 percent to 10 percent in terms of number and from 33 percent to 14.5 percent in terms of value. Second, investment incentives were also reformed with the promulgation of the Omnibus Investment Code of 1981 which consolidated government incentives for investment and exports. Further simplification and consolidation were implemented through Executive Order 225 of Feb 1987.

During the 1990s, more market-oriented reforms were implemented. First, the second tariff reform was implemented in July 1991 under Executive Order 470 which provided for the reduction in the number of commodity lines with high tariffs, the increase in the number of commodity lines with low tariffs over a five-year period, and for the reduction of the average tariff rate from 28 percent to 18 percent. Second, the Foreign Investment Act of 1991 liberalized investment regulations by allowing foreign equity participation up to 100 percent in all areas not specified in the Foreign Investment Negative List, by identifying in advance the areas or sectors where foreign investment was allowed or restricted, and by reducing government bureaucratic procedures involved in cases where foreign equity participation exceeded 40 percent. Third, more market-oriented reforms were implemented which include further liberalization of: laws on foreign investment, on entry of foreign banks, on foreign ownership of property, on opening of infrastructure building to foreign participation; of key sectors like telecommunications, power, insurance, shipping, and the capital market; interest rates and eliminating preferential and credit targeting. Thus, the industrial policies since the 1980s indicate the considerable diminishing role of the government and the rising importance of market-oriented policies.

Malaysia

Several studies have analyzed the industrialization process in Malaysia.[6] The Malaysian economy has undergone tremendous structural changes away from being a primary commodity producer into an increasingly diversified economy with an expanding industrial base. To a significant extent, this transformation is attributed to the accelerated industrialization drive of the Malaysian economy.

Since its independence in 1957, the Malaysian economy has adopted two phases of industrialization, an ISI phase followed by an EOI phase. Like many developing countries initiating the first phase of their industrialization program, Malaysia adopted an ISI strategy, which involved the introduction of various industrial policies in order to encourage the development of domestic industries, particularly, the manufacture of simple consumer goods like canned food and beverages for the domestic market. The policy instruments include tariff protection, fiscal incentives and the establishment of industrial estates. The Pioneer Industries Ordinance was introduced in 1958 which provided generous tax relief and tariff protection to selected local industries.

In the 1960s, several government institutions were created to provide conducive environment for industrialization. In order to provide or generate industrial finance, the government established the Malaysian Stock Exchange and the Malaysian Industrial Development Finance Berhad. In addition, the Tariff Advisory Board was established to formalize the system of tariff protection. It should be noted, however, that Malaysia's experience, in terms of tariff protection, was different from other developing countries as import substitution in Malaysia did not result in excessively high tariffs. The average rate of tariff protection in Peninsular Malaysia rose from 15 percent in 1962 to 45 percent in 1969 which was relatively low compared with those in other countries where the rate was as high as 250 percent.[7] In 1968, Malaysia's industrialization took a different route when the government shifted towards EOI strategy because of the limited size of its domestic market and the need to generate jobs in order to absorb the rapidly rising the labor force. In order to create a more conducive investment environment for industrial development, the Investment Incentives Act was broadened in 1968. With the adoption of an EOI policy, the import-substitution gradually lost its significance in terms of output and employment generation, although it continued to co-exist with the former[8]

---

6 These studies include Sundaram Jomo, *Growth and Structural Change in the Malaysian Economy*, London: Macmillan Press, 1990; Imran Lim and Helen Nesadurai, "Managing the Malaysian Industrial Economy" in Seiichi Masuyama, Donna Vandenbrink, and Siow Yue Chia (eds.), *Industrial Policies in East Asia*, Japan: Nomura Research Institute and Singapore: Institute of Southeast Asian Studies, 1997, pp.185-215; Sundaram Jomo, Rajah Rasiah, Rokiah Alavi and Jaya Gopal. "Industrial Policy and the Emergence of Internationally Competitive Manufacturing Firms in Malaysia," in Kazuo Takahashi (ed.) *Asia's Development Experiences – How Internationally Competitive National Manufacturing Firms Have Developed in Asia*, Tokyo, Japan: Foundation for Advanced Studies on International Development, 1998, pp.178-261; Vijayakumari Kanapathy, "Industrial Restructuring in Malaysia: Policy Shifts and the Promotion of New Sources of Growth," in Seiichi Masuyama, Donna Vandenbrink, and Siow Yue Chia (eds.), *Industrial Restructuring in East Asia,* Japan: Nomura Research Institute and Singapore: Institute of Southeast Asian Studies, 2001, pp.139-165.

7 Bank Negara, "The Accelerated Industrialization Drive," *Bank Negara Annual Report*, 1991,pp.53-63.

8 Sundaram Jomo, Rajah Rasiah, Rokiah Alavi and Jaya Gopal, "Industrial Policy…," 1998.

In 1971, the New Economic Policy (NEP) was introduced giving emphasis on industrialization as the main vehicle to achieve its objectives particularly in terms of employment generation and equity restructuring. Under the First Outline Perspectives Plan (OPP1) for the period 1971-1990, the manufacturing sector would act as the main engine of economic growth. The NEP and the OPP1 were implemented aimed at promoting growth to restructure the Malaysian society and to foster national unity.

During the 1970s, the Malaysian government participated heavily in the industrialization process through the following activities. These include the establishment of Non-financial Public Enterprises (NFPEs), the regulation of commercial and industrial activities, and the promotion of private investment in the manufacturing industry. In addition, with the passage of the Free Trade Zone Act in 1971, the government set up export-processing or free-trade zones (FTZs) where companies were given fiscal incentives including tax holidays, exemptions from import and export duties, and unrestricted and tax-free remittances of profits and dividends. This Act attracted mainly export-oriented labor-intensive industries like electric/electronic, textile/garment, and rubber industries. In the subsequent years, the FTZs were occupied mainly by highly organized multinational subsidiaries dealing with the assembly of electrical machinery, appliances, parts and components. In 1975, the controversial Industrial Co-ordination Act (ICA) was adopted aimed at ensuring the orderly development and growth of the manufacturing sector with the end-in-view of inducing Bumiputra participation towards Malaysian industrial development.

In the early 1980s, the government began its second phase of ISI policy with its launching of the "big push" on heavy industry projects led by the Heavy Industries Corporation of Malaysia (HICOM). Because of large capital outlays and long gestation periods, both the government and the private sector jointly participated in a number of heavy industrial projects which included iron and steel, cement, the national car, and small engine plants. However, bulk of these projects was financed by heavy foreign borrowings. In 1982, the Malaysian economy experienced a twin-deficit problem so that a structural adjustment was implemented which involved the reduction of government spending and encouraging the private sector to act as the main engine of growth. Thus, in 1984, the government began its move towards deregulating the economy, reducing the role of its public sector and, more importantly, adopting an EOI-strategy.

From 1985 to 1987, the government implemented some reforms towards greater economic liberalization. First, amendments were made to the guidelines on the issuance of licenses as provided for in the Industrial Coordination Act of 1975. Second, the Promotion of Investments Act was introduced in 1986 which replaced the Investment Incentives Act of 1968. This Act broadened the scope of incentives to include small- and medium-scale industries, tourist and hotel projects.

Those reforms resulted in a comprehensive review of industrial policies and led to the launching of the Industrial Master Plan (IMP) to chart the industrialization strategy for the period 1986-95. It aimed to promote outward-oriented industries with particular emphasis on three things, namely, (a) the continued promotion of resource-based industries like processed palm oil, cut logs and timber, rubber products, and petroleum and liquefied natural gas industries, as these industries were expected to help improve Malaysia's trade balance and promote inter-sectoral linkages, (b) the diversification of non-resource based industries (like electronics and electrical products, machinery, metal products, transport equipment, plastics and basic metals) in order to serve as important sources of growth, and (c) the promotion of several heavy industries (like automobiles, cement, and iron and steel products) which were seen as vital in industrializing Malaysia.

In 1991, Malaysia embarked on a renewed economic development path with the formulation of new development plans called the Second Outline Perspective Plan (OPP2) and the Sixth Malaysia Plan (6MP). These plans would be implemented within the overall framework of the National Development Policy (NDP, the successor to NEP). With the NDP, the government eliminated all limits on minimum percentage of Bumiputra participation in approved projects. In order to provide a favorable investment climate, the government has also supported the development of facilities like infrastructure projects in super-highways, well-equipped industrial estates, industrial parks, and airport and port upgrading.

The development plans adopted since the 1990s aimed to set the pace for Malaysia to become a developed nation by 2020. The manufacturing sector would become the main driving force of the Malaysian economy, following its 'Look East' policy – that is, based on the successful development experiences of the dynamic East Asian economies which includes South Korea, Taiwan, Hong Kong and Singapore which centered on the development of human resources. Thus, in order to achieve its 'Vision 2020' target which projects sustained rapid growth over the next 30 years, Malaysia would need to strengthen its drive towards the development of its human resources. This would enable Malaysia to make the transition towards a more sophisticated industrial base.

Singapore

Singapore's industrial development, policies, and experiences have been extensively chronicled.[9] Since 1960, the industrialization program in Singapore has followed several phases. In the first phase from 1960 to 1965, ISI policy was pursued because of the anticipated merger of Singapore into a larger Malaysian common market. The first protective tariffs were implemented in 1960 and tariff protection was extended and accelerated during Singapore's tenure in Malaysia between 1963-65. In 1961, the government created the Economic Development Board in order to lead the industrialization drive through industrial investment promotion, development of industrial infrastructure and facilities, participation in industrial financing, and administering tax incentives.

---

9 These studies include Siow Yue Chia, "Direct Foreign Investment and Industrialization in Singapore," in Chong-Yah Lim and Peter Lloyd (eds.), *Singapore Resources and Growth,* Singapore: Oxford University Press, 1986, pp.79-117; Linda Lim, "Foreign Investment, the State and Industrial Policy in Singapore," in Howard Stein (ed.), *Asian Industrialization and Africa,* St. Martin's Press, New York, 1995, pp.205-238; Poh Kam Wong and Chee Yuen Ng, "Singapore's Industrial Policy to the year 2000," in Seiichi Masuyama, Donna Vandenbrink and Siow Yue Chia (eds.), *Industrial Policies in East Asia*, Japan: Nomura Research Institute and Singapore: Institute of Southeast Asian Studies, 1997, pp. 121-141; Poh-Kam Wong, Sock-Yong Phang, Jong-Say Yong and Meng-Kng Chng, "Development of Internationally Competitive Indigenous Manufacturing Firms in Singapore," in Kazuo Takahashi (ed.), *Asia's Development Experiences – How Internationally Competitive National Manufacturing Firms Have Developed in Asia,* Tokyo, Japan: Foundation for Advanced Studies on International Development, 1998, pp. 372-447; and Siow Yue Chia, "Singapore: Towards a Knowledge-based Economy," in Seiichi Masuyama, Donna Vandenbrink and Siow Yue Chia (eds.), *Industrial Restructuring in East Asia*, Japan: Nomura Research Institute and Singapore: Institute of Southeast Asian Studies, 2001, pp.170-208.

Following its separation from Malaysia in August 1965, the ISI phase was clearly not sufficient to sustain manufacturing growth in Singapore given its small domestic market. Thus, the second phase of Singapore's industrialization strategy began in 1965 when the government dismantled its ISI policy and switched towards export-oriented and labor-intensive industrialization. The labor-intensive export-manufacturing strategy was chosen taking into account Singapore's scarcity of land and natural resources for extraction, small domestic market, and the need for mass employment creation. The unemployment rate reached a record high of 10 percent in 1965, with population and labor force growing by 3.3 percent and 5.0 percent, respectively.[10] Moreover, given Singapore's lack of domestic entrepreneurial class and lack of foreign capital and technology, the government assigned a strong role to foreign corporations through foreign direct investment. Thus, the three leading export-oriented industries were petroleum refining, transport equipment and oil rigs, and electronic products and components, which by 1971 accounted for a combined share of 43.6 per cent of total manufacturing value added.

During the second phase, government intervention in the domestic economy was pervasive and extensive and took two forms: first, involving infrastructural activities, and second, direct establishment of wholly-owned or partly-owned industrial and commercial ventures including the national shipping line, the airlines, the Development Bank of Singapore, the Singapore Petroleum Company, the National Iron and Steel Mills, a large trading and investment company.

The third phase began in 1979 when an economic restructuring program was launched that would upgrade established industries and develop new ones that would utilize more capital, high technology, and skilled labor in the production of high-value manufactured goods and services for export. This policy was aimed at using Singapore's scarce labor resources more effectively and efficiently. The shift in emphasis stemmed from the tight labor market conditions and rising domestic costs of production as these would hurt the competitiveness of domestically-produced goods. Under the so-called Second Industrial Revolution, the government restructured its economy by upgrading the technology employed in the local manufacturing industries and by investing heavily in these industries. The government also followed a high-wage policy in order to reduce its dependence from labor-intensive manufacturing industries.

Singapore's industrialization program, however, met some difficulties in the mid-1980s as the economy experienced a recession. The Report of the Economic Committee headed by BG Lee Hsien Loong stated that the high costs of production severely affected the operations of multinational corporations (MNCs) in Singapore, which in turn was attributed mainly to the high-wage policy. Thus, the 1985-86 recession limited the extent in the implementation of the restructuring policy and significantly weakened the manufacturing production. Several policy measures were implemented including wage restraint and adoption of favorable investment incentives.

In the early 1990s, the government launched its vision of Singapore as a developed nation in a document called *The Next Lap* which envisioned Singapore to be in tough competition with advanced, developed nations towards the end of the century. Then, the government formulated a *Strategic Economic Plan* (SEP) which paved the way for the implementation of

---

[10] Poh-Kam Wong, Sock-Yong Phang, Jong-say Yong and Meng-Kng Chng, "Development of Internationally Competitive Indigenous Manufacturing Firms...," 1998.

several specific program initiatives.[11] First, the *Manufacturing 2000* program aims to sustain manufacturing's share of GDP at more than 25 percent and its share of employment at more than 20 percent in the medium to long term.

Second, the *International Business Hub* aims to enhance Singapore's position as a gateway to the Asia-Pacific region for business services like financial services, tourism, operational headquarters, logistics distribution, media/telecommunications, commodity trading, international arbitrage, exhibition and convention, tertiary education and training, and medical services.

Third, *Regionalization 2000* program aims to build an external economy which is closely linked to and which enhances the Singapore economy by participating in the growth of the Asian region.This program provides incentives and assistance for Singapore-based companies to invest in the region, and for Singapore to co-invest and co-manage large-scale industrial parks in the region.

Fourth, the *National Technology Plan* aims to develop Singapore into a center of excellence in select fields of science and technology through intensified research and development activities.

Fifth, the *IT2000 Vision* and the *National Information Infrastructure* initiatives aims to turn Singapore into an intelligent island through innovations in information technology (IT) and development of advanced telecommunications and information infrastructure.

Sixth, with the *Local Enterprises 2000* program, the government aims to promote the development of local enterprises through grants, loans, preferential interest rates, and tax incentives. In addition, the government utilizes the Local Industry Upgrading Program in which MNCs are asked to help upgrade the local companies which are their suppliers and business partners. Moreover, the government intends to help develop a group of promising local enterprises and turn them into future MNCs and industry leaders.

Seventh, the *Co-Investment Program* enables the Singapore government to co-invest in more technology-intensive and capital-intensive large scale projects like the semiconductor wafer fabrication industry, petrochemicals, and biotechnology. Finally, with the *Industry Cluster* Fund, the government established a S$2 billion fund aimed at promoting integrated industry clusters as exemplified by the co-investment program. Thus, the industrial policies cited above emphasize three main concerns, namely, internationalization, technological innovations, and creation and growth of industries.

---

11 Poh-Kam Wong and Chee Yuen Ng, "Singapore's Industrial Policy…," 1997.

Thailand

Several studies analyzed the extent of industrialization in Thailand.[12] Modern industrialization in Thailand began in the early 1960s. During the period from 1960-1971, import substitution was the main objective of Thailand's industrial policy-makers in order to reduce its dependence on imported consumer goods. In the 1960s, domestic manufacturing activities were concentrated on food processing as it accounted for a third of total manufactured products. Local industries were protected through higher tariffs on imported goods.

The ISI period coincided with the First and Second National Economic Development Plans, 1961-66 and 1967-71, respectively. These plans were implemented by government agencies like the Ministry of Finance which set import tariffs, the Ministry of Commerce which imposed quota restrictions, and the Board of Investment which promoted investment through government incentives like exemption from import duties on capital goods, lower or zero duties on imported raw materials and intermediate inputs, and exemption from corporate taxes. The government's protection of the domestic manufacturing sector resulted in different effective rates of protection – lower for machinery products, and moderate to high range for consumer products. On the other hand, resource-based activities were subject to export tariffs. Thus, Thailand's tariff structure was made favorable to the domestic manufacturing sector at the expense of the export sector.

By the end of the 1960s, the Thai economy began to falter and its balance of payments started to worsen due to rapid growth in the importation of machinery and raw materials, stagnation of primary exports, and the decline in foreign investment. Thus, the government adopted the Third National Development Plan (1972-77) which emphasized a change in its industrial policy towards promotion of manufactured exports, the deepening of the import substitution process for intermediate goods and raw materials, the promotion of small-scale and labor-intensive industries, and the dispersion of industries into the rural areas.

Throughout the 1970s and the first half of the 1980s, Thailand's external deficits persisted and worsened. The government responded by emphasizing the urgency of promoting exports of manufactured goods in the fourth and fifth plans (1977-1981 and 1982-1986, respectively) The government explicitly stated its commitment to promote exports of manufactured goods as the main source of growth. The fifth plan had strongly emphasized the

---

12 These studies include Atchaka Sibinruang and Peter Brimble, in Seiji Naya (ed.), *Direct Foreign Investment Theories and Export Promotion:Policies and Experiences in Asia*, Southeast Asia Central Bank Research and Training Center, Kuala Lumpur, 1987, pp. 317-357; Jean-Christophe Simon, "The Thai Manufacturing Sector: New Patterns of Expansion," in Michael Parnwell (ed.), *Uneven Development in Thailand*, Aldershot, UK: Avebury, 1996, pp.82-108; Nipon Poapongsakorn and Belinda Fuller, "Industrial Location Policy in Thailand: Industrial Decentralization or Industrial Sprawl," in Seiichi Masuyama, Donna Vandenbrink and Siow Yue Chia (eds.), *Industrial Policies in East Asia*, Japan: Nomura Research Institute and Singapore: Institute of Southeast Asian Studies, 1997, pp.146-184; Patcharee Siroros and Wilaiwan Wannitikul, "International Competitiveness of Indigenous Firms: Case Studies of the Gems and Jewelry Industry and the Siam Cement Group," in Kazuo Takahashi (ed.), *Asia's Development Experiences – How Internationally Competitive National Manufacturing Firms Have Developed in Asia*, Tokyo, Japan: Foundation for Advanced Studies on International Development, 1998, pp.264-310; Nipon Poapongsakorn and Somkiat Tangkitvanich, "Industrial Restructuring in Thailand: a Critical Assessment", in Seiichi Masuyama, Donna Vandenbrink, and Siow Yue Chia (eds.), *Industrial Restructuring in East Asia*, Japan: Nomura Research Institute and Singapore: Institute of Southeast Asian Studies, 2001, pp.109-138.

restructuring of certain existing and new industries in order to achieve higher levels of efficiency and enhance the competitiveness in both external and internal markets. The sixth plan (1987-91) also called for the promotion of export-oriented industries, small-scale industries, rural industries located in areas outside Bangkok and its vicinity, agro-based industries, and basic industries like engineering, petrochemical, iron and steel industries. The seventh plan (1992-96) targeted the textile and garment industries although Thailand has lost its comparative advantage in labor-intensive industries. Thailand's eighth development plan was for the period from 1997-2001. Thailand claimed to be an emerging newly industrializing economy.

Thus, from the above discussions, Thailand's industrialization has been based on a series of 5-year development plans. However, its industrialization drive has met some criticisms, particularly with regard to inconsistencies between the development plans and strategies. As for the ISI phase, three inconsistencies were identified. First, there was incompatibility between making ISI as major industrialization strategy and calling for the promotion of labor-intensive industries. Second, the development plans called for the promotion and utilization of domestic raw materials, but the tariff structure discriminated against resource-based activities. Third, the development plans call for the promotion of household and small-scale industries, but the BOI favored large-scale, capital-intensive industries to support import substitution. As for the export-orientation phase, it was pointed out that inconsistency arose from the development plan of making exports as an engine of growth in the early 1970s but in reality, the trade regime remained largely the same (ie. anti-export bias) until the late 1970s given higher effective rates of protection for import-substituting industries.

The shift in Thailand's industrialization strategy from ISI to EOI has resulted in a changing structure of its merchandise exports in two ways. First, there was a shift away from primary commodities and towards manufactured goods. The year 1985 was very significant as exports of manufactured goods surpassed agricultural exports for the first time. Second, the exports of medium- and high-technology products surpassed exports of labor-intensive products for the first time in 1993.

The petroleum product industry registered a slower growth of 34 percent per year during the 1980-88 period. By 1993, it accounted for only 1.4 percent of GDP. On the other hand, the manufacturing sector grew at an average of about 10 percent per year during the period from 1960-1988. As the largest sector, manufacturing accounted for 26 percent of GDP in 1988 and 29 percent in 1993. Intermediate products like machinery, metal products, and iron and steel expanded rapidly. The textiles and garment products became the most important industry during the 1986-88 period. In 1989, the manufacturing industry expanded by 15 percent arising from the government's export-oriented policy, and also because of stable oil prices, interest rates and exchange rates. Moreover, Thailand has also developed supporting industries such as the construction of automotive engine plants and developing a major petrochemical complex that would provide inputs for the manufacturing sector. An important milestone in Thailand's manufacturing history was achieved when the 'Made in Thailand' Mitsubishi cars were exported to Canada, Portugal and Cyprus.

Indonesia

The Indonesian manufacturing sector has undergone four phases of development since the New Order in 1965.[13] The first phase was from 1967 to 1973 in which the Indonesian economy was driven mainly by liberalization and the return to normal conditions. Suharto's government inherited a badly damaged economy including an excess capacity, low level of foreign trade, and a 600 percent inflation rate. The new government undertook some economic liberalization measures which involved a shift in policy orientation away from heavy intervention towards a more market-oriented economy. These include liberalization of foreign exchange and trade policies, dismantling of the import licensing system, introduction of a new export bonus scheme, launching of foreign and domestic investment laws, rehabilitation of financial state banks, and introduction of a banking law. The economic reforms were very effective as inflation fell sharply to 17 percent in 1969, foreign exchange constraint was eased, and real manufacturing output expanded by 9 percent in 1968 and by 14 percent in 1969. The reforms continued until 1972 which included devaluation, unification of a multiple exchange rate system, simplification of export and import procedures, and elimination of international capital controls. However, despite these reform measures, major industrial sectors like textiles and automotive products received heavy protection.

The second phase in the development of the manufacturing sector in Indonesia was the petroleum years during the 1973-1982 period when the prices of crude oil rose significantly – first, in 1973-1974 and again, in 1978-1979. During this period, Indonesia followed an inward-oriented ISI regime. The oil boom led to a fundamental reappraisal of industrial policy objectives as the government took a more interventionist path through a more restrictive foreign investment policy. The more liberal foreign investment policy prior to the oil boom period generated significant inflows of FDI which in turn created resentment among Indonesian nationalists. This resentment reached its peak during the 1974 visit of former Japan's PM Tanaka in Indonesia. The massive oil bonanza also enabled the Indonesian government to intervene heavily through (i) an extension of credit subsidies to favored clients by the state banks, (ii) direct engagement in production by the state-owned enterprises particularly in upstream, capital-intensive industries like cement and fertilizer, and (iii) imposition of non-tariff barriers for imports, especially for planned heavy industries. Thus, the late 1970s was characterized with an extensive state-guided industrial intervention.

The third phase took place during the 1982-85 period following the decline in oil prices, which created a balance of payments crisis. Thus, it was realized that making oil exports as an engine of growth was limited and hence there was an urgency of shifting towards non-oil, manufacturing exports as sources of economic growth. Faced with economic difficulties, the government followed a prudent macroeconomic management including a re-scheduling in the

---

[13] Some of the more recent studies on Indonesian industrial development, policies and experiences include Hal Hill, "Indonesia's Industrial Policy and Performance: Orthodoxy Vindicated," *Economic Development and Cultural Change*, 1996, pp.147-174; Hal Hill, *Indonesia's Industrial Transformation,* Singapore: Institute of Southeast Asian Studies, 1997; Haryo Aswicahyono, "Transformation and Structural Change in Indonesia's Manufacturing Sector," in Mari Pangestu and Yuri Sato (eds.), *Waves of Change in Indonesia's Manufacturing Industry,* Tokyo: Institute of Developing Economies, 1997, pp.1-28; Karseno, Arief Ramelan, "Perspectives on Government Policy for Industrial Competitiveness in Indonesia," in Seiichi Masuyama, Donna Vandenbrink, and Siow Yue Chia (eds.), *Industrial Policies in East Asia*, Japan: Nomura Research Institute and Singapore: Institute of Southeast Asian Studies, 1997, pp.216-232.

development of capital-intensive industries, a significant devaluation of the rupiah by 27.5 percent in March 1983, and major banking reforms which included lifting of interest rate controls on state banks and credit ceilings. On the other hand, the government had become even more protectionist in terms of further restrictive trade and industrial policies through the increased use of NTBs over this period. In 1982, the government introduced a system called approved importers system which had become an instrument for quantitative restrictions on imports. Thus, the implementation of these protectionist measures resulted in a high-cost economy. Consequently, public discussions took place on the costs of protection, on pervasive regulations, and on inefficient state-owned companies.

In the fourth stage, from 1986 to the present, industrial policy has taken the form of deregulation and reforms. In 1986, Suharto's New Order government considered for the first time making non-oil exports and private sector industries as the main engines of growth in Indonesia. Thus, from an inward-looking strategy during the third phase, the government has shifted towards an outward-oriented economy in terms of trade and foreign investments. This change in policy stance resulted from the government's anticipated increase in global competition and from the successful export promotion experiences of high-performing East Asian economies like Taiwan, Hong Kong, South Korea and Singapore. The policy shift was implemented through a series of deregulatory measures including across-the-board reduction in nominal tariffs, and a reorganization of customs, parts and shipping operations. The government also adopted substantive trade reforms which resulted in the elimination of the import monopolies of plastic and steel, and cotton, and also in a more transparent quota allocation system for textile. Moreover, financial reforms were implemented in 1988 which resulted in increased competition among banks. In addition, both foreign and domestic investments were liberalized particularly for export-oriented FDI by allowing 95 percent foreign ownership and domestic distribution.

CONCLUSION

The five Southeast Asian economies followed an ISI-policy before switching to an EOI policy. The Philippines began the industrialization of the region through the creation of import-substituting industries in the late 1940s. A decade after, Malaysia, Singapore and Thailand followed the Philippine example while Indonesia joined in only two decades later. However, Singapore switched to an EOI-policy in the late 1960s given its separation from Malaysia in 1965, its small domestic market, and its lack of natural resources. This has proved to be successful for Singapore as it has resulted in rising trade, output, income and standards of living.

During the 1970s and the 1980s, other Southeast Asian economies relied less on ISI policy and began to follow the EOI policy adopted by East Asian economies like Singapore, Hong Kong, South Korea and Taiwan. Some factors which accounted for this change in industrialization policy include the limited success of ISI, the declining and fluctuating prices of primary commodities, and the consequent pursuit of export-diversification policy. The need to diversify is reflected in the changing structure of trade - away from primary and toward manufactured exports and the rising dependence on manufactured imports.

In order to promote an outward-oriented industrialization policy, the Southeast Asian governments have provided strong support through a package of incentives including tax exemptions, improvement of the investment climate and provision of industrial infrastructure including the establishment of industrial parks and export-processing zones which have offered a variety of fiscal and financial incentives to investors.

QUESTIONS FOR DISCUSSION

1. The Southeast Asian economies have pursued two types of industrialization policy: (a) outward-oriented policy which promotes free and open trade and investments, and (b) an inward-looking policy which involves heavy government protection of the domestic manufacturing sector. Compare and contrast these policies in terms of their costs and benefits.
2. Despite efforts to promote and develop the agricultural sector in Southeast Asia, it has remained backward, stagnant and unproductive. On the other hand, the non-agricultural (manufacturing and services) sector has become modern, more developed and productive.
   (a) Explain why such structural dualism has existed in Southeast Asia.
   (b) Explain whether or not you would expect this dualism to persist.
3. In order to promote and develop the industrial sector in Southeast Asia, particularly the manufacturing sector, some countries have adopted import-substitution policies while others have followed export-oriented policies. Discuss why these countries differ in their approaches to industrialization.
4. "To industrialize or not to industrialize – is the policy issue. Various countries in Southeast Asia have taken up the challenge of industrialization by adopting strategies that would suit their own respective economies. Among Southeast Asian economies, Singapore has achieved a higher level of industrial development than others. It is therefore to the advantage of all Southeast Asian economies to follow the policies that Singapore has adopted." Do you agree with the given statements? Explain.

SUGGESTED MATERIALS FOR CASE STUDIES

Indonesia

Rock, Michael, 1999, "Reassessing the Effectiveness of Industrial Policy in Indonesia: Can the Neoliberals be Wrong?" *World Development,* Vol.27, No.4, pp.691-704.

Asia

Quibria, M.G., Shamsun Ahmed, Ted Tschang, Mari-Len Reyes-Macasaquit, 2003, "Digital Divide: Determinants and Policies with special reference to Asia," *Journal of Asian Economics,* Vol.13, No.6, pp.811-825.

REFERENCES FOR CHAPTER 4

Antonio Jr., Emilio, 1997, "Industrial Policies in the Philippines: Growing Reliance on Market Mechanisms," in Seiichi Masuyama, Donna Vandenbrink, and Siow Yue Chia (eds), *Industrial Policies in East Asia*, Japan: Nomura Research Institute and Singapore: Institute of Southeast Asian Studies, pp.233-252.

Aswicahyono, Haryo, 1997, "Transformation and Structural Change in Indonesia's Manufacturing Sector," in Mari Pangestu and Yuri Sato (eds.), *Waves of Change in Indonesia's Manufacturing Industry,* Tokyo: Institute of Developing Economies, pp.1-28.

Bagchi, Amiya Kumar, 1989, "Industrialization," in John Eatwell, Murray Milgate and Peter Newman (eds.), *Economic Development,* London and Basingstoke, UK: The Macmillan Press, pp.160-173.

Bank Negara, 1991, "The Accelerated Industrialization Drive," *Bank Negara Annual Report*, pp.53-63.

Bautista, Romeo, John Power and Associates, 1979, *Industrial Promotion Policies in the Philippines*, Manila: Philippine Institute for Development Studies.

Chia, Siow Yue, 1986, "Direct Foreign Investment and Industrialization in Singapore," in Chong-Yah Lim and Peter Lloyd (eds.), *Singapore Resources and Growth,* Singapore: Oxford University Press, pp.79-117.

Chia, Siow Yue, 2001, "Singapore: Towards a Knowledge-Based Economy," in Seiichi Masuyama, Donna Vandenbrink and Siow Yue Chia (eds.), *Industrial Restructuring in East Asia*, Japan: Nomura Research Institute and Singapore: Institute of Southeast Asian Studies, pp.170-208.

Hill, Hal, 1996, "Indonesia's Industrial Policy and Performance: Orthodoxy Vindicated," *Economic Development and Cultural Change*, Vol.45, No.1, pp.147-174.

Hill, Hal, 1997, *Indonesia's Industrial Transformation,* Singapore: Institute of Southeast Asian Studies.

Jomo, Sundaram, 1990, *Growth and Structural Change in the Malaysian Economy*, London: Macmillan Press.

Jomo, Sundaram, Rajah Rasiah, Rokiah Alavi and Jaya Gopal, 1998, "Industrial Policy and the Emergence of Internationally Competitive Manufacturing Firms in Malaysia," in Kazuo Takahashi (ed.), *Asia's Development Experiences – How Internationally Competitive National Manufacturing Firms Have Developed in Asia*, Tokyo, Japan: Foundation for Advanced Studies on International Development, pp.178-261.

Kanapathy, Vijayakumari, 2001, "Industrial Restructuring in Malaysia: Policy Shifts and the Promotion of New Sources of Growth," in Seiichi Masuyama, Donna Vandenbrink, and Siow Yue Chia (eds.), *Industrial Restructuring in East Asia,* Japan: Nomura Research Institute and Singapore: Institute of Southeast Asian Studies, pp.139-165.

Karseno, Arief Ramelan, 1997, "Perspectives on Government Policy for Industrial Competitiveness in Indonesia," in Seiichi Masuyama, Donna Vandenbrink, and Siow Yue Chia (eds.), *Industrial Policies in East Asia*, Japan: Nomura Research Institute and Singapore: Institute of Southeast Asian Studies, pp.216-232.

Lim, Imran and Helen Nesadurai, 1997, "Managing the Malaysian Industrial Economy" in Seiichi Masuyama, Donna Vandenbrink, and Siow Yue Chia (eds.), *Industrial Policies in*

East Asia, Japan: Nomura Research Institute and Singapore: Institute of Southeast Asian Studies, pp.185-215

Lim, Linda, 1995, "Foreign Investment, the State and Industrial Policy in Singapore," in Howard Stein (ed.), *Asian Industrialization and Africa,* St. Martin's Press, New York, pp.205-238.

Medalla, Erlinda, Gwendolyn Tecson, Romeo Bautista and John Power, 1995, *Catching Up with Asia's Tigers,* Vol.1, Main Report, Manila: Philippine Institute for Development Studies.

Myrdal, Gunnar, 1956, *An International Economy*, Harper & Bros., New York.

Poapongsakorn, Nipon and Belinda Fuller, 1997, "Industrial Location Policy in Thailand: Industrial Decentralization or Industrial Sprawl," in Seiichi Masuyama, Donna Vandenbrink and Siow Yue Chia (eds.), *Industrial Policies in East Asia*, Japan: Nomura Research Institute and Singapore: Institute of Southeast Asian Studies, pp.146-184.

Poapongsakorn, Nipon and Somkiat Tangkitvanich, 2001, "Industrial Restructuring in Thailand: a Critical Assessment", in Seiichi Masuyama, Donna Vandenbrink, and Siow Yue Chia (eds.), *Industrial Restructuring in East Asia*, Japan: Nomura Research Institute and Singapore: Institute of Southeast Asian Studies, pp.109-138.

Sibinruang, Atchaka and Peter Brimble, 1987, in Seiji Naya (ed.), *Direct Foreign Investment Theories and Export Promotion:Policies and Experiences in Asia*, Kuala Lumpur: Southeast Asia Central Bank Research and Training Center, pp. 317-357

Simon, Jean-Christophe, 1996, "The Thai Manufacturing Sector: New Patterns of Expansion," in Michael Parnwell (ed.), *Uneven Development in Thailand*, Aldershot, UK: Avebury, pp.82-108.

Siroros, Patcharee and Wilaiwan Wannitikul, 1998, "International Competitiveness of Indigenous Firms: Case Studies of the Gems and Jewelry Industry and the Siam Cement Group," in Kazuo Takahashi (ed.), *Asia's Development Experiences – How Internationally Competitive National Manufacturing Firms Have Developed in Asia*, Tokyo, Japan: Foundation for Advanced Studies on International Development, pp.264-310.

Saw, Swee Hock (ed.), 1980, *ASEAN Economies in Transition*, Singapore: Singapore University Press, pp.169-242.

Wong, Poh Kam and Chee Yuen Ng, 1997, "Singapore's Industrial Policy to the year 2000," in Seiichi Masuyama, Donna Vandenbrink and Siow Yue Chia (eds.), *Industrial Policies in East Asia*, Japan: Nomura Research Institute and Singapore: Institute of Southeast Asian Studies, pp. 121-141.

Wong, Poh-Kam, Sock-Yong Phang, Jong-Say Yong and Meng-Kng Chng, 1998, "Development of Internationally Competitive Indigenous Manufacturing Firms in Singapore," in Kazuo Takahashi (ed.), *Asia's Development Experiences – How Internationally Competitive National Manufacturing Firms Have Developed in Asia,* Tokyo, Japan: Foundation for Advanced Studies on International Development, pp. 372-447.

World Bank, 1976, *The Philippines: Priorities and Prospects for Development.* Washington DC: The World Bank.

Chapter 5

THE FINANCIAL MARKETS AND INSTITUTIONS IN SOUTHEAST ASIA

ABSTRACT

This chapter examines the financial sector in Southeast Asian economies and discusses its contribution to the transformation process of these economies. It discusses the various financial markets and institutions in Southeast Asia based on individual country experiences.

INTRODUCTION

This chapter aims to provide an analysis of the financial sector in Southeast Asia focusing on the developments in the financial markets and financial intermediaries including problems and policies. The financial sector in Southeast Asia has contributed significantly to the economic development of their economies. There exists a positive relationship between economic and financial development.[1] As the real economy grows and develops, the financial sector also grows and becomes more developed as it provides the financial requirements of the real sector. The assets of both bank and non-bank financial institutions increase. The financial markets grow rapidly and become diversified. More and diverse financial instruments are demanded and supplied. Table 5.1 shows the importance of the financial sector to the economies in Southeast Asia. As a proportion of real GDP, the financial services in Southeast Asia increased during the 1970-99 period. The contribution of the financial

---

1 Some of the studies which examine this relationship include Anis Chowdry and Iyanatul Islam, "Financial Development and Economic Performance," in Anis Chowdry and Iyanatul Islam, *The Newly Industrializing Economies of East Asia*, London: Routledge, 1993; Serene Tay, *Financial and Economic Development in ASEAN*, Singapore: National University of Singapore, 1993; Daniel Lian and Tsao Yuan Lee, "Financial Development in ASEAN," in Joseph Tan and Zhaohong Luo (eds.), *ASEAN-China Economic Relations*, Institute of World Economics and Politics, and Singapore: Institute of Southeast Asian Studies; Maxwell Fry, "Financial Development in Asia: Some Analytical Issues," *Asian-Pacific Economic Literature*, Vol.9, No.1, 1995, pp.40-57; and Dipendra Sinha and Joseph Macri, "Financial Development and Economic Growth: The Case of Eight Asian Countries," *Economia Internazionale*, Vol.55, pp.219-234.

sector is particularly higher for the more developed economies of Singapore and Malaysia than for the less developed economies of Indonesia, the Philippines and Thailand.

Table 5.1. Share of Financial Services to Real GDP, in percent

Year	Indonesia	Malaysia	Philippines	Singapore	Thailand	ASEAN
1970	3.0	...	...	13.9	...	8.4
1975	3.9	8.4	3.5	15.6	6.5	7.6
1980	4.8	8.3	3.9	20.5	7.6	9.0
1985	6.4	8.9	3.0	27.4	3.2	9.8
1990	8.1	9.8	4.1	26.3	5.5	10.8
1995	9.2	10.4	4.2	23.9	7.6	11.1
1999	7.3	12.1	5.0	23.3	8.0	11.1

Source: ADB, *Key Indicators of Developing Asian and Pacific Countries*, Manila: Asian Development Bank, Various Issues.

The increasing importance of the financial sector can also be determined by the extent of financial deepening which involves the monetization of an economy as well as the rise of financial institutions. As the financial sector deepens, savings are increasingly held in financial rather than in non-financial instruments. The extent of financial deepening is determined by tracing the evolution of key financial variables like M1 or M2 ratios to GDP. This is shown in Table 5.2.

The ratio of M2/GDP more than doubled from 40 percent in 1970 to 89 percent in 1999 for the Southeast Asian region. This reflects the significant deepening that has taken place in Southeast Asia. However, the extent of deepening differs considerably between the richer, more developed countries of Singapore, Malaysia and Thailand and the poorer, less-developed countries of Indonesia and the Philippines. A higher M2/GDP ratio for Singapore, Malaysia and Thailand indicates that a large amount of loanable funds circulates through the organized financial sector in these countries. As Table 5.2 shows, the ratios of quasi-money (savings and time deposits) to GDP are very high for these countries. A lower ratio for Indonesia and the Philippines implies slower financial deepening where savings are held either in non-financial, rather than on financial, assets like savings and time deposits. Thus, the ratio of quasi-money to GDP for Indonesia and the Philippines are much lower than Singapore, Malaysia and Thailand. Moreover, a low ratio indicates that the Thais and the Filipinos rely less on financial institutions for intermediation between savers and borrowers. This is especially so in the many rural areas in the Philippines and Thailand.

Financial Markets

The financial markets channel resources from surplus holders to those who have shortage of funds. These markets can be classified into two types; namely, debt and equity markets, and money and capital markets. Some examples of a **debt instrument** are bonds or mortgage loans. **Equities** come in the form of common stocks in which owners of these stocks share in the net income (including dividends) and assets of a firm. In a **money market**, short-term debt instruments are traded. Some examples are government Treasury Bills which have lesser price fluctuations, are safer investments as they are government-guaranteed, and are often held by banks and corporations to earn interest on their surplus funds. Money market instruments also include negotiable certificates of deposits (NCDs), short-term government securities, bills of exchange, and commercial papers. **Capital market** deals with longer-term debt and equity instruments which are often held by insurance companies and pension funds because of the predictable nature of their cash flows.

Table 5.2. Indicators of Financial Deepening

Year	Indonesia	Malaysia	Philippines	Singapore	Thailand	ASEAN
	Ratio of Narrow Money to GNP (M1/GNP)					
1970	7.6	...	11.2	26.9	14.2	15.0
1975	10.3	20.1	9.0	26.0	11.7	15.4
1980	11.5	19.0	9.2	25.3	10.9	15.2
1985	10.9	18.9	6.4	21.8	8.3	13.3
1990	11.8	21.9	8.2	22.4	9.0	14.7
1995	11.9	24.5	9.4	20.9	9.4	15.2
1999	12.1	25.8	12.5	20.1	12.6	16.6
	Ratio of Quasi-Money to GNP (QM/GNP)					
1970	...	...	11.0	37.6	19.6	13.6
1975	6.0	26.1	16.2	35.1	26.3	21.9
1980	6.2	35.5	13.7	41.0	27.4	24.8
1985	14.0	51.2	16.1	48.0	48.8	35.6
1990	30.2	53.9	19.2	68.4	61.8	46.7
1995	38.5	69.3	29.1	63.1	71.0	54.2
1999	50.7	92.2	30.5	92.7	94.0	72.0
	Ratio of Broad Money to GNP (M2/GNP)					
1970	...	...	22.2	64.5	33.8	40.2
1975	16.4	46.2	25.3	61.2	38.0	37.4
1980	17.7	54.5	23.0	66.4	38.3	40.0
1985	24.9	70.0	22.5	69.8	57.1	48.8
1990	42.0	75.8	27.5	90.8	70.8	61.4
1995	50.5	93.8	38.6	84.0	80.4	73.1
1999	62.8	118.0	43.0	112.8	106.4	88.6

Source: ADB, *Key Indicators of Developing Asian and Pacific Countries*, Manila: Asian Development Bank, Various Issues.

In Southeast Asia, there exists a sharp contrast in the development of capital markets with those in Indonesia, Thailand and the Philippines lagging behind those in Singapore and Malaysia. This is evident in Table 5.3.

Table 5.3. Equity Market Capital and GDP in Southeast Asia

	Equity Market Capital (US$ billion)		GDP (US$ billion)		Equity-market capital/GDP ratio (percent)	
	1995	2000	1995	2000	1995	2000
Jakarta	66.5	26.8	196.6	153.3	34	17.5
Kuala Lumpur	213.8	113.02	82.4	89.3	259	126.7
Philippines	58.8	25.3	72.6	74.7	81	33.8
Singapore	151.0	155.1	77.5	92.3	195	168.2
Thailand	135.9	29.2	142.9	122.2	95	23.9

Source: World Federation of Exchanges Annual Reports, 1996 and 2001 issues.

As a proportion of GDP, the equity market capitalization in Indonesia, Thailand and the Philippines were significantly much lower than those in Singapore and Malaysia. All countries experienced marked reductions in the ratios of their equity market capital to output (proxied by GDP). The drastic fall was mainly due to the marked decrease in their equity market capital as a result of the 1997/98 financial crisis in which many companies had incurred massive losses. The wide gaps in the development of the capital markets in Southeast Asia are also attributed to the differentials in the level of transaction costs particularly in the equity markets. Table 5.4 shows the results of the Elkins/McSherry analysis of transaction costs for the fourth quarter of 1997. The Philippines had the highest transaction costs among the Southeast Asian economies mainly because of its relatively high commissions, fees and taxes. Next in line was Indonesia with a total cost of 101.26 basis points. Thailand and Malaysia had much lower transaction costs, but about 20-25 percent higher than the world average cost. Singapore had the lowest cost among ASEAN countries, which was about the same as the world average cost.

Indonesia

Indonesia's domestic bond market is relatively underdeveloped.[2] This applies to both government and corporate bond markets. The Government has been effectively prohibited from issuing bonds since 1967 because of the balance-budget requirement. The corporate sector was likewise prohibited from issuing bonds until 1988. Despite the lifting of the prohibition in 1988, the market was slow to take off until the Capital Markets Law was promulgated in 1995 which set a clearer regulatory framework. In contrast, the equity market expanded rapidly. For example, as at mid-1997, the equity market capitalization reached 302 trillion rupiahs (Rp) while corporate bonds were valued at Rp 16 trillion, or a mere 5 percent of the equity capital. The differential in the development of the bond and equity markets in Indonesia reflects the greater interest among foreign investors in equities as these investments offer exposure to the long-run growth potential of the Indonesian economy whereas bonds

---

[2] For an excellent analysis of capital markets in Indonesia, see Stephen Wells, "Moving Toward Transparency: Capital Market in Indonesia," in *Rising to the Challenge in Asia: A Study of Financial* Markets (Volume 6 – Indonesia), Manila: Asian Development Bank, 1999, pp.74-111.

have no upside, only downside risk. The pension funds, insurance companies, corporations, and more recently, the mutual funds have been the major investors in bonds.

Table 5.4. Global Transaction Costs in the Equity Markets 4th Quarter 1997 (Basis Points)

Economy	Commission, Fees and Taxes	Market Impact*	Total Cost
Indonesia	77.90	23.38	101.28
Malaysia	71.36	16.36	87.72
Philippines	104.03	6.76	110.79
Singapore	55.32	16.64	71.96
Thailand	66.79	20.66	87.45
Hong Kong	46.45	9.46	55.91
India	20.70	49.53	70.23
Korea	60.77	158.81	219.58
Taipei	52.55	21.15	73.70
Average	61.76	35.86	97.62
New York Stock Exchange	12.36	22.11	34.47
World	44.28	27.17	71.45

*Market impact is measured by comparing the trade price with some measure of the underlying price – the price that would have prevailed had the trade not taken place. It measures the skill of execution and liquidity of the market. Normally, the larger the trade, the more impact will be. See Elkins/McSherry Co. Inc. as cited in Stephen Wells, "Solid Crust with Soft Center: A Problem of Enforcement in the Philippine Capital Market," in *Rising to the Challenge in Asia: A Study of Financial* Markets (Volume 10 – Philippines), Manila: Asian Development Bank, 1999, pp.83

During the 1992-97 period, the bond market in Indonesia grew rapidly when listed bonds increased their market capitalization by 700 percent. Issuance was particularly rapid from 1996 until the onset of the crisis. However as shown in Table 5.5, the corporate bond market was small with a market capitalization of Rp7 trillion (about 5 percent of equity market capitalization and just 4 percent of bank loans). On the other hand, bank finance was the dominant source of non-equity capital.

In terms of the equity market, the Jakarta Stock Exchange (JSX) is the most dominant. There was a significant increase in the number of companies listed in the JSX from 123 in 1990 to 287 companies in 1997 as entry requirements were seen as reasonable including a minimum requirement of 200 shareholders and a requirement of two years' profitability. The market value likewise rose markedly from Rp14 trillion to Rp160 trillion during the same period. Issuers on the JSX include private companies, government enterprises, and subsidiaries of listed holding companies. The Surabaya Stock Exchange (SSX) is a smaller market in which 11 companies have sought listing.

Table 5.5. Asset Values in Indonesian Financial Markets, Mid-1997

Type of Asset	Value (Rp Trillion)
Bank loans	375.8
Equity market capitalization	301.6
Bank Indonesia Certificates (BIS)	7.0
Corporate Bonds (market capitalization)	15.8
Rupiah commercial paper	0.8
US$ Medium-term notes, floating rate notes, etc.	7.0

Source: Pefindo, as cited in Stephen Wells, "Moving Toward Transparency: Capital Market in Indonesia," in *Rising to the Challenge in Asia: A Study of Financial* Markets (Volume 6 – Indonesia), Manila: Asian Development Bank, 1999, p.84.

Malaysia

The capital market in Malaysia has undergone a robust development since the late 1980s following the delisting of Malaysian and Singaporean companies from their respective stock exchanges at the end of 1989.[3] The proliferation of privatization projects and the equity boom in 1993 have resulted in Malaysia's capital market capitalization to exceed that of Singapore by the mid-1990s. Thus, the Malaysian market has become one of the fastest growing in the region. For example, in 1995, the equity market capitalization in Malaysia reached US$214 billion while in Singapore, the value reached US$151 billion. Some of the big privatized companies listed in the Kuala Lumpur Stock Exchange (KLSE) included Telecom Malaysia Berhad and Tenaga Nasioni Berhad. The 1997/98 crisis, however, impacted Malaysia's equity market severely as share prices collapsed. Like banks, Malaysia's stockbrokers incurred massive losses because of their customers' loan defaults and hence some brokers were suspended by the KLSE. The Bank Negara Malaysia (BNM) announced controls on foreign exchange by fixing the US dollar at RM3.80 on September 2, 1998. This was aimed at regaining monetary independence and protecting the Malaysian economy from further worsening. For its part, the KLSE declared that all Malaysian shares would be traded only within the KLSE, and that foreigners should hold on to their Malaysian shares for at least one year so that they could convert the proceeds from selling them into foreign currency. These measures were aimed at restoring confidence on the Malaysian equity market.

As for the bond market, the Malaysian government has encouraged private and public bodies to issue bonds for generating funds, while Bank Negara Malaysia has been supportive in developing the market infrastructure for bond issues. By the end of the 1980s, the Malaysian primary market for government bonds was relatively developed. To develop the secondary market for government bonds, a principal dealer system and an auction system for government securities were introduced.

As for private bonds, the first Cagamas bonds[4] were released in 1987, but it did not develop until the mid-1990s. Several measures were introduced by the Malaysian government

3 For a thorough analysis of capital markets in Malaysia, see Yutaka Shimomoto, "The Capital Market in Malaysia," in *Rising to the Challenge in Asia: A Study of Financial* Markets (Volume 8 – Malaysia), Manila: Asian Development Bank, 1999, pp.80-112.

4 Cagamas bonds are issued by Cagamas Berhad, a secondary mortgage market institution.

to help develop the private bond market including, among others, the establishment of a credit rating agency, tax exemption on interest income, and scripless trading for unlisted bonds. The outstanding amount of private bonds rose sharply from RM15 billion in 1993 to RM63 billion in 1997 because of their AAA rating and because these bonds are eligible assets for liquidity requirements of commercial banks and finance companies. Since 1994, Islamic bonds have accounted for the biggest share of private debt securities in Malaysia. These bonds are issued through private placements but are allotted to government institutions. For example, in 1996, when the Kuala Lumpur International Airport Berhad (KLIA) issued a RM2.2 billion Islamic bond, it was able to get financial support from the Malaysian government (through the Employees Provident Fund) as it was a national project.

Philippines

The capital market in the Philippines can be characterized as follows.[5] Firstly, the equity primary market is relatively underdeveloped given that the Philippine Stock Exchange (PSE) lists only some 200 companies and that less than 100 of the country's top 1000 largest corporations have a listing. This was attributed to the nature of the Philippine industrial organization, that is, the Philippine companies are tightly held and generate most of their capital requirements from captive banking institutions. These companies are generally cautious in releasing information and have very little pressures from their shareholders. As at Feb 1998, the top ten most active stocks include Manila Electric Company, Philippine Long Distance Telephone, Ayala Land, Metro Bank, San Miguel Corporation, Belle, Ayala Corporation, SM Prime, Digitel Telecom, and Metro Pacific.

Secondly, the Philippines has a relatively more developed bond market than some other ASEAN countries as it has offered diverse financial instruments and long-term debt instruments. It has a significant public bond market because of the need to fund chronic fiscal deficits. The various features of both public and private bonds are shown in Table 5.6. Since mid-1998, the Government bond market has been regulated by the Bureau of Treasury rather than by its central bank known as Bangko Sentral ng Pilipinas (BSP). Currently, the market is almost all short term (mostly three-month bills) and hence generates a liquid secondary market supported by a scripless settlement system. On the other hand, the Philippine corporate bond market is very much smaller than the public bond market. The corporate bond market is regulated by the Securities Exchange Commission.

---

5 For an excellent study of Philippine capital markets, see Stephen Wells, "Solid Crust with Soft Center: A Problem of Enforcement in the Philippine Capital Market," in *Rising to the Challenge in Asia: A Study of Financial* Markets (Volume 10 – Philippines), Manila: Asian Development Bank, 1999, pp.80-105.

Table 5.6. Assets of Philippine Bond Market

	Public		Private	
Item	Short-Term Treasury Bills	Long-Term Treasury Bonds	Short-term Commercial Paper	Long-Term Commercial Paper
Term	91-364 days	1-20 years	Up to 365 days	Over 1 year-mostly 5 years
Interest	Fixed	Floating-reset quarterly	Fixed	Floating-reset quarterly
Issue Method	Weekly auction by BTr	Fortnightly auction by BTr	Underwritten or private placement Underwriting fees P100 – 150 billion	
Trading	OTC – liquid		OTC – illiquid	
Settlement	Scripless, electronic run by BTr		Currently interoffice, paper based. Proposal to transfer to scripless	
Regulator	Bureau of Treasury (BTr)		SEC- registration required	
Investors	Insurance companies, banks, mutual funds, wealthy individuals, state pension systems (SSS and GSIS), which are required to invest heavily in government securities			
Issuers			Prime corporations from manufacturing, finance and especially property/real estate sectors	
Other Features			CP requires no shareholder approval, in contrast to bonds	

Note: OTC = over the counter, GSIS = Government Service Insurance System, SSS = Social Security System, SEC=Securities and Exchange Commission. Source: Stephen Wells, "Solid Crust with Soft Center: A Problem of Enforcement in the Philippine Capital Market," in *Rising to the Challenge in Asia: A Study of Financial* Markets (Volume 10 – Philippines), Manila: Asian Development Bank, p.91.

Singapore

The Singapore bond market consists of corporate bonds, Asian dollar bonds, and government securities. Since independence in 1965, the Singapore government has run persistent surpluses which have had a significant impact on the development of government and corporate bond markets. The secondary bond market in Singapore is considered anemic as compared with the equity market.[6] Outside of the commercial banks, there is virtually no

[6] For an interesting discussion of the bond market in Singapore, see Edward Ng, "Central Provident Fund in Singapore: A Capital Market Boost or Drag?" in *Rising to the Challenge in Asia: A Study of Financial* Markets, (Volume – Singapore), Manila: Asian Development Bank, 1999, pp.56-80. See also Chwee

secondary government bond market. The government issues two broad types of debt securities: Treasury Bills and the Singapore Government Securities (SGS). Having been issued under the Local Treasury Bills Act of 1923 (amended in 1992), the T-bills have different maturity periods - 91days, 182 days, 273 days, and 364 days. The SGS are issued to finance current expenditure under the Government Securities Act or to finance infrastructure development under the Development Loan Act. The Monetary Authority of Singapore (MAS) manages the sale of SGS. The four discount houses acted as dealers in the SGS market until July 1, 1987 and sold these securities to commercial banks to meet their liquidity reserve requirements. In 1987, as the discount houses were abolished, the commercial banks themselves have performed as primary dealers for SGS. There are 8 primary dealers and 38 secondary dealers among banks, merchant banks and stockbroking firms.

Historically, a large proportion of SGS outstanding has been held by the Central Provident Fund (CPF) Board for a minimum share of 65 per cent in 1969 to a maximum share of 85 percent in 1967. In 1996, it held a share of about 72 percent. Over the years, the other holders are commercial banks and POSBank, with shares of 16 percent and 4 percent in 1996, respectively. As for the corporate bond market, a total of 48 issues of corporate bonds which raised S$5.9 billion in 1997, as compared with 31 issues worth S$3 billion in 1996.[7]

On February 28, 1998, the government implemented several measures to stimulate the domestic bond market. These measures include, among others, granting tax exemptions for income earned by financial institutions which arrange debt securities, and granting a concessionary tax rate of 10 percent for interest income earned by bond holders including financial institutions and corporations. The MAS and other government bodies (like Jurong Town Corporation, Public Utilities Board, Housing Development Board, Land Transport Authority) will also be issuing more government securities. Moreover, foreign institutions are encouraged to issue Singapore dollar bonds.

The development of stock market in Singapore can be traced back to as early as the 19th century when stock brokers bought and sold shares of rubber and tin companies.[8] In 1929, the Singapore Stockbrokers Association was created to regulate the conduct of stockbrokers. In 1960, several companies from Singapore, Kuala Lumpur, Penang and Ipoh jointly established the Malayan Stock Exchange. In 1961, the Singapore and Kuala Lumpur trading rooms were connected by direct telephone lines, and had therefore acted effectively as a single market and was known as the Stock Exchange of Malaysia until 1965 when Singapore obtained its independence. Subsequently, it was renamed Stock Exchange of Malaysia and Singapore. Then, in 1973, the Malaysian government ended the inter-changeability between the Malaysian ringgit and Singapore dollar and split the joint stock exchange. On May 24, 1973, the Stock Exchange of Singapore was set up with many of the 300 companies being co-listed in the Kuala Lumpur Stock Exchange. In 1987, the SES introduced a second board called SESDAQ (Stock Exchange of Singapore Dealing and Automated Quotation) for smaller companies to raise funds. Consequently, the KLSE de-listed some 180 Malaysian companies from the SES main board in 1989, which resulted in a significant reduction of the stock market capitalization in Singapore. To remedy the situation, an over-the-counter market

Huat Tan, *Financial Markets and Institutions in Singapore,* Singapore: Singapore University Press, 1999.

7 Chwee Huat Tan, Financial Markets and Institutions in Singapore…, 1999, p.234.

8 Chwee Huat Tan, Financial Markets and Institutions in Singapore, 1999, p.243.

(known as Clob International) was introduced by the SES to facilitate trading of Malaysian shares and later on Hong Kong and Philippine shares, too. Because of the severe impact of the July 1997 financial crisis on Malaysia's stock market, the KLSE announced on August 31, 1998 that all Malaysian securities had to be traded through the KLSE or through an exchange allowed by the KLSE. Other measures including foreign exchange controls were imposed by Malaysia so that by September 16, 1998, the SES ended trading Malaysian shares on Clob International. The SES and KLSE worked on procedures to transfer Clob International accounts to accounts with the Malaysian Central Depository.

Thailand

Thailand lacks an active government bond market.[9] In 1990, the government stopped issuing new bonds as it started running consecutive budget surpluses. Thus, the Government's outstanding baht liabilities significantly dropped from almost 200 billion baht (Bt) in 1990 to only Bt 14 billion by the end of 1997. Thus, the government bonds as at end-1997 accounted for a mere 3 percent of all outstanding bonds. While the Thai government ceased to issue bonds directly, State enterprises increased their share of outstanding bonds to 55 percent by the end of 1997, valued at Bt 288 billion.

Secondly, the private sector corporations in Thailand have not been active borrowers in the bond market as they have preferred bank loans or equity finance for their external long-term borrowing requirements. Because of these financing patterns which could be found in other Southeast Asian countries, Thailand's corporate bond market has remained limited in size and scope. This was attributed to the institutional settings which could be found in Thailand as well as other Southeast Asian countries in which there exists a close and interlocking links between banks, companies and governments.[10] Banks are often part of the major conglomerates that dominate the corporate sector in Southeast Asia. There is also an interlocking relationship between governments and the business families that control the conglomerates and banks. Thus, these institutional settings have given strong incentives for companies to depend heavily on banks for their financing requirements.

The corporate bond market started to take off in 1992 when the Securities and Exchange Act (SEA) was passed, which gives limited companies the right to offer bonds to the general public. Spurred by these developments, the primary issue activity expanded quickly and corporate bonds accounted for 36 percent of all outstanding bonds by the end of 1997. Unlike other Southeast Asian countries, Thailand has been successful in establishing a thriving corporate bond market over a relatively short period of time.

As for sectoral distribution, Table 5.7 shows that bond issuers came primarily from the financial and property sectors. In 1997, almost half of existing corporate bonds were issued by banks and finance companies, which reflected the asset bubble. Another 22 percent was accounted for by the real estate and construction industries.

---

9 For a detailed discussion of capital market in Thailand, see Richard Werner, "Capital Market in Thailand: Issues and Opportunities," in *Rising to the Challenge in Asia: A Study of Financial* Markets (Volume 11 – Thailand), Manila: Asian Development Bank, 1999, pp.106-134.

10 Krishnan Sharma, *The Underlying Constraints on Corporate Bond Market Development in Southeast Asia*, United Nations: Development Policy and Analysis Section, 2002. [http://www.combinet.net/wldecnmy/oct2000/KrishnaSharma/constraints.htm]

Table 5.7. Bond Issues in Thailand by Sector

Sector	Outstanding value, as of Dec 31, 1997 (Bt million)	Share in corporate bonds (% of total)
Banking	33,510	25.3
Finance companies	30,532	23.1
Property development	21,972	16.6
Energy	11,406	8.6
Holding company	8,541	6.4
Construction	6,748	5.1
Others	19,791	14.9
Total	132,500	100.0

Source: Thai Bond Dealing Center. As cited in Richard Werner, "Capital Market in Thailand: Issues and Opportunities," in *Rising to the Challenge in Asia: A Study of Financial* Markets (Volume 11 – Thailand), Manila: Asian Development Bank, 1999, pp.110.

The local stock market has become a major source of capital for the Thai companies. While the financial crisis of July 1997 has affected the primary issue activity in the stock market, there has been no major crisis in the regulatory and supervisory system. Given that there have been no major bankruptcies or irregularities among brokers or securities companies, the Thai equity market has been much better regulated and supervised than the banking sector. Fifty-six finance companies and securities companies were permanently closed down in December 1997 because of their exposure to non-performing loans rather than because of their securities business. Table 5.8 shows the market capitalization of the Stock Exchange in Thailand (SET). Although half of the stock market capitalization was concentrated in finance and property sectors in 1996, this concentration was less than that of the bond market. Capital mobilization dropped significantly in 1997 as the stock market was hit by the crisis. As at end-1997, 431 companies were listed in the Stock Exchange of Thailand.

FINANCIAL INTERMEDIARIES

More advanced economies have wider range of both bank and non-bank financial institutions which provide diverse and specialized services. These financial institutions can be classified into (a) money generating, (b) other deposit type, (c) contractual savings, (d) development type, and (e) investment-type institutions.

Money-Generating Institutions

These include the central banks and commercial banks. Central banks generate money by issuing currency and notes. Commercial banks generate money by accepting deposits and make these deposits available for loans. In its narrow definition, money (M1) refers to the sum of currency in circulation (C)and demand deposits (D), that is, M1 = C + D. Table 5.9 shows the evolution of M1 in Southeast Asia and its components. Over a period of three decades, the proportion of currency to M1 has fallen for the more developed countries like

Singapore and Malaysia indicating their move towards cashless societies. Thailand has been very dependent on the usage of currency as its proportion to M1 rose from 61 percent in 1970 to 82 percent in 1999.

Table 5.8. Market Capitalization of the Stock Exchange of Thailand As of December 1996

Sector	Market capitalization (Bt billion)	Percent of total
Banking and finance	894.8	34.9
Property and construction	369.3	14.4
Communication	308.2	12.0
Energy	225.7	8.8
Entertainment	89.9	3.5
Transportation	83.9	3.3
Chemicals and plastics	78.0	3.0
Commerce	63.2	2.5
Food and beverage	40.3	1.6
Others	409.9	16.0
Total	2563.2	100.0

Source: Stock Exchange of Thailand. As cited in Richard Werner, "Capital Market in Thailand: Issues and Opportunities," in *Rising to the Challenge in Asia: A Study of Financial* Markets (Volume 11 – Thailand), Manila: Asian Development Bank, 1999, pp.115.

Central Banks in Southeast Asia

The establishment of central banks in Southeast Asia had some elements of foreign intervention and characteristics. In 1942, the Bank of Thailand was established by the Japanese. In 1949, the Philippine Central Bank was created based on the central banks of Paraguay and Guatemala. In 1953, the central bank of Indonesia was founded following the nationalization of a Dutch commercial bank called the Java Bank. Then, in 1968, a new central bank bill was passed by the Suharto government which reconstituted what is now known as the Bank of Indonesia. In 1959, the Malaysian central bank was established following the British and Australian central banking models. Following its breakaway from the Federation of Malaya, the sole right of currency issue in Singapore has been conferred to the Board of Commissioners of Currency. By an Act of Parliament, the Monetary Authority of Singapore (MAS) was established in 1971 to be the banker and financial agent of the Government, to promote stability in monetary, credit and exchange rate conditions, and to develop and strengthen the financial markets and institutions in Singapore. In 1984, the MAS Act was amended in which its role of being a banker and financial agent to the government was extended to government company and statutory boards.

Table 5.9. Narrow Money (M1) in Southeast Asia

Year	1970	1980	1990	1995	1999
Indonesia					
M1	241	4995	23819	52677	124633
Currency	64	43	38	40	47
Demand Deposits	36	57	62	60	53
Malaysia					
M1	2032	9761	24241	51924	72318
Currency	49	49	42	34	34
Demand Deposits	51	51	58	66	66
Philippines					
M1	4697	22537	89012	184931	394129
Currency	51	45	70	60	55
Demand Deposits	49	55	30	40	45
Singapore					
M1	1574	6135	15260	25349	31109
Currency	43	51	47	39	36
Demand Deposits	57	49	53	61	64
Thailand					
M1	19448	71595	195414	388276	575000
Currency	61	64	70	73	82
Demand Deposits	39	36	30	27	18

Note: The values of M1 are expressed in national currencies: billion Indonesian rupiah, million Malaysian ringgit, million Philippine pesos, million Singapore dollars, and million Thai baht. The currency in circulation and demand deposits are expressed in percent (as shares of total money, M1) for each country. Source: ADB, *Key Indicators of Developing Asian and Pacific Countries*, Manila: Asian Development Bank, Various Issues.

The central banks in Southeast Asia have the following features. First, they were initially one of the largest financial institutions. Second, the share of their assets relative to the total assets of the financial system has decreased over time as seen in Table 5.10. Third, currency as a proportion of central bank liabilities has fallen as other types of financial institutions grow much faster. This is shown in Table 5.11.

Functions of the Central Banks

Aside from issuing currency and notes, the central bank performs two important functions. First, it formulates and implements monetary policy on interest rates, money supply and exchange rates. Another function that central banks perform is to supervise and regulate financial institutions, both banks and non-banks. Each of these functions will be discussed for each Southeast Asian country.

Table 5.10. Assets of the Financial System in Southeast Asia

Year	1970	1980	1990	1995	1999
Indonesia					
Total assets	1018	19927	181668	383235	1305087
Central Bank	52	49	27	19	38
Deposit banks	48	51	73	81	62
Malaysia					
Total assets	6681	45180	170199	380687	621730
Central Bank	33	29	24	23	24
Deposit banks	67	71	76	77	76
Philippines					
Total assets	6003	199615	985418	1863074	3732687
Central Bank	100	33	45	27	26
Deposit banks	n.a.	67	55	73	74
Singapore					
Total assets	5041	44765	167922	293247	434202
Central Bank	-	26	20	23	25
Deposit banks	5041	74	80	77	75
Thailand					
Total assets	73272	448121	2287676	6139118	9485690
Central Bank	41	32	21	17	26
Deposit banks	59	68	79	83	74

Note: Total assets are expressed in national currencies: billion Indonesian rupiah, million Malaysian ringgit, million Philippine pesos, million Singapore dollars, and million Thai baht. Assets of central bank and deposit banks are expressed as shares of total assets. Source: These information were obtained from the individual country reports found in the ADB, *Key Indicators of Developing Asian and Pacific Countries*, Manila: Asian Development Bank, Various Issues.

Indonesia

As for Indonesia's monetary policy, the Bank of Indonesia (BI) increased the SBI rate in 1995 in response to the speculative attack on the rupiah brought about by the Mexican crisis. Real interest rates rose which encouraged inflows of short-term foreign capital, which in turn, led to significant expansion of money supply. Consequently, to restrict short-term capital inflows, BI widened the band for exchange rate intervention five times from 3 percent in January 1996 to 12 percent in July 1997. Moreover, the BI pursued a more market-oriented interest rate for SBIs. However, the intervention came too late as Indonesia's external indebtedness skyrocketed to US$108 billion by end-1995 and as the current account deficit deteriorated. By March 1997, private sector foreign borrowings rose to US$61 billion from US$48 billion at end-1995. When the July 1997 crisis had spread to Indonesia, BI initially tried to defend the rupiah by intervening in the foreign exchange market and by raising the SBI rates. Eventually, BI decided to float the rupiah and lifted the exchange rate intervention bands on August 14, 1997. This led to a 30 percent depreciation of the rupiah by mid-October 1997. Thus, the BI set high interest rates to support the rupiah against the US dollar and to contain money-supply growth through open market issues of SBIs.

Table 5.11. Currency as a Proportion of Central Bank Liabilities in SE Asia

Year	1970	1980	1990	1995	1999
Indonesia					
Currency (C)	155	2153	9094	20807	58353
Liabilities (L)	531	9805	49045	74617	490069
C/L ratio	29	22	18	28	12
Malaysia					
- Currency (C)	1000	4758	10059	17479	24873
Liabilities (L)	2221	12994	40914	88475	147048
C/L ratio	45	37	25	20	17
Philippines					
- Currency (C)	2410	10174	61921	110892	218476
Liabilities (L)	6003	65447	444893	501914	970141
C/L ratio	40	16	14	22	23
Singapore					
Currency (C)	682	3137	7108	9907	11315
Liabilities (L)	-	10845	33920	68668	108164
C/L ratio	-	29	21	14	10
Thailand					
Currency (C)	11863	45900	137500	284100	472400
Liabilities (L)	30314	142727	481112	1072572	2512326
C/L ratio	39	32	29	26	19

Note and source: As in Table 5.10.

As for its second function, the Bank of Indonesia (BI) regulates and supervises all banking financial institutions. For example, the Bapindo scandal prompted BI to phase in more prudential regulations to ensure bank soundness. These include reporting requirements, self regulation of banks, capital adequacy, asset quality, and others. The BI also undertook a major revamp of its banking supervision division in 1994, which consisted of 28 teams covering the commercial banks and 8 teams to cover the rural banks. The BI has joined forces with the Ministry of Finance in supervising non-bank financial institutions (NBFIs) like finance companies, insurance companies and pension funds, and in closely monitoring banks affiliated with NBFIs. With the passage of Capital Markets Law in 1995, the BI was tasked to regulate and supervise the money markets and banks, while the Capital Market Supervisory Agency (Bapepam) was assigned to regulate debt securities with maturity of more than one year

Malaysia

As for its first function, the Bank Negara Malaysia (BNM) announced a new monetary policy in March 1998 with changes from direct instruments (direct lendings/borrowings) to indirect instruments through open market operations using short-term instruments like Treasury Bills, Bank Negara Bills, short-term securities and negotiable certificates of deposits. Because of the worsening crisis situation, BNM relaxed monetary policy on August 27, 1998 by reducing the reserve requirement from 13.5 percent to 4 percent in order to increase liquidity in the system. On September 1, 1998, BNM announced capital control measures aimed at eliminating speculative capital flows that had attacked the ringgit and the stock market, and at obtaining monetary independence that would allow a progressive reduction of interest rates. On September 2, 1998, the foreign exchange rate was fixed at RM3.80 against the US dollar. This measure enables BNM to determine the interest rates, which in fact, were reduced to stimulate the Malaysian economy following the July 1997 crisis. Then, on September 3, 1998, BNM slashed its 3-month intervention rate from 9.5 to 8 percent and then to 7.5 percent, and also reduced the reserve requirement from 6 percent to 4 percent to increase liquidity in the system.

As for its second function, BNM regulates and supervises the first group of institutions consisting of commercial banks as well as non-bank financial institutions like finance companies, merchant banks, discount houses, foreign banks representative offices, and offshore banks in the International Offshore Financial Center in Labuan. From May 1, 1988, insurance companies have also been regulated and supervised by BNM. The second group of institutions under the supervision of various government departments and agencies includes development finance institutions, savings institutions, provident and pension funds, and other financial intermediaries. Following the July 1997 crisis, the BNM has implemented various controls on banking institutions aimed at strengthening of prudential regulation and supervision. These measures, among others, include greater transparency in monetary operations, increased requirements for capital adequacy ratios, and re-classification of non-performing loans from six months to three months.

Philippines

As for the conduct of monetary policy in the Philippines, the interest rates are not market-determined as these are mainly administered by auctions held by the central bank, Bangko Sentral ng Pilipinas (BSP). The loan rates are set by banks in a cartel-like manner. In March 1998, the BSP agreed with the Bankers Association of the Philippines to decrease reserve requirements on the condition that banks would reduce their loan rate margins. The interest rates have been held high to support the Philippine peso against the US dollar thereby encouraging short-term borrowing and dependence on foreign lenders.

As for its second function, the BSP is responsible for the regulation and prudential supervision of the financial system which consists of banks and non-bank financial intermediaries (NBFIs). The Securities and Exchange Commission (SEC) oversees the conduct of the corporate stock and bond markets, and to the extent that banks and NBFIs participate in these markets, the SEC works with the BSP in supervising and regulating these institutions.[11] For public sector bonds, the BSP was the regulator. Subsequently, however, the Bureau of Treasury has taken over the regulation and supervision. But for banks and NBFIs which participate in public sector bonds, the Bureau of Treasury works with the BSP as it has direct control over these institutions.

Following the 1997/98 crisis, the BSP has implemented comprehensive reform measures in order to strengthen the prudential and supervisory systems, and to deal effectively with problem banks and safeguard the soundness of the banking system. These measures include,

---

11 For an excellent analysis of Philippine banking, see Maria Socorro Gochoco-Bautista, "The Past Performance of the Philippine Banking Sector and Challenges in the Post-crisis Period," in *Rising to the Challenge in Asia: A Study of Financial* Markets (Volume 10 – Philippines), Manila: Asian Development Bank, 1999, pp.30-78.

among others, increasing the minimum capital requirements of banks by 20-67 percent from end-1998 levels, in two equal rounds to be completed by end-December 2000, requiring banks to set up a 2 percent loan-loss provision, redefining loans classified as non-performing loans - from six months to three months for loans payable in monthly installments, and from three quarters to one quarter for loans payable in quarterly installments.

Singapore

As for its first function, the Monetary Authority of Singapore (MAS) formulates and implements the country's monetary policy. It works very closely with the Ministry of Finance so that monetary policy would form an integral part of the overall national economic policy. The MAS develops and implements its monetary policy in order to impact on monetary aggregates and money market conditions which would have the intended effects on the real production and trade sectors.

As for its second function, the MAS regulates and supervises both banks and non-bank financial institutions. In February 1998, the MAS announced several reforms which included a review of its regulatory framework to provide a more conducive regulatory environment. Some of the regulatory reforms implemented were those that apply to banking like raising bank disclosure standards, liberalizing guidelines on Singapore dollar loans for regionalization projects, lowering minimum cash balance from 6 percent to 3 percent, and raising limits on offshore banks' loans to residents from S$200 million to S$300 million.[12] Other regulatory reforms applied to insurance, fund management, equity and futures markets, and bond market – all aimed at improving the competitiveness of Singapore as a financial center.

Thailand

As for its first function, the use of open market operations as a monetary policy tool is impeded since the government bond market is relatively undeveloped. Consequently, the Bank of Thailand (BOT) has relied on three instruments to regulate credit in the economy such as the Equalization Exchange Fund (EEF), the use of discount window, and the bonds issued by the BOT, the Financial Institutions Development Fund (FIDF) and the Property Loan Management Organization (PLMO). The EEF was created by the Bank of Thailand in 1984 to peg the baht to a basket of currencies of its major trading partners which was dominated by the US dollar. Since July 1997, the baht has been floated and determined in the market, but the BOT may intervene to preserve exchange rate stability. In 1995, the Thai government commenced issuing FIDF and PLMO bonds in order to provide liquidity to ailing banks and finance companies.

As for its second function, the BOT acts as the caretaker and overseer of the banking system.[13] It has regulatory and supervisory jurisdiction over all commercial banks, both locally-incorporated banks and branches of foreign banks. All commercial banks operate under the Commercial Banking Act B.E. 2505 of 1962 which was amended in 1979, 1992, 1997 and 1998. The Act authorizes the BOT together with the Ministry of Finance issue

---

[12] For a detailed discussion of the regulatory and supervisory functions of the MAS, see Chwee Huat Tan, *Financial Markets and Institutions in Singapore...*, 1999, pp.345-358.

[13] For an analysis of the supervisory function of the Bank of Thailand, see BOT, *Supervision Report*, Thailand: Bank of Thailand, 2000.

regulatory guidelines on the type of business, prudential requirements and reporting standards which apply to all commercial banks. The BOT also has authority over some NBFIs like finance companies, finance and securities companies, credit foncier companies and asset management companies. Unlike banks, finance companies, finance and securities companies, and credit foncier obtain their funding by issuing promissory notes, extend credit facilities which are not trade-related, and are not allowed to engage in foreign exchange services. The asset management companies (AMCs) were set up in 1998 following the crisis whose main role is to manage the assets transferred to them from financial distressed institutions.

Other NBFIs in Thailand are under the regulation and supervision government bodies other than the BOT. The Securities and Exchange Commission of Thailand (SEC) looks after securities companies, mutual fund management companies and provident fund. Beginning in 1999, the Ministry of Finance (MOF) is in charge of eight specialized financial institutions owned by the government. (Prior to the 1997 crisis, these institutions were under the authority of the BOT). The Ministry of Agriculture and Cooperatives regulates and supervises savings and agricultural cooperatives. The Ministry of Commerce handles all life insurance companies. The social security fund is looked after by the Ministry of Labor and Social Welfare.

Deposit-Money Banks in Southeast Asia

These banks, mostly commercial banks, dominate over all types of financial institutions in terms of assets, deposits mobilized, and number of head offices and branches. These information are shown in Table 5.12. Both assets and liabilities of commercial banks in Southeast Asia expanded significantly. The number of local banks decreased in Indonesia, Malaysia and Singapore indicating closures and/or mergers. On the other hand, the number of foreign banks rose in the Philippines and Singapore which indicates further opening of these countries to foreign banks. For all countries, the number of branches of commercial banks increased reflecting the availability of these institutions and their products and services over a wider geographical space.

The commercial banks in Southeast Asia have the following features. First, the share of their assets relative to total assets of the financial system has risen over the years. (This was seen earlier in Table 5.10). Second, the share of non-interest earning demand deposits to total deposits has fallen in importance while the share of interest-bearing instruments, like savings and time deposits, has increased. This is shown in Table 5.13.

Table 5.12. Commercial Banks in Southeast Asia, 1994 and 1999

	Assets	Deposit Liabilities	Number of Institutions	Number of Branches
	1994/1999	1994/1999	1994/1999	1994/1999
Indonesia				
Deposit Money Banks				
State banks	99 (576)	64 (338)	7 (5)	1171 (1858)
Pte national banks	115 (300)	85 (254)	166 (92)	3203 (4343)
Regional banks	8 (26)	6 (14)	27 (27)	431 (825)
Foreign/JV banks	25 (103)	9 (72)	40 (40)	83 (104)
Malaysia				
Banking Institutions				
Commercial banks	239 (475)	160 (333)	37 (33)	1283 (1767)
Domestic banks	184 (366)	124 (257)	23 (20)	1139 (1623)
Foreign banks	55 (109)	36 (75)	14 (13)	144 (144)
Islamic Bank	3 (9)	3 (7)	1 (1)	60 (81)
Philippines				
Banking Institutions				
Commercial Banks	1059 (2758)	693 (1752)	34 (52)	2890 (4274)
Domestic Banks	972 (2398)	671 (1593)	30 (41)	2885 (4263)
Foreign Banks	87 (360)	22 (159)	4 (11)	5 (11)
Singapore				
Total Banks	202 (326)	99 (174)	139 (139)	
Local			12 (8)	
Foreign			127 (131)	
Full banks			22 (23)	
Restricted banks			14 (16)	
Offshore banks			91 (92)	
Thailand				
Commercial Banks	4025 (6922)	2761 (4672)	29 (34)	2857 (3290)

Note: Assets and liabilities are expressed in national currencies: trillion Indonesian rupiah, billion Malaysian ringgit, billion Philippine pesos, billion Singapore dollars, and billion Thai baht. Source: These information were obtained from the individual country reports found in the Financial Statistics Yearbook published by the Southeast Asian Central Banks for Training and Research (SEACEN) based in Kuala Lumpur (July 1995 and July 2000 issues).

Indonesia

The Indonesian financial sector has undergone deregulation since 1983, when interest rate ceilings and direct credit targets were lifted. The present banking system has been shaped mainly by two laws: PAKTO 1988 and Banking Act of 1992.[14] The reform measures aimed to encourage competition by lowering the barrier to entry and to promote banks as the major vehicle for funds mobilization. These measures include drastically cutting the reserve requirement from 15 to 2 percent of deposit liabilities, more relaxed procedures in opening branches and the conversion to foreign exchange bank status. These measures contributed to the explosive growth of the banking sector. The number of commercial banks rose

14 For an excellent analysis of Indonesian banks, see Catherine Chou, "Indonesian Banks: Survival Of The Fittest," In *Rising To The Challenge In Asia: A Study Of Financial* Markets (Volume 6 – Indonesia), Manila: Asian Development Bank, 1999, Pp.36-72.

considerably from 111 two months after PAKTO 1988 was passed to 208 by end-1992. The number of bank offices likewise increased from 1,957 to 5,495 during the same period. A large number of the new banks are small and joint-venture banks which resulted in bank fragmentation and intense competition for funds. During the 1988-92 period, the assets and credits of private banks expanded by 60 percent and 40 percent, respectively. However, the unsoundness of the banking system came to light when two banks collapsed – the Bank Duta in 1990 because of foreign exchange losses and Bank Summa in 1992. Consequently, the Bank of Indonesia introduced prudential regulations in 1991 by incorporating the capital adequacy ratio into the revised Banking Act of 1992, thereby increasing the minimum paid-up capitalization for private national banks to Rp50 billion (US$25 million). More prudential regulations and supervisory tools were phased in during the 1993-96 period which were largely consistent with those recommended by the Basle Committee and largely comparable with the western standards.

Table 5.13. Deposit Liabilities of Deposit Money Banks in SE Asia

Year	1970	1980	1990	1995	1999
Indonesia					
Total Deposits	166	4323	60875	162761	474860
-Demand Deposits	52	66	24	20	14
-Sav. & Time Dep.	48	34	76	80	86
Malaysia					
Total Deposits	3	23	61	160	280
-Demand Deposits	31	22	23	22	17
-Savings Deposits	18	18	22	15	12
-Time Deposits	51	60	55	63	71
Philippines					
Total Deposits	8	71	305	867	1709
-Demand Deposits	30	17	9	9	10
-Savings Deposits	50	32	59	67	60
-Time Deposits	20	51	32	24	30
Singapore					
Total Deposits	3	15	62	106	172
-Demand Deposits	29	19	13	15	11
-Savings Deposits	13	11	16	22	35
-Time Deposits	58	70	71	63	54
Thailand					
Total Deposits	31	211	1431	3170	4640
-Demand Deposits	24	12	4	3	2
-Savings Deposits	9	13	28	23	24
-Time Deposits	67	75	68	74	74

Note: Total deposits are expressed in national currencies: billion Indonesian rupiah, billion Malaysian ringgit, billion Philippine pesos, billion Singapore dollars, and billion Thai baht. Demand, savings and time deposits are expressed as shares of total deposits for each country. Source: These information were obtained from the individual country reports found in the ADB, *Key Indicators of Developing Asian and Pacific Countries*, Manila: Asian Development Bank, Various Issues.

Aside from private national banks, the seven State banks are the major players in Indonesia's banking system as they have historically played an important role in the allocation of subsidized credit to priority social and economic sectors designated by the Bank of Indonesia. These sectors included sugar estates and refineries, rubber and palm oil plantations, and construction. However, the entire State banking sector was financially devastated in 1994 when the Bank Pembangunan Indonesia's (Bapindo) massive loan assistance to businessman Edi Tansil proved to be disastrous – a scandal which led to a substantial deterioration in the quality of the State bank assets.

On the lending side, the seven State banks' share of the total outstanding credit was around 65 percent during the 1983-88 period and 56 percent in 1991. The private bank credit expanded by around 40 percent during the 1988-92 period. During the 1993-97 period, bank loans expanded by 26 percent. The aggressive lending activities of the seven State Banks and the numerous private national banks during the 1988-93 period resulted in a high level of non-performing loans (NPLs) – at 20 percent of total State bank credits in 1993 and 12 percent for all commercial banks in 1994.

On the sourcing side, commercial banks in Indonesia relied heavily on foreign borrowings (offshore funding) for various reasons. First, there was a need to bridge the maturity mismatch of their funds. Around 95 percent of rupiah deposits in commercial banks are short term (one year or less) while around 20 percent of their loans are long term (more than one year). Second, Indonesian banks found it cheaper to borrow more from overseas because the large differentials between local and international interest rates. Third, the rupiah proved to be stable with a nominal depreciation of about 3-5 percent before the July 1997 crisis. Thus, the foreign currency liabilities of commercial banks rose by 160 percent in 1993, and amounted to about 30 percent of their total liabilities by June 1997.

The 1997/98 crisis severely weakened the Indonesian banking system. For example, the number of banks (state and private) was drastically cut. As at mid-1998, 23 commercial banks were closed, 7 were nationalized, and 40 more were closely supervised by the Indonesian Bank Restructuring Agency. IBRA was created to help the banking sector recover and to work towards making Indonesian banks comparable to internationally accepted standard.

Malaysia

The number of domestic banks fell from 23 in 1994 to 20 in 1999 as shown in Table 5.12. However, the number of branches increased from 1139 in 1994 to 1623 in 1999. On the other hand, the number of foreign banks decreased from 14 to 13 while the number of branches remained unchanged during the same period and hence indicates Malaysia's policy of keeping its borders relatively closed to foreign banks unlike Singapore and the Philippines where the number of foreign banks increased as part of the financial liberalization measures.

In Malaysia, there is a clear separation of functions for the different financial institutions.[15] Only commercial banks are allowed to accept deposits from the public and undertake foreign exchange transactions. Merchant banks concentrate on investment banking business. Finance companies deal with hire-purchase lending. Several banks are subsidiaries of large corporate groups, while many finance companies and merchant banks are subsidiaries

[15] For a more complete discussion of the banking sector in Malaysia, see Soo-Nam Oh, "Towards a Sustainable Banking Sector in Malaysia," in *Rising to the Challenge in Asia: A Study of Financial* Markets (Volume 8 – Malaysia), Manila: Asian Development Bank, 1999, pp.34-78.

of commercial banks. The two largest commercial banks in Malaysia are Maybank and Bank Bumiputra, with the latter being owned by the government.

In 1994, Bank Negara Malaysia introduced a two-tier structure for commercial banks in order to consolidate the banking sector and make them internationally competitive. By imposing higher capital requirements, banks in tier 1 would be stronger and more efficient than those in tier 2. At end-1997, 10 commercial banks were accorded tier-1 status and were allowed to undertake other activities subject to prudential limits and conditions set by the BNM.[16] These banks have been allowed to issue negotiable certificates of deposits up to five times their capital funds, participate in equity derivatives, undertake securities borrowing and lending, and set up additional branches and offices.

In terms of their resources, total assets of Malaysian banks expanded about four times on average during the 1990-97 period. Total lending by commercial banks expanded by 25 percent per annum during the 1993-97 period because of a lax monetary policy regime in the 1990s and the two-tier classification of banks. However, bulk of the loans was given to the property and manufacturing sectors – an indication of overexposure by commercial banks on these sectors. Thus, following the 1997 financial crisis, the non-performing loans (NPLs) of Malaysian banks surged from 5.7 at end-1997 to 8.5 percent of total loans at end-May 1998 as the Malaysian economy went through recession and as the property and stock markets collapsed. The more fundamental reasons for the large NPLs were state-directed loan policies, lack of competition, and lack of prudential regulations.[17] Consequently, BNM implemented a number of measures a number to help strengthen prudential regulations and transparency. These include, among others, those measures concerning NPL classification and provisioning standards, capital adequacy ratios, lending to the property sector and for the purchase of stocks and shares, and disclosure and monitoring.

Moreover, on July 16, 1998, the government set up a national asset management company called Danaharta, with a paid capital of RM250 million. It was expected to raise about RM25 billion through government bond flotations in order to acquire the assets behind almost all NPLs in the system (about RM42 billion). To complement Danaharta, a special purpose vehicle to recapitalize and consolidate the banking sector was created called Danamodal. With a proposed investment budget of RM16 billion, Danamodal will serve as an interim funding vehicle for the infusion of funds into financially-distressed banking institutions

Philippines

Table 5.12 shows that the number of commercial banks in the Philippines rose from 34 in 1994 to 52 in 1999. Eleven new local banks and 7 new foreign banks entered the Philippine banking system. The number of branches of local banks almost doubled from 2885 to 4263 during the 1994-1999 period. The number of branches of foreign banks also increased from 5 to 11 during the same period. In 1999, the central bank endorsed reforms that would allow up to 100 percent foreign ownership of banks. The large number of banks and the large number of branches resulted from the fact that interest rates are being administered and cartelized and hence generate cheaper sources of finance. Lending rates are set by the banks in a cartel-like fashion while savings deposits pay very low rates (even negative real rates) as there are no

16 Soo-Nam Oh, "Towards a Sustainable Banking Sector in Malaysia…," 1999, p.36.

17 Soo-Nam Oh, "Towards a Sustainable Banking Sector in Malaysia…," 1999, p.36.

other institutions which could compete for small retail deposits. Thus, banks dominate the retail savings market in the Philippines. As they are usually part of large conglomerates, banks raise finance for these groups. Having been captives of these groups, banks' lending is generally concentrated and therefore risky.

The Philippine banking system has been hit by several crises.[18] First, in 1981, a Filipino Chinese named Dewey Dee absconded with a large amount of money borrowed from various investment houses and finance companies. This led to a financial crisis as investors moved out their funds from these institutions into large commercial banks. This scandal further resulted in the insolvencies of several investment houses and finance companies. Second, in 1983, former Senator Benigno Aquino was assassinated upon his return to the Philippines from exile in the United States. This led to a much bigger crisis than that of 1981 because of the significant erosion of domestic and international confidence on the whole financial system in the Philippines. There was massive capital flight combined with severe current account deficits thereby prompting the central bank to devalue the peso, declare a moratorium on the payments of foreign borrowings, ration foreign exchange, and increase interest rates. Third, the July 1997 crisis adversely impacted the banking sector as evidenced by the dramatic declines in their profitability, with their returns on equity falling from 12.4 percent in 1997 to about 7 percent at end-1998, and to about 2 percent in March 1999. The crisis also led to bank closures from 14 in 1997 to 22 in 1998. Nevertheless, it was commonly perceived that the Philippine banking system was relatively unscathed by the crisis because of several factors including the financial reforms reforms that were implemented since the 1980s, the lower growth rates of the Philippine economy as compared to other Southeast Asian economies, the higher level of exports and private consumption that helped offset the fall in private investment, and the improvement in the foreign debt exposure of the Philippines.

Singapore

In 1992, all locally incorporated commercial banks in Singapore were required to maintain a capital adequacy ratio (CAR) of 12 percent Tier 1 capital. In fact, all locally incorporated banks have complied with the minimum CAR of 8 percent set by the Bank for International Settlements in 1992.[19] Three local banks, namely, OCBC, DBS and UOB, were ranked among the world's strongest banks with an estimated CAR of 17 percent, 16.2 percent, and 15.5 percent, respectively. The number of local commercial banks dropped from 12 in 1994 to 8 in 1999 because of merger and acquisition activities. In 1998, the DBS Bank acquired POSB Bank while Keppel and Tat Lee merged to form Keppel TatLee Bank. In 2002, the United Overseas Bank merged with the Overseas Union Bank.

The MAS has given license to foreign commercial banks to operate in Singapore. On May 17, 1999, the MAS made several policy announcements including liberalization of the banking sector due to the rapid development in the global electronic banking and the internet in which foreign banks have a competitive advantage and because of the need to encourage local banks to strengthen their management and improve corporate governance.

---

18 For a complete discussion of the banking sector in the Philippines, see Maria Socorro Gochoco-Bautista, "The Past Performance of the Philippine Banking Sector and Challenges in the Post-crisis Period," in *Rising to the Challenge in Asia: A Study of Financial* Markets (Volume 10 – Philippines), Manila: Asian Development Bank, 1999, pp.30-78.

19 For detailed discussion of commercial banks in Singapore, see Chwee-Huat Tan, *Financial Markets and Institutions in Singapore...,* 1999, pp.61-100.

Within a five-year plan (1999-2004), the MAS will allow the entry of more foreign banks including a new category called Qualifying Full Bank (QFB), increasing the number of restricted banks, and give offshore banks greater flexibility in S$ wholesale business. As at end-1999, the number of foreign banks rose from 127 in 1994 to 131 in 1999 which indicates Singapore's continuing implementation of liberalization policy. The MAS increased the number of foreign banks in all categories in 1999: (23 full, 16 restricted, and 92 offshore) as compared to those in 1994 (22 full, 14 restricted, and 91 offshore). The full license banks deal with the whole range of banking activities for both personal and corporate customers. The restricted license banks operate mainly in wholesale corporate, not personal, banking. As such, they source their funds from the interbank market. Offshore license banks transact business with banks and approved financial institutions. They were authorized to deal in foreign exchange and to operate Asian Currency Units, but not offer current, savings or time deposits.

Thailand

Commercial banks in Thailand dominated the financial sector, accounting for 64 percent of total financial assets, 69 percent of total deposits, and 67 percent of total credits extended at end-1996.[20] The number of banks increased from 29 in 1994 to 34 in 1999. In 2000, the number of banks remained at 34 consisting of 13 locally incorporated and 21 are branches of foreign banks. Because of the July 1997 crisis, foreign ownership in locally-incorporated banks rose significantly. To be able to attract new capital for troubled banks, the government issued an emergency decree on June 27, 1997 which relaxed the foreign ownership of commercial banks by allowing 100 percent shareholding for foreign investors. At end-2000, there were two banks which are majority owned by foreigners: the Bank of Asia was 75 percent acquired by ABN-Amro in September 1998, and the DBS Thai Danu Bank, 48.73 percent acquired by the DBS Bank of Singapore in March 1998.

The number of commercial banks' branches/offices increased from 2,857 to 3,290 during the 1994-99 period as shown in Table 5.12. As at end-2000, the total number of branches/offices even rose further to 3,807.[21] The commercial banks are allowed to deal in normal banking activities but they are not allowed to engage in securities or trust services.

As a proportion of GDP, the volume of credit extended by the financial sector expanded significantly from 83 percent in 1990 to 147 percent in 1996. As at end-1996, commercial bank loans went to manufacturing (27 percent) and trade (25 percent), construction and real estate (14 percent), and personal consumption (13 percent). The problem arose when the financial institutions increasingly depended on borrowings to supplement the insufficient deposits in order to extend loans to the private sector. This led rising loan to deposit ratios from around 100 in 1991 to about 140 in 1997. Thus, the financial sector became very vulnerable to flight of deposits, decrease in non-deposit borrowing, and poor quality of loans which led to rising NPLs.

---

[20] A thorough analysis of the banking sector in Thailand is found in Masahiro Kawai and Ken-ichi Takayasu, "The Economic Crisis and Banking Sector Restructuring in Thailand," in *Rising to the Challenge in Asia: A Study of Financial* Markets (Volume 11- Thailand), Manila: Asian Development Bank, 1999, pp.38-103.

[21] Bank of Thailand, *Supervision Report*, Thailand: BOT, 2000.

The Thai banking sector had two weaknesses which led to the July 1997 crisis. First, there was excessive lending without prudent management of assets and liabilities. On the asset side, a large proportion of loans were directed to non-productive and speculative investments such as real estate, construction, and consumer loans for automobiles, stock purchases, and hire purchases. Moreover, loans were also directed to companies with problems of rising debt-equity ratios since lending was given based on collateral submitted by these companies rather than on their projected profitability. On the liability side, commercial banks depended heavily on domestic and foreign borrowings in which the latter accounted for a larger share. Second, there were inadequate regulatory and supervisory frameworks. By end-1996, non-performing loans (NPLs) of all commercial banks were estimated to reach Bt 487 billion.

Other Deposit-Type Institutions

These include savings banks, finance companies, credit unions and cooperatives, and rural banks. Table 5.14 shows some information on their assets, liabilities, number of institutions, and number of branches. They have the following features. First, they accept savings deposits, time deposits, and negotiable certificates of deposits (NCDs). Second, their clientele includes households, non-corporate and non-financial entities. Third, the deposits that they generated have contributed to a significant expansion of broad money (M2), where M2 is the sum of M1 and quasi-money, which in turn is the sum of savings deposits and fixed deposits.

Table 5.15 shows the evolution of M2 and its components. For all countries, the proportion of M1 to M2 has fallen markedly over the years. On the other hand, the proportion of quasi-money to M2 has significantly increased indicating their clientele's preference for interest-bearing instruments.

Indonesia

Prior to October 1995, finance companies were allowed to conduct various types of businesses like leasing, factoring, consumer finance, credit card finance, and venture capital activities. In October 1995, venture capital was categorized separately because of the higher risks associated with their activities. Among its various activities, factoring experienced the sharpest growth during the 1992-95 period. Subsequently, leasing took the lead with a share of 46 percent of total business in 1996. Consumer finance grew by 43 percent per annum during the 1992-96 period. Credit card finance was almost wiped out by the stiff competition from the commercial banks.

Finance companies are required to have a minimum paid-in capital of Rp10 billion (US$4 million) by October 1998. Finance companies are not allowed to accept deposits from the public, issue promissory notes or engage in security business. Because of these restrictions on fund sourcing, finance companies in Indonesia have relied heavily on domestic and offshore borrowings. In 1996, their total funds reached Rp36 trillion of which 35 percent came from bank loans and 32 percent came from offshore borrowings.

Table 5.14. Other Deposit-type Institutions in Southeast Asia, 1994 and 1999

	Assets	Deposit Liabilities	Number of Institutions	Number of Branches
	1994 /1999	1994 /1999	1994 /1999	1994 /1999
Indonesia				
Finance companies	19.1 n.a.	12.6 n.a.	206 n.a.	n.a. n.a.
Malaysia				
Finance companies	73.5 (116)	57.3 (90.2)	40 (23)	860 (944)
National Savings Bank	5.4 (8.8)	4.3 (8.0)	1 (1)	478 (439)
Urban Credit Coop.	6.2 (3.7)	1.3 -	- (503)	
Rural Credit Coop.	4.0 (8.4)	2.9 -		
Philippines				
Finance Companies	26.5 (27.4)	- -	128 (147)	72 (55)
Savings Banks	69.3 (136.2)	42.2 (87.2)	12 (35)	335 (718)
Stock S&L Associations	8.9 (18.5)	6.1 (11.4)	51 (42)	158 (249)
Rural Banks	28.2 (63.1)	17.5 (36.2)	784 (806)	490 (1079)
Singapore				
Finance Companies	19 (20)	14 (14)	23 (14)	
Post Office SavingsBank	n.a.	n.a.	144 -	
Thailand				
Finance Companies	1201 (734)	747 (360)	91 (22)	59 n.a.
Gov't Savings Bank	184 (425)	158 (378)	1 (1)	538 (578)
Agri'l Cooperatives	27 n.a.	4.4 n.a.	2474 n.a.	- -
Savings Cooperatives	127 n.a.	27 n.a.	1045 n.a.	- -
Bank Agri & Agri Coop.	123 (279)	61 (158).	1 (1)	362 (659)

Note: Assets and liabilities are expressed in national currencies: billion Indonesian rupiah, million Malaysian ringgit, million Philippine pesos, billion Singapore dollars, and million Thai baht.

Source: These information were obtained from the individual country reports found in the Financial Statistics Yearbook published by the Southeast Asian Central Banks for Training and Research (SEACEN) based in Kuala Lumpur (July 1995 and July 2000 issues).

Malaysia

Bank Negara Malaysia extended in 1996 the two-tier structure to finance companies and merchant banks. (This structure was initially introduced in December 1994 to commercial banks). The introduction of the two-tier system led to the rapid growth in loans and advances. Lending by finance companies had expanded by 24 percent per annum during the 1993-97 period. Consumption credit (primary lending to finance hire-purchase activities of consumers) accounted for about 35 percent of the loans granted by finance companies in Malaysia. Property loans also got a significant share of about 30 percent. Thus, finance companies were overexposed to consumer financing and property sector which had contributed to the weakening of the financial sector in Malaysia.

Following the severity of the July 1997 crisis, the Malaysian government announced in Jan 1998 a merger plan for finance companies instead of closing them down like in Korea and Thailand. The government intended to merge 38 finance companies into eight – a plan which was perceived by the market to be less successful since stronger finance companies will lose out if they merge with weaker ones.

Table 5.15. Broader Money (M2) in Southeast Asia

Year	1970	1980	1990	1995	1999
Indonesia					
M2	321	7691	84630	222638	646205
M1	75	65	28	24	19
Quasi-Money	25	35	72	76	81
Malaysia					
M2	4130	27652	83903	198873	330908
M1	49	35	29	26	22
Quasi-Money	51	65	71	74	78
Philippines					
M2	9388	55431	297307	755191	1357907
M1	50	41	30	24	29
Quasi-Money	50	59	70	76	71
Singapore					
M2	3783	16065	61845	101967	174474
M1	42	38	25	25	18
Quasi-Money	58	62	75	75	82
Thailand					
M2	46170	251801	1529115	3310558	4854700
M1	42	28	13	11	12
Quasi-Money	58	72	87	89	88

Note: The values of M2 are expressed in national currencies: billion Indonesian rupiah, million Malaysian ringgit, million Philippine pesos, million Singapore dollars, and million Thai baht. M1 and quasi-money are expressed as shares of total money, M2, for each country. Source: These information were obtained from the individual country reports found in the ADB, *Key Indicators of Developing Asian and Pacific Countries*, Manila: Asian Development Bank, Various Issues.

Singapore

Finance companies mushroomed during the 1960s due to an increased demand for consumer credit to finance their purchases of consumer durables on buy-now-pay-later schemes. The increase in demand was due to the growing affluence of the Singaporeans and the rising standards of living, and the cartelization of bank interest rates. Because of the growing business of the finance companies, commercial banks formed own subsidiary finance companies in order to compete for deposits. In 1967, the Finance Companies Act was passed to regulate them because of the alarm generated by the depositors on the risky investment activities of the finance companies like dealing in real estate and speculating in the stock exchange. The number of finance companies dropped from 34 in 1976 to 23 in 1994 and to 14 in 1999 due to mergers and acquisition activities. Most of them are affiliated to the six major finance groups such as DBS, OCBC, UOB, OUB, Hong Leong and Keppel. The total assets of the finance companies rose slightly from S$19 billion in 1994 to S$20 billion in 1999 while their deposit liabilities remained relatively constant during the same period. The Finance Companies Act was amended twice: in 1984 in which the changes restricted their lending activities, and in 1994 in which the changes were related to the management of capital fund and investment.

Thailand

Finance companies were the next largest group of financial institutions as at end-1996, with a share of 21 percent of total assets, 19 percent of total deposits and 21 percent of total credits. While some finance companies were independent, others were affiliates of commercial banks to provide specialized services that banks were not allowed to engage in like issuing large denomination promissory notes, NCDs, and bills of exchange. As at end-1996, the assets of finance companies were dominated by loans (77 percent of all assets) and securities investment and receivables (18 percent). As they could not compete for the mainstream businesses of the commercial banks, the finance companies had allocated a larger share of their asset portfolio to high risk areas like construction and real estate (28 percent) and personal consumption loans (26 percent). As in the case of commercial banks in Thailand, the NPLs of finance companies reached an enormous amount of Bt 225 billion at end-1996, which was equivalent to 15 percent of gross loans.

The financial crisis started as early as March 1997 when the Thai Danu Bank (TDB) announced its planned takeover of the largest finance company called Finance One which experienced management difficulties. However, the takeover did not push through because of the bad financial record of Finance One. Consequently, the Bank of Thailand publicized the names of ten distressed finance companies sending the financial markets in disarray as funds began to leave the institutions which were considered as weak. Thus, the BOT began to inject liquidity support to the affected finance companies.

As the Thai financial markets experienced a sharp decline in confidence, the BOT suspended the operations of insolvent and liquidity-strapped finance companies - 16 on June 27, 1997 and 42 on 4 August 4, 1997 - a total of 58 out of 91 companies. As part of the IMF rescue package, these companies were required to submit their rehabilitation plans. Based on the recommendations of the Financial Sector Restructuring Authority (FRA), 56 out of 58 finance companies were permanently closed and liquidated under the supervision of the FRA through auctions. The Asset Management Corporation (AMC) was created by the Thai government in November 1997 to act as a bidder of last resort for the impaired assets of the 56 finance companies which were auctioned by the FRA. As at end-2000, the AMC held total assets of Bt 25.8 billion. At end-1999, there were 22 finance companies in Thailand. This is shown in Table 5.14. Their assets fell significantly from Bt 1,201 billion in 1994 to Bt 734 billion in 1999. The deposit liabilities likewise decreased markedly from Bt 747 billion to Bt 360 billion during the same period.

Contractual Savings Institutions

These include provident and pension funds, and insurance companies. Table 5.16 shows some information on their assets, deposit liabilities, and the number of institutions and branches. The inflows and outflows of their funds are predictable since these are based on their members' contributions and payment claims. The contributions and insurance premiums are compulsory. These institutions invest their funds on equities, bonds, bank deposits, and central bank securities.

Indonesia

The Pension Funds Act of 1992 led to the establishment of pension fund schemes including government schemes for its employees like PT Taspen for civil service employees and Asabri for members of the Armed Forces, a general State social security scheme known as Jamsostek which is required for all employees, private company schemes, and schemes operated by financial institutions like banks and insurance companies. In December 1996, there were 261 pension funds, in which 239 were employer managed and 22 were operated by financial institutions. As at end-1996, about 16 million workers were covered by these schemes out of a total labor force of 80 million indicating a low penetration rate of 20 percent. Indonesia has some 90 life insurance companies which is expected to increase further. As at end-1996, Indonesia's pension funds and insurance companies invested their funds in equities and bonds for a combined share of about 14 percent of their total assets valued at Rp32.2 trillion. The bulk (about 97 percent in 1996) was invested in short-term assets like bank deposits, negotiable certificates of deposits, and Bank of Indonesia Certificates of Indebtedness (SBIs) because of their high yield and a lack of suitable long-term assets.

Table 5.16. Contractual Savings Institutions in Southeast Asia, 1994 and 1999

	Assets	Deposit Liabilities	Number of Institutions	Number of Branches
Indonesia	1994 /1999	1994 /1999	1994 /1999	1994 /1999
Pension Funds (Rp trillion)	8.9 n.a.	n.a. n.a.	n.a. n.a.	n.a. n.a.
Insurance Cos. (Rp trillion)	14.4 n.a.	n.a. n.a	150 n.a.	n.a. n.a.
Malaysia				
. Provident & Pension Funds				
-Employees Provident Fund	84.5 (169)		1 (1)	n.a (35)
-Social Security Org.	3.8 (7.9)		1 n.a.	
-Armed Forces Fund	3.0 (5.0)		1 n.a.	
-Other Funds	5.0 (15.6)			
. Insurance Companies	21.0 (46.5)		63 n.a.	536 n.a.
-Domestic Companies	11.2 n.a.		52 n.a.	443 n.a.
-Foreign Companies	9.7 n.a.		9 n.a.	85 n.a.
-Islamic Insurance Co.	0.1 n.a.		2 n.a.	8 n.a.
Philippines				
.Pension Funds	n.a. n.a.	n.a. n.a.	n.a. n.a.	n.a. n.a.
.Insurance Companies	n.a. n.a.	n.a. n.a.	n.a. n.a.	n.a. n.a
Singapore				
.Insurance Companies	n.a. n.a.	n.a. n.a.	141 n.a.	n.a. n.a.
.Pension Funds	n.a. n.a.	n.a. n.a.	n.a. n.a.	n.a. n.a.
Thailand				
.Life Insurance Companies	104.5 (215.3)	77.1 (170.2)	12 (25)	1166 (1151)

Note: Assets and deposit liabilities are measured in national currencies: trillion rupiah for Indonesia, billion ringgit for Malaysia, and billion baht for Thailand. Source: These information were obtained from the individual country reports found in the Financial Statistics Yearbook published by the Southeast Asian Central Banks for Training and Research (SEACEN) based in Kuala Lumpur (July 1995 and July 2000 issues).

From 1992, when the Insurance Law was promulgated, the number of insurance companies in Indonesia rose from 145 to 171 in 1997, with assets expanding by 25 percent per annum. The expansion was attributed to the increase in the number of joint venture companies from 19 to 40 during the same period. The minimum paid-in capital requirement for insurance companies by 1998 was Rp2 billion for life insurance, Rp3 billion for non-life insurance, and Rp10 billion for reinsurance. Life and non-life insurance accounted for bulk of the insurance business. At end-1996, total assets of the insurance companies reached Rp22 trillion. Bulk (55 percent) of their investible funds went into time deposits and 15 percent into SBIs.

Malaysia

The government established a compulsory saving scheme known as the Employees Provident Fund (EPF) which has been investing aggressively in equities. With the passage of EPF Act in June 1991, the investment portfolio of EPF has been diversified including eligible securities like fully-guaranteed government loans, short-term Bank Negara Bills (BNBs), and other short-term investments issued by state government or local authorities. The EPF has been the biggest investor in government bonds. For example, as at end-1997, EPF's holding of government bonds reached RM38.1 billion, or 29.4 percent of the total funds managed by the EPF. However, due to fiscal surpluses, the issuance of government bonds has declined which led to a shortage of eligible securities managed by the EPF.

Philippines

The government set up a national pension scheme for all public sector employees through the Government Service Insurance Scheme and for private sector employees through the Social Security System. With contributions from both employers and employees, these schemes are currently in surplus. The pension funds have been invested almost entirely in bank deposits, housing loans, and government bonds. In 1997, a Social Security Act was passed which limits the portfolio allocation of these pension funds to, among others, 30 percent for government bonds to fund infrastructure, 30 percent for bonds issued by government financial institutions or corporations, 40 percent for bonds or deposits of good quality banks, 35 percent for bonds issued by housing corporations, and other limits for different types of bonds. However, no limit was set for bonds issued by the Philippine government. In the Philippines, there is no framework for private pension schemes unlike in Indonesia and Thailand.

Singapore

The Central Provident Fund (CPF) has been established as a national funded scheme since 1955. It has kept its main role as a pension fund for retirement of both government and private sector employees. However, its functions have expanded considerably to include medical expenses, property and financial investments. From a combined 10 percent contribution rate by employers and employees, the CPF combined rate rose to 13 percent of the employee's salary in 1968. It increased gradually over the years to reach 30 percent in 1974 and to 50 percent in 1984. From 1991-99, the combined contribution rate was 40 percent. The CPF pension fund has generated enormous funds which have been invested in various financial instruments the bulk of which (about 70 percent) has been in government securities. Since 1981, the CPF Board has invested in other forms of securities like floating-rate notes, negotiable certificates of deposits, fixed deposits, and even equities. Other types of investment activities were undertaken like trading in Singapore government-registered stocks in the secondary market, and investing in Singapore government stocks and placing funds as advanced deposits with the Monetary Authority of Singapore pending the issue of such stocks.

Thailand

The provident fund industry began in 1983. In 1987, the Provident Fund Act was passed which established the legal framework for its expansion. Private pension funds have been established on a voluntary basis by companies for the social security and pension benefits of their employees. The number of provident fund schemes rose markedly from 159 in 1984 to 950 in 1997. As at end-1997, some one million workers from the public and private sectors have joined the pension funds, which accounted for about 13 percent of Thai's labor force, which is even lower than the 20 percent penetration rate found in Indonesia. This implies that more than 85 percent of Thai's employees (and 80 percent of Indonesia's employees) are not covered by any pension fund scheme. By August 1997, provident funds had accumulated 123 billion baht (or about 2 percent of GDP). These funds were invested in cash or bank deposits (32 percent), debt instruments (61 percent), equities (5 percent), and other assets (2 percent). About 80 percent of these funds were invested in short-term instruments.

Development-Type Institutions

Development banks have been established due to lack of medium- and long-term funds to finance industrial development. Thus, their assets consist mainly of medium- and long-term loans, and investments in agricultural and industrial sectors. Table 5.17 shows some information on their assets, deposit liabilities, and on the number of institutions and branches.

Investment-Type Institutions

These include investment companies, merchant banks, mutual funds and unit trusts, which source funds from savings of a large number of people. Table 5.18 shows some information on their assets and liabilities, and on the number of institutions and branches.

Indonesia

The mutual funds were allowed in 1988. However, they took off slowly until the Capital Markets Law was passed in 1995. From 7 funds in mid-1996, the number rose to 77 by end-1997. Their clientele include high-net-worth individual investors and institutional investors. By-end 1997, there were 200,000 individual investors each investing an average of Rp8 million (or total assets of Rp1.6 trillion). By mid-1997, 60 funds had an estimated total capitalization of Rp5 trillion in which about 60 percent came from banks (the major investor) given that these funds are tax-exempt on income and capital gains. The mutual funds companies invest their funds mainly in high-yielding bank deposit instruments (60 percent), equities (15 percent), and money market instruments (25 percent). As banks have been the major investors in tax-free mutual funds, it is tantamount to saying that the banks were buying their own deposits through mutual funds for tax avoidance. Pension funds and insurance companies also invest in mutual funds.

Malaysia

Because of Moslem teachings which do not allow payment of interest (the *riba* issue), many Moslems are reluctant to invest in interest-yielding instruments. Thus, the government established the Permodaran Nasional Berhad (PNB) to increase bumiputras' shareholdings up to 30 percent by 1990. As the biggest unit trust company, it aims to encourage the bumiputras, who are mostly Moslems, to mobilize their financial savings through unit trusts which invest mostly in equities. The PNB owns sizable investments in listed companies in different sectors including manufacturing, banking, transport, services, mining, construction, plantation and conglomerates.

Table 5.17. Development-Type Institutions in Southeast Asia, 1994 and 1999

	Assets	Deposit Liabilities	Number of Institutions	Number of Branches
	1994 /1999	1994 /1999	1994 /1999	1994 /1999
Indonesia	n.a. n.a.	n.a. n.a.	n.a. n.a.	n.a. n.a.
Malaysia				
Dept Finance Instns.	9.7 (22.4)	3.09 -	1 (8)	n.a. (179)
Housing Credit Instns.	26.0 (26.9)	0.9 -	4 (3)	n.a. (25)
Philippines				
Devpt Bank of Phils.	59.9 n.a.	10.0 n.a.	1 1	67 n.a.
Private Devpt Banks	28.5 69.0	16.9 33.8	37 41	228 393
Govt Non-banks	50.4 385.3	- -	5 7	- -
Nat'l Home Mortgage	35.2 n.a.	- -	1 1	- -
National Devpt Co's.	10.8 n.a.	- -	1 1	- -
Singapore	n.a. n.a.	n.a. n.a.	n.a. n.a.	n.a. n.a.
Thailand				
Gov't Housing Bank	111.8 338.3	60.5 186.9	1 1	32 112
Industrial Finance Co.	90.2 187.2	- -	1 1	9 27
Small Indust'l Finance	0.7 4.0	- -	1 1	1 1

Note: Assets and deposit liabilities are measured in national currencies: billion ringgit for Malaysia, billion pesos for the Philippines, and billion baht for Thailand. Source: These information were obtained from the individual country reports found in the Financial Statistics Yearbook published by the Southeast Asian Central Banks for Training and Research (SEACEN) based in Kuala Lumpur (July 1995 and July 2000 issues).

Philippines

The mutual fund companies find it difficult to compete with banks for deposits from high net-worth individual investors. These better-off investors tend to favor deposit investments like common trust funds (CTFs) run by the banks. Consequently, the mutual funds target the less well-off, less sophisticated and less return-conscious individual investors. For example, one group known as Kabuhayan intends to collect 200 pesos per month from each investor to be kept in interest-yielding account until a minimum holding of 5,000 pesos is reached. This amount can then be withdrawn for emergency or schooling needs, or be kept with the funds.

Table 5.18. Investment-type Institutions in Southeast Asia, 1994 and 1999

	Assets	Deposit Liabilities	Number of Institutions	Number of Branches
Indonesia	1994 /1999	1994 /1999	1994 /1999	1994 /1999
Merchant Banks	n.a. n.a.	n.a. n.a.	n.a. n.a.	n.a. n.a
Malaysia				
Merchant Banks	23.6 39.2	14.6 25.9	12 12	17 22
Unit Trusts	49.2 33.3	- -	74 n.a.	- -
Philippines				
Investment Houses	15.3 83.9	- -	26 52	11 26
Investment Companies	16.8 13.9	- -	65 64	- -
Securities Dealers	8.8 11.2	- -	129 130	- -
Singapore				
Asian Currency Units*	416345 480399	65788 121319	207 194	
Merchant Banks	7000 7900	n.a. n.a.	77 64	
Thailand				
Merchant Banks	n.a. n.a.	n.a. n.a.	n.a. n.a.	n.a. n.a.

Note: Assets and deposit liabilities are measured in national currencies: trillion rupiah for Indonesia, billion ringgit for Malaysia, and million S$ for Singapore merchant banks. *Assets and liabilities of ACUs are expressed in US$ million. Source: These information were obtained from the individual country reports found in the Financial Statistics Yearbook published by the Southeast Asian Central Banks for Training and Research (SEACEN) based in Kuala Lumpur (July 1995 and July 2000 issues).

Singapore

There were some 160 institutions in 1997 which conducted fund management activities mainly unit trusts in which the financial resources of small investors are being pooled and invested in securities by professional fund managers. For some small investors, unit trusts investment can start from S$500 which is much lower than the S$1000 minimum requirement for investing in ordinary shares. The price of the units changes depending on the appreciation or depreciation of the securities. In 1997, the total amount of funds managed was S$124 billion most of which were invested in equities (S$69 billion) and the rest (S$55 billion) were invested in bonds, deposits, and other instruments.

Thailand

The first mutual fund was introduced in 1977. Since then until 1992, the mutual fund industry was controlled by a single company called the Mutual Fund Company. Subsequently, following the liberalization of this industry, the number of mutual funds has expanded from 37 to over 200 by 1998. The total assets managed by the mutual funds increased significantly from 58 billion baht to the June 1997 level of 167 billion baht. However, because of the July 1997 crisis, the total assets managed fell to B107 billion by December 1997. About 65 percent of the mutual fund investors are private individuals and about 35 percent are institutional investors. It was estimated that about 800,000 individuals (or about 1.5 percent of the Thai population) had invested in mutual funds. These companies have invested their funds in equity markets and more recently in fixed-income markets. As at end-1997, about half (47 percent) of the mutual funds was invested in fixed-income assets while 43 percent was allocated exclusively on equities.

CONCLUSION

The financial sector in Southeast Asia has grown and developed over the years as evidenced by a higher degree of monetization, the rise of financial institutions and financial markets, and the availability of more financial instruments to suit the requirements of both savers/investors and borrowers. It has contributed significantly to the economic development of the Southeast Asian economies because the deepening process results in more loanable funds circulating in the real economy through the financial sector to finance agriculture, industry, trade and investment activities.

However, one common feature among Southeast Asian financial markets is the relatively undeveloped bond markets relative to equity markets. This is due to the institutional setting found in Southeast Asia where there exists interlocking relationships between the financial institutions, the business conglomerates, and the government.

Despite undertaking financial reforms in the past, the Southeast Asian financial markets have become vulnerable to several crises, the most recent of which was the July 1997 crisis which hit Thailand initially, but immediately spread to other economies in the region. These economies suffered severely, particularly impacting their financial markets (stock and foreign exchange markets) and their financial institutions mainly banks and finance companies as these institutions have large exposure to non-performing loans. Several measures have been implemented in response to the crisis in order to strengthen the financial system including, among others, closures and mergers, recapitalization, and tighter regulations and supervision of financial institutions.

QUESTIONS FOR DISCUSSION

1. How significant is the financial sector in the economic development of Southeast Asia? Discuss.
2. Discuss why there has been uneven development of financial markets in Southeast Asia, in particular, the capital markets.
3. Identify the various financial intermediaries in Southeast Asia. Compare and contrast them in terms of their functions, sources and uses of funds.

SUGGESTED MATERIALS FOR CASE STUDIES

Asia

Fase, M.M.G. and R.C.N. Abma, 2003, "Financial Environment and Economic Growth in Selected Asian Countries," *Journal of Asian Economics,* Vol.14, No.1, pp.11-21.

Stiglitz, Joseph, 2000, "Capital Market Liberalization, Economic Growth, and Instability," *World Development,* Vol.28, No.6, pp.1075-1086.

Philippines

Agabin, Meliza, 1993, "The Informal Credit Markets in the Philippines," *Asian Economic Journal,* Vol.7, No.2, pp.209-247.

Indonesia

Patten, Richard, Jay Rosengard and Don Johnston, Jr., 2001, "Microfinance Success amidst Macroeconomic Failure: The Experience of Bank Rakyat Indonesia during the East Asian Crisis," Vol.29, No.6, pp.1057-1069.

References for Chapter 5

Agabin, Meliza, 1993, "The Informal Credit Markets in the Philippines," *Asian Economic Journal,* Vol.7, No.2, 1993, pp.209-247.

ADB, Various Issues, *Key Indicators of Developing Asian and Pacific Countries*, Manila: Asian Development Bank.

BOT, 2000, *Supervision Report*, Thailand: Bank of Thailand.

Chowdry, Anis and Iyanatul Islam, 1993, "Financial Development and Economic Performance," in Anis Chowdry and Iyanatul Islam, *The Newly Industrializing Economies of East Asia*, London: Routledge.

Chou, Catherine, 1999, "Indonesian Banks: Survival of the Fittest," in *Rising to the Challenge in Asia: A Study of Financial Markets,* (Volume 6 – Indonesia), Manila: Asian Development Bank, pp.36-72.

Fase, M.M.G. and R.C.N. Abma, 2003, "Financial Environment and Economic Growth in Selected Asian Countries," *Journal of Asian Economics,* Vol.14, pp.11-21.

Fry, Maxwell, 1995, "Financial Development in Asia: Some Analytical Issues," *Asian-Pacific Economic Literature*, Vol.9, No.1, pp.40-57.

Gochoco-Bautista, Maria Socorro, 1999, "The Past Performance of the Philippine Banking Sector and Challenges in the Post-crisis Period," in *Rising to the Challenge in Asia: A Study of Financial Markets,* (Volume 10 – Philippines), Manila: Asian Development Bank, pp.30-78.

Kawai, Masahiro and Ken-ichi Takayasu, 1999, "The Economic Crisis and Banking Sector Restructuring in Thailand," in *Rising to the Challenge in Asia: A Study of Financial* Markets (Volume 11- Thailand), Manila: Asian Development Bank, pp.38-103.

Lian, Daniel and Tsao Yuan Lee, "Financial Development in ASEAN," in Joseph Tan and Zhaohong Luo (eds.), *ASEAN-China Economic Relations*, Institute of World Economics and Politics, and Singapore: Institute of Southeast Asian Studies.

Ng, Edward, 1999, "Central Provident Fund in Singapore: A Capital Market Boost or Drag?" in *Rising to the Challenge in Asia: A Study of Financial Markets,* (Volume – Singapore), Manila: Asian Development Bank, 1999, pp.56-80.

Oh, Soo-Nam, 1999, "Towards a Sustainable Banking Sector in Malaysia," in *Rising to the Challenge in Asia: A Study of Financial Markets* (Volume 8 – Malaysia), Manila: Asian Development Bank, pp.34-78.

Patten, Richard, Jay Rosengard and Don Johnston, Jr., 2001, "*Microfinance Success amidst Macroeconomic Failure: The Experience of Bank Rakyat Indonesia during the East Asian Crisis*," Vol.29, No.6, pp.1057-1069.

SEACEN, 1995 and 2000 issues, *Financial Statistics Yearbook*, Kuala Lumpur, Malaysia: The Southeast Asian Central Banks for Training and Research (SEACEN).

Sharma, Krishnan, 2002, *The Underlying Constraints on Corporate Bond Market Development in Southeast Asia*, United Nations: Development Policy and Analysis Section. [http://www.combinet.net/wldecnmy/oct2000/KrishnaSharma/constraints.htm]

Shimomoto, Yutaka, 1999, "The Capital Market in Malaysia," in *Rising to the Challenge in Asia: A Study of Financial Markets* (Volume 8 – Malaysia), Manila: Asian Development Bank, pp.80-112.

Sinha, Dipendra and Joseph Macri, "Financial Development and Economic Growth: The Case of Eight Asian Countries," *Economia Internazionale*, Vol.55, pp.219-234.

Stiglitz, Joseph, 2000, "Capital Market Liberalization, Economic Growth, and Instability," *World Development,* Vol.28, No.6, pp.1075-1086.

Tan, Chwee Huat, 1999, *Financial Markets and Institutions in Singapore,* Singapore: Singapore University Press, 1999.

Tay, Serene, 1993, *Financial and Economic Development in ASEAN*, Singapore: National University of Singapore Department of Economics and Statistics.

Wells, Stephen, 1999, "Moving Toward Transparency: Capital Market in Indonesia," in *Rising to the Challenge in Asia: A Study of Financial Markets* (Volume 6 – Indonesia), Manila: Asian Development Bank, pp.74-111.

Wells, Stephen, 1999, "Solid Crust with Soft Center: A Problem of Enforcement in the Philippine Capital Market," in *Rising to the Challenge in Asia: A Study of Financial Markets* (Volume 10 – Philippines), Manila: Asian Development Bank, pp.80-105.

Werner, Richard, 1999, "Capital Market in Thailand: Issues and Opportunities," in *Rising to the Challenge in Asia: A Study of Financial Markets* (Volume 11 – Thailand), Manila: Asian Development Bank, pp.106-134.

PART III: THE EXTERNAL ECONOMY OF SOUTHEAST ASIA

Chapter 6

FOREIGN TRADE IN SOUTHEAST ASIA: THEORIES, POLICIES AND AFTA

ABSTRACT

This chapter examines the trade sector in Southeast Asian economies. It discusses the theories of trade including the absolute advantage, comparative advantage, Heckscher-Ohlin model, and competitive advantage. Some illustrations of these concepts in the context of Southeast Asia are discussed. This is followed by a discussion of the various trade policies including tariffs and non-tariff barriers. This chapter also analyzes the geographical and industrial patterns of Southeast Asia's exports and imports. Finally, it discusses the trade liberalization schemes followed by the Southeast Asian economies including the creation of the ASEAN Free Trade Area (AFTA).

INTRODUCTION

The appropriate role of trade and trade policy in economic development has been controversial for a long period of time. Greenaway and Morgan (1998) provides an excellent review of the core theoretical canons on trade policy and economic development.[1] As they stated further, based on multi-country and country-specific studies, the empirical evidence on the relationship between trade strategy and economic performance has been viewed from several different angles. First, some address the relationships between exports and economic growth on the assumption that more outward-oriented trade strategies are associated with higher exports. Second, some address the relationship between liberalization and exports - which is a narrower focus. Third, some attempts to use 'composite indicators of trade strategy and link these to indicators of economic performance.

In the case of Southeast Asian economies, exports have played a significant role in their economic development and transformation. Fukuda and Toya (1995) reported that the successful promotion of exports has been primarily responsible for rapid industrialization in

---

[1] See David Greenaway and Wyn Morgan, "Trade Orientation and Economic Development: Theory and Evidence," in David Sapsford and John-ren Chen (eds), *Development Economics and Policy,* London, UK: Macmillan Press, 1988, pp.113-132.

the Asian newly-industrialized economies and even in the case of Southeast Asian countries.[2] This was true particularly for Thailand and Malaysia in the late 1980s when the growth rate of exports was more than twice as large as the rate of GNP growth between 1987 and 1990. The contribution of exports was less conspicuous in the Philippines and Indonesia, but their export-GNP ratios were higher than the Latin American countries, and even went up steadily in the late 1980s.

The remainder of this chapter is organized as follows. The next section discusses the various theories of trade. The third section describes briefly some trade policies. The fourth and fifth sections provide an analysis of the industrial and geographical trends and patterns of trade in Southeast Asia, respectively. The sixth section traces the trade liberalization policies in Southeast Asia focusing on the ASEAN Free Trade Area (AFTA).

THEORIES OF TRADE

Among the different theories of trade, this section discusses only four theories and are illustrated in the context of Southeast Asia. The first three are absolute advantage, comparative advantage and the Heckscher-Ohlin model.[3] The fourth model is based on the competitive advantage framework.

Absolute Advantage

Adam Smith postulated that two nations could trade based on absolute advantage. When one country (I) produces more efficiently than another country (II) in producing one good (X), then country I has an absolute advantage in the production of that good X. When Country II produces more efficiently than country I in producing the second good (Y), then country II has an absolute advantage in the production of good Y. Thus, country I will specialize in the production of good X and country II will specialize in the production of good Y. Both countries I and II can gain by exchanging part of their output for these goods. Trade is thus created. Through specialization, resources are used efficiently as they are re-allocated away from inefficient towards efficient commodity. Through trade, more output of both goods can be produced.

Assume that we have two countries; namely, Singapore and Indonesia. Because of labor conditions, Singapore is more efficient in the production of computers but inefficient in the production of textiles. Thus, Singapore has an absolute advantage in the production of computers. On the other hand, Indonesia is more efficient in the production of textiles but inefficient in the production of computers. Thus, Indonesia has an absolute advantage in the production of textiles. Both Singapore and Indonesia would gain by each producing the good of its absolute advantage and exchange them. Singapore would specialize in the production of computers by manufacturing more of them and exchange them for textiles manufactured in

---

2 See Shin-ichi Fukuda and Hideki Toya, "Conditional Convergence in East Asian Countries: The Role of Exports in Economic Growth," in Takatoshi Ito and Anne O. Krueger (eds), *Growth Theories in Light of the East Asian Experience,* Chicago, USA: The University of Chicago Press, 1995, pp.247-265.

3 For a complete discussion of these three trade theories, see Dominick Salvatore, *International Economics*, New York: Macmillan Publishing Co., 1990.

Indonesia. Consequently, more of computers and textiles would be manufactured and both countries would gain from trading.

To illustrate, consider the following example in Table 6.1. Assume that one hour of labor produces 6 units of computer in Singapore but only three in Indonesia. On the other hand, one hour of labor produces 6 yards of textiles in Indonesia, but only three in Singapore. Hence, Singapore is more efficient than Indonesia in the production of computers. Indonesia is more efficient than Singapore in the production of textiles. Both countries would gain by trading.

Table 6.1. Absolute Advantage

	Singapore	Indonesia
Computers (units/man-hour)	6	3
Textiles (yards/man-hour)	3	6

Comparative Advantage

In his book titled "Principles of Political Economy and Taxation" published in 1817, David Ricardo presented a very important concept called the law of comparative advantage, which has many practical applications. According to this law, if country I is more efficient than country II in the production of both goods X and Y, it still benefits to trade, as long as country II is not equally less productive in the production of both goods. Each country should specialize, produce and export the good in which it has a comparative advantage.

This is illustrated in Table 6.2. Singapore has absolute advantage in both lines of production as it produces higher computer and textile output than Indonesia. However, in terms of comparative advantage, Singaporean labor is twice as productive as Indonesian labor in the production of computers, but only one and a half times as productive as Indonesia in textiles. Equivalently, Indonesian labor is half as productive as Singaporean labor in computer production, but two-thirds as productive as Singaporean labor in textiles. Singapore's absolute advantage is greater in the production of computers and Indonesia's absolute advantage is greater in the production of textiles. Thus, we say that Singapore has a comparative advantage in the production of computers while Indonesia has a comparative advantage in the production of textiles. Singapore and Indonesia would need to specialize in the production of computers and textiles, respectively. Both would gain by trading.

Table 6.2. Comparative Advantage

	Singapore	Indonesia
Computers (units/man-hour)	6	3
Textiles (yards/man-hour)	3	2

The law of comparative advantage could also be explained in the context of opportunity costs. The opportunity cost of the first good (X) is the cost of a second commodity (Y) that needs to be given up in order to release sufficient resources to produce one additional unit of the first commodity (X). Without trade, Singapore needs to give up ½ of a unit of textile to produce one unit of computer domestically. Thus, the opportunity cost of a computer is one-half of a unit of textile (1C = ½ T in Singapore). This is shown in Table 6.3. Without trade, Indonesia needs to give up two-thirds of a unit of textile to produce one unit of computer domestically. Thus, the opportunity cost of a computer is two-thirds of a unit of textile (1C = 2/3 T in Indonesia). Hence, Singapore has the lower opportunity cost of computer in terms of the amount of textiles that has to be given up. Singapore would have a comparative (cost) advantage in the production of computers and Indonesia, in textiles. Singapore needs to specialize in the production of computers and exchange some of it for Indonesia's textiles.

Table 6.3. Comparative Advantage (Opportunity costs of one unit of computer)

	Singapore	Indonesia
Computers (units/man-hour)	6/6 = 1	3/3 = 1
Textiles (yards/man-hour)	3/6 = 0.5	2/3 = 0.67
Opportunity cost	1C = 0.5 T	1 C = 0.67 T

Heckscher-Ohlin Trade Model

According to this theory, nations trade as a result of the differences in their factor endowments; namely, labor and capital. The theory states that capital-abundant countries will produce and export capital-intensive goods and labor-abundant countries will produce and export labor-intensive goods.

But what is the meaning of factor abundance? There are two alternative definitions. The first definition is in terms of factor prices. Country I is capital-abundant if the price of its capital (P_C) relative to the price of its labor (P_L) is lower than that in Country II.

$$\frac{P_{C,I}}{P_{L,I}} < \frac{P_{C,II}}{P_{L,II}}$$

It also follows that if capital is cheaper in country I than in country II, then country I is abundant in capital. If labor is cheaper in country II than in country I, then country II is abundant in labor. As such country I will produce and export capital-intensive good while country II will produce and export labor-intensive goods. Some countries in Southeast Asia are more capital abundant such as Singapore and Malaysia, others are more labor abundant such as Indonesia, the Philippines and Thailand, with a population of about 205 million, 74 million and 62 million, respectively. Thus, according to this theory, the price ratio of capital to labor in Singapore is lower than that of Indonesia. As a result of this difference in factor intensity, Singapore will produce and export capital-intensive goods like computers while Indonesia will produce and export labor-intensive goods like textiles.

The second definition is stated in terms of the physical endowments of labor and capital. Country I is abundant in capital if the ratio of capital to labor is larger in country I than in country II.

$$\frac{C_I}{L_I} < \frac{C_{II}}{L_{II}}$$

where C_I and L_I are the total amounts of capital and labor, respectively, in country I and C_{II} and L_{II} are the total amount of capital and labor, respectively, in country II. This definition implies that from the production side, there is a bias in country I (the capital-rich country) towards producing capital-intensive good X. The opportunity cost of producing good X is lower in country I than in country II. For labor-abundant country II, there is a bias from the production side towards producing labor-intensive good Y as the opportunity cost of producing it is lower than in country I. From the demand side, demand in country I will be biased towards the capital-intensive good X and as such, in isolation, good X will be more expensive in country I than in country II. Demand in country II will be biased towards labor-intensive good Y and as such, in isolation, good Y will become more expensive in country II than in country I. With trade, country I will export labor-intensive good Y and country II will export capital-intensive good Y on the assumption that demand factors offset the production bias.

Therefore, the two definitions of factor abundance – first, based on price ratios of capital to labor, and second, based on the physical endowments of capital and labor – do not give equivalent theoretical results. It is only in the context of the first definition of factor abundance that a capital-abundant country will produce and export capital-intensive goods and that labor-abundant country will produce and export labor-abundant goods.

Theory of Competitive Advantage

Economists use "competitiveness" in various ways. One is purely macroeconomic in which the lack of competitiveness is treated as a real exchange rate problem which arises when a country at full employment runs a "persistent (and unwelcome) current account deficit which would in due course require adjustment, usually via a mixture of deflation and depreciation."[4] In this context, competitiveness is measured in terms of relative price and/or cost indices.

A broader definition of competitiveness used by most analysts is the one which focuses on structural factors affecting medium- to long-term economic performance such as productivity, innovation, skills and so on.[5] In this context, Porter (1990) developed a new paradigm which takes into account the changes in the nature of competition, and which challenges the traditional theory of comparative advantage.[6] As described by Singaravelu and

4 A. Boltho, "The Assessment: International Competitiveness," *Oxford Review of Economic Policy,* Vol.12, No.3, 1996, p.2, as cited in Sanjaya Lall, "Competitiveness Indices and Developing Countries: An Economic Evaluation of the Global Competitiveness Report," *World Development,* Vol.29. No.9, 2001, pp.1503.

5 J. Fagerberg, "Technology and Competitiveness," *Oxford Review of Economic Policy,* Vol.12, No.3, 1996, pp.39-51, as cited in Lall (2001: 1503).

6 For an excellent analysis of Porter's theory of competititive advantage and its application to Southeast Asia, see Ananda Singaravelu and Loh Shen Lee, "Competitive Advantage: The US and ASEAN," in Tan Teck Meng, Low Aik Meng, John Williams and John Webster (eds), *US-ASEAN Relations: Implications for Business,* Nanyang Business Report Series, Singapore: Prentice Hall, 1997, pp.73-97.

Loh, Porter's theory of national competitive advantage consists of various determinants as shown in Fig.6.1. It has four sets of variables which affect the ability of a firm to establish and sustain its competitive advantage in the global markets. These include factor conditions, demand conditions, related and supporting industries, and firm strategy, structure and rivalry. Factor conditions refer to a country's position in terms of factors of production like skilled labor or infrastructure which are necessary to compete in a given industry.

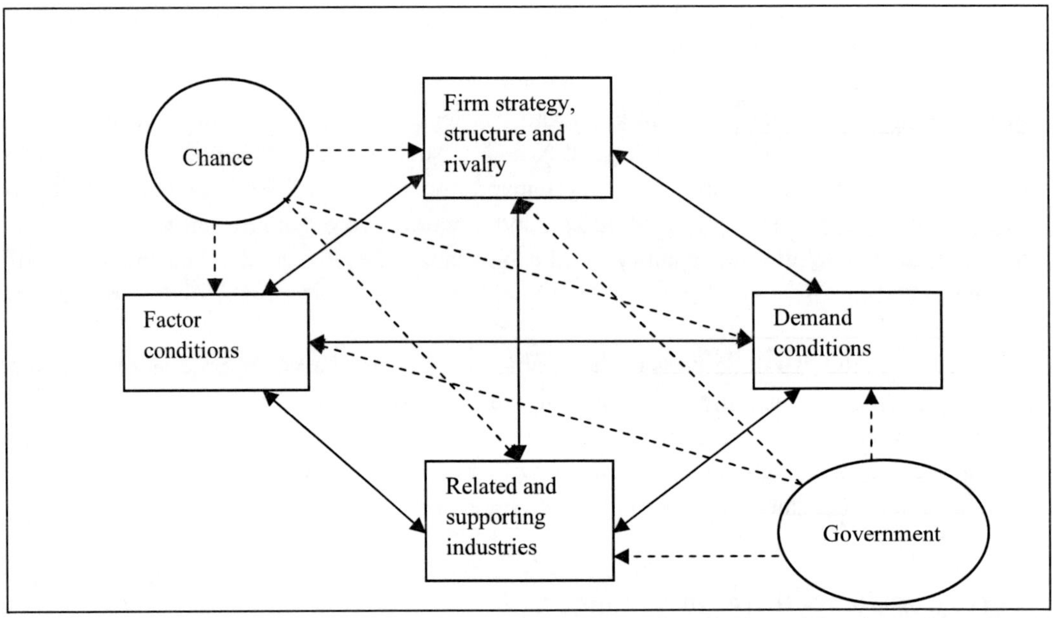

Fig.6.1 – The Porter Diamond of Competitive Advantage. Source: Porter, 1990, as shown in Singaravelu and Loh (1997:184).

Demand conditions refer to the nature of domestic demand for the industry's product or service. Related and supporting industries refer to the presence or absence of supplier and related industries in a country which are internationally competitive. Firm strategy, structure and rivalry are concerned with the conditions in a country that govern the ways companies are created, organized and managed, and the nature of domestic rivalry. These four sets of conditions interact with one another and that they also interact with government influence and chance. Government influence is evident in the policies that impact each of these determinants. Chance is concerned with developments and events which are outside of the control of a firm and sometimes, the government.

Using his framework, an index labelled as the *Business Competitiveness Index* (BCI) was first introduced in *The Global Competitiveness Report 2000.*[7] The argument is that an economy cannot be competitive unless firms doing business there are competitive, whether

---

7 For an excellent discussion of competitiveness and its measurement, see Xavier Sala-i-Martin, Executive Summary, *Global Competitiveness Report 2003-2004,* p.xi-xxiv. However, Sanjaya Lall (2001:1501-1525) assesses the index used in this report and finds several deficiencies including broad definitions, biased approach, flawed methodology, and vague qualitative measures. He further argues that these weak theoretical and empirical foundations reduce the value of the indices for analytical or policy purposes.

they are domestic companies or affiliates of foreign companies.[8] However, the sophistication and productivity of companies is linked with the quality of the national business environment. As such, the BCI index is measured based on two sub-indices: (a) the sophistication of company operations and strategy, and (b) the quality of the national business environment.

How competitive are the Southeast Asian economies with other Asian economies? Table 6.4 shows the BCI for the top 10 and for some Asian countries based on a survey of 102 countries conducted by the World Economic Forum in collaboration with its 104 partner institutes. Among Asian countries, Singapore ranked 8th. It even ranked 4th in terms of the quality of the national business environment. Among Southeast Asian countries, Malaysia (26) and Thailand (31) are far much more competitive than Indonesia (60) and the Philippines (65). The Philippines ranked 74th in terms of the quality of the national business environment.

Table 6.4. – The Business Competitiveness Index

Country	BCI ranking	Company operations and strategy ranking	Quality of the national business environment ranking
Finland	1	4	1
United States	2	2	2
Sweden	3	3	5
Denmark	4	7	3
Germany	5	1	9
United Kingdom	6	8	6
Switzerland	7	5	8
Singapore	**8**	**12**	**4**
Netherlands	9	10	11
France	10	9	14
		BCI for Asian countries	
Japan	12	6	20
Taiwan	15	16	16
Hong Kong	19	22	15
Korea	23	19	25
Malaysia	**26**	**26**	**24**
Thailand	**31**	**31**	**32**
India	37	40	36
China	46	42	44
Vietnam	**50**	**53**	**48**
Indonesia	**60**	**62**	**61**
Philippines	**65**	**48**	**74**

Source: Cited in Xavier Sala-I-Martin, "Executive Summary," The Global Competitiveness Report, Switzerland: World Economic Forum, 2003-2004, pp.xviii-xx. The BCI Index was measured based on a survey of 102 countries.

8 The concept of national competitiveness is, however, viewed as elusive by Paul Krugman. In his article titled "Competitiveness: A Dangerous Obsession" (Foreign Affairs, 1994: 28-45), Krugman stated that when we say that a corporation is uncompetitive, we mean that its market position is unsustainable – that unless it improves its performance, it will cease to exist. He further argues that countries, on the other hand, do not go out of business as they may be happy or unhappy with their economic performance, but they have no well-defined bottom line.

A second measure of competitiveness is the Growth Competitiveness Index (GCI) which was developed by Jeffrey D. Sachs and John McArthur. This index determines the capacity of the national economy to achieve sustained economic growth over the medium and long-term term. The GCI is based on three sub-indices, namely, the macroeconomic environment, the quality of public institutions, and technology. How competitive are Southeast Asian economies with other Asian economies? Table 6.5 shows the GCI in 2003 for the top 10 countries and for some Asian countries based on a survey of 102 countries conducted by the World Economic Forum in collaboration with its 104 partner institutes. Among Asian countries, Taiwan ranked 5th, followed by Singapore. Singapore ranked 1st in terms of macroeconomic environment, but in terms of technology index, Taiwan, Japan and Korea ranked better than Singapore. Among Southeast Asian countries, Malaysia (29) and Thailand (32) are again far much more competitive than the Philippines (66) Indonesia (72). In terms of the quality of public institutions, Indonesia ranked 76th while the Philippines ranked 85th.

Table 6.5. – The Growth Competitiveness Index, 2003

Countries	GCI Ranking	Macroeconomic environment index	Public institutions index	Technology index
Finland	1	2	2	2
United states	2	14	17	1
Sweden	3	8	7	4
Denmark	4	5	1	8
Taiwan	5	18	21	3
Singapore	**6**	**1**	**6**	**12**
Switzerland	7	6	8	7
Iceland	8	16	3	15
Norway	9	4	16	13
Australia	10	7	4	19
GCI for Asian Countries				
Japan	11	24	30	5
Korea	18	23	36	6
Hong Kong	24	15	10	37
Malaysia	**29**	**27**	**34**	**20**
Thailand	**32**	**26**	**37**	**39**
China	44	25	52	65
India	56	52	55	64
Vietnam	**60**	**45**	**61**	**73**
Philippines	**66**	**60**	**85**	**56**
Indonesia	**72**	**64**	**76**	**78**

Source: As in Table 6.4, pp.xi-xvii. The GCI Index was measured based on a survey of 102 countries.

TRADE POLICIES

The flow of international trade is limited by various trade policies through restrictions and regulations generally known as trade or commercial policies which include tariffs and non-tariff trade barriers (NTBs). The General Agreement on Tariffs and Trade (GATT) was established in 1947 to achieve a substantial reduction of tariffs and NTBs to trade and thus to secure freer access of countries to to international markets.[9] While tariffs have been declining over the years, particularly on manufactured goods, nations worldwide have been dependent on NTBs which include quotas, voluntary export restraints (VERs), and technical, administrative and other regulations.[10]

A **tariff** is a tax or duty which is imposed on a commodity that crosses national boundaries. Tariffs can be imposed on imported or exported commodity. Import tariffs are the more common source of tax revenues particularly for the lower income countries in Southeast Asia. The more developed countries like Singapore relies more on personal and corporate income taxes as the major source of revenue. Export tariffs are commonly imposed by developing countries on their traditional primary commodities including agricultural commodities. The average tariff rates in ASEAN have declined substantially by as much as 51 percent since 1986.[11] In the context of the regional trade liberalization initiatives (discussed further in section 6 of this chapter), after ten years since 1993, the ASEAN Free Trade Area (AFTA) has been virtually realized. Regional tariffs on 99.60 percent of products in the CEPT Inclusion List (IL) of ASEAN-6 (Brunei Darussalam, Indonesia, Malaysia, the Philippines, Singapore and Thailand) are now within the 0-5 percent range, compared to 96.2 percent in 2002.[12] The average CEPT rate for ASEAN-6 has gone down from 12.8 percent in 1993 to 2.4 percent in 2003.

Import quotas are the most important non-tariff trade barrier which restricts the quantity of the imported commodity. They are usually imposed to protect the domestic industry like agriculture or manufacturing and/or for balance of payments purposes. For example, the European Union (EU) countries have imposed quotas on textiles imported from Southeast Asian countries. The EU and Vietnam have signed a 3-year agreement that gives Vietnam an increase in textile and clothing quotas worth 200 million euros (about US$215 million) a year.[13] In return, Vietnam is committed to lower its customs duties for EU imports of textile and clothing products progressively to 20 percent for clothing, 12 percent for fabrics, 7 percent for yarns and 5 percent for fibers by 2005.[14]

---

9 Amelia Santos-Paulino, "The Effects of Trade Liberalization on Imports in Selected Developing Countries," *World Development,* Vol.30, No.6, 2002, p.959.

10 For a complete discussion of the various types of trade policies, see Dominick Salvatore, *International Economics*, New York: Macmillan Publishing Co., 1990, pp.207-286.

11 See Chulia Azarcon, "Comparative Tariff Policies of ASEAN Member Countries," *Journal of Philippine Development,* Number 43, Vol.24, No.1, First Semester, 1997, pp.93-135.

12 ASEAN Secretariat, "Joint Media Statement," released during the 17th meeting of the AFTA Council, September 1, 2003, Phnom Penh, Cambodia, September 1, 2003. The acronym CEPT refers to Common Effective Preferential Tariffs, a scheme introduced since 1993 towards trade liberalization in the ASEAN region.

13 *Textile World Asia,* "EU and Vietnam sign quota agreement," Spring 2003. (See http://www.textile worldasia.com/News.htm?CD=1846&ID=5025)

14 *Textile World Asia,* "EU and Vietnam ..."

Voluntary export restraints (VER) is another type of non-tariff barrier whereby the importing nation induces another nation to "voluntarily" reduce its exports of a commodity. Should the exporting nation export of this commodity, the viabillity of the commodity in the importing nation will be affected, not only in terms of domestic production, but also employment in that industry. VERs have been negotiated by developed countries like the United States since the 1950s to restrict imports of textiles, cars, steel and other commodities from Japan and other exporting countries. In 1984, the US was able to negotiate VERs with major steel exporters which set its imports to about 20 percent of the US steel market which in turn was able to save some 35,000-40,000 jobs. However, with Japan signing a free trade agreement (FTA) with Mexico, Japan will be able to export more cars and steel to the United States and Europe via Mexico.[15] As part of the agreement, Mexico will import Japanese vehicle parts and steel to assemble cars and electronic appliances for export to the US and Europe.

Technical, administrative and other regulations are other forms of NTB which include safety regulations, health regulations, and labelling requirements. Some examples of these standards are as follows: (i) an EU ban since 1989 on US exports of meat products from animals treated with growth-promoting hormones, which has effectively blocked U.S. meat (mainly beef) exports valued at about $100 million annually, (ii) an EU prohibition against US exports of poultry meat because the EU will not recognize as safe the U.S. processors' system for washing carcasses in chlorinated water, (iii) Korean border clearance procedures that can delay imported perishable products for several weeks, compared with several days elsewhere in Asia, and (iv) an EU decision, effective November 1, 1997, that human foods must be labeled to indicate whether they were produced from genetically modified corn and soybeans.[16]

International cartel is an organization of international producers who agree to restrict production and exports of a commodity to maximize profits. The Organization of Petroleum Exporting Countries (OPEC) is an example. It decided to restrict its output and exports of oil and this led to a four-fold increase in the world price of crude oil in 1973-74. Southeast Asian countries, particularly the oil-importers like the Philippines, Thailand and Singapore were the worst hit among the oil importing developing countries. Oil-producers like Brunei, Indonesia and Malaysia benefited through significant increase in their foreign exchange reserves.

Export subsidies are given to the country's exporters or would-be exporters through direct payments, tax reliefs or subsidized loans. Export subsidies in the form of low-interest rate loans can also be given to foreign buyers to boost the country's exports. In the case of the European Union, the subsidies being poured into the sugar industry have cost the EU taxpayers US$1.7 billion every year.[17] This is in the form of extremely high guaranteed prices for EU sugar producers which lead to overproduction. This has proved to be harmful to the major sugar exporting countries from the developing world including Brazil, Thailand, South Africa and Guatemala. In its study titled "The Great EU Sugar Scam," Oxfam pointed out that

---

15 The Straits Times, "Japan to use Mexico as trade gateway to US, EU," March 15, 2004, p.A15.

16 Geoffrey Becker, Agricultural Exports: Technical Barriers to Trade, CRS Report for Congress, Oct 21, 1997. (see the National Council for Science and the Environment website http://www.ncseonline.org/NLE/CRSreports/Agriculture/ag-43.cfm)

17 Asia Times, "Propping up sugar prices a bitter prospect," May 27, 2003. See http://www.atimes.com/atimes/Southeast_Asia/EE27Ae01.html

European consumers and taxpayers are paying to destroy livelihoods in some of the world's poorest countries and that they are paying for a system that rewards a handful of sugar producers in Europe, while undermining markets and opportunities for farmers and agricultural laborers in the developing world.[18] For their part, the Cairns Group (an informal bloc of big and medium-sized developed and developing country agricultural exporters that includes, among others, Southeast Asian countries, Argentina and New Zealand) has urged for a broader and faster liberalization of agricultural markets via increased market access, an end to export subsidies, and a decrease in production subsidies in the North.[19] Thus, the Southeast Asian governments have taken sides with the United States in pressuring for market opening in Japan and the termination of direct income subsidies for EU farmers.

Dumping is the practice of exporting a good at below cost or selling the good overseas at a lower price than in the home country. For example, the US International Trade Commission has imposed anti-dumping duties on shrimp from Thailand, Brazil, Ecuador, India, China and Vietnam in order "to create fair trading" and protect its American producers.[20] These countries are said to have 'dumped" frozen and canned shrimp and prawn in the US market. Because of the US move, the Thai shrimp exports are expected to fall by 20-30 percent, according to Thiraphong Chansiri, secretary-general of the Thai Frozen Foods Association. Unlike other exporting countries, however, Thailand is not likely to feel the impact because most of the shrimp products have premium quality which commands higher prices. Another country which is affected by the US move is Vietnam which exported US$467 million worth of shrimp to the United States in 2003.[21] Accordingly, the Vietnam Association of Seafood Exporters and Producers (Vasep) estimates that in order to fight US anti-dumping move, it will cost about US$1.2 million to US$1.5 million. In 2003, Vietnam lost against the US anti-dumping case on Vietnam's exports of catfish to the US market. Consequently, the US import tariff on catfish rose to 60 percent. The Vietnamese have temporarily stopped exporting the catfish fillet to the United States and instead diverted their exports of catfish to Asian countries such as Hong Kong, Singapore, European destinations as well as Australia.[22]

Industrial Patterns of Trade

Based on the Standard International Trade Classification (SITC) as shown below, trade classification has enabled analysts and policy makers to determine the changes in the structure of exports and imports that take place overtime, and hence make important policy decisions including diversification policy.

0 Food & live animals

1 Beverage & tobacco

18 See Asia Times, "Propping up sugar prices a bitter prospect," May 27, 2003. (http://www.atimes.com/atimes/Southeast_Asia/EE27Ae01.html)

19 See Walden Bello, "Asia, Asian Farmers and the WTO," Focus on Trade, No.36, Transnational Institute (TNI), July 1999. (http://www.tni.org/archives/bello/asiawto.htm)

20 *The Nation,* "Are anti-dumping duties justified?" Editorial, Feb 21, 2004.

21 See Intellasia, "Vietnam ready to tackle possible US antidumping lawsuit," Jan 1, 2004 (http://www.intellasia.com/news_today/2004/020104.htm)

22 See Asia Times, "Vietnamese catfish firm shifts exports from US," Feb 15, 2003 (http://www.atimes.com/atimes/Southeast_Asia/EB15Ae06.html)

2 Crude materials
3 Minerals & fuels
4 Animal oils & fats
5 Chemicals
6 Basic manufactures
7 Machines, transport and equipment
8 Miscellaneous manufactures
9 Miscellaneous transactions

For analysis of trade structure, sectors 0 to 4 are considered primary products and sectors 5 to 8, manufactured products. Tables 6.6 and 6.7 shows the composition of Southeast Asian exports and imports, respectively. The structure of exports for all countries shifted away from primary products and towards manufactured goods. Indonesia, the Philippines, Thailand and Malaysia were very much dependent on primary exports as shown by their shares in 1975 at 98 percent, 78 percent, 76 percent and 69 percent, respectively. However, Indonesia showed the fastest change over a 26 year period with its share of manufactured goods rising to 58 percent in 2001. For Singapore, its share of manufactured goods more than doubled to 85 percent in 2001. Southeast Asia's dependence on manufactured imports continued to increase.

Table 6.6. – Composition of Trade: Merchandise Exports

	Indonesia		**Malaysia**		**Philippines**		**Singapore**		**Thailand**	
	1975	**2001**	**1975**	**2001**	**1975**	**2001**	**1975**	**2001**	**1975**	**2001**
Total Exports (US$ mil)	7102	56318	3830	88032	2295	32150	5376	121687	2208	65118
0 Food and live animals	5.2	5.8	6.4	2.0	36.1	4.1	7.2	1.3	59.1	14.9
1 Beverage and tobacco	0.5	0.5	0.3	0.4	1.6	0.2	0.3	0.8	1.3	0.3
2 Crude materials	14.9	7.4	35.0	2.3	28.4	1.3	13.3	0.7	15.1	3.7
3 Mineral fuels, etc.	74.8	25.3	10.5	9.7	1.6	0.8	27.0	7.6	0.6	2.8
4 Animal, vegetableoils & fats	2.3	2.6	16.3	3.7	10.2	1.3	1.9	0.2	0.1	0.2
PRIMARY PRODUCTS	**97.7**	**41.6**	**68.5**	**18.1**	**77.9**	**7.7**	**49.7**	**10.6**	**76.2**	**21.9**
5 Chemicals	0.3	5.0	0.9	4.3	1.0	1.0	3.7	8.1	0.5	5.8
6 Basic manufactures	1.3	19.9	17.6	7.2	10.4	3.9	8.5	3.9	14.3	11.7
7 Machines, transport equipment	0.5	16.2	6.2	60.6	0.5	74.3	22.7	64.4	1.3	42.0
8 Misc. manufactures	0.3	16.5	5.7	8.8	4.4	12.9	6.9	8.7	3.5	15.2
MANUFACTURED PRODUCTS	**2.3**	**57.6**	**30.4**	**80.9**	**16.3**	**92.1**	**41.8**	**85.1**	**19.6**	**74.7**
9 Miscellaneous producs	0.0	0.8	1.1	1.1	5.9	0.2	8.4	4.3	4.3	3.5

Sources: ASEAN Secretariat (*www.aseansec.org*); Bank of Thailand (*www.bot.or.th*); UN COMTRADE (unstats.un.org); ADB, *Key Indicators of Developing Asian and Pacific Countries 2002* (*www.adb.org*); IE Singapore (*www.iesingapore.gov.sg*); Bank of Korea *(www.bok.or.kr)*.

Table 6.7. Composition of Trade: Merchandise Imports

	Indonesia		Malaysia		Philippines		Singapore		Thailand	
	1975	2001	1975	2001	1975	2001	1975	2001	1975	2001
Total Imports (US$ mil)	**4770**	**30962**	**3554**	**73098**	**3756**	**29551**	**8134**	**115919**	**3280**	**62072**
0 Food and live animals	12.1	8.1	16.4	4.4	9.6	7.4	8.6	2.5	2.9	4.0
1 Beverage and tobacco	0.3	0.8	1.4	0.3	0.7	0.7	0.7	0.9	1.1	0.4
2 Crude materials	3.4	10.3	6.5	2.5	4.0	3.3	6.4	0.6	6.0	4.1
3 Mineral fuels	5.4	17.8	12.0	5.3	21.7	11.4	24.6	12.6	21.3	12.0
4 Animal, veg oils and fats	0.1	0.1	0.3	0.3	0.2	0.2	1.3	0.2	0.2	0.1
PRIMARY PRODUCTS	**21.3**	**37.1**	**36.6**	**12.8**	**36.2**	**23.0**	**41.6**	**16.8**	**31.5**	**20.6**
5 Chemicals	16.9	17.4	8.3	7.4	11.3	8.9	5.8	5.9	13.6	10.7
6 Basic manufactures	22.5	13.7	16.3	10.7	13.2	11.9	18.2	7.3	15.8	16.1
7 Machines, transport eqpt	37.2	29.2	32.5	60.3	31.7	52.3	26.2	59.7	34.6	45.3
8 Miscellaneous manufactures	2.1	2.5	5.5	5.7	2.1	3.9	6.9	8.9	3.2	5.3
MANUFACTU-RED PRODS	**78.7**	**62.8**	**62.6**	**84.1**	**58.3**	**77.0**	**57.1**	**81.8**	**67.2**	**77.4**
9 Miscellaneous products.	0.0	0.03	0.8	3.1	5.6	0.1	1.4	1.4	1.3	2.0

Sources: As in Table 6.6.

GEOGRAPHICAL PATTERNS OF TRADE

As Table 6.8 shows, by region, Asia is the top destination of Southeast Asia's exports. Indonesia, Malaysia, the Philippines and Singapore are increasingly more dependent on the Asian region as Asia's share of their exports rose in 2000 relative to 1976. Thailand's exports to Asia fell, but remained high at 46 percent in 2000. Thus, we could see that there is a growing trade between Southeast Asia and the Asian region, particularly with the Northeast Asian region and even within the Southeast Asian region itself, which is an indication of rising intra-ASEAN regional exports. The North American Free Trade Agreement (NAFTA) and the European Union (EU) regions are the other two leading regional destinations of Southeast Asia's exports. Within NAFTA, the US is the largest beneficiary. Within EU, the main export partners are UK, Germany, France and the Netherlands. The UK's major role in Southeast Asia emanates to some extent from the historical relationship between it and its former colonies: Brunei, Malaysia and Singapore. On the other hand, Indonesia and the Philippines have shown decreasing dependence on their former colonial masters, Netherlands and Spain, respectively,[23] which is a reflection of their nationalistic attitudes departing from

[23] Teofilo C. Daquila, 1997, "Obstacles to Closer Trade and Investment Links: An ASEAN Viewpoint," in Chia Siow Yue and Joseph L.H. Tan (eds), *ASEAN and EU: Forging New Linkages and Strategic Alliances*, Singapore: Institute of Southeast Asian Studies, and Paris: OECD, p.104.

the colonial pattern in the past.[24] By country, the major export partners of Southeast Asia are US, Japan, and UK.

Table 6.8 Direction of Trade: Merchandise Exports (% of Total Exports)

From	INDONESIA		MALAYSIA		PHILIPPINES		SINGAPORE		THAILAND	
To	1976	2000	1976	2000	1976	2000	1976	2000	1976	2000
Total Exports (US$ Million)	8547	62124	5297	98135	2574	39783	6594	137804	2980	61924
ASIA	**57.3**	**61.4**	**48.2**	**57.2**	**31.7**	**46.0**	**45.0**	**60.2**	**53.6**	**46.2**
***N.E. Asia**	**43.8**	**40.9**	**25.0**	**27.7**	**28.2**	**30.7**	**19.7**	**28.9**	**34.0**	**25.7**
-Japan	41.7	23.2	21.1	13.0	24.3	14.1	10.3	7.5	25.8	14.8
-South Korea	1.8	7.0	1.8	3.3	9.0	2.9	1.1	3.6	1.0	1.8
-Hong Kong	0.3	2.5	1.2	4.5	1.5	4.8	7.8	7.9	5.0	5.0
-China	…	4.5	0.8	3.1	1.5	1.7	0.6	3.9	2.1	4.1
-Taiwan	…	3.8	…	3.8	…	7.2	…	6.0	…	0.0
***ASEAN-10**	**13.1**	**17.5**	**22**	**26.6**	**2.6**	**15.0**	**21.1**	**27.4**	**18.0**	**18.7**
- Indonesia	-	0.0	-	1.7	…	0.5	-	0.0	5.2	1.9
-Malaysia	0.3	3.2	-	0.0	0.2	3.5	15.2	18.2	4.2	4.2
-Philippines	1.1	1.3	1.5	1.8	…	0.0	7.9	2.5	1.0	1.6
-Singapore	11.7	10.6	18.2	18.4	2.2	7.9	-	0.0	6.8	8.7
-Thailand	…	1.7	1.3	3.6	0.3	3.0	3.0	4.3	-	0.0
-Brunei	…	0.0	0.7	0.3	…	0.0	1.5	0.4	0.1	0.1
-Vietnam	…	0.6	…	0.5	…	0.2	0.2	1.5	…	1.2
-Laos	…	0.0	…	0.0	…	0.0	…	0.0	0.6	0.6
-Myanmar	…	0.1	0.2	0.2	…	0.0	0.3	0.3	0.1	0.0
-Cambodia	…	0.1	…	0.1	…	0.0	…	0.3	…	0.5
South Asia	**0.4**	**2.8**	**1.1**	**2.8**	**0.4**	**0.2**	**1.9**	**3.3**	**1.6**	**1.7**
Other Asia	**0**	**0.2**	**0.1**	**0.1**	**0.5**	**0.1**	**2.3**	**0.6**	**…**	**0.1**
EUROPEAN UNION	**7.5**	**13.0**	**17.3**	**13.7**	**19.6**	**17.2**	**15.4**	**13.2**	**23.0**	**15.7**
-U. Kingdom	0.5	2.4	…	3.1	2.8	3.8	3.7	2.6	1.6	3.4
-Germany	2.4	2.3	4.3	2.5	4.1	3.3	4.0	3.1	3.3	2.4
-Netherlands	2.7	3.0	6.6	4.2	8.2	7.5	1.7	3.0	13.3	3.3
-France	0.4	1.2	1.8	0.7	2.3	0.7	2.5	1.6	1.3	1.3
-Italy	0.9	1.2	2.1	0.6	0.6	0.4	1.3	0.4	1.2	1.2
-Belgium	0.2	1.3	0.9	0.9	0.5	0.3	0.5	0.5	0.7	1.6
-Other EU	0.4	1.5	1.6	1.6	1.1	1.0	1.7	2.1	1.6	2.6
NAFTA	**28.9**	**14.7**	**16.6**	**22.0**	**37.0**	**30.2**	**16.1**	**18.3**	**10.4**	**22.9**
-United States	28.7	13.7	15.6	20.5	36.0	28.7	14.6	17.3	10.0	21.3
-Canada	0.2	0.7	0.8	0.8	1	0.9	1.3	0.4	0.4	1.1
-Mexico	…	0.4	0.2	0.6	…	0.7	0.3	0.6	…	0.6
CER	**0.4**	**2.4**	**2.6**	**2.8**	**2.0**	**0.8**	**6.1**	**2.6**	**1.1**	**2.6**
- Australia	0.4	2.4	2.2	2.5	1.7	0.8	5.1	2.3	1.0	2.3
- New Zealand	…	0.0	0.4	0.4	0.3	0.0	1.0	0.3	0.1	0.3
MERCOSUR	**…**	**0.6**	**0.4**	**0.4**	**…**	**0.1**	**0.9**	**0.3**	**0.1**	**0.4**
Rest of the World	**6.0**	**7.9**	**14.8**	**3.9**	**9.5**	**5.6**	**16.4**	**5.3**	**11.9**	**12.1**

Source: IMF, *Direction of Trade Statistics Yearbook,* Washington D.C.: International Monetary Fund, Various Issues.

24 Teofilo C. Daquila, 1997, "Obstacles to Closer …," p.122.

Table 6.9. Direction of Trade: Merchandise Imports (% of Total Imports)

To	INDONESIA		MALAYSIA		PHILIPPINES		SINGAPORE		THAILAND	
From	1976	2000	1976	2000	1976	2000	1976	2000	1976	2000
Total Imports (US$ Million)	5674	33515	3831	82199	3952	33808	9070	134545	3572	61924
ASIA	**49.0**	**54.7**	**45.5**	**62.9**	**37.7**	**51.8**	**41.6**	**58.9**	**43.8**	**56.0**
***NE. Asia**	**30.5**	**33.1**	**27.6**	**37.8**	**30.0**	**36.5**	**22.3**	**33.1**	**36.3**	**34.5**
-Japan	26.2	16.1	21.2	21.1	27.1	17.8	16.0	17.2	32.4	23.8
-South Korea	0.8	6.2	0.7	4.4	0.5	7.0	0.9	3.6	0.8	3.4
-Hong Kong	1.2	1.0	2.2	2.8	1.3	3.6	2.4	2.6	1.0	4.5
-China	2.3	6.0	3.5	3.9	1.0	2.3	2.9	5.3	2.0	2.8
-Taiwan	...	3.8	...	5.6	...	5.8	...	4.4	...	...
***ASEAN-10**	**15.7**	**19.2**	**16.3**	**24.1**	**6.5**	**14.7**	**17.8**	**20.0**	**4.9**	**20.0**
- Indonesia	-	...	-	2.8	3.0	2.0	...	...	0.1	1.8
-Malaysia	0.3	3.4	-	0.0	2.3	3.4	14.3	17.0	0.5	5.4
-Philippines	0.3	0.3	0.3	2.4	-	0.0	0.4	2.5	0.2	1.7
-Singapore	10.0	11.3	8.7	14.3	0.6	6.3	-	-	2.5	9.7
-Thailand	3.7	3.3	4.2	3.9	0.7	2.5	2.3	4.3	-	-
-Brunei	...	0.0	2.0	...	0.1	...	0.2	0.2	1.4	0.8
-Vietnam	0.1	0.9	...	0.6	...	0.5	0.3	0.6	...	0.5
-Laos	...	...	0.7	...	...	0.0	...	...	0.1	0.1
-Myanmar	1.6	...	0.5	0.1	...	...	0.2	0.1	0.1	...
-Cambodia	...	0.0	...	...	...	...	...	0.1	...	...
South Asia	**2.6**	**2.0**	**1.7**	**0.9**	**0.7**	**0.5**	**1.2**	**1.0**	**1.5**	**1.3**
-India	2.2	1.6	1.5	0.9	0.6	0.5	0.8	0.8	1.2	1.0
Other Asia	**0.2**	**0.3**	**0.1**	...	**0.5**	...	**0.3**	**4.8**	**1.1**	**0.2**
EUROPEAN UNION	**21.8**	**12.4**	**18.8**	**10.8**	**12.9**	**8.8**	**11.5**	**10.2**	**14.3**	**10.0**
-U. Kingdom	3.1	1.7	7.4	2.0	3.4	1.0	3.8	2.0	3.6	1.4
-Germany	8.5	3.7	5.6	3.0	3.4	2.2	3.3	3.1	4.8	2.8
-Netherlands	3.0	1.3	0.7	0.7	1.1	1.0	1.0	1.0	1.2	1.5
-France	3.5	1.2	1.6	1.7	2.5	1.0	1.3	1.6	1.3	1.1
-Italy	1.2	1.0	0.9	0.7	0.7	0.5	0.8	0.1	1.3	0.8
-Belgium	1.6	0.7	0.7	0.4	0.6	0.4	0.3	0.5	0.5	1.1
-Other EU	0.9	2.8	1.9	2.4	1.2	2.7	1.0	1.8	1.6	1.3
NAFTA	**18.4**	**12.1**	**13.8**	**17.3**	**23.5**	**16.5**	**13.7**	**15.8**	**14.8**	**11.4**
-United States	17.4	10.1	12.7	16.6	22.2	15.8	13.2	15.1	13.5	10.7
-Canada	1.0	1.9	1.1	0.5	1.2	0.6	0.5	0.4	1.3	0.6
-Mexico	0.1	0.1	...	0.2	0.1	0.1	...	0.3	0.1	0.1
CER	**3.7**	**5.8**	**8.0**	**2.4**	**4.5**	**2.9**	**3.0**	**1.8**	**2.5**	**2.1**
- Australia	3.3	5.1	7.1	2.0	3.5	2.4	2.6	1.7	2.1	1.8
- New Zealand	0.4	0.7	0.9	0.4	1.0	0.5	0.4	0.1	0.4	0.3
MERCOSUR	**0.2**	**1.0**	**0.4**	**0.4**	**0.8**	**0.3**	**0.4**	**0.2**	**0.3**	**0.8**
Rest of the World	**7.0**	**14.0**	**13.5**	**6.2**	**20.7**	**19.0**	**29.8**	**13.0**	**24.2**	**19.7**

Source: IMF, *Direction of Trade Statistics Yearbook,* Washington D.C.:International Monetary Fund, Various Issues.

TRADE LIBERALIZATION AND AFTA

Economic globalization is broadly defined as the shrinkage of economic distances between nations which consists of two separate but not necessarily mutually exclusive trends: globalization of production and trade and globalization of finance and capital flows.[25] It is the closer integration of the countries and peoples of the world which has been brought about by the enormous reduction of costs of transportation and communication, and the breaking down of artificial barriers to the flows of goods, services, capital, knowledge, and (to a lesser extent) people across borders.[26] Various international institutions have been responsible in pushing for the global removal of barriers to free trade and the closer integration of national economies. The General Agreement of Tariffs and Trade (GATT) and its successor, the World Trade Organization (WTO) have been in charge of promoting free trade in goods and services on a global scale. The International Monetary Fund (IMF) has been responsible for removing the barriers to global finance and capital.

This section discusses the evolution of trade liberalization in Southeast Asia. The idea of trade liberalization and economic co-operation in Southeast Asia began with the UN team's report whose terms of reference were the promotion of free trade. The UN report recommended a comprehensive action plan which consisted of trade liberalization and industrial co-operation. Trade liberalization can take either a maximal approach which envisaged a free trade area with total elimination of tariff barriers, or a minimal approach which involves a gradual item-by-item approach. The UN recommended the latter.[27]

In 1974, Singapore's former minister, Mr. S. Rajaratnam emphasized that trade was the logical framework for economic activities in Southeast Asia. There was disagreement on the pace and method of trade liberalization. Singapore favored a free trade area via across-the-board tariff cuts to be implemented at a faster pace. This was supported by the Philippines. Indonesia and Malaysia, however, favored a cautious step-by-step approach. Thailand was neutral, but tended to lean towards across-the-board approach.

Following the first ASEAN summit meeting in 1976, trade liberalization measures were implemented since 1977 through a preferential trading arrangement (PTAs) which granted tariff preferences. Items covered were based on voluntary offers and product-by-product negotiations, followed by a sectoral approach. This was then changed to across-the-board approach in 1980 which provided for a minimum preferential tariff cut of 20 percent to all intra-ASEAN imports. The implementation of PTAs, however, was not very effective and had very minimal impact on trade. It covered only 2 percent of of intra-ASEAN trade in 1980 and 5 percent in 1986. Only 337 of 12,783 items offered in the PTA list were granted tariff preferences in 1987. This low utilization rate was commonly attributed to various factors, including a long exclusion list, too detailed dis-aggregation and inclusion of irrelevant items.

---

25 Rajan, Ramkishen Rajan, Economic Globalization and Asia: Trade, Finance and Taxation, Discussion Paper No.0108, Centre for International Economic Studies, University of Adelaide, 2001, p.1.

26 Joseph Stiglitz, *Globalization and its Discontents,* England: The Penguin Press, 2002, p.9.

27 For a discussion of the early attempts at ASEAN economic cooperation, see Marjorie Suriyamongkol, *Politics of ASEAN Economic Cooperation,* Singapore: Institute of Southeast Asian Studies, and Oxford University Press, pp.45-111.

Intra-ASEAN Trade

Historically, intra-ASEAN trade has remained very low at around 15-20 percent mainly accounted for by trade between Singapore, Indonesia and Malaysia. This is shown in Tables 6.10 and 6.11. It reveals that intra-ASEAN exports as a proportion of global exports increased from 12.7 percent in 1970 to 19.7 percent in the year 2000. Intra-ASEAN imports as a proportion of ASEAN's global imports rose from 5.5 percent to 19.1 percent during the same period. However, if we exclude Singapore from the picture, intra-ASEAN exports and imports would be extremely low, rising from 3.3 percent to 7.0 percent for the former and from 4.0 to 8.2 percent for the latter. Thus, the calculations would highlight the significant role of Singapore in intra-ASEAN trade and why Singapore encourages a faster pace of trade liberalization.

Table 6.10. Intra-ASEAN Exports (% of ASEAN's global exports)

From\To	INDO	MSIA	PHILS	SPORE	THAI	ASEAN-5	ASEAN-4
Indonesia							
1970		...	2.4	15.8	0.02	**18.2**	**2.4**
2000		3.2	1.3	10.6	1.7	**16.8**	**6.2**
Malaysia							
1970	0.6		1.7	21.6	0.9	**24.8**	**3.2**
2000	1.7		1.8	18.4	3.6	**25.5**	**7.1**
Philippines							
1970	0.2	...		0.7	0.3	**1.2**	**0.4**
2000	0.5	3.5		7.9	3.0	**14.9**	**7.0**
Singapore							
1970	n.a.	1.0	0.3		3.3	**4.6**	
2000	n.a.	18.2	2.5		4.3	**25.0**	
Thailand							
1970	2.3	5.6	0.1	6.6		**14.6**	**8.0**
2000	1.9	4.2	1.6	8.7		**16.4**	**7.7**
ASEAN-5							
1970	**3.1**	**6.6**	**4.5**	**44.7**	**4.5**	12.7	
2000	**4.1**	**29.1**	**7.2**	**45.6**	**12.6**	19.7	
ASEAN-4							
1970	**3.1**	**4.5**	**4.2**		**1.2**		3.3
2000	**4.1**	**10.9**	**4.7**		**8.3**		7.0

ASEAN-4 excludes Singapore. Source: IMF, *Direction of Trade Statistics Yearbook,* Washington D.C.:International Monetary Fund, Various Issues.

Other factors were responsible for the low intra-ASEAN trade. First, ASEAN imports from developed countries faced lower tariffs as these were mostly producer/capital goods while imports of manufactured goods from ASEAN faced higher tariffs as these were mainly final consumer goods Second, ASEAN countries have historically depended on countries outside ASEAN for its trade, FDIs and technology. Third, there were differences in the pace of industrialization. During the 1950s and 1960s, ASEAN countries adopted an import-substitution policy which restricted imports through high tariff rates. The Philippines had the longest IS policy experience while Singapore, the shortest. Given a limited market size, scarce financial resources, massive unemployment, and lack of domestic entrepreneurs, Singapore has shifted to outward-orientation of its economy since the late 1960s through an industrialization policy which relied heavily on export-oriented labor-intensive FDIs. Since 1979, however, Singapore has re-directed its industrialization policy by encouraging more capital-intensive, highly-skilled, high-tech and high-value added industries. Since the 1970s, having learned from the successful experiences of Singapore, other ASEAN countries have switched to export-oriented industrialization policy which is dependent on FDIs.

Table 6.11. Intra-ASEAN Imports (% of ASEAN's global imports)

To\From	INDO	MSIA	PHILS	SPORE	THAI	ASEAN-5	ASEAN-4
Indonesia							
1970		1.0	0.2	…	1.6	**2.8**	**2.8**
2000		3.4	0.3	11.3	3.3	**18.3**	**7.0**
Malaysia							
1970	4.8		0.2	7.5	3.6	**16.1**	**8.6**
2000	2.8		2.4	14.3	3.9	**23.4**	**9.1**
Philippines							
1970	2.4	…		0.4	0.04	**2.9**	**2.5**
2000	2.0	3.4		6.3	2.5	**14.2**	**7.9**
Singapore							
1970	n.a.	…	0.4		2.0	**2.4**	
2000	n.a.	17.0	2.5		4.3	**23.8**	
Thailand							
1970	1.5	0.5	0.3	1.0		**3.3**	**2.3**
2000	1.8	5.4	1.7	9.7		**18.6**	**8.9**
ASEAN-5							
1970	**8.7**	**1.5**	**1.1**	**8.9**	**7.2**	5.5	
2000	**6.6**	**29.2**	**6.9**	**41.6**	**11.4**	19.1	
ASEAN-4							
1970	**8.7**	**1.5**	**0.7**		**5.2**		4.0
2000	**6.6**	**12.2**	**4.4**		**9.7**		8.2

Note: n.a. = not available. ASEAN-4 excludes Singapore. Source: IMF, *Direction of Trade Statistics Yearbook*, Washington D.C.:International Monetary Fund, Various Issues

Towards the ASEAN Free Trade Area (AFTA)

As Greenaway and Morgan stated, the 1980s and 1990s have seen a remarkable wave of unilateral liberalization which has involved developing countries, newly independent states in Central and Eastern Europe, and even some developed market economies most notably Australia and New Zealand.[28] In the case of Southeast Asia, the idea of free trade was proposed during the Manila summit in 1987 but was not well-received. However, the idea was revived in 1991 by Thailand's former PM Anand Panyarachun and was supported by

Singapore's former PM Goh Chok Tong. Some feasibility studies were undertaken by some sectors in the region. The academe recommended the use of a differentiated approach to provide grace periods for countries not ready yet for fast-track liberalization. The private sector proposed a 40-percent ASEAN content rule. On the government side, committees were set up to consider the idea and to develop a practical working scheme. Discussions and deliberations were conducted through formal and informal dialogue sessions.

During the 22nd ASEAN Economic Ministers meeting, Indonesia proposed a trade instrument known as the Common Effective Preferential Tariff or CEPT which was adopted during the 1992 summit meeting in Singapore. The most significant step to promote intra-ASEAN trade was the decision of this summit to establish AFTA by the year 2008. The ASEAN member countries agreed in September 1994 to accelerate the establishment of AFTA by shortening the initial time frame from 15 years to 10 years. The primary objectives of AFTA include the promotion of intra-ASEAN trade, intra-ASEAN investment, greater FDIs in ASEAN, and also to promote ASEAN as a competitive production base.

The achievement of AFTA is not without problems. First, there is a lack of commitment from the private sector. Second, it will generate unemployment from inefficient industries. Third, there is a lack of harmonized safety and technical standard and customs clearance regulation. Fourth, there are differences in tariff structures, with Indonesia, the Philippines and Thailand having higher tariff rates. Moreover, a reduction in tariffs will result in loss of revenues particularly for the poorer countries in Southeast Asia.

To achieve AFTA, the CEPT scheme has been implemented since 1993. It covers manufactured products, capital goods and processed agricultural goods. Under the CEPT scheme, there are two groups of commodities covered, namely, the 'priority goods' and the 'other goods.' The 15 priority products included in the fast-track scheme are pulp, cement, fertiliser, vegetable oil, gems and jewellery, rubber products, pharmaceuticals, copper cathodes, leather products, wooden and rattan furnitures, plastics, textiles, chemicals, electronics, and ceramics and glass products.

For the priority goods, tariffs should be reduced to 0-5 percent at a faster pace than the other goods. The original members of ASEAN are expected to achieve the AFTA required tariff rates of 0-5 percent by the year 2003. The CEPT scheme has provided the most comprehensive coverage with the inclusion of more than 90 percent of total ASEAN tariff lines and the coverage of more than 85 percent of intra-ASEAN trade values and about 86 percent of the overall trade of ASEAN member countries. By the year 2000, more than 95 percent of the total ASEAN tariff lines were placed under CEPT.

Each member of ASEAN has a 10-year time frame of tariff reduction program under AFTA. By 2003, the older ASEAN-6 countries have experienced a tariff regime of not more than 5 percent tariff rate. The newer ASEAN members (Cambodia, Laos, Myanmar and Vietnam) are given a longer period to achieve this reduction in light of their current level of economic development. Vietnam is targeted to fully implement the AFTA in 2006, while the target year for Laos and Myanmar is 2008, and 2010 for Cambodia. Thus, the CEPT has been expected to boost intra-ASEAN trade significantly.

Trade liberalization measures since 1993 have proved to be effective as indicated by the rising level of intra-ASEAN trade. Intra-ASEAN trade grew significantly by 40 percent from

---

[28] See David Greenaway, Wyn Morgan, and Peter Wright, "Trade Liberalization and Growth in Developing Countries: Some New Evidence," *World Development,* Vol.25, No.11, 1997, p.1885.

US$79 billion in 1993 to US$111 billion in 1994. In 1995, it rose to US$140 billion which is about 25 percent of ASEAN's global trade. The adoption by ASEAN economies of outward-oriented trade policies, and pragmatic exchange rate policies, combined with rapid expansion of exports, have indicated that ASEAN's path replicated that of the newly industrialized countries in the 1960s and the 1970s.

Benefits of AFTA

The formation of AFTA offers several benefits. First, trade creation exists when a member country imports products or inputs from a more efficient exporting member country rather than from a less efficient non-member country. However, a negative effect is also possible in the form of trade diversion which refers to the condition when a member country imports products or inputs from a less efficient exporting member country rather than from a more efficient non-member country.

Second, it provides for a free flow of goods and services. The ASEAN region offers a large market size as it has some 500 million population. Third, AFTA will generate economies of scale. Regional producers will produce commodities according to comparative advantage which will lead to greater specialization, increased production and cost reduction. Fourth, AFTA will attract more foreign direct investments particularly those which are trade-related given that there will be reduced tariffs ranging from 0 to 5 percent. More multinational corporations will invest in the region to avail of the huge consumer base and reduced tariffs.

Conclusion

This chapter discusses the various theories and policies of trade with some applications to Southeast Asia. Among the various policies, tariffs are the most commonly used to generate revenues and protect domestic industries. This chapter also provides an analysis of the geographical and industrial patterns of Southeast Asian exports and imports. We have seen that Southeast Asia's major trading partners by region are Asia, North America and the European Union. It is important to note that Asia has increasingly become a significant regional partner of Southeast Asia. By industry, we have seen that Southeast Asia's trade has experienced a structural change away from primary exports towards manufactured exports, and a continuing dependence on manufactured imports. The Southeast Asian region has also implemented various measures aimed at liberalizing trade within the region through schemes like preferential trading arrangements and the Common Effective Preferential Tariffs – aimed at achieving AFTA by 2003 for the older members of the regional grouping and at various stages for other members. AFTA would certainly bring some benefits to the member countries but there will also be costs involved and problems along the way.

Questions for Discussion

1. To what extent are trade theories relevant in the real world? Discuss your answer with reference to Southeast Asia.

2. Intra-ASEAN regional trade has been historically at low levels compared to those with countries/region outside ASEAN mainly, the United States, Japan and the European Union. Why?
3. Would ASEAN's trade dependence on the US, Japan and the EU persist?
4. Trade liberalization policies have resulted in lower tariffs globally. However, non-tariff barriers (NTBs) have risen particularly those which are imposed by the developed world against the developing nations including the ASEAN Asian region. Give examples of these NTBs and discuss their implications on the ASEAN economies.

SUGGESTED MATERIALS FOR CASE STUDIES

Malaysia and Thailand

Reinhardt, Nola, 2000, "Back to Basics in Malaysia and Thailand: The Role of Resource-Based Exports in Their Export-led Growth," *World Development,* Vol.28, No.1, pp.57-77.

Vietnam

Hill, Hal, 2000, "Export Success Against the Odds: A Vietnamese Case Study," *World Development,* Vol.28, No.2, pp.283-300.

REFERENCES FOR CHAPTER 6

Alam, Asad, 1995, "The New Trade Theory and its Relevance to the Trade Policies of Developing Countries," *The World Economy,* Vol.18, No.3, pp.367-385.

Azarcon, Chulia, 1997, "Comparative Tariff Policies of ASEAN Member Countries," *Journal of Philippine Development,* Number 43, Vol.24, No.1, pp.93-135.

Boltho, A., 1996, "The Assessment: International Competitiveness," *Oxford Review of Economic Policy,* Vol.12, No.3, pp.1-16.

Daquila, Teofilo C., 1997, "Obstacles to Closer Trade and Investment Links: An ASEAN Viewpoint," in Chia Siow Yue and Joseph L.H. Tan (eds), *ASEAN and EU: Forging New Linkages and Strategic Alliances*, Singapore: Institute of Southeast Asian Studies, and Paris: OECD, pp.103-134.

Daquila, Teofilo C., 2000, "Japanese Economic Policy in Asia: An Asian Perspective," in Verena Blechinger and Jochen Legewie (eds), *Facing Asia – Japan's Role in the Political and Economic Dynamism of Regional Cooperation,* Munich:Germany, Iudicium Verlag, pp.175-198.

Fagerberg, J., 1996, "Technology and Competitiveness," *Oxford Review of Economic Policy,* Vol.12, No.3, pp.39-51

Fukuda, Shin-ichi and Hideki Toya, 1995, "Conditional Convergence in East Asian Countries: The Role of Exports in Economic Growth," in Takatoshi Ito and Anne O.

Krueger (eds), *Growth Theories in Light of the East Asian Experience,* Chicago, USA: The University of Chicago Press, pp.247-265.

Greenaway, David and Wyn Morgan, 1998, "Trade Orientation and Economic Development: Theory and Evidence," in David Sapsford and John-ren Chen (eds), *Development Economics and Policy,* London, UK: Macmillan Press, pp.113-132.

Greenaway, David, Wyn Morgan and Peter Wright, 1997, "Trade Liberalization and Growth in Developing Countries: Some New Evidence," *World Development,* Vol.25, No.11, pp.1885-1892.

Hill, Hal, 2000, "Export Success Against the Odds: A Vietnamese Case Study," *World Development,* Vol.28, No.2, pp.283-300.

IMF, Various Issues, *Direction of Trade Statistics Yearbook,* Washington D.C.: International Monetary Fund.

James, William, 1998, "Trade and Financial Market Reforms in ASEAN," *ASEAN Economic Bulletin,* Vol.14, No.3, pp.224-237.

Krugman, Paul, 1994, "Competitiveness: A Dangerous Obsession," *Foreign Affairs,* Vol.73, No.2, pp.28-45.

Lall, Sanjaya, 2001, "Competitiveness Indices and Developing Countries: An Economic Evaluation of the Global Competitiveness Report," *World Development,* Vol.29. No.9, pp.1501-1525.

Le, Quoc-Phuong, Duc-Tho Nguyen, and J.S. Bandara, 1996, "Vietnam's Foreign Trade in the Context of ASEAN and the Asia-Pacific Region," *ASEAN Economic Bulletin,* Vol.13, No.2, pp.185-199.

Lincoln, Edward J., 1987, *Japan's Economic Role in Northeast Asia*. Asian Agenda Report No. 10. Maryland: University Press of America & the Asia Society, pp.xviii-xi.

Porter, Michael, 1990, *The Competitive Advantage of Nations,* New York: The Free Press.

Rajan, Ramkishen, 2001, Economic Globalization and Asia: Trade, Finance and Taxation, Discussion Paper No.0108, Centre for International Economic Studies, University of Adelaide.

Reinhardt, Nola, 2000, "Back to Basics in Malaysia and Thailand: The Role of Resource-Based Exports in their Export-led Growth," *World Development,* Vol.28, No.1, pp.57-77.

Reynolds, Christopher, 2002, "The Southeast Asian Economic Miracle and International Trade Theory," in *Global Logic: The Challenge of Globalization for Southeast Asian Business,* Singapore: Prentice Hall, pp. 89-118.

Sala-I-Martin, Xavier, 2003-2004, "Executive Summary," The Global Competitiveness Report, Switzerland: World Economic Forum, pp.xi-xxiv.

Salvatore, Dominick, 1990, "Trade Restrictions: Tariffs," in *International Economics*, New York: Macmillan Publishing Co., pp.207-286.

Santos-Paulino, Amelia, 2002, "The Effects of Trade Liberalization on Imports in Selected Developing Countries," *World Development,* Vol.30, No.6, pp.959-974.

Singaravelu, Ananda and Loh Shen Lee, 1997, "Competitive Advantage: The US and ASEAN," in Tan Teck Meng, Low Aik Meng, John Williams and John Webster (eds), *US-ASEAN Relations: Implications for Business,* Nanyang Business Report Series, Singapore: Prentice Hall, pp.73-97.

Sodersten, Bo, 1980, "The Theory of Comparative Advantage and the Gains from Trade," *International Economics,* New York: St. Martin's Press, pp.11-27.

Stiglitz, Joseph, 2002, *Globalization and its Discontents,* England: The Penguin Press.

Suriyamongkol, Marjorie, 1988, *Politics of ASEAN Economic Cooperation,* Singapore: Institute of Southeast Asian Studies, and Oxford University.

The Nation, "Are Anti-Dumping Duties Justified?" Editorial, Feb 21, 2004.

The Straits Times, "Japan to use Mexico as trade gateway to US, EU," March 15, 2004, p.A15.

Internet Sources

ADB, Key Indicators of Developing Asian and Pacific Countries 2002 *(www.adb.org*).

Asia Times, "Vietnamese catfish firm shifts exports from US," Feb 15, 2003 (*http://www.atimes.com/atimes/Southeast_Asia/EB15Ae06.html)*

Asia Times, "Propping up sugar prices a bitter prospect," May 27, 2003. (*http://www.atimes.com/atimes/Southeast_Asia/EE27Ae01.html*)

ASEAN Secretariat *(www.aseansec.org*).

ASEAN Secretariat, 2003, "Joint Media Statement," released during the 17th meeting of the AFTA Council, Phnom Penh, Cambodia, September 1. (*http://www.aseansec.org/15070.htm*)

Bank of Korea *(www.bok.or.kr*).

Bank of Thailand *(www.bot.or.th)*

Becker, Geoffrey, 1997, Agricultural Exports: Technical Barriers to Trade, CRS Report for Congress, October 21. (see the National Council for Science and the Environment website: *http://www.ncseonline.org/NLE/CRSreports/Agriculture/ag-43.cfm*)

Bello, Walden, 1999, "Asia, Asian Farmers and the WTO," Focus on Trade, No.36, Transnational Institute (TNI). (*http://www.tni.org/archives/bello/asiawto.htm*)

IE Singapore *(www.iesingapore.gov.sg*)

Intellasia, "Vietnam ready to tackle possible US antidumping lawsuit," Jan 1, 2004 *(http://www.intellasia.com/news_today/2004/020104.htm*)

Textile World Asia, "EU and Vietnam sign quota agreement," Spring 2003. (*http://www.textileworldasia.com/News.htm?CD=1846&ID=5025)*

UN COMTRADE (*unstats.un.org*)

Chapter 7

FOREIGN DIRECT INVESTMENT IN SOUTHEAST ASIA: TRENDS, PATTERNS AND DETERMINANTS

ABSTRACT

This chapter discusses the role of FDI in the economic growth and development of Southeast Asian economies. It analyzes the various theories that relate to FDI, namely, the theory of the firm, the theory of factor endowment, and FDI-cum-trade approach. It also analyzes the geographical and industrial patterns of FDI in each of these economies. It also discusses the various motives and determinants of FDI in the context of the theories discussed.

INTRODUCTION

Foreign direct investment (FDI) has both positive and good points. On the positive front, FDI accelerates host countries' growth by augmenting domestic savings and investment, helping transfer of technology from the "leaders," increasing competition in the host country's domestic market, increasing exports and earning foreign exchange, and imparting several other types of positive externalities (spillovers) to the economy at large.[1] Moreover, FDI has given the global integration process a major impetus by helping link markets for capital and labor and raise relative wages and productivity of capital in recipient countries.[2] Indeed, the optimism associated with the prospects for capital flows, technology transfer, management know-how, access to export markets, and faster economic growth has given birth to renewed interest in the role of transnational corporations (TNCs) as engines of economic growth.[3] According to UNCTAD, some 40,000 parent firms and approximately

---

1 Rati Ram and Kevin Honglin Zhang, "Foreign Direct Investment and Economic Growth: Evidence from Cross-Country Data for the 1990s," *Economic Development and Cultural Change,* Vol.51, No.1, 2002, p.205. See also Stephen Thomsen, *Southeast Asia: The Role of Foreign Direct Investment Policies in Development,* Working Papers on International Investment, Paris: Organization for Economic Cooperation and Development (OECD), 1999.

2 IFC, "Foreign Direct Investments," *Lessons of Experience*, No.5, 1997, Washington DC, USA: International Finance Corporation, p.14.

3 Momtaz Uddin Ahmed, "Foreign Direct Investment and Technology Flows in Asia and the Pacific Region in the 1990s: An Analysis of Trends, Patterns and Policies," in Behrman, J.R, M.Dutta, S.L.

270,000 foreign affiliates controlled an FDI stock of US$2.7 trillion, equivalent to 10% of the world GDP in 1995.[4] This gives recognition to the enormous benefits brought by FDI.

However, FDI may repatriate funds almost to the same extent as it brings funds, transfer technologies that are inappropriate for the host country's factor proportions, kill indigenous enterprise through an intense competition, especially due to the strong economic power of large foreign companies that bring FDI, primarily target the host country's domestic market and thus not increase exports, cause distortions in the host country's policies so as to benefit the foreign investors, and create distortions in the host country's social and economic structures by infusing inappropriate social and cultural norms and behavior patterns.[5]

As IFC (1997:20) stated, the largest economies naturally attract FDI, but experience shows that it can be an important part of even the smallest, poorest economies. There is no doubt that FDI has played a significant role in the economic development of Southeast Asia, particularly in small economies like Singapore. Since its independence in 1965, Singapore has explicitly and pragmatically relied on an outward-oriented industrialization policy by encouraging FDI and promoting trade. Singapore's heavy dependence on FDI was due to its lack of natural resources, small domestic market, lack of domestic entrepreneurs, and lack of domestic savings.[6] Other countries such as Indonesia, Malaysia, the Philippines and Thailand have relied on FDI to a lesser extent than Singapore because of their bigger domestic markets and the presence of natural resources that they can depend on. However, having realized the significant contribution of FDI in the economic transformation of Singapore, the other Southeast Asian countries have increasingly relied on the inflows of FDI into their economies. From a poor, underdeveloped country with a per capita GNP of less than US$500 and a 14 percent unemployment rate in 1960, Singapore has become a newly industrialized economy with a per capita income of about US$25,000 in the year 2000.

This chapter provides an analysis of FDI in Southeast Asia. In the next section, the theories of FDI are discussed to understand the conceptual framework that governs FDI – why FDI takes place. The third section discusses the three types of FDI which include natural-resource investment, investment to serve the host market, and export-oriented investment. The fourth section identifies the various government institutions in the respective countries in Southeast Asia which are responsible for investment promotion and facilitation activities. The fifth and sixth sections analyse the geographical and industrial patterns of FDI in the five Southeast Asian countries. Because of the inconsistency in the reporting of the data on FDI by geographical and sectoral basis, analysis is done on an individual country basis. The seventh section explains the motives and determinants of FDI in Southeast Asia.

Husted, Sumalee, C. Suthiphand, and P. Wiboonchutikula, *Restructuring Asian Economics for the New Millenium,* JAI – Elsevier Science, 2001, p.643.

4 Ahmed, "Foreign Direct Investment …, p.643.

5 Rati Ram and Kevin Honglin Zhang, "Foreign Direct Investment and Economic Growth …," p.205.

6 When a domestic resource gap exists, that is, when gross domestic investment exceeds gross domestic savings, this can be financed by foreign borrowings or foreign direct investment. The main difference between the two forms of external financing is that the former involves repayment of principal and interests. FDI involves the transfer of, not only financial capital but also physical resources (eg. machineries and equipment) from the investing countries. While FDI does not require repayment of principal and interest in the case of foreign loans, it involves payment and remittance of dividends to foreign investors.

THEORIES OF FDI

Several explanations have been put forward to analyse the three tasks related to FDI; namely, the determinants (why investment takes place), the impact on the host country, and the impact on the investing country. However, as what most studies have done, this section focuses on the first task, that is, to explain the determinants of FDI. Among the various theories of FDI, three theories are discussed here; namely, the factor endowment approach, the profit maximization approach, and the FDI-cum-trade approach.[7]

Factor Endowment Approach

The motive for foreign direct investment is a higher rate of return to the factor (i.e. capital) transferred through FDI. This model assumes that that capital moves from capital-abundant countries with relatively low returns to capital-scarce countries with relatively high returns to capital. However, this approach is constrained by the fact that it cannot explain the investment flows between capital-abundant countries such as those between the United States and Japan, and between Europe and Japan. Moreover, this model blurs the differences between FDI and other types of capital flows.

Theory of the Firm Approach

This approach focuses on the profit maximization behavior of the firm. Among the various theories that fall under this category, Dunning's eclectic theory (1977) has been the most comprehensive approach that integrates both international trade and production theories.[8] It assumes that there are three sets of determinants; namely, the ownership advantages, locational advantages, and advantages that would arise from internalization. In general, this approach argues that these advantages must outweigh the costs of operating in foreign markets.

Firstly, what do foreign investors have or what can they offer? Foreign investors should possess some form of ownership advantages over their competitors or potential competitors in the host country, which may take the form of either a monopoly over a product or a brand name, a patent on a production process or technology, superior knowledge of the host market, management skills or marketing expertise.

Secondly, what do the host countries offer? The foreign investors should be able to derive benefits from the locational advantages that are available in the host country which include their ability to access the host market or to make the host country a production and/or export platform for their products or services. A host country can provide a comparative advantage over the other countries in terms of abundance of high-quality low-wage labor, low transport

7 For a very comprehensive survey of these theories, see Udom Kerdpibule and Eric Ramsetter, "Foreign Investment Theories and Policy Issues," in Seiji Naya (ed.), *Direct Foreign Investment and Export in Asia,* Kuala Lumpur: SEACEN, 1987, pp.1-23. See also ADB, 'Foreign Direct Investment: An Explanation," *Asian Development Outlook,* Manila: Asian Development Bank, p.47.

8 For further discussion, see John Dunning, *International Production and the Multinational Enterprise*, London: Allen & Unwin, 1981, chapters 2-4.

costs, excellent infrastructure, a strategic geographical location, and favorable investment incentives, among others. In the absence of these locational advantages, the foreign investor would choose exporting the product instead of direct investment for him to exploit his ownership advantage.

Lastly, aside from ownership and location advantages, there should be an internalization advantage which encourages the foreign investors to choose direct investment over other types of arms-length arrangements such as production licensing and franchising. Foreign investors usually bring technology with them as part of FDI package, which host countries would like to be unbundled. However, unbundling becomes difficult because of problems related to the definition of the technology component to be sold and the price of the component.

FDI-Cum-Trade Approach

The trade-oriented nature of FDI has been very important for many countries including Japan, the newly-industrialized economies (NIEs) of South Korea, Hong Kong, Taiwan and Singapore, and the more developed countries of Southeast Asia like Malaysia and Thailand. With FDI, trade is stimulated. In this case, FDI is viewed as a complement to trade. This view is explained in two ways. First, according to the factor endowments theory, foreign direct investment is viewed as complement to trade if trade volume increases after the inflow of FDI takes place. This is true as long as differences in technologies exist between the investing country and the recipient country. Thus, the trade-oriented nature of this type of FDI exists.

The second view is according to the product cycle hypothesis.[9] Both Akamatsu and Vernon suggested that, in the context of the product cycle hypothesis, leading economies typically develop new products and export them to lesser developed countries (LDCs). As production becomes standardized, it is transferred to 'host' LDCs via FDI, until the production of the goods is carried out mainly in the LDCs. The goods are then exported back to the investing countries, known as the boomerang effect.

Kojima analysed the trade-oriented nature of Japanese FDI. There is a progression from industries in which Japan loses its comparative advantage, and the host country gains an advantage, presumably while new products and industries generate new areas of competitiveness for Japan. This process would result in Japanese FDI being 'trade-oriented'. Japan, the investing country, would benefit if it disinvests from a comparatively disadvantaged, marginal domestic industry, in order to produce the same product in a host country at costs much lower than in Japan. The product can then be exported to the investing country (Japan) as well as to other markets.

---

9 For full discussion, see Kaname Akamatsu, ''A Historical Pattern of Economic Growth in Developing Countries,'' *The Developing Economies*, The Preliminary Issue, No.1, 1962a, p.3-25; Kaname Akamatsu, "A Theory of Unbalanced Growth in the World Economy," *Weltwirtschafliches Archiv*, Heft 86, Band 2, 1962b, pp523-544; Raymond Vernon, "International Investment and International Trade in the Product Cycle", *Quarterly Journal of Economics,* Vol.80, No.2, 1966, pp.190-207; Kiyoshi Kojima, *Direct Foreign Investment: A Japanese Model of Multinational Business Operations*, New York: Praeger, 1978; and Kiyoshi Kojima, "A Model of Trade-Oriented Foreign Investment," in Seiji Naya (ed.), *Direct Foreign Investment and Export Promotion Policies: Policies and Experiences in Asia,* Kuala Lumpur: Southeast Asia Central Banks Research and Training Center and Hawaii: East-West Resource Systems Institute, 1987, pp. 159-183.

Types of FDI

There are basically three types of FDI particularly in developing countries; namely, (a) investment in natural resources, (b) investment to serve the domestic market of the host country, and (c) investment in export-oriented industries. An example of natural-resource investment is British investment in the oil and gas sector in Brunei. The locational advantage is present in Brunei because of the abundance of oil and gas there. The ownership advantage of the British is also present because they have the high capital and technology requirements of natural resource extraction. The internalization advantage is also present but not as strong as in other sectors.

The second type of investment to serve the host country market took place during the 1950s and 1960s when developing countries followed import-substitution policies to protect their domestic industries. As imports of consumer goods of the protected industries were restricted, FDI became a means to circumvent import restrictions. More recently, FDI to serve the host markets include those in the services sectors like banking and finance, insurance and tourism. In these sectors, both ownership and locational advantages are present.

The third type of investment in export-oriented industries has occurred since the 1970s and 1980s when massive FDI from Japan and the United States came into Asia particularly the NIEs and then to Southeast Asia making these countries the production and export bases for the products of the foreign investors. The locational advantage was present in the form of low-cost labor and investment incentives. The ownership advantage was also present as foreign investors had inside knowledge of the labor-intensive consumer products like electronics products. One significant impact of this type of investment was the ability of the host countries, like the NIEs, to become foreign investors themselves in other host countries in Southeast Asia like Malaysia, Thailand and Indonesia as locational advantages and ownership advantages were both present.

Investment Agencies in Southeast Asia

Generally, there are two types of lists which many developing countries have utilized in restricting FDI. First, there is a positive list which specifies sectors open to FDI. Second, there is a negative list which specifies the industries closed to FDI. The sectors permitted or banned were sometimes specified in concrete terms and sometimes imprecisely that "threaten the economic interests of the state."[10] There also geographical restrictions as specified in these lists, that is, which regions or areas will ban or allow FDI.

In many countries, including Southeast Asia, FDI are usually subject to official approvals by government agencies. We can classify the investment agencies in Southeast Asia into two groups. The first group consists of Indonesia's BKPM and Thailand's BOI given that these agencies primarily perform their conventional functions of investment promotion and facilitation. The second group consists of Malaysia's MIDA, the Philippines' BOI and Singapore's EDB. Not only these agencies perform their traditional functions, but also they are involved significantly in shaping the industrial development of their economies.

---

[10] IFC, "Foreign Direct Investments…, p.30.

In Indonesia, the Badan Koordinasi Penanaman Modal (BKPM), known as the the Investment Coordinating Board, is the main government agency which handles the statistics and other information on foreign direct investment in Indonesia. It was created in 1973 to effectively implement the enactment of law on foreign and domestic investment.[11] It has been operating directly under the Office of the President. Its main functions include investment promotion, facilitation and policy formulation. It grants investment incentives, circumscribe investment areas and assist investors in setting up their businesses.

The Malaysian Industrial Development Authority (MIDA)[12] is the principal government agency which promotes and coordinates industrial development and investment in Malaysia. Since its establishment in 1965, it was primarily engaged in protecting and promoting industries before it assumed a larger role of investment promotion with the passage of the Promotion of Investments Act in 1986. Having been under the Ministry of International Trade and Industry, MIDA recommends trade policies and strategies relevant to the promotion and development of industries.

The Board of Investment (BOI)[13] is the main government agency which is responsible for the promotion of investments in the Philippines. It is a unit under the Ministry of Trade Industry, whose functions include investment promotion and industry planning. It also undertakes sectoral analysis, industry planning, and preparation of the annual Investment Priorities Plan. It also facilitates investment application, processing and approval through a "One Stop Action Centre." It also provides traditional services like granting incentives and project monitoring.

The Singapore Economic Development Board (SEDB)[14] was one of the oldest investment agencies in Southeast Asia, having been set up in 1961 as a statutory board under the Ministry of Trade and Industry. Since then, the SEDB has been mainly responsible for steering the growth of domestic industries particularly in the manufacturing and trade services. Its activities have been guided by its main focus which is to ensure a conducive and competitive business environment and to work with the government so that relevant infrastructure and manpower capabilities for the industries and businesses would be met. It has also provided a one-stop investment facilitation – from assisting investors to establish their businesses in Singapore, securing infrastructure and manpower, to connecting with regional business partners. Thus, SEDB has performed not only its conventional investment promotion and facilitation role, but also its economic developmental role.

The Board of Investment of Thailand (BOI)[15] is the principal investment agency in Thailand. Having been established with the passage of the Investment Promotions Act of 1977, it reports directly to the Prime Minister of Thailand. Its main functions include the promotion of investment in Thailand and providing business-related services to prospective investors.

---

[11] For more information, see Indonesia's BKPM website, http://www.bkpm.go.id

[12] For more information, see MIDA's website: http://www.mida.gov.my.

[13] For more information, see Philippine BOI website: http://www.boi.gov.ph.

[14] For more information, see Singapore's EDB website: http://www.sedb.com.

[15] For more information, see Thailand's BOI website: http://www.boi.go.th.

GEOGRAPHICAL PATTERNS OF FDI

As a general guiding principle, FDI is defined as 'investment that is made to acquire a lasting interest in an enterprise operating in an economy other than that of the investor.'[16] For statistical purposes, the International Monetary Fund defines foreign investment as direct (FDI) when the investor holds 10 percent or more of the equity of an enterprise, which as a rule of thumb, is usually enough to give the investor a say in the management of the enterprise.[17]

Indonesia

Table 7.1. shows the approved foreign investment projects in Indonesia by sources of origin as reported by Indonesia's Investment Coordinating Board called Badan Koordinasi Penanaman Modal (BKPM). By region, Europe is the largest investing group with a share of 39.4 percent in 1998, followed closely by Asia with a share of about 34 percent. A far third is North America whose share was about one-tenth of Europe's share. In 1999, we observe a significant decrease in Europe's and North America's shares while Asia's share markedly increased to about 60 percent. In 2000, we have a completely different picture as Europe's share rebounded more than five times, while Asia's share dropped to about half of its share in 1999. An important observation from Table 7.1 is the significant contribution of Northeast Asia mainly because of Japan, Taiwan and Korea. As a group, it accounted for about a fifth of FDI in Indonesia during the 1998-2000 period. By country sources, UK was the largest investor in 1998 whose share was even a lot more than the combined shares of the other three top investors, namely, Japan, Singapore and the US. But in 1999, both UK and the US were out of the top four investors, as Australia and Taiwan took the top two positions. In 2000, UK again took the top spot but Singapore and the US dropped to lower positions as the Netherlands and Germany garnered the third and fourth ranks.

Malaysia

Table 7.2 shows the approved foreign investments in Malaysia as reported by the Malaysian Industrial Development Authority (MIDA). By region, North America was the leading investor during the 1998-1999 period, with an average share of about 46 percent. However, its share fell in the year 2000 to about 38 percent. Asia was the second largest investing group in both 1998-99 period, but managed to take the lead in the year 2000 as it accounted for about two-fifths of the total FDI. Europe was consistently the third placer with an average share of about 18 percent during the 1998-2000 period. It even showed an increasing trend as its share more than doubled in the year 2000 relative to that of 1998. Within Asia, it is again interesting to note that Northeast Asia was a significant player as it accounted for about a quarter of the total FDI in 1998 and 2000. However, its share had more than halved in 1999 because of the reductions in Japanese and Taiwanese investments. As for

16 Hal Hill, "Foreign Investment and East Asian Economic Development," *Asian-Pacific Economic Literature,* Vol.4, No.2, 1990, p.23.

17 IFC, "Foreign Direct Investments," ... p.9.

country sources, the United States was the top investor accounting for about 40-50 percent during the 1998-2000 period. Japan took the second position with an average share of about 12 percent during the same period. The other top investors during this period were Taiwan (1998), Singapore (1998-2000), Netherlands (1999-2000) and Germany (2000).

Table 7.1. Geographical Distribution of Approved FDI in Indonesia (in mil USD)

Country	1998	% share	1999	% share	2000	% share
Total	**13563**	**100**	**10890**	**100**	**15413**	**100**
Asia	**4594**	**33.9**	**6486**	**59.6**	**3820**	**24.8**
- ASEAN	**n.a.**	**-.**	**n.a.**	**-**	**n.a.**	**-**
Malaysia	n.a.	-.	n.a.	-	n.a.	-
Philippines	n.a.	-	n.a.	-	n.a.	-
Singapore	1267	9.3	731	6.7	536	3.5
- Northeast Asia	**2247**	**16.5**	**2473**	**22.7**	**2878**	**18.7**
Hong Kong	549	4.0	77	0.7	105	0.7
Japan	1331	9.8	644	5.9	1954	12.7
Taiwan	165	1.2	1489	13.7	131	0.8
South Korea	202	1.5	263	2.4	688	4.5
China	n.a.	-	n.a.	-	n.a.	-
-Other Asia	**1079**	**8.0**	**3282**	**30.1**	**405**	**2.6**
Europe	**5346**	**39.4**	**773**	**7.1**	**5980**	**38.8**
- European Union	**5311**	**39.1**	**731**	**6.7**	**5938**	**38.5**
Belgium	12	0.1	10	0.1	0.5	...
France	8	0.1	23	0.2	65	0.4
Germany	71	0.5	87	0.8	960	6.2
Netherlands	412	3.0	49	0.4	1159	7.5
United Kingdom	4745	35.0	507	4.7	3645	23.6
- Switzerland	35	0.3	42	0.4	42	0.3
North America	**576**	**4.2**	**140**	**1.3**	**244**	**1.6**
Canada	8	...	3	...	2	...
United States	568	4.2	137	1.3	242	1.6
Australia	**85**	**0.6**	**2458**	**22.6**	**48**	**0.3**
Other countries	**2718**	**20.0**	**1006**	**9.2**	**4776**	**31.0**

Source of basic data: Badan Koordinasi Penanaman Modal as cited *in Indikator Ekonomi (Economic Indicators*), Busan Pusat Statistik, Jakarta –Indonesia, March 2001, p.58.

Philippines

Table 7.3 provides the data on approved foreign investments in the Philippines as reported by its Board of Investments. By region, Europe, North America and Asia were the top investors in the Philippines during the 1997-1999 period. While Europe accounted for bulk of FDI in 1997, its share fell drastically to 32 percent in 1998 and to 9 percent in 1999. The complete opposite was shown by North America as its share more than tripled in 1999 relative to 1997. As for Asia, its share more than tripled in 1998, but dropped to about a third in 1999. Table 7.3 also shows that Africa had substantial investment in the Philippines during the 1997-98 period. As for country sources, no country breakdown was available. However, it has been known that the United States has been a major investor in the Philippines historically. Japan was also one of the top investors.

Table 7.2. Geographical Distribution of Approved FDI in Malaysia (in mil RM)

Country	1998	% share	1999	% share	2000	% share
Total	**13063**	**100**	**12274**	**100**	**19819**	**100**
Asia	**4427**	**33.9**	**2366**	**19.3**	**8142**	**41.1**
- ASEAN	**1028**	**7.9**	**934**	**7.6**	**1861**	**9.4**
Indonesia	55	0.4	32	0.3	66	0.3
Brunei	1	...	...	...	...	...
Philippines	2	0.01	...	...	...	...
Singapore	968	7.4	902	7.3	1778	9.0
Thailand	2	0.01	...	...	16	0.08
- Northeast Asia	**3328**	**25.5**	**1383**	**11.3**	**4897**	**24.7**
Japan	1868	14.3	1006	8.2	2879	14.5
Taiwan	1001	7.7	267	2.2	916	4.6
South Korea	76	0.6	35	0.3	723	3.6
China	361	2.8	74	0.6	379	1.9
Hong Kong	22	1.7	-	-	-	-
-Other Asia	**71**	**5.4**	**49**	**0.4**	**1384**	**7.0**
Europe	**1543**	**11.8**	**2104**	**17.1**	**4847**	**24.4**
- European Union	**1382**	**10.6**	**1335**	**10.9**	**4755**	**24.0**
France	14	1.1	8	0.07	3	0.01
Germany	152	1.2	187	1.5	1655	8.4
Netherlands	628	4.8	772	6.3	2174	11.0
United Kingdom	479	3.7	192	1.6	747	3.8
- Switzerland	141	1.1	708	5.8	91	0.4
North America	**6475**	**49.5**	**5273**	**43.0**	**7494**	**37.8**
Canada	42	0.3	115	0.9	2	0.01
United States	6433	49.2	5159	42.0	7492	37.8
Australia	**117**	**0.9**	**52**	**0.4**	**130**	**0.7**
Other countries	**501**	**3.8**	**2479**	**20.2**	**793**	**4.0**

Source of basic data: MIDA, *Statistics on the Manufacturing Sector*, Kuala Lumpur: Malaysian Industrial Development Authority, 1994-98 issue; and MIDA, *Report on the Performance of the Manufacturing Sector* 2000, Kuala Lumpur: Malaysian Industrial Development Authority, February 6, 2001, p.124.

Table 7.3. Geographical Distribution of Approved FDI in Philippines (in mil pesos)

Country	1997	% share	1998	% share	1999	% share
Total	**58716**	**100**	**37299**	**100**	**21180**	**100**
Asia	7498	12.8	14571	39.1	2869	13.5
North America	10522	17.9	7998	21.4	13921	65.7
Central America	-	-	-	-	-	-
South America	-	-	-	-	1920	9.1
Europe	32335	55.1	11968	32.1	1990	9.4
Australia	296	0.5	267	0.7	3	0.01
Africa	4366	7.4	2198	5.9	39	0.2
Middle East	-	-	87	0.2	-	-
Others	3698	6.3	209	0.6	438	2.1

Source of basic data: NSCB, *Philippine Statistical Yearbook,* Manila: National Statistical Coordinating Board, 2000, p.6-17

Singapore

The EDB reports the amount of approved FDI in Singapore. However, the analysis here is based on the stock of FDI at end-1980, end-1990 and end-1999 (latest data available) as reported by the Department of Statistics in Singapore. By region, Europe, Asia and North America were the top three investing groups in Singapore during the 1980-99 period. While Europe and Asia accounted for about a third each, North America shared about a fifth of the total FDI in Singapore. Within Asia, the Northeast Asian group was been a significant investor as it accounted for about a quarter of FDI in Singapore.

On a country basis, the United Kingdom was the leading investor in Singapore in 1980 as it accounted for about a quarter of total FDI, followed closely by the US. A far third was Japan with a share of about one-tenth. However, in 1990, Japan overtook both the UK and the US as its share almost doubled relative to 1980. In 1999, Japan and the US maintained the first two positions, but their shares dropped to about 15 percent each. During the 1980-99 period, the other significant investors were Malaysia (about 4-6 percent), Hong Kong (but its share dropped from 12 percent in 1980 to about 3 percent in 1999), the Netherlands (whose share rose more than 7 times in 1999 relative to 1980), and Switzerland (whose share more than doubled in 1999 relative to 1980).

Thailand

The Board of Investments report the data on the approved FDI in Thailand. However, the analysis here is based on the actual investments as reported by the Bank of Thailand on a net flow basis (inflows minus outflows) given its availability. This is seen in Table 7.5. By region, Asia has been a significant investing group as it accounted for bulk of FDI in Thailand. From 51 percent in 1998, its share fell to about 40 percent in 1999, but rose to 67 percent in the year 2000. North America and Europe were the other leading investing groups in Thailand. Europe's share, however, dropped significantly to almost 7 percent in 2000 from a high of 40 percent in 1999. On the other hand, the North American share almost doubled in

2000 relative to 1999. Like in other Southeast Asian countries, the Northeast Asian group has been a major investing group as it accounted for about 25-40 percent during the 1998-2000 period, which was mainly due to huge investments coming from Japan, Hong Kong and Taiwan.

Table 7.4. Geographical Distribution of FDI In Singapore (S$ Million)

Country	1980	% share	1990	% share	1999	% share
Total	**11,201.7**	**100.0**	**49,830.6**	**100.0**	**150,451.9**	**100.0**
Asia	**3,659.1**	**32.7**	**17,301.6**	**34.7**	**40,367.1**	**26.8**
- ASEAN	**827.2**	**7.4**	**3,002.7**	**6.0**	**8,028.0**	**5.3**
Brunei Darussalam	33.8	0.3	71.4	0.1	202.6	0.1
Indonesia	71.1	0.6	245.1	0.5	1,441.3	1.0
Malaysia	684.3	6.1	2,109.7	4.2	4,956.7	3.3
Philippines	11.3	0.1	159.3	0.3	638.4	0.4
Thailand	26.6	0.2	417.3	0.8	762.0	0.5
-Northeast Asia	**2718.7**	**24.2**	**14154.8**	**28.5**	**31812.8**	**21.2**
Hong Kong	1,357.4	12.1	3,267.1	6.6	4,044.7	2.7
Japan	1,311.8	11.7	10,662.7	21.4	23,102.1	15.4
China	-	-	61.5	0.1	877.6	0.6
South Korea	-	-	-61.7	-0.1	724.0	0.5
Taiwan	49.5	0.4	225.2	0.5	3,064.4	2.0
Europe	**4,286.3**	**38.3**	**13,465.2**	**27.0**	**57,220.9**	**38.0**
- European Union	**3,709.4**	**33.1**	**10,564.3**	**21.2**	**40,255.4**	**26.8**
Germany	416.5	3.7	884.1	1.8	1,554.7	1.0
Netherlands	217.4	1.9	4,072.3	8.2	21,433.8	14.2
United Kingdom	2,947.7	26.3	4,639.0	9.3	10,479.9	7.0
- Switzerland	506.1	4.5	2,262.4	4.5	15,362.3	10.2
North America	**2515.7**	**22.5**	**11096.4**	**22.2**	**25895.7**	**17.2**
Canada	-	-	2,506.2	5.0	4,127.9	2.7
United States	2,515.7	22.5	8,590.2	17.2	21,767.8	14.5
Australia	**269.3**	**2.4**	**2,953.1**	**5.9**	**2,687.7**	**1.8**
Other countries	**471.3**	**4.2**	**5014.4**	**10.2**	**24280.5**	**16.1**

Source: Department of Statistics, *Foreign Equity Investment in Singapore*, Singapore: Department of Statistics, Various Issues

By country sources, Table 7.5 reveals that the top investors in Thailand were Japan, the United States and Singapore. After falling from about a quarter of total FDI in 1998 to about 18 percent in 1999, the US share of investment almost doubled in 2000. Japan's share showed a similar trend: falling from about a third in 1998 to about 14 percent in 1999 and then rising to about a quarter in 2000. Singapore's share more than doubled in 2000 relative to 1998. The other significant players in Thailand were Hong Kong (4th in 1998 and 2000) and Netherlands (1st in 1999).

Table 7.5. Geographical Distribution of Actual Foreign Investment in Thailand (on a net flow basis, million baht)

Country	1998	% share	1999	% share	2000	% share
Total	**209,888**	**100**	**134,592**	**100**	**107,281**	**100**
Asia	**107955**	**51.4**	**53385**	**39.7**	**72304**	**67.4**
- ASEAN	**23817**	**11.3**	**21260**	**15.8**	**24587**	**22.9**
Indonesia	111	0.1	46	0.03	37	0.03
Malaysia	711	0.3	1044	0.8	742	0.7
Philippines	320	0.2	123	0.1	0.9	...
Singapore	22674	10.8	20047	14.9	23807	22.2
- Northeast Asia	**84138**	**40.1**	**32125**	**23.9**	**47447**	**44.2**
Hong Kong	16571	7.9	8862	6.6	13645	12.7
Japan	60478	28.8	18558	13.8	26318	24.5
Taiwan	4073	1.9	4581	3.4	7466	6.9
South Korea	2799	1.3	205	0.2	-169	-0.2
China	217	0.1	-81	-0.1	187	0.2
Europe	**40648**	**19.4**	**54209**	**40.3**	**6960**	**6.5**
- European Union	**37570**	**17.9**	**51941**	**38.6**	**7201**	**6.7**
Belgium	1297	0.6	-1380	-1.0	-987	-0.9
France	10926	5.2	8983	6.7	-133	-0.1
Germany	4073	1.9	10973	8.2	2603	2.4
Netherlands	13836	6.6	24584	18.3	-3898	-3.6
United Kingdom	4815	2.3	7009	5.2	8248	7.7
- Switzerland	3078	1.5	2268	1.7	-241	-0.2
North America	**51928**	**24.7**	**24250**	**18.0**	**33396**	**31.2**
Canada	128	0.06	113	0.1	190	0.2
United States	51800	24.7	24137	17.9	33206	31.0
Australia	**1526**	**0.7**	**490**	**0.4**	**693**	**0.6**
Other countries	**7829**	**3.7**	**2256**	**1.7**	**-5802**	**-5.4**

Source: Bank of Thailand, *Quarterly Bulletin*, Bangkok: Bank of Thailand, Dec 2000, p.90

INDUSTRIAL PATTERNS OF FDI

Indonesia

Table 7.6 shows that the industrial sector was the major recipient of FDI in Indonesia as it had accounted for about three-quarters of the total FDI. Among all the economic sectors, the manufacturing sector is the most dominant having received about 50-70 percent of total FDI during the 1996-2000 period. Investments in the electricity, gas and water industry had been significant particularly during the 1996-99 period, but it dropped markedly in the year 2000. The services sector accounted for about a fifth of total FDI.

Table 7.6. Approved Foreign Investment Projects in Indonesia (US$ million)

	1996	1997	1998	1999	2000
Total Investment	**29,929**	**33,833**	**13,563**	**10,891**	**15,413**
Agricultural sector	**1522** **(5.1)**	**464** **(1.4)**	**998** **(7.3)**	**491** **(4.5)**	**443** **(2.9)**
Industrial sector	**21784** **(73.1)**	**25165** **(74.4)**	**10381** **(76.5)**	**9406** **(86.4)**	**10930** **(70.9)**
Mining, quarrying	1697 (5.7)	2 (...)	0.3 (...)	14 (0.1)	2 (0.01)
Manufacturing	16072 (53.7)	23017 (68.0)	8388 (61.8)	6929 (63.6)	10703 (69.4)
Electricity, gas & Water	3808 (12.7)	1839 (5.4)	1795 (13.2)	2310 (21.2)	0.4 (...)
Construction	297 (1.0)	307 (0.9)	198 (1.4)	153 (1.4)	225 (1.4)
Services Sector	**6533** **(21.8)**	**8204** **(24.2)**	**2183** **(16.1)**	**993** **(9.1)**	**4040** **(26.2)**
Wholesale, retail trade, restaurants, Hotels	1762 (5.9)	472 (1.4)	673 (5.0)	508 (4.7)	1671 (10.8)
Transport, storage, communications	695 (2.3)	5900 (17.4)	79 (0.6)	103 (0.9)	1219 (7.9)
Finance, insur., real estate, business services	3000 (10.0)	1398 (4.1)	1271 (9.4)	179 (1.6)	302 (1.9)
Community, social & personal services	1076 (3.6)	434 (1.3)	160 (1.2)	203 (1.9)	848 (5.5)

Note: Figures in the parentheses refer to percentage share of each sector to total FDI for each year.
Source of basic data: *Economic Indicators*, Badan Pusat Statistic, Indonesia, March 2001, p.55.

Malaysia

There is no sectoral breakdown of FDI in Malaysia. Table 7.7 only shows the industrial breakdown of the actual FDI in the manufacturing sector based on manufacturing surveys at end-1997 compared with that at end-1993. These data were collected from the 1990-94 and 1994-98 data series. The 1998-2002 data are not yet available at the time of writing. To make the data more meaningful for analysis, the sectoral classification based on capital intensity was adopted. It is interesting to observe that the bulk of FDI in Malaysia had been in high-capital intensive industries particularly in the electrical and electronics industry, and petroleum and coal products. The low- and medium-capital intensive industries shared about 20 percent and 25 percent, respectively. The more significant sectors were food manufactures, non-metallic products, and fabricated metal products within the medium-capital intensive group. The textiles and textile products, wood and wood products, and plastic and plastic products were the more significant sectors within the low-capital intensive sectors.

Table 7.7. Industrial Distribution of FDI (paid-up capital) in Malaysia

	End-1993		End-1997	
	Mil RM	% share	Mil RM	% share
Total	**13500**	**100**	**20665**	**100**
High -capital intensive	**6890**	**51.0**	**11329**	**54.8**
Electr. & electronic prods.	4207	31.2	6686	32.3
Scientific & measuring inst.	255	1.9	357	1.7
Chemicals & chem prods.	885	6.6	1202	5.8
Petroleum & coal products	883	6.5	1877	9.1
Basic metal products	660	4.9	1208	5.8
Medium-capital Intensive	**4025**	**29.8**	**5088**	**24.6**
Transport Equipment	539	4.0	675	3.3
Machinery manuf'ging	390	2.9	896	4.3
Food Manufactures	1,251	9.3	1185	5.7
Beverages & tobacco	472	3.5	578	2.8
Fabricated metal products	635	4.7	780	3.8
Non-metallic mineral prod.	738	5.5	974	4.7
Low -capital Intensive	**2585**	**19.2**	**4247**	**20.6**
Rubber products	455	3.4	552	2.7
Plastic products	433	3.2	568	2.7
Textile & textile products	825	6.1	1914	9.3
Leather & leather products	35	0.3	22	0.1
Wood & wood products	469	3.5	698	3.4
Furnitures & fixtures	95	0.7	103	0.5
Paper, printing & publish'g	131	1.0	217	1.0
Miscellaneous	142	1.0	174	0.8

Source of basic data: Malaysian Industrial Development Authority, *Statistics on the Manufacturing Sector,* Kuala Lumpur: MIDA, 1990-94 and 1994-98 issues.

Philippines

Table 7.8 shows that, in 1997, the services sector received about two-thirds of FDI in the Philippines because of the enormous investments in the public utilities for a share of about 57 percent. However, investments in the services sector fell drastically to about a third in 1998 and then to 6 percent in 1999. On the other hand, the industrial sector experienced a marked increase as its share rose by about three times to 94 percent in 1999. This was mainly due to a hefty increase in manufacturing investments which accounted for about 84 percent in 1999.

Table 7.8. Industrial Distribution of Approved FDI in the Philippines(mil pesos)

	1997		1998		1999	
Grand Total	**58737**	**100**	**37299**	**100**	**21180**	**100**
Agricultural Sector	**337**	**0.6**	**182**	**0.5**	**24**	**0.1**
Industrial Sector	**19385**	**33.0**	**28912**	**77.5**	**19844**	**93.7**
-Mining	4379	7.4	1332	3.6	161	0.8
-Manufacturing	8136	13.9	16380	43.9	17709	83.6
-Energy-related	6726	11.4	11006	29.5	1928	9.1
-Motor vehicle program	144	0.2	12	0.03	46	0.2
Service Sector	**39014**	**66.4**	**8386**	**22.5**	**1310**	**6.2**
-Public Utilities	33435	56.9	-	-	24	0.1
-Export traders	68	0.1	3	...	-	-
-Service exporters	65	0.1	-	-	6	0.02
-Tourism-oriented	376	0.6	140	0.4	-	-
-Infrastructure/ individual services	4903	8.3	7845	21.0	517	2.4
- R & D projects	9	0.01	-	-	-	-
-Environment protection	122	0.2	350	0.9	736	3.5
-Regional Headquarters	36	0.06	48	0.1	27	0.1

Source of basic data: Philippine Board of Investments, as cited in NSCB, *Philippine Statistical Yearbook* Manila: National Statistical Coordination Board, 2000, p.6-16.

Singapore

Table 7.9 shows the sectoral classification of FDI as reported by the Department of Statistics. While the industrial sector accounted for the bulk of FDI in 1980, its share showed a declining trend: falling to about 41 percent in 1990 and to about 37 percent in 1999. This was due mainly to the declining share of the manufacturing sector from about 57 percent in 1980 to about 36 percent in 1999. On the other hand, the share of the services sector reflected an increasing trend: from 42 percent in 1980 to 59 percent in 1990 and to 63 percent in 1999. The significant increase was experienced in the financial and business services sectors as their combined shares more than doubled in 1999 relative to 1997. This pattern is consistent with the long-term target of transforming Singapore into a financial and business hub in the region. It can be recalled that the services sector has accounted for about 60 percent of Singapore's GDP.

Thailand

Table 7.10 shows that the service sector has accounted for the bulk of FDI in Thailand for a share ranging from 52 percent in 2000 to about 70 percent in 1999. This was due to the large contributions of the trade and services sectors. Investment in financial institutions was about 20 percent in 1998, but its share dropped in the two subsequent years. The industrial sector accounted for about two-fifths of the total FDI in 1998 and 2000, dropping to 31 percent in 1999. The manufacturing sector continued to be the dominant sector during the 1998-2000 period.

Table 7.9. Industrial Distribution of FDI In Singapore (S$Million)

Industry	1980		1990		1999	
Total	**11202**	**100**	**49831**	**100**	**150452**	**100**
Agricultural sector	5	0.04	117	0.02	48	0.03
Industrial sector	6517	58.2	20317	40.8	55316	36.8
Mining & Quarrying	11	0.1	-44	-0.08	-14	...
Manufacturing	6340	56.6	19760	39.7	53893	35.8
Electricity, gas & water	-	-	-	-	-	-
Construction	165	1.5	601	1.2	1437	1.0
Services Sector	4680	41.7	29398	58.9	95159	63.3
Commerce	1800	16.1	6517	13.1	21996	14.6
Transport, Storage & Telecommunications	385	3.4	1230	2.4	4323	2.9
Financial, insurance, real estate, business services	2457	21.9	21531	43.2	68840	45.8
Social & Personal services	38	0.3	120	0.2	-70	-0.04

Source: Department of Statistics, *Foreign Equity Investment in Singapore*, 1980-89, 1990-92, 1998-99 (latest issue), Singapore: Department of Statistics.

Table 7.10. Industrial Distribution of Approved FDI in Thailand (on a net flow basis, in billion bahts)

	1998	% share	1999	% share	2000	% share
Total	**182.8**	**100**	**134.0**	**100**	**111.1**	**100**
Agricultural sector	**0.002**	**...**	**0.069**	**0.05**	**0.016**	**0.01**
Industrial sector	**80.6**	**44.1**	**41.6**	**31.0**	**52.3**	**47.1**
- Mining &quarrying	3.3	1.8	2.7	2.0	0.3	0.3
- Manufacturing	74.1	40.5	43.2	32.2	52.2	47.0
- Construction	3.2	1.8	-4.3	-3.2	-0.2	-0.2
Service Sector	**102.2**	**55.9**	**92.4**	**69.9**	**58.9**	**52.9**
-Financial institution	34.5	18.9	9.3	6.9	2.8	2.5
-Trade	34.1	18.7	38.8	29.9	22.8	20.5
-Real Estate	0.6	0.3	5.6	4.2	3.5	3.1
-Services	11.9	6.5	17.9	13.4	31.9	28.7
-Others	21.1	11.5	20.8	15.5	-2.1	-1.9

Source of basic data: Bank of Thailand, *Quarterly Bulletin*, Bangkok: Bank of Thailand, December 2000, p.90

MOTIVES AND DETERMINANTS OF FDI

From the analysis of geographical trends in the fifth section, we can conclude that FDI in Southeast Asia has come mainly from Japan, the United States, and the United Kingdom. The other significant players are Singapore, Germany, the Netherlands, and Switzerland. Table 7.11 also reveals that the top 10 foreign affiliates in the five Southeast Asian countries by sales were mainly Japanese companies (39 out of the top 50 TNCs). This is followed by the EU(5 companies)[18], US (3 companies), Singapore (2 companies), and USA/Hong Kong (1 company).

The question then is: what are the factors that can explain the inflows of FDI from these investing countries? We can use the various approaches discussed in section 2 of this chapter. The theory of the firm states that foreign firms want to maximize profits. The factor endowment approach states that foreign capital, through FDI, will flow from capital-abundant to capital-short countries where the rate of returns to capital would be higher. According to the eclectic approach, foreign investors certainly have ownership advantage as they possess monopoly over brand names, products, production processes, technology, excellent knowledge of the market and marketing techniques.

These leading investors have certainly generated an enormous amount of revenues and profits. Evidence is seen, for example, in the returns on foreign equity. However, Singapore is the only country which reports this kind of data as shown in Table 7.12. In 1980, the Dutch investors had the highest return of about 56 percent on their equities in Singapore, followed by the Americans (about 35 percent), Germany (26 percent), UK (24 percent) and Switzerland (19 percent). Japanese investors had a return of about 10 percent lower than Hong Kong investors' return of 17 percent. In 1990, the returns on equities of these foreign investors remained high particularly for the American and European investors. However, in 1998, the returns on their equities fell significantly. However, in 1999, while some investors experienced an improvement in their returns such as the Germans, Dutch, Swiss, and Americans, other investors continued to suffer lower returns. By industrial classification, foreign equity investments in the manufacturing sector generated higher returns particularly the electronics and the machinery sectors a shown in Table 7.12.

---

18 These were mainly from UK, Netherlands and Denmark.

Table 7.11. The Ten Largest Foreign Affiliates in SE Asia By Sales (million US$)

Company	Home Economy	Industry	Sales	Year
Indonesia				
.Japan Indonesia Oil Co. Ltd	Japan	Petroleum	1127	1992
.Lasmo Oil (Malacca Strait) Ltd.	United Kingdom	Petroleum	361	1991
.Indomobil Suzuki International,	Japan	Transport Equipment	356	1991
.International Nickel Indonesia,	Japan	Chemicals	223	1991
.Tembaga Mulia Semanan	Japan	Electrical Equipment	134	1991
.Mitsubishi Krama YudhaMotors	Japan	Transport Equipment	132	1991
.Panen Lestari Internusa (Sogo),	Japan	Distributive Trade	121	1992
.Bridgestone TireIndonesia	Japan	Rubber	110	1992
.Yamaha Indonesia Motor Mfg.	Japan	Electrical Equipment	108	1991
.Teijin Indonesia Fibre Corp.	Japan	Textiles	107	1992
Malaysia				
.Perusahaan Otomobil Nasional	Japan	Transport Equipment	1180	1993
.Shell Refining Co. Bhd	UK/Netherlands	Petroleum	882	1992
.Amalgamated Steel Mills Bhd	Singapore	Metals	656	1992
.Esso Malaysia Bhd	United States	Petroleum	635	1992
.Nissho Iwai Corp.	Japan	Distributive Trade	630	1992
.Marubeni Corp.	Japan	Distributive Trade	560	1992
.Genting Bhd.	Singapore	Diversified	444	1992
.Oriental Holdings Bhd.	Japan	Motor Vehicles	422	1992
.Rothmans Pall Mall (Malaysia)	USA/Hong Kong	Tobacco	373	1992
.HitachiSemiconductor Malaysia	Japan	Electrical Equipment	367	1993
Philippines				
.Pilipinas Shell Petroleum Corp.	UK/Netherlands	Petroleum	1159	1992
.Philippines Automotive Mfg.	Japan	Motor vehicles	244	1992
.Shell Gas Eastern Inc.	UK/Netherlands	Coal and petroleum	199	1992
.Philippine Automotive Mfg.Co.	Japan	Transport Equipment	166	1991
.Toyota Motor Philippines Corp.	Japan	Transport Equipment	161	1991
.Texas Instruments Philippines	United States	Diversified	159	1992
.Matsushita Communication	Japan	Electrical Equipment	140	1992
.Matsushita Electric Philippines	Japan	Electrical Equipment	127	1992
.Nissan Motor Philippines, Inc.	Japan	Transport Equipment	101	1990
.Sharp (Philippines) Corp.	Japan	Electrical Equipment	88	1992
Singapore				
.Nissho Iwai Petroleum Spore	Japan	Distributive trade	3064	1993
.Cosmo Oil International PteLtd	Japan	Petroleum	2187	1992
.Itochu Petroleum Co.(Spore)	Japan	Petroleum	1728	1992
.ITOCHU Petroleum co.(Spore)	Japan	Distributive trade	1512	1993
.Marubeni Singapore Pte Ltd	Japan	Distributive trade	1506	1993
.Hitachi Asia Pte Ltd	Japan	Distributive trade	1495	1993
.Marubeni International Petrol	Japan	Distributive trade	1300	1993
.Hitachi Asia Pte Ltd	Japan	Distributive trade	1155	1992
.Kanemasu Oil Singapore Pte	Japan	Petroleum	1037	1992
.Takashimaya (Singapore) Ltd	Japan	Distributive trade	905	1993

Table 7.11. Continued.

Company	Home Economy	Industry	Sales	Year
Thailand				
.Toyota Motor Thailand Co. Ltd.	Japan	Transport Equipment	1893	1993
.Marubeni Thailand co. Ltd	Japan	Distributive Trade	1704	1993
.Thai Oil Co. Ltd	UK/US/Netherlds.	Petroleum	1554	1992
.Mitsiam International Ltd.	Japan	Distributive Trade	1442	1992
.MMC Sittipol co., Ltd.	Japan	Transport Equipment	1188	1993
.Seagate Technology (Thailand)	United States	Motor Vehicles	826	1992
.Thai Honda Mfg Co. Ltd.	Japan	Motor Vehicles	434	1992
.Minebea Thai Ltd.	Japan	Electrical Equipment	381	1992
Thai Arrow Products Co. Ltd.	Japan	Transport Equipment	320	1993
Sukosol and Mazda Co. Ltd.	Japan	Transport Equipment	317	1993

Source: UNCTAD

We can also apply the eclectic approach considering the locational advantages of the host countries made available to the foreign investors. These investors have been able to access the Southeast Asian market whose population has risen from 160 million in 1960 to 202 million in 1970. Currently, the combined Southeast Asian market has a population of about 550 million. Moreover, the rising per capita incomes of the Southeast Asian economies has been an important incentive for the foreign investors. The Southeast Asian region also offers other locational advantages or 'pull' factors including abundance of high quality, low-wage labor, low transportation costs, generous investment incentives and political regional stability. However, some of these pull factors have begun to affect some foreign investors like the Japanese manufacturers. According to the Straits Times, 13 September 1996 issue, a survey of 977 firms revealed that most Japanese manufacturers cited labor-related issues and rising wage levels as the most pressing problem they had faced in the region. The survey was done by the Japan External Trade Organization (JETRO), which sent out 2200 questionnaires to Japanese- owned or joint venture manufacturers and received 977 replies. Respondents were involved in electronics and electrical equipment, metal, chemical, and pharmaceutical products, textiles and transport equipment. A tabulation of the results of this survey is presented in Table 7.13. These results are consistent with the study by Tham (1998).[19] Moreover, in order to attract FDI into the Southeast Asian region, their governments have initiated or sponsored the so-called "growth triangles" which include the SIJORI (involving Singapore, Johor in Malaysia and Riau in Indonesia), the IMT (Indonesia, Malaysia and Thailand), and the EAGA (East ASEAN Growth Area, involving Eastern Malaysia, Southern Philippines, Brunei and Eastern Indonesia).[20] In addition, the creation of the ASEAN Free Trade Area (AFTA) is another incentive to attract FDI into the region.

---

19 Tham Siew Yean, "Competition and Cooperation for Foreign Direct Investment: An ASEAN Perspective," *Asia-Pacific Development Journal,* Vol.5, No.1, 1998, p.9.

20 Hadi Soesastro, "Policies Towards Foreign Direct Investment – New Challenges Facing Asian Developing Countries," *The Indonesian Quarterly,* Vol.24, No.2, 1996, p.166. See also G. Naidu, "Johor-Singapore-Riau Growth Triangle: Progress and Prospects," in Myo Thant, et.al. 1994, pp.218-242.

Table 7.12. Returns on Foreign Equity Investments in Singapore, %

	1980	1990	1998	1999
		By investing countries, %		
United States	**34.7**	**20.7**	**6.2**	**11.4**
Europe	**25.6**	**24.5**	**8.7**	**17.3**
-UK	23.7	25.5	22.5	11.8
-Germany	25.5	23.1	-108.7	36.4
-Netherlands	56.4	19.8	11.3	21.6
-Switzerland	18.5	26.2	18.8	26.4
Asian	**15.2**	**15.2**	**-8**	**2.3**
-Japan	9.6	17.4	-3.5	6.6
-ASEAN	17.1	12.7	-4.5	1.9
-Taiwan	6.6	5.3	-14.2	-7.7
-Hong Kong	16.8	12.3	-14.6	1.0
		By sectoral investment, %		
Manufacturing	21.0	18.3	17.4	15.6
-Electronics	28.4	20.8	20.1	21.0
-Electricals	-	-	10.2	14.2
-Machinery	25.9	11.9	12.0	16.5
-Chemicals	19.5	27.9	21.9	10.0
-Food products	11.1	12.3	4.8	15.4
-Textiles	0.3	5.0	2.6	7.0
Financial Service	16.4	9.4	-8.5	5.0
Business Services	8.2	10.3	-5.5	5.0
Commerce	15.9	16.4	0.8	11.6
Construction	-13.8	-9.2	-23.2	-3.6

Note: (a)Returns on equity investment is a measure of the profitability of the equity investment, and is calculated as the ratio of the current year's earnings to the average of the stock of equity capital invested in the current year and the preceding year. See Department of Statistics, *Foreign Equity Investments in Singapore*, 1980-89, pp.14. Source: Department of Statistics, *Foreign Equity Investment in Singapore,* Singapore: Department of Statistics, Various Issues.

In the context of the FDI-cum-trade approach, since the 1970s, the Southeast Asian region has become, not only a production base to serve the domestic markets, but also a distribution base for export-oriented FDI. The domestic costs of production in Japan rose significantly as the yen appreciated strongly in 1985.[21] Japanese manufacturers then exported their industries by relocating their factories outside Japan including Southeast Asian countries where costs of production were lower. As Fukushima and Kwan (1995) stated, the three main factors that made this shift to the Southeast Asian region are as follows: (a) Japanese firms have already established themselves in the region, particularly in Singapore, (b) there has been successful technology transfer from Japanese electronic companies to the region since the 1980s, and (c) Southeast Asian countries are ready to receive the transfer of higher technology products and production process through investment in social infrastructures such

---

21 Because of rising production costs in the newly industrializing economies (NIEs) triggered by higher wages and currency appreciation in the late 1980s, the NIEs were no longer the major target for Japanese FDI.

as transportation network and the development of supporting industries for FDI firms.[22] Southeast Asian affiliates have produced manufactured goods, mostly intermediate parts and components which are then exported to parent companies in Japan for the final assembly of high value products and hence indicates an international division of labor. This process generates what has been known as 'boomerang effect.'[23]

Table 7.13. Results of JETRO's Survey

INVESTMENT FACTORS		
Here are the key factors influencing Japanese investment decisions in the ASEAN region (in order of importance)		
	Positive factors	**Negative factors**
Singapore	political and social stability, infrastructure, quality of labor force, foreign investment incentives, potential of domestic market, low labor cost	rise in wages, labor-related problems, exchange rate fluctuations, competition with other manufacturers and suppliers, unfavorable market conditions
Indonesia	low labor cost, potential of domestic market, political and social stability, quality of labor force, foreign investment incentives, infrastructure	bureaucracy/red tape, exchange rate fluctuations, tariff and customs procedures, taxes, rise in wages
Malaysia	political and social stability, infrastructure, foreign investment incentives, low labor cost, quality of labor force, potential of domestic market	labor-related problems, rise in wages, exchange rate fluctuations, difficulty in obtaining visas or work permits, competition with other manufacturers
Thailand	political and social stability, low labor cost, quality of labor force, potential of domestic market, foreign investment incentives, infrastructure	rise in wages, labor-related problems, tariff and customs procedures, exchange rate fluctuations, quality control
Philippines	quality of labor force, low labor cost, foreign investment incentives, potential of domestic market, political and social stability, infrastructure	labor-related problems, rise in wages, exchange rate fluctuations, poor infrastructure, tariff and customs procedures

Source: The Straits Times, September 13, 1996.

22 Kiyohiko Fukushima and C.H.Kwan, "Foreign Direct Investment and Regional Industrial Restructuring in Asia," in NRI and ISEAS (compilers), *Foreign Direct Investment in Asia,* Tokyo: Tokyo Club Foundation for Global Studies and Singapore: Institute of Southeast Asian Studies, 1995, p.7.

23 The 'boomerang' effect is a term to describe the impact on the Japanese economy of increased imports of goods resulting from Japanese overseas investment in manufacturing (Shinohara 1982 as cited in Meng Kng Chng and Ryokichi Hirono, *Asean Japan Industrial Cooperation: An Overview*, Jakarta: ASEAN Secretariat, Japan Institute of International Affairs, and Singapore: Institute of Southeast Asian Studies, 1987, pp.87.

Conclusion

This chapter discusses the geographical and industrial distribution of foreign direct investments in Southeast Asia. The top leading investors in the region are the Japanese, Americans, and British. The other significant investors are the Singaporeans, Dutch, Germans, and Swiss. In terms of the industrial analysis, the manufacturing sector has been the dominant sector as it receives bulk of FDI in Southeast Asia, except in Singapore, where the services sector has increasingly hosted more foreign investments. The various determinants of FDI are discussed including the profit maximization approach, factor endowment approach, the eclectic approach, and FDI-cum-trade approach. All these models were found to be highly relevant in explaining FDI in Southeast Asia.

Questions For Discussion

1. Why do foreign direct investments (FDI) take place? Discuss.
2. To what extent are FDI concepts relevant to the developing world? Discuss your answer with reference to Southeast Asia?
3. Among the Southeast Asian economies, Singapore is the most dependent on FDI. Why?
4. Would it be possible for Southeast Asian economies to grow and develop without FDI? Discuss.

Suggested Materials for Case Studies

Soesastro, Hadi, 1996, "Policies Towards Foreign Direct Investment – New Challenges Facing Asian Developing Countries," *The Indonesian Quarterly,* Vol.24, No.2, pp.161-180.

Ram, Rati and Kevin Honglin Zhang, 2002, "Foreign Direct Investment and Economic Growth: Evidence from Cross-Country Data for the 1990s," *Economic Development and Cultural Change,* Vol.51, No.1, pp.205-215.

References for Chapter 7

ADB, 'Foreign Direct Investment: An Explanation," *Asian Development Outlook,* Manila: Asian Development Bank.

Ahmed, Momtaz Uddin, 2001, "Foreign Direct Investment and Technology Flows in Asia and the Pacific Region in the 1990s: An Analysis of Trends, Patterns and Policies," in Behrman, J.R, M.Dutta, S.L. Husted, Sumalee, C. Suthiphand, and P. Wiboonchutikula, *Restructuring Asian Economics for the New Millenium,* JAI – Elsevier Science, pp.643-668.

Akamatsu, Kaname, 1962a, ''A Historical Pattern of Economic Growth in Developing Countries,'' *The Developing Economies*, The Preliminary Issue, No.1, pp.3-25.

Akamatsu, Kaname, 1962b, "A Theory of Unbalanced Growth in the World Economy," *Weltwirtschafliches Archiv*, Heft 86, Band 2, pp.523-544.

Chng, Meng Kng and Ryokichi Hirono, 1987, *Asean Japan Industrial Cooperation: An Overview*, Jakarta: ASEAN Secretariat, Japan Institute of International Affairs, and Singapore: Institute of Southeast Asian Studies.

Dunning, John, 1981, *International Production and the Multinational Enterprise*, London: Allen & Unwin.

Fukushima, Kiyohiko and C.H.Kwan, 1995, "Foreign Direct Investment and Regional Industrial Restructuring in Asia," in NRI and ISEAS (compilers), *Foreign Direct Investment in Asia,* Tokyo: Tokyo Club Foundation for Global Studies and Singapore: Institute of Southeast Asian Studies, pp.3-39.

Hill, Hal, 1990, "Foreign Investment and East Asian Economic Development," *Asian-Pacific Economic Literature,* Vol.4, No.2, pp.21-58.

IFC – International Finance Corporation, 1997, "Foreign Direct Investments," *Lessons of Experience*, No.5, Washington DC, USA: International Finance Corporation.

Ismail Md Salleh, 1995, "Foreign Direct Investment and Technology Transfer in the Malaysian Electronics Industry," in NRI and ISEAS (compilers), *Foreign Direct Investment in Asia,* Tokyo: Tokyo Club Foundation for Global Studies and Singapore: Institute of Southeast Asian Studies, pp.133-159.

Kerdpibule, Udom and Eric Ramsetter, 1987, "Foreign Investment Theories and Policy Issues," in Seiji Naya (ed.), *Direct Foreign Investment and Export in Asia,* Kuala Lumpur: Southeast Asia Central Banks Research and Training Center (SEACEN) and Hawaii: East-West Resource Systems Institute, pp.1-23.

Kojima, Kiyoshi, 1978, *Direct Foreign Investment: A Japanese Model of Multinational Business Operations*, New York: Praeger.

Kojima, Kiyoshi, 1987, "A Model of Trade-Oriented Foreign Investment," in Seiji Naya (ed.), *Direct Foreign Investment and Export Promotion Policies: Policies and Experiences in Asia,* Kuala Lumpur: Southeast Asia Central Banks Research and Training Center and Hawaii: East-West Resource Systems Institute, pp. 159-183.

Naidu, G., 1994, "Johor-Singapore-Riau Growth Triangle: Progress and Prospects," in Myo Thant, Min Tang, and Hiroshi Kakazu (eds.), *Growth Triangles In Asia:A New Approach To Regional Economic Cooperation*, Hong Kong: Oxford University Press, pp.218-242.

Ram, Rati and Kevin Honglin Zhang, 2002, "Foreign Direct Investment and Economic Growth: Evidence from Cross-Country Data for the 1990s," *Economic Development and Cultural Change,* Vol.51, No.1, pp.205-215.

Soesastro, Hadi, 1996, "Policies Towards Foreign Direct Investment – New Challenges Facing Asian Developing Countries," *The Indonesian Quarterly,* Vol.24, No.2, pp.161-180.

Tham, Siew Yean, 1998, "Competition and Cooperation for Foreign Direct Investment: An ASEAN Perspective," *Asia-Pacific Development Journal,* Vol.5, No.1, pp.9-36.

Thomsen, Stephen, 1999, *Southeast Asia: The Role of Foreign Direct Investment Policies in Development,* Working Papers on International Investment, Paris: Organization for Economic Cooperation and Development (OECD).

Vernon, Raymond, 1966, "International Investment and International Trade in the Product Cycle", *Quarterly Journal of Economics,* Vol.80, No.2, pp.190-207.

Internet Sources

Indonesia's Investment Coordinating Board, Badan Koordinasi Penanaman Modal (BKPM) website, *http://www.bkpm.go.id*

Malaysian Industrial Development Authority (MIDA's website: *http://www.mida.gov.my.*

Philippine Board of Investment (BOI) website: *http://www.boi.gov.ph.*

Singapore's Economic Development Board (EDB website: *http://www.sedb.com*)

Thailand's Board of Investment (BOI website: *http://www.boi.go.th*)

Chapter 8

REGIONAL ECONOMIC INTEGRATION IN SOUTHEAST ASIA: CASE OF ASEAN[1]

ABSTRACT

This chapter examines the regional integration process that has taken place in Southeast Asia through the ASEAN regional grouping. It analyzes the initiatives that have been undertaken by ASEAN to foster closer regional economic integration. It also identifies and explains the different factors which have affected the ASEAN integration process. Finally, it identifies ASEAN's linkages with the global economy at the multilateral, regional and bilateral levels including the present and future schemes which may impact on the ASEAN regional grouping.

INTRODUCTION

The governance of international trade on a multilateral level rests mainly with the GATT and its contracting parties, and now the WTO and its members. As the only international body which deals with the rules of trade between nations, the WTO is centered on its agreements, the legal ground-rules for international commerce and for trade policy. The agreements aim mainly to help trade flow as freely as possible, to achieve further liberalization gradually through negotiation, and to set up an impartial means of settling disputes.[2] The multilateral trading system is based on a set of fundamental principles which include non-discrimination, freer trade, predictable policies, encouraging competition, and extra-provisions for less-developed countries.

Article 1 of the GATT establishes the central requirement that signatory governments shall extend unconditionally to all contracting parties (members) any advantage, favor, privilege, rules and procedures that they give to products originating in or destined for any other country.[3] Thus, under this 'most-favored nation' (MFN) clause, no country is to give

---

1 Earlier versions of this chapter were presented as invited conference papers at the following institutions: Chulalongkorn University (2001, 2002), Vienna Institute for International Economic Studies (2003), and published as a journal article written jointly with Le Huu Huy, titled "Singapore and ASEAN in the Global Economy: The Case of Free Trade Agreements," in the *Asian Survey*, Vol.43, No.6, pp.908-928.

2 See WTO website: http://www.wto.org.

3 WTO, *Regionalism and the World Trading System*, Geneva: World Trading Organization, 1995, p.5.

special trading advantages to another or to discriminate against it: all are on equal basis and share the benefits of any moves towards lower trade barriers.[4] However, there are exceptions to this MFN clause such as Article XXIV of the GATT 1947, which is the principal agreement dealing with customs unions and free trade areas – a provision on regional trading agreements (RTAs). It provides a number of rules governing such agreements, including notification and review by the contracting parties acting jointly. Agreements must meet the "substantially-all-trade" requirement, and members of a regional agreement must have a trade policy with respect to third countries that is not on the whole higher or more restrictive than the individual policies prior to the agreement.[5]

Multilateral trade liberalization in the postwar period has been paralleled by a process of integration through regional agreements.[6] Nearly all of the WTO members have concluded RTAs with other countries. In the period 1948-1994, GATT contracting parties notified 108 RTAs relating to trade in goods, of which 38 in the five years ending 1994.[7] However, during this period, the West European countries were parties in 76 out of 108 instances. During the 1995-1999 period, 67 additional RTAs were notified, some of which in the area of trade in services. Out of 194 RTAs notified to the GATT/WTO, 107 are presently in force. These RTAs have at times been concluded by countries in the same geographic region, and in other cases, have involved countries in different regions. These RTAs include the European Community, the European Free Trade Area (EFTA), NAFTA, Mercosur, Australia-New Zealand CER, and the ASEAN Free Trade Area (AFTA).

This chapter broadly seeks to analyze the regional integration process that has taken place in ASEAN. The following section provides an analysis of the initiatives that have been undertaken by ASEAN to foster closer regional economic integration. The third section identifies and explains the different factors which have affected the regional integration process in ASEAN. The fourth section identifies ASEAN's linkages with the global economy, namely, at the multilateral, regional and bilateral levels including a discussion of the present and future schemes which may impact on the ASEAN regional grouping.

ASEAN ECONOMIC INTEGRATION

To promote closer economic cooperation/integration, ASEAN has undertaken both widening and deepening economic activities.[8]

---

4 WTO, *Trading Into the Future,* Geneva: World Trading Organization.

5 WTO, *Regionalism* …, 1995, p.7.

6 For an interesting discussion of the co-existence between multilateralism and regionalism, see Sung-Hoon Park, "East Asian Economic Integration – Finding a Balance between Regionalism and Multilateralism", EIAS Briefing Paper, February 2002, Brussels: European Institute for Asian Studies. Among others, he discussed instances in which regionalism is viewed as a stumbling block or a building block to multilateralism. For an earlier discussion of the same subject matter with reference to ASEAN, see Mohamed Ariff, "Economic Regionalism versus Multilateralism: Dilemmas for Southeast Asia?" Paper presented at ISEAS 30th anniversary conference on Southeast Asia in the 21st Century: Challenges of Globalization, Singapore, 1998.

7 WTO website: http://www.wto.org/wto/develop/regional.htm – Regional Integration and the Multilateral Trading System, printed on 01 October 1, 1999.

8 For a discussion of these regional initiatives, see Teofilo Daquila, "Towards Strengthening ASEAN Integration: Challenges, Strategies and Prospects", in Apirat Petchsiri, Alfred Kellerman, Charit

Enlargement

The ASEAN region expanded from ASEAN-5 in 1967 to ASEAN-6 in 1984 to include Brunei. In 1995, the admission of Vietnam enlarged the region to ASEAN-7 and then to ASEAN-9 in 1997 with the entry of Laos and Myanmar. The grouping saw its fifth enlargement in 1999 to ASEAN-10 with the inclusion of Cambodia. On a positive note, the expansion of the ASEAN region brings together some 550 million people and a regional income of about US$550 billion. The huge regional market and the rising per capita income of the ASEAN people offer tremendous trade and investment opportunities for the rest of the world. However, the expansion of ASEAN to include non-democratic countries was met with criticisms and harsh attitudes from the other countries. Unlike the EU which prescribes democratization as a prerequisite for membership admission, the ASEAN regional grouping does not impose this criterion following its policy of non-interference in domestic affairs.

Trade Liberalization

ASEAN has pursued efforts aimed at liberalizing trade through tariff reductions and lessening/elimination of non-tariff barriers. These measures (were already discussed in chapter 6) include Preferential Trading Arrangements (PTAs), the Common Effective Preferential Tariff (CEPT) scheme, and AFTA.

ASEAN has also undertaken measures to liberalize trade in services. As the region grows and per capita income increases, the ASEAN people demand more goods and services. More services and institutions have been created to meet this rising demand, which is reflected in the growing importance of the services sector, particularly, in financial services, transportation and communications. The ASEAN Framework Agreement on Services was signed by the ASEAN Trade and Industry ministers in December 1995 to liberalize trade in services in seven sectors: air transport, business services, construction, financial services, maritime transport, telecommunications and tourism. During the 4th ASEAN informal summit meeting in Singapore in November 2000, the leaders signed the e-ASEAN Framework Agreement which provides for the liberalization of intra-regional trade in information and communications technology (ICT) products and services by eliminating duties and non-tariff barriers in three stages - 2003, 2004 and 2005, for the original members. For Cambodia, Laos, Myanmar and Vietnam, the three stages will take effect in 2008, 2009 and 2010.

Investment Liberalization

ASEAN has also undertaken measures to liberalize foreign direct investment (FDI). First is the ASEAN Investment Area (AIA) scheme which will encourage greater private sector participation in welcoming foreign investors. The second initiative is known as the ASEAN

Tingsabadh and Pornsan Watananguhn (eds.), *Strengthening ASEAN Integration: Lessons from the EU's Rule of Law*, Thailand: Chulalongkorn University's Interdisciplinary Department of European Studies, the Center for European Studies, and TMC Asser Institute of the Netherlands, 2001, pp.77-87. For more recent analysis, see Teofilo Daquila, "ASEAN Economic Performance: Revisiting the Past, Looking to the Future," *Harvard Asia Quarterly*, Mass.: Harvard University, Vol. 6, No.3, 2002, pp.9-14, online exclusive.

Industrial Cooperation (AICO) scheme which allows joint ventures between ASEAN nationals and foreign investors whose products or services will be given tariff preferences. Third is a type of Growth Triangle sub-regional cooperation scheme like the Singapore-Johor (Malaysia)-Riau (Indonesia) growth triangle, popularly known as SIJORI. This scheme exemplifies the positive synergy of factor endowments and comparative advantage, whereby Singapore provides excellent infrastructure and skilled labor, while Johor and Riau provide land and lower-cost labor. The success of the SIJORI growth triangle has led to its expansion to include other parts of Indonesia and Malaysia, which is an indication of its positive spillover effects. This concept has been replicated in other parts of the ASEAN region. including (i) the East ASEAN Growth Area (EAGA) scheme which involves Brunei, Indonesia, Malaysia and the southern Philippines, and (ii) the inter-state areas along the West-East Corridor (WEC) of the Mekong Basin in Vietnam, Laos, Cambodia and North-eastern Thailand under the ASEAN Mekong Basin Development Cooperation scheme.

Financial Cooperation

There are also developments arising from the recent economic crisis which provide lessons for ASEAN in terms of the need to strengthen their financial co-operation. Some of the proposed strategies include the use of domestic currencies in trade settlements and the setting up of the Asian Monetary Fund (AMF) by Japan. The proposed establishment of the AMF, to be capitalized at US$100 billion, aims to provide immediate financial assistance to crisis-hit countries in the future. However, the United States dismissed the proposal, fearing that it would diminish the effectiveness of the IMF and its policies in Asia, and the AMF proposal was rejected in the fifth APEC meeting in Manila. However, Malaysia's former PM Mahathir brought up the AMF idea again during the World Economic Forum in Singapore in 1999 and a modified version of the AMF proposal was discussed in the informal summit meeting of the ASEAN Finance Ministers in Manila in 1999. More recently, a network of bilateral swap arrangements among ASEAN countries, China, Japan and the Republic of Korea has been negotiated to assist ASEAN members in times of temporary balance-of-payments crises. Following the agreement on the Chiang Mai Initiatives (CMI), ASEAN agreed to enlarge the size of the ASEAN Swap Agreement to US$1 billion effective in November 2000. Substantial agreements on the bilateral swap arrangements have been reached between Korea and Japan, Malaysia and Japan, and Thailand and Japan.

Factors Affecting ASEAN Regional Integration

Intra-ASEAN economic cooperation has proceeded very slowly particularly during the 1967-75 period. However, during the 1976 to 1992 period, some changes in the ASEAN machinery and more frequent summit meetings had improved the extent of economic cooperation. It was also during this period that specific areas and actions of economic cooperation were identified. However, it was only in 1992 following the Singapore Declaration that ASEAN heads of government formally decided to achieve AFTA and agreed on the enhancement of economic cooperation.

What then are the things that have worked in ASEAN, or equivalently, the strong points of ASEAN economic integration? What are those things that did not work, or equivalently, the weak points of economic integration?[9]

First is the ASEAN institutional machinery. In 1967, the individual member states of ASEAN were hesitant to accord it with strong powers over the members, preferring a high level of individual sovereignty.[10] Thus, this resulted in an organizationally loose structure which avoided the trappings of a strong regional organization. The supreme decision-making authority was vested on the Foreign Ministers of the five ASEAN states during the annual ministerial meetings held in the capital cities of member countries on a rotational basis. The initial structure consisted of the Annual Ministerial Meetings, the ASEAN standing committee, ad hoc and permanent committees and the national secretariats. The decentralized and overlapping bureaucratic structure generated some obstacles for ASEAN as an organization like delays, and many suggestions were never considered nor realized. Moreover, there was no high level body directly in charge of making decisions and executing economic policies. Thus, the narrow structure of the initial ASEAN machinery was one of the contributory factors to the low level of economic cooperation particularly during the 1967-1975. Having realized this, the institutional structure was expanded in 1976 during the Bali summit to include economic and other ministers, as well as the establishment of an ASEAN Secretariat in Jakarta to provide a central administrative and coordinating body. The ASEAN Economic Ministerial Meetings has been the decision-making organ for economic matters. Since 1976, the supreme decision-making authority is the ASEAN Heads of Government Meeting, also known as the ASEAN Summits, which were held as and when necessary.

Second is the consensus style. As ASEAN was established on loose foundations, it has developed and evolved through a cumulative, gradual process whose decisions and actions have been carried out on a consensus style, popularly known as the 'ASEAN way" of doing things which relies to a large extent on the personal approach in contrast to the more legalistic and structural ways in the western countries. The consensus approach is embodied in two Malay terms: *musyawarah,* the process of decision-making through discussion and consultation, and *mufakat*, the unanimous decision that is arrived at.[11] The consensus approach is viewed as a weak point of ASEAN as decision-making has been delayed due to differences in attitudes and views of member countries, and differences in their levels of development and economic structures. However, some have argued that the consensus approach brings the ASEAN member countries closer and that direct conflicts have been avoided. But even when a consensus has been reached, not all members are obliged to participate in the decision since ASEAN allows bilateral and other types of cooperative arrangements (like sub-regional growth areas). In other cases, ASEAN provides for a membership-minus-x principle in which only able members can implement the agreement at the time while other members may join when they are able to do so. In light of the impact of the Asian financial crisis in 1997/98, outgoing ASEAN Secretary-General Rodolfo Severino

---

9 For discussion of these problems, see Teofilo Daquila, "The ASEAN Experience of Economic Cooperation," Paper presented at "The East African Forum on the East African Community: Economic Aspects of Integration," organized by Friedrich Ebert Foundation, 27-29 Sept 1999, Kampala, Uganda.

10 For an excellent analysis of ASEAN's organizational structure, see Paul Davidson, *ASEAN: The Evolving Legal Framework for Economic Cooperation*, Singapore: Times Academic Press, 2002, pp.14-50.

11 Paul Davidson, ASEAN: The Evolving Legal Framework..., 2002, p.41.

has suggested that ASEAN needs to move away from a 'relationship-based' way of doing things and creating wealth to one that was more rules-based and market-driven.[12] Within ASEAN, a rationalization of the framework for economic cooperation and the development of rules to set the guidelines within which this cooperation can take place is occurring.[13]

Third is political commitment. During the 1967-1992 period, there were only four irregular summit meetings which took place in Bali (1976), Kuala Lumpur (1977), Manila (1987) and Singapore (1992). The holding of only four and irregular summits within 25 years since its formation in 1967 was an indication of the lack of political commitment. Having learned from this shortcoming, the summit meeting has been institutionalized since 1992 to take place once every three years with informal meetings in between. Outgoing ASEAN secretary-general Rodolfo Severino called for more political commitment within ASEAN in order to achieve greater economic integration. He said that ASEAN "seems to have stuck in framework agreements, work programs and master plans."

Fourth, the problems associated with various schemes and instruments of economic cooperation in industry, banking and finance, agriculture and trade. The early scheme of industrial cooperation through the ASEAN Industrial Projects (AIP) was relatively ineffective because of lack of feasibility studies, lack of financing, lack of political commitment, lack of private sector participation, and rigidity in equity requirements. Given these shortcomings, other schemes like AIC and AIJV had evolved through time providing for flexibility in the requirements allowing the participation of foreign investors and the private sector. On trade cooperation, the low utilization rate and hence the ineffectiveness of the PTAs was attributed to various problems such as a long exclusion list, too detailed disaggregation and inclusion of irrelevant items. With these shortcomings and having realized the need to enhance economic cooperation in the midst of rising protectionism in other parts of the world (like EU and NAFTA), the ASEAN heads of government agreed and committed in 1992 to carry out deeper and meaningful trade liberalization measures through CEPT to pave the way for AFTA in the year 2003.

Fifth, the dominance of national interests over regional interests also accounts for the low level of regional economic integration. ASEAN's economic performance has been shaped to a large extent by the national economic policies of their respective governments particularly on trade and FDI.

On the trade front, ASEAN economies have largely embraced free trade, but with varying degrees of openness as reflected by the differences in their tariff structures, the extent of protectionism and trade liberalization measures. Being a highly open export-oriented economy, Singapore has the lowest tariffs. Thailand has the highest tariffs, due to its ISI policy which protects domestic manufacturing industries. Indonesia, Malaysia and the Philippines have tariff structures somewhere between Singapore and Thailand. More open economies like Singapore have preferred a faster pace of tariff cuts than the more closed

---

12 Paul Davidson, *ASEAN: The Evolving Legal Framework...*, 2002, p.43.

13 Paul Davidson, *ASEAN:The Evolving Legal Framework...*,2002, p.158-159. Some examples of the agreements which are forming the "rules" of an evolving legal framework are: The Framework Agreement for Enhancing ASEAN Economic Cooperation, the Agreement on the Common Effective Preferential Tariff (CEPT) scheme for the ASEAN Free Trade Area, the ASEAN Industrial Cooperation Scheme, the ASEAN Investment Area, the ASEAN Framework Agreement on Services, and the ASEAN Framework Agreement on Intellectual Property Cooperation.

economies like Indonesia and Thailand. However, since most ASEAN countries rely on tariffs as a major source of government revenues, tariff reductions have proceeded slowly.

On the investment front, ASEAN governments have opened their economies to FDI to various degrees. With no natural resources and a limited domestic market, Singapore is the most reliant upon FDI. The Philippines, Indonesia, Malaysia and Thailand have natural resources and much larger domestic markets, and therefore could afford to be less dependent upon FDI. Indonesia and Malaysia are oil and gas producers and have benefited substantially from the oil price hikes in the 1970s. However, declining oil prices combined with the fact that oil is a non-renewable resource have convinced both Indonesia and Malaysia to diversify their economies and increase their dependence on FDI. Over the years, ASEAN governments have followed Singapore's experiences by relaxing regulations on investments and foreign equity ownership for export firms. Most ASEAN governments now allow 100% foreign ownership as long as the business produces mainly for exports.

ASEAN AND THE GLOBAL ECONOMY

ASEAN has been more historically dependent on countries/groupings outside the region particularly Japan, the United States and the European Union for trade, FDI, technology and foreign aid. For example, while intra-EU trade hovers around 50-60 percent of its global trade, intra-ASEAN trade has been around 15-20 percent of its global trade. As such, ASEAN has been linked more to the global economy particularly in the areas of liberalization, facilitation and cooperation through multilateral, regional and bilateral schemes.

Multilateral Links

ASEAN has been linked to the WTO. In ASEAN, Singapore hosted the first WTO meeting in December 1996. It brought together ministers and representatives of member countries. It was a very significant gathering as they came up with a crucial document known as the 'Information Technology Agreement' which will liberalize the information technology industry on a global scale. The WTO meeting is a victory of consensus and compromise between the North and South.

The WTO replaced the General Agreement on Tariffs and Trade (GATT) as a result of the Uruguay Round multilateral trade negotiation which lasted for seven years (1986-1993). The WTO aims to implement the results of this round, namely, (a) that member countries implement tariff reductions commitments in industrial products, (b) that quotas on agricultural imports and imports of textiles and apparel are replaced with less restrictive tariffs, (c) that the Multi-Fibre Agreement will be dismantled, (d) that trade in textiles and clothing will be integrated into the normal GATT rules, and (e) that the dispute settlement mechanism be strengthened. These trade liberalization measures have certainly brought both benefits and costs to the ASEAN region as it will compete with other countries in some products particularly in agricultural and textile products but can complement in other manufactures.

The WTO has also taken initiatives to liberalize trade in services. In 1995, the export of services was valued at US$1,234 billion. The EU is the largest service exporter with a share of 46 per cent. Accounting for a share of 17 percent, the United States offered to liberalize its financial sector by giving foreign companies unrestricted market access not only to existing operations of foreign companies but also to all foreign institutions and to new or expanded financial services. The ASEAN region accounted for 5.4 percent (US$67 billion) of the global exports of services. Singapore and Thailand were the main beneficiaries as they shared 44 percent and 22 percent of the region's service exports, respectively. The Philippines, Malaysia and Indonesia accounted for 14 percent, 10 percent and 9 percent, respectively.

Extra-Regional Links

ASEAN has been linked to the global economy through its membership in regional fora like the Asia-Pacific Economic Cooperation (APEC) and the Asia-Europe Meeting (ASEM). Through APEC, the ASEAN countries have been involved with two of its major trading and investment partners namely, Japan and the United States. In APEC, ASEAN has been considered as the cornerstone for the successful implementation of an open-regionalism strategy that would pave the way for the successful achievement of the goal of Bogor Declaration which is to free trade and investments in the region in 2010 for developed countries and 2020 for developing countries. In 1996, APEC leaders agreed to back a global deal which will eliminate most tariffs on information technology products by the year 2000 including computers, semi-conductors, software and telecommunications equipment. The global information technology package is worth US$500 billion on a global scale, with APEC members accounting for 80 percent of the total trade. ASEAN should be proactive and should lead APEC in realising this goal. APEC should complement, and not compete with the WTO.

ASEAN has also been linked with the European Union through the Asia-Europe Meeting (ASEM), which is a trans-atlantic and trans-pacific regional forum initiated by Singapore's former PM Goh Chok Tong. The first meeting was held in Bangkok in March 1996. As it brought together leaders of the ASEAN, EU-15, China, Japan and Korea, it was an important step towards more meaningful and enhanced relationship between Asia and Europe. ASEAN is also considered as the cornerstone of ASEM and it should continue to do so. ASEAN should push for the institutionalization of the summit meeting to put a greater political commitment and dedication from all leaders involved.

Bilateral Links Through FTAs

Given the slow pace of trade liberalization undertaken by the WTO on a multilateral level[14] and by ASEAN on a regional basis, and in light of the uncertainties arising from global developments, some ASEAN countries have undertaken or are considering bilateral

[14] In his speech titled "Regionalism in Place of or Together with Multilateralism" delivered before the Economic Society of Singapore on 9 July 1992, Professor Rolf Langhammer identified three strands of a weakening multilateralism. First, there was the decline of the American superpower in politics and of the loss of the functions of a "leading economy" in economics. Second, apart from lacking sanction mechanism, he cites two additional weaknesses: GATT mixes allocation targets and distribution targets by giving special and differential treatment to developing countries. Third, the heterogeneity of membership in the GATT has increased with the number of members increasing to more than one hundred, [*which hampers decision-making*].

Free Trade Agreements (FTAs) with countries outside the ASEAN. Singapore has concluded FTAs with New Zealand, Japan, EFTA, Australia and the United States. Singapore also has on-going negotiations with Mexico, Canada, Korea, Jordan and India. Other countries are also interested in FTAs. As for Malaysia, its Minister for International Trade and Industry announced that the Malaysian government is already studying the costs and benefits of forging bilateral FTAs, but those which are focused on services like telecommunications. The United States has also proposed FTAs each with Thailand and the Philippines. Australia is also negotiating an FTA with Thailand. Inspired by Japan-Singapore FTA, President Gloria Arroyo had officially proposed the establishment of an FTA during her third visit to Japan on 4 December 2002.[15]

Singapore's Bilateral FTA's

Singapore's bilateral FTA's can be grouped into three categories, namely, completed FTAs, on-going FTAs, and future FTAs (see Fig.8.1). On the first category, Singapore has completed its negotiations for an FTA each with New Zealand, Japan, the European Free Trade Area (EFTA), Australia and the United States. The *Agreement between New Zealand and Singapore on a Closer Economic Partnership (ANZSCEP)* was the first FTA concluded by Singapore in August 2000 after six rounds of negotiations. It was signed by New Zealand's Prime Minister (PM) Helen Clark and Singapore's former PM Goh Chok Tong on November 14, 2000, and has been implemented since January 2001. It was the second FTA for Singapore after AFTA. Launched in October 2000, the *Agreement between Japan and the Republic of Singapore for a New-Age Economic Partnership (JSEPA)* was concluded in October 2001 after 12 rounds of substantive negotiations. It was signed on January 13, 2002 by the Japanese PM Junichiro Koizumi and former PM Goh and went into effect on November 30, 2002.[16]

With the initiative floated in December 2000, the *EFTA-Singapore Free Trade Agreement* (ESFTA) was signed on June 26, 2002 by Singapore's former Trade and Industry Minister Brigadier-General (BG) George Yeo and Ministers of EFTA, after three rounds of negotiations. The agreement came into force on January 1, 2003.[17]

---

15 It is expected that the proposed Japan-Philippines FTA would go beyond the usual FTA to maximize the many areas of complementarity between them. President Arroyo cited examples like Japan can utilize Filipino health care workers given Japan's aging population and Japanese high tech firms can hire skilled young Filipino workers. For details, see *Philippine Star* online issue December 4, 2002: http://www.philstar.com/philstar/print.asp?article=103628.

16 The JSEPA comprises provisions for liberalization and facilitation, partnership and cooperation, and dispute settlement, among others. For more discussion, see section titled "JSEPA: a backdoor for Japanese products?"

17 The ESFTA is EFTA's 19th FTA and Singapore's 3rd after FTAs with New Zealand and Japan. It is a historical achievement given that it is the first FTA between Europe and Asia which is expected to hasten economic linkages between the two continents. EFTA consists of Switzerland, Iceland, Liechtenstein and Norway.

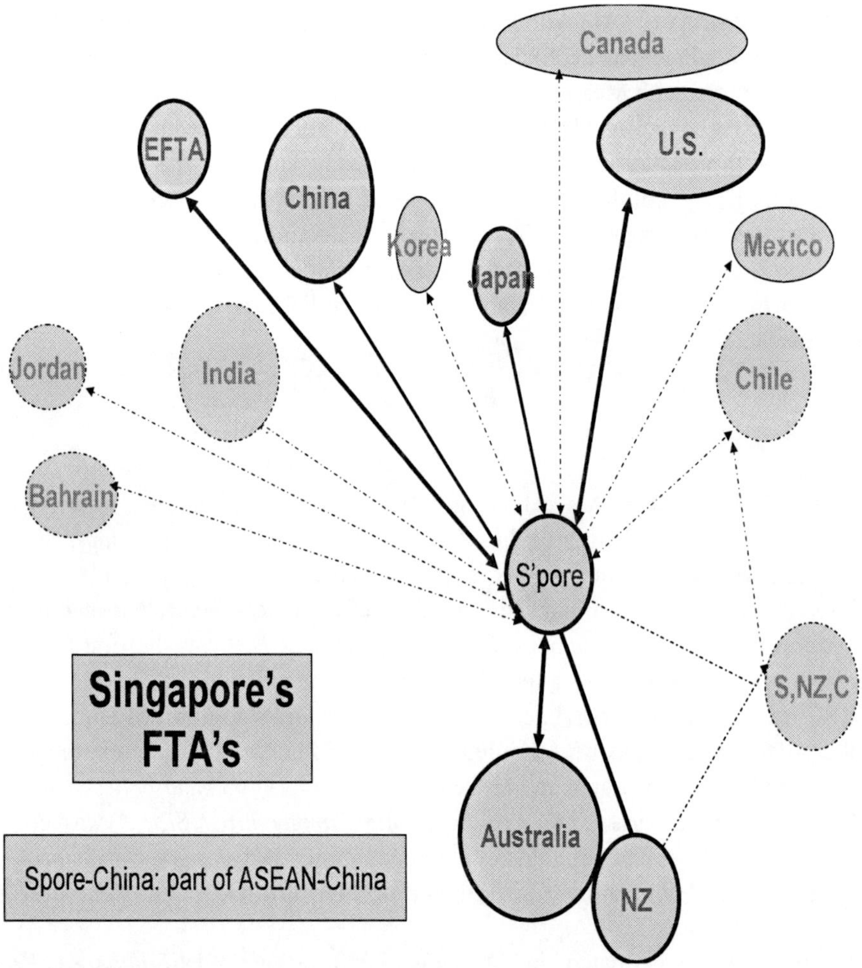

Fig. 8.1. – Singapore's Free Trade Agreements (FTAs)

During the APEC Summit 2000 in Brunei, former US President Bill Clinton and Singapore's former PM Goh agreed to commence negotiations towards the establishment of the *United States-Singapore Free Trade Agreement* (USSFTA). After several rounds of lengthy negotiations during a two-year period, some 50 negotiators from the Singapore side, led by Singapore's Ambassador-at-large, Professor Tommy Koh, had 'traversed thousands of miles locked in talks – in Washington, Singapore and London.'[18] The deal was completed in January 2003 with President George Bush formally notifying the US Congress that he intends to enter into an FTA with Singapore. It is the first FTA of the US with Asia.[19] The agreement passed smoothly through the US Congress. It came into force by the start of the year 2004. As Singapore is a regional hub for many American companies, the bilateral deal is viewed as a model for trade liberalization throughout the region which could pave the way for multilateral liberalization.

---

18 See The Straits Times, "How the FTA was won," November 23, 2002, p.28.

19 Singapore was the US 11th largest trading partner with total two-way trade in goods and services valued at US$38.8 billion in 2001. See The Straits Times, "Bush gives go-ahead for FTA pact with S'pore," February 1, 2003, p.A12.

On the second category of FTAs, Singapore has on-going bilateral trade discussions with Canada and Mexico. On June 5, 2000, Canada's former International Trade Minister Pierre Pettigrew and Singapore's former Trade and Industry Minister BG George Yeo announced the possibility of negotiating *Canada-Singapore Free Trade Agreement* (CSFTA) between the two countries. Three rounds of negotiations were already completed on a range of issues such as trade in goods, services, financial services, investment, government procurement, dispute settlement, and competition.[20] On September 13, 1999, Mexico's former President Ernesto Zedillo Ponce de Leon and Singapore's former PM Goh agreed in-principle to negotiate *Mexico-Singapore Free Trade Agreement* (MSFTA) which could draw the two regions (Latin America and Southeast Asia) closer together. Having completed four rounds of negotiations since July 2000, progress has been made covering areas like trade in goods and services, investment, and government procurement.

On the third category of FTAs, Singapore plans to commence bilateral talks with South Korea, India and the European Union. The Trade Ministers of Singapore and Korea jointly announced on November 14, 2002 about the creation of a study group to look into the scope of the *Korea-Singapore Free Trade Agreement* (KSFTA). The joint study group, consisting of government officials, businessmen and academics, commenced in January 2003.[21] South Korea was Singapore's eighth largest trading partner in 2002. Singapore's exports to Korea included S$734 million of integrated circuits and S$466 million of computers, disk drives, printers and peripherals in the period from January to September 2002.[22] While the Korean-Chile trade pact dragged on for three years because of agricultural concerns, the KSFTA is expected to be completed at a faster pace given Singapore's experience and know-hows in FTA negotiations.

In April 2002, India's former PM Atal Behari Vajpayee and Singapore's former PM Goh agreed to set up a study group consisting of senior Singapore and Indian officials to look into establishing a comprehensive economic partnership agreement which is expected to be far more wide-ranging than the regular free trade deals.[23] During his visit to Singapore in February 2003, India's former Deputy PM Lal Khrisna Advani said that "Singapore evokes admiration for the manner that it transformed its economy thanks to the vision of its leaders and enterprise of its people" and that "we *[Indians]* are exerting to replicate these attributes in our country" to make India a developed nation by 2020.[24] PM Goh visited India in April 2003

---

20 Having been asked about the relationship between APEC and FTAs, BG Yeo stated that the proposed CSFTA will help both sides of the Pacific closer together to achieve the APEC's Bogor vision of free trade and investments. In a symposium about Singapore's FTAs on March 7, 2003, Mr. Aubeck Kam, a director in Singapore's Ministry of Trade and Industry, pointed out that the proliferation of FTAs across the Asia-Pacific region could serve as building blocks to achieve the Bogor goals of free and open trade and investments in the region.

21 See The Straits Times, "Spore-Seoul free trade talks to begin next year," November 15, 2002.

22 The Straits Times, "Spore-Seoul free trade...," p.A38.

23 Trade between the two countries has been growing rapidly and hit an all-time high of S$6.9 billion last year. Singapore's former PM Goh Chok Tong stated that the EPA is expected to provide access for Indian companies in the ASEAN region while giving greater confidence to Singapore companies that want to invest in India. The agreement is expected to be sealed between the two countries within a year. See The Straits Times, "S'pore, India for economic partnership," April 9, 2002, p.1.

24 The Vajpayee's government undertook some landmark decisions in its push for economic liberalization. These included a program for the road network connecting the major metropolitan centers, a drive to develop the IT software industry, and a new plan to interlink the major rivers in India, and most

during which negotiations for the *India-Singapore Comprehensive Economic Cooperation* was launched.

Danish PM Anders Fogh Rasmussen told Singapore's former PM Goh Chok Tong during his visit to Copenhagen that he is in favor of an FTA between Singapore and the EU.[25] As Professor Jayakumar, Singapore's former Foreign Affairs Minister, stated, "Singapore remained convinced that one way to forge stronger links [*between ASEAN and the EU*] was through the conclusion of an EU-ASEAN free trade pact … and … that the clinching of a Singapore-EU free trade deal could be a first step towards a wider pact with ASEAN."[26] He further noted that "while the EU side was not yet ready to enter into free-trade agreements with Singapore or the *[ASEAN]* bloc as a whole, ASEAN's series of free-trade arrangements with China, India, Japan, Korea and the United States, struck a resonance with the Europeans."[27]

Given the benefits and potential opportunities offered by FTAs, Singapore, New Zealand and Chile have even moved on to a higher plane by jointly announcing a new trilateral FTA initiative during the APEC summit held in Los Cabos, Mexico in October 2002.[28] It was described as "a win-win situation" by New Zealand's PM Helen Clark, "path-breaking" by Singapore's former Trade and Industry Minister BG George Yeo, and "difficult but could be overcome" by Chile's President Ricardo Lagos.[29] It is viewed as a pioneering attempt at linking the Americas and the Asia-Pacific region to liberalize trade consistently with APEC and the WTO. This agreement will also pave the way for the three partners to access the three regions to which they belong – Latin America, Asia and the Pacific.

The Pros and Cons of Singapore's FTAs

In theory, FTAs come into effect when two or more countries come together and negotiate towards the removal of trade restrictions on goods and services against each other. FTA signatories enjoy the benefits which include the removal of tariff and non-tariff barriers which will lead to foreign exchange savings. Moreover, FTAs will give members greater access to their respective markets and therefore create a larger internal market which increases the degree of competition among FTA suppliers. A larger internal market also creates opportunities for exploitation of scale economies by allowing for a higher degree of specialization in production. The free flow of goods and services will allow countries to further capitalize on their comparative strengths and hence the optimal allocation of resources. On the strategic front, establishing FTAs could also help to anchor the presence of the signatories in their respective territories or regions. Moreover, FTAs could also be forged

importantly, the creation of a feeling of confidence and optimism that India can be a front-ranking nation. See The Straits Times, "S'pore and India plan talks on free-trade pact," February 4, 2003.

25 Denmark is one of the 15 EU countries which has been studying the possibility of a Singapore-EU FTA. See The Straits Times, "Denmark backs Singapore-EU free trade pact," April 18, 2002, p.6.

26 The Business Times, "EU, ASEAN pledge to boost trade, political ties," February 24, 2003.

27 The Straits Times, "EU and ASEAN ministers pledge closer trade and intelligence ties," January 29, 2003, p.A6.

28 The Straits Times, "Singapore, NZ and Chile go for 3-way trade talks," October 28, 2002.

29 The Straits Times, "Singapore, NZ and Chile…" p.A18.

for geopolitical reasons like serving as a confidence measure to promote harmony towards closer political integration.

While Singapore has always advocated the promotion of free trade on multilateral and regional levels, various factors have contributed to Singapore's bilateral trade policy. *First,* the pace of ASEAN regional integration is too slow, below what Singapore expects for its own benefit and for the prosperity of ASEAN. In particular, ASEAN countries have struggled among themselves to bring down their tariffs to achieve the ASEAN Free Trade Area (AFTA) by 2003.[30] Moreover, AFTA has lost its momentum due to the Asian financial crisis of 1997 and political disarray in countries like Indonesia and the Philippines.

Having been a founding member of ASEAN, Singapore is indeed committed to AFTA. However, in view of the slow-moving regional integration process, it is imperative for Singapore to seek fulfillment of its objectives through bilateral channels, to complement Singapore's multilateral and regional trade liberalization initiatives. Singapore's former PM Goh said that "those who can run faster should run faster...and should not be restrained by those who don't want to run at all."[31] Singapore's economic viability depends on its geo-strategic position as the port of call in the Asia-Pacific linking Europe, the Middle East, the African continent, the South Asian continent, through to the Pacific islands and the Americas. It is important to view Singapore's status as a bustling port of call. In reality, Singapore's port faces increasing competition from the developments of other port facilities in Thailand, Hong Kong, China and particularly Malaysia.[32]

Second, ASEAN has been slow in building free-trade linkages with the United States, Japan and the EU. In his meeting with the editors of 11 Asian newspapers at the *Istana* [Singapore's Presidential Palace], former PM Goh said that "we would like ASEAN to move faster; I'm impatient because I believe ASEAN is taking a lot of time in just looking at ASEAN, whereas it should be looking outside ASEAN."[33] PM Goh's view is valid since trade outside the regional grouping (extra-ASEAN) has been far more significant at around 70-75 percent of ASEAN's global trade during the past 2-3 decades. However, because of the weak economic conditions in Japan, US and the EU, ASEAN should latch on with the rising economies of India and China to avail of the benefits and opportunities from their linkages.[34]

---

30 The Agreement for Common Effective Preferential Tariff (CEPT) scheme leading to AFTA was implemented on January 1, 1993. The original members of ASEAN were expected to achieve the AFTA required tariff rates of 0-5% by the year 2003. During its 15th meeting, the AFTA Council announced that each of the original five members (Indonesia, Malaysia, the Philippines, Singapore and Thailand) had reduced tariffs to 0-5% on at least 90% of its tariff lines in the inclusion list. The newer ASEAN members are given a longer period to achieve this reduction in light of their current level of economic development. Each member of ASEAN has a 10-year time frame of tariff reduction program under AFTA. Vietnam is targeted to fully implement AFTA in 2006, while the target year for Laos and Myanmar is 2008, and 2010 for Cambodia.

31 Asian Economic News, "Singapore free trade pact worrisome, Mahathir says," March 5, 2001.

32 Singapore has faced growing competition from the Malaysian Port of Tanjung Pelepas (PTP) which lured away Danish Maersk Sealand in 2000 and Taiwan's largest shipping company, Evergreen Marine in 2002. See The Straits Times, "PSA's cargo volume down 8.9% last year," January 19, 2002.

33 The Straits Times, "ASEAN 'slow' on free-trade links," May 3, 2002, p.1.

34 Despite being fierce competitor in some sectors, China's growth and prosperity will benefit ASEAN in some ways. ***First,*** ASEAN can zoom in on China's growing middle-class who will demand more foreign goods and more foreign tours. For example, Singapore's booming two-way trade with China posted a significant increase of 39.5 percent in non-oil domestic exports in 2002 to S$6.2 billion, with petrochemicals, electronics and precision engineering products as main exports to China. ***Second,***

Third, there has been greater progress in the trade liberalization and enlargement activities in the Western Hemisphere such as the creation of the North American Free Trade Agreement (NAFTA) which encompasses the US, Canada and Mexico; the widening of the EU to include some Central and Eastern European countries; and the establishment of the Free Trade Area of Americas (FTAA) in 2005 to include North, South and Central Americas. These developments were emphasized in a speech delivered by Ms. Ng Bee Kim, director of Singapore's Ministry of Trade and Industry (MTI) and Singapore's chief negotiator for EFTA-Singapore FTA:

> We argued that with the worldwide trend towards FTAs, we could not afford to be left out of the game. The EU, already a huge FTA in itself, was in the process of enlargement. The EU also has FTAs with many Central and East European, African and South American countries. The US, Canada and Mexico have NAFTA. And then you have the massive and ambitious Free Trade Area of the Americas (or FTAA), whereby more than 30 North and South American countries intend to form the world's largest FTA. We felt that these compelling developments merited a refinement of our trade policy. If, through FTAs, everyone else was part of a selective club where the members got special trading privileges, then Singapore had better ensure that we had membership too. Otherwise, our *[Singapore's]* companies would be seriously disadvantaged.[35]

Fourth, Singapore's FTAs are expected to serve both economic and strategic interests. On the economic front, FTAs could provide certain predictability for Singapore businessmen and investors, lower barriers to trade and investment, and open up considerable opportunities for Singapore's business community. As Ms Ng Bee Kim of Singapore's Ministry of Trade and Industry declared:

> FTAs could achieve the following: Reduced tariffs would save costs for our exporters. Our companies could be guaranteed access to the services markets of other countries. All other sorts of barriers that our companies faced in selling goods and services to foreign markets could be reduced or eliminated. Having solid investment rules would also be an added attraction for MNCs to set up shop and invest in Singapore, creating jobs for our people in the process.[36]

Fifth, Singapore's FTAs could promote the liberalization and integration of regional markets and hasten global free trade within the context of the WTO. On January 17, 2000,

---

ASEAN exports to China are already bigger than the region's exports to any other part of the world as pointed out by Mr Tharman Shanmugaratnam, Singapore's Senior Minister of State for Trade and Industry and Education. ***Third,*** the number of tourists from China who visited ASEAN had increased by 30-35 percent a year including 400,000 Chinese visitors to Malaysia in 2001. Tourist arrivals in Singapore from China in October 2002 rose by 35.4 percent. Vietnam received over 700,000 Chinese tourists in 2002. ***Fourth***, Malaysia's former PM Dr Mahathir Mohamad said that there would be some products that China cannot produce that ASEAN could capitalize on like the potential huge demand for paper and palm oil products. (See The Straits Times, "ASEAN must latch on to China's growth," May 7, 2002, p.A6, and The Straits Times, "Chinese tourists heading for Southeast Asia," December 14, 2002, p.A2),

35 Taken from her speech delivered in a seminar on FTAs organized by the Icelandic Chambers of Commerce, June 24, 2002. See Singapore's MTI website: < http://www.mti.gov.sg/public/FTA/frm_FTA_Default.asp?sid=37&cid=1183 >

36 See Singapore's MTI website: < http://www.mti.gov.sg/public/FTA/frm_FTA_Default.asp?sid=37&cid=1183 >

Singapore's former Minister of Trade and Industry, BG George Yeo, was asked if Singapore's pursuit of bilateral FTAs reflects Singapore's dissatisfaction with the pace of global trade liberalization. He replied that 'to some extent, yes" and warned that the failure of the WTO Ministerial Meeting in Seattle may cause the momentum of trade liberalization to falter and embolden protectionist measures.[37] Also, when asked in a Singapore symposium about how Singapore's pursuit of bilateral FTAs may affect Singapore's WTO commitments, Mr. Raymond Lim, Singapore's Minister of State for Foreign Affairs and Trade and Industry, said that 'both are equally important and resources are dedicated to both, and that they are not mutually exclusive.'[38] On another occasion, Mr. Lim emphasized that the pursuit of bilateral arrangements is parallel and complementary to the multilateral system.[39] Moreover, Mr. Chan Beng Seng, Deputy Director of Singapore's Ministry of Trade and Industry, maintained that Singapore would always focus on multilateral trade negotiations whereas FTAs would constitute a complementary and dynamic force. Mr. Khaw Boon Wan, former head of Singapore's Trade and Industry Ministry, also believed that suitably designed regional and bilateral pacts could stimulate further global trade liberalization in the WTO.[40]

Singapore's FTAs also contain a strategic angle. Establishing FTAs with various countries around the world could help to anchor the presence of these countries in the region, and keep Singapore and ASEAN on their radar screen. This is especially important for a small nation like Singapore.

However, Singapore's dual move towards AFTA and FTAs has been quite controversial among its ASEAN fellows. There have been concerns that such FTAs may undermine the strength of AFTA and complicate future negotiations of ASEAN with other strategic partners like China and Japan. Malaysia's Foreign Minister Syed Hamid Albar said that "when we do something outside the ASEAN context which could weaken the organization, we must think twice."[41] Mr. Jose Ampeso, a Filipino diplomat who was formerly based at the Philippine Embassy in Singapore, stressed that a FTA, like the one between Singapore and Japan, could undermine the strength of AFTA as the rest of ASEAN would perceive Singapore as Japan's favorite trading partner.

Singapore's go-it-alone move has been viewed by others as against the spirit of ASEAN. While no sanctions are imposed on Singapore's participation in trade negotiation with countries outside the ASEAN regional grouping, Singapore should not ignore the political, social, cultural and economic implications of its policies including FTAs. For instance, Malaysia has expressed its criticisms against Singapore's FTA policy.[42] According to the

---

37 See The Business Times, "Bilateral pacts could have catalytic effects: BG Yeo," January 18, 2000.

38 "Singapore's position has always been that FTAs create the 'competitive dynamics' towards greater liberalization. Moreover, FTAs represent 'competitive liberalization' rather than "competitive protectionism." See The Straits Times, "S'pore values both WTO deals, FTAs," February 21, 2003, p.A18.

39 Speech delivered in an International Symposium on "FTAs: JSEPA and Beyond," organized by the Japan Economic Foundation and the Singapore Institute of International Affairs, held in Singapore on March 7, 2003.

40 Hardev Kaur, "Amid globalization trend, Pacific Rim sees a bellweather on bilateral trade," *The WorldPaper,* [accessed 21 April 2003] < http://www.worldpaper.com/2001/may01/tradeblocs4.html >

41 Hardev Kaur, "By reaching out."

42 Prior to her independence in 1965, Singapore was part of the Federation of Malaya. Singapore is connected to Malaysia in the north by a causeway carrying road, rail and water supply links. Malaysia has always been Singapore's major trading partner. However, their relationship has been strained

Malaysian Foreign Minister, Syed Hamid Albar, "Singapore may not have done anything wrong in legal terms but morally, the *[Singapore]* Republic's action showed that it had undermined friendship in ASEAN."[43] Moreover, a Malaysian newspaper, *Berita Harian Malaysia*, argued that Singapore's FTA with non-ASEAN countries could "provide a third route or back door for them to penetrate AFTA markets."[44]

More interestingly during a lunch talk before the members of the Singapore International Chamber of Commerce, Malaysia's Minister of International Trade and Industry, Rafidah Aziz, highlighted that Singapore's special trade pacts with several countries are not FTAs but bilateral agreements.[45] In her opinion, there is a huge difference between an FTA and a bilateral agreement. An FTA involves tariff negotiations, but a bilateral agreement does not as it is only concerned with trade facilitation and the promotion of trade.[46] With her definition of bilateral trade agreement, Ms Rafidah said that "all of us do that" which presumably refers to all trading nations in the world including ASEAN. She further argued that if trade negotiation is undertaken by an ASEAN member country including offers of tariff cuts to a non-ASEAN country, the same offers should be made to the rest of ASEAN and this could therefore nullify the benefit of having bilateral FTAs because the rest of ASEAN could also benefit.[47] She further stated that the non-ASEAN country being offered concessions cannot come into ASEAN through the bilateral agreement because of the ASEAN local content rule of at least 40 percent. When asked what if Singapore's bilateral trade pacts with various countries had tariff negotiations, she said that "… they [Singapore and her bilateral partners] have to go back to ASEAN provisions, and the ASEAN Secretariat will alert them on this … then whatever provisions in the Act will then apply."[48]

However, by now, it should be clear that Singapore's bilateral trade agreements do in fact involve trade negotiations and tariff cuts. With the passing of time, Malaysia's earlier stance against Singapore's bilateral FTAs has changed given Ms. Rafidah Aziz's announcement that the Malaysian government is already studying the costs and benefits of forging bilateral FTAs, but those which are focused on services like telecommunications. Malaysia's former PM Dr. Mahathir Mohamad also announced during his visit to Tokyo in December 2002 that his country would be having an FTA with Japan.[49] The proliferation of FTAs and their benefits and opportunities may have led to Malaysia's policy-makers taking a second look at bilateral pacts.

---

because of various historical disputes over several overlapping territorial claims, border customs and the negotiation of a new agreement for Malaysia to supply water to Singapore.

43 The Hindu, "Malaysia Cautions on Trade Pacts," November 23, 2000.

44 The Business Times, "Singapore won't be back door to AFTA," May 3, 2001.

45 The Business Times, "S'pore's trade pacts are not FTAs," October 12, 2001.

46 The Business Times, "S'pore's trade pacts," p.7.

47 The Business Times, "S'pore's trade pacts," p.7.

48. According to Ms Rafidah Aziz, a FTA would be subject to rules agreed by the ASEAN countries under the two regional arrangements – the Common Effective Preferential Treatment (CEPT) scheme and the ASEAN Investment Area (AIA). The CEPT scheme enables tariff negotiations under AFTA. See The Business Times, "S'pore's trade pacts," p.7

49 The Business Times, "The paradox of Asia's FTAs," December 18, 2002. Japan is Malaysia's second most important trading partner after the United States. Bilateral trade between Japan and Malaysia reached a total of RM99 billion (S$46 billion) in 2001. Japan is also the second largest foreign investor in Malaysia. See The Straits Times, "Malaysia aims for first free-trade deal with Japan," December 13, 2002, p.A22.

Towards ASEAN's Bilateral FTAs

Given the different stages of policy developments among ASEAN countries, the convergence towards full trade liberalization could be a long way to go unless ASEAN countries, either individually or jointly, do something. In this context, aimed at complementing her regional and global trade liberalization policies, Singapore, as discussed in the previous section, has concluded several FTAs, has on-going trade negotiations, and intends to establish more FTAs. For example, the Singapore–US bilateral FTA is expected to benefit not only Singapore but also the other ASEAN countries, like Indonesia, as Singapore's exports to the US can make use of ASEAN-manufactured components.[50] As such, Singapore's FTA could create a win-win environment for ASEAN with more trade opportunities as well as economic and political stability. While the process for ASEAN regional integration is irreversible, AFTA members will benefit from Singapore's bilateral FTAs once they are catalyzed by such an impetus to restructure their economies and external trade to cope with the new challenges of a globally competitive world.

It is interesting to observe that other ASEAN countries are also keen in forging FTAs. As stated earlier, Malaysia is now considering to form a bilateral FTA with Japan. Also inspired by the Japan-Singapore FTA, Philippine President Gloria Arroyo officially proposed the establishment of a FTA during her third visit to Japan on December 4, 2002.[51] The United States has also proposed bilateral FTAs each with Thailand and the Philippines. Australia is also working towards commencing negotiations for an FTA with Thailand. In addition to planned FTAs between some ASEAN member countries and non-ASEAN countries, the ASEAN regional grouping itself is keen in establishing FTAs with countries outside the regional grouping like China, US and India because of the potential benefits and opportunities offered by FTAs.

During the ASEAN-China summit in November 2000, China's former Premier Zhu Rongji first proposed the establishment of the *ASEAN-China Free Trade Area* (ACFTA). It was mainly for strategic and economic reasons.[52] At the November 2001 ASEAN+China Summit, the leaders agreed to start negotiations for the ACFTA and to establish it within 10 years. After six rounds of negotiations, the Framework Agreement on Comprehensive Economic Cooperation between ASEAN and the People's Republic of China was signed by the leaders on November 4, 2002 in Phnom Penh, Cambodia. The agreement includes provisions for cooperation in economic liberalization as well as economic cooperation. The central liberalization element in the agreement is the "early harvest" in which ASEAN and China are committed to reduce tariffs for early harvest products mainly agricultural products.

---

50 The Straits Times, "FTA 'customs union' to benefit Southeast Asia, " March 17, 2002

51 It is expected that the proposed Japan-Philippines FTA could be beyond the usual FTA to maximize the many areas of complementarity between them. President Arroyo cited examples like Japan can utilize Filipino health care workers given Japan's aging population and Japanese high tech firms can hire skilled young Filipino workers. For details, see "Arroyo pushes free trade with Japan," *Philippine Star,* December 4, 2002:

52 Razeen Sally stated that "both political and economic factors lie behind the new form of regionalism – the formation of bilateral FTAs. China views FTAs as a means to exercise strategic leadership in the East Asian region. The economic motivation are mostly defensive. With the WTO being stuck in the drift and deadlock over the past few years, there is a race to secure preferential access to the markets of the major powers, and to defuse trade tension by locking into strong bilateral and regional partnerships." See The Straits Times, "Asia gets onto bandwagon of regionalism," January 28, 2003, p.16.

Tariffs on these products will be eliminated over three years, beginning January 1, 2004. When concluded, ACFTA will be the largest FTA in the world with a regional GDP of US$2 trillion. It is expected that ASEAN could attract FDI in the region to serve the Chinese market. Moreover, with a huge market of 1.2 billion people, China promises an export boom for ASEAN as the latter's exports to China was estimated to grow by almost 50 percent.

Within days after the ASEAN-China FTA was formally inked, the United States announced the *Enterprise for ASEAN Initiative* (EAI) which could give ASEAN countries broader access to the US market. It will be based on the high standards set in the US-Singapore FTA. The EAI offers prospects of bilateral free trade pacts between the US and ASEAN countries which are WTO members. Should the EAI be implemented, ASEAN countries could penetrate the US markets more for its goods and services. However, Dr Frank-Jurgen Richter, the World Economic Forum's director for Asia, argued that the US's EAI initiative was mainly to counterbalance a rising China and that the US does not want to be left out in the cold. Moreover, given that APEC's free trade agenda is not moving as fast as it should, he predicts that APEC will be set back by the EAI – the US may believe that it can achieve more with the ASEAN economies through the EAI than with a sluggish APEC.[53]

Japanese PM Junichiro Koizume and the ASEAN leaders signed the *ASEAN-Japan Comprehensive Economic Partnership* (AJCEP) deal during the 8th ASEAN summit in Cambodia on November 10, 2002. According to Mr. Tsugami, a senior fellow at Japan's Research Institute of Economy, Trade and Industry (RIETI), this announcement was viewed as Japan's immediate response to the launching of the China-ASEAN FTA negotiation exactly a year ago which caught many Japanese political and business leaders by surprise.[54] It was a shocking news to Japan and that some sentiments which prevailed in Japan then were the fear that China might exclude Japan from the East Asian economic development and political circle, the question of why ASEAN countries abandon their "balancing diplomacy between major powers in the region," and the fear that Japan could be further left behind from the East Asian move because of the delay in the much needed domestic reforms.[55]

Japan and ASEAN have a combined population of 590 million (11 percent of the world's total population) and a combined GDP of US$4.9 trillion (18 percent of the world's total GDP). Unlike China's push for free trade, the AJCEP focuses on human resource development and investment promotion. Unlike ASEAN-China FTA, Japan's proposal will be implemented based on bilateral deals as any ASEAN member could commence talks with Japan to form a bilateral pact. Japan has already concluded an FTA with Singapore, and intends to form similar arrangements with Thailand, the Philippines, Indonesia and Malaysia.

India's former PM Atal Behari Vajpayee offered to commence negotiations for an *ASEAN-India Free Trade Area* (AIFTA) which could be completed in 10 years. He

53 The Business Times, "The paradox of Asia's FTAs," December 18, 2002.

54 Toshiya Tsugami, "On ASEAN-China Free Trade Agreement – a personal view from Japan," Presented at a symposium on "FTAs: JSEPA and Beyond", organized by the Japan Economic Foundation and Singapore Institute of International Affairs, Singapore, March 7, 2003.

55 However, several counter-sentiments were cited as follows: (a) that it was Japan who shocked China first with its idea of launching "Japan-Korea FTA" in 1998 and JSEPA in 1999, (b) that it is not fair for Japan to complain to ASEAN for their "China shift" because Japan is shifting towards China more rapidly, (c) that ASEAN's move does not mean ignoring its "balancing diplomacy" but more of an indication to Japan to accelerate its economic reforms, and (d) that China does not intend to leave Japan as evidenced by the proposed formation of a trilateral FTA among Japan, China and Korea.

announced this proposal on November 5, 2002, a day after the signing of the ASEAN-China FTA. It was a surprised but welcome offer given that India is a relatively closed economy with high tariffs for its imports. Using an analogy, Singapore's former PM Goh Chok Tong said that the ASEAN jumbo jet is now ready to take off with one wing in the making in the East through agreements with China and Japan, and with India providing the second wing. Bilateral trade between India and ASEAN is expected to double within ten years from its present level of US$10 billion. Moreover, ASEAN is a strategic partner for India as it could provide a link to Northeast Asia. India could somehow provide a balance between ASEAN and Northeast Asia.

TOWARDS ASEAN OR EAST ASIAN ECONOMIC COMMUNITY?

In the future, the ASEAN regional grouping can form a common market to be known as *ASEAN Economic Community (AEC)* or an *East Asian Economic Community (EAEC)*. Singapore's former PM Goh proposed for the establishment of an AEC by 2020 during the 8th ASEAN summit in Cambodia in November 2002.[56] His proposal, along the lines of the European Economic Community, received a strong support from Thailand's PM Thaksin Shinawatra. As a single market with 500 million people, the AEC could allow the 10 member countries to enjoy free movement of goods and services, and a free movement of factors of production including capital and labor particularly professionals. Having had a number of economic initiatives on trade, tourism and services, the AEC could serve as the end vision for all these agreements. It is expected that the AEC could help in bridging the economic gap between and among ASEAN members which include high-income countries like Singapore, Brunei and Malaysia and lower-income ones like Laos, Cambodia and Myanmar.

Alternatively, the ASEAN+3 countries comprising 10 ASEAN countries, Japan, China and South Korea, can form an *East Asian Economic Community* (EAEC).[57] They can move away from being merely dialogue partners towards becoming more economically integrated. This could initially be in the form of an *East Asian Free Trade Area* (EAFTA), an idea which was first proposed by the East Asian Vision Group in its report presented during the ASEAN+3 summit in Brunei in November 2001. EAFTA could be achieved in 2006 as suggested by Mr. Noboru Hatakeyama, Chairman and CEO of Japan Economic Foundation.[58] He suggested that the ASEAN+3 Economic Ministers should recommend to their Leaders to commence the actual study on EAFTA from 2003 and enter into negotiation from 2004 with the goal of concluding it by the end of 2006. However, Professor Chia Siow Yue, former director of the Institute of Southeast Asian Studies, argued during the open forum on Singapore's FTAs, that Mr Hatakeyama's suggestion is very optimistic but not realistic. She

---

56 ASEAN and the EU are two different groups. For example, intra-regional trade in the former has hovered around 20-25 percent of ASEAN's global trade in the last two decades, while in the latter, intra-regional trade historically has been around 50-60 percent of EU's global trade. Despite this difference, ASEAN could learn from the EU on the different stages of its regional economic integration.

57 China, Japan and South Korea are currently ASEAN's dialogue partners under the ASEAN+3 framework. For an excellent discussion of this framework, including its origins, evolution and potentials, see Richard Stubbs, "ASEAN plus three: emerging East Asian regionalism?" *Asian Survey*, Vol.42, No.3, 2002.

58 Noboru Hatakeyama, "EAFTA not a dream, but a reality," Presented at the symposium on "FTAs; JSEPA and Beyond," Singapore, March 7, 2003.

further raised the idea that the more likely scenario is the one proposed by Mr. Long Yongtu, Vice Minister of China's Ministry of Foreign Trade and Economic Cooperation (MOFTEC), for the establishment of an East Asia Comprehensive Economic Partnership which includes trade facilitation and economic cooperation rather than trade liberalization. Whatever form it may take initially, the ASEAN+3 grouping should work towards becoming more fully integrated as a common market in the long-run.

The formation of an East Asian bloc is justified on several grounds. First, the integration of Southeast Asia with Northeast Asia could become one of the driving forces in the global economy as it provides a market of more than 2 billion people (a third of the world's population) and a fifth of global trade. Second, with China being ASEAN's fifth largest trading partner and emerging giant, economic ties with ASEAN for Japan and South Korea could be a means to counteract China's growing economic power. Third, the ASEAN regional grouping could be losing its attractiveness to foreign investors in light of China's rising economic might.[59]

Given all the existing regional agreements and FTAs, what is the best way to arrive at EAFTA? Dr Chulsu Kim, President of Korea's Sejong University, suggested a number of alternative scenarios for the process leading to EAFTA. These include (a) negotiating a region-wide FTA directly among all countries in the region, (b) phasing in EAFTA through the formation of various bilateral FTAs between ASEAN and Northeast Asian countries, and (c) forming a trilateral FTA among China, Japan and Korea and then move in the direction of consolidating with ASEAN.[60]

But what is the probability of forming an East Asian regional economic grouping. For one, Razeen Sally believes that an East Asian bloc forming around either China and/or Japan seems plausible given that the East Asian countries have relatively liberal trade policies and are reasonably well-integrated into the global economy.[61] However, he pointed out that the East Asian countries are hugely different in terms of their outward-orientation with Singapore and Hong Kong being free ports, with South Korea and Taiwan having liberalized substantially in recent years, with Thailand's protectionism remaining high, with Indonesia and the Philippines being mired in political and economic instability, with Myanmar, Vietnam, Cambodia and Laos having higher levels of protection, with Japan having a defensive trade policy particularly its agricultural sector, and with China narrowing the trade policy gap with other developing countries bringing average tariffs down to Southeast Asian

59 In recent years, China's buoyant economic performance has diverted FDI away from ASEAN. In 2001, ASEAN attracted only US$13.1 billion which paled in comparison with China's US$47 billion. See The Straits Times, "ASEAN may become an East Asia grouping," Oct 12, 2002, p.28. On the contrary, however, a study by Singapore's Ministry of Trade and Industry reported that FDI in ASEAN and China have moved in tandem during the 1989 to 2001 period – that is, "the trends and patterns of global FDI flows to ASEAN and China have not shown that growth in China's FDI has been at the expense of ASEAN. Moreover, Japan, US and the EU have consistently invested more in ASEAN than in China, except in 1998." See The Straits Times, "China's rise has not been at ASEAN's expense," November 19,2002, p.A16. The results were also published by Friedrich Wu and Kok Keong Puah, "Foreign Direct Investment in China and Southeast Asia: Has ASEAN been losing out?" *Journal of Asian Business,* Vol.18, No.3, 2002.

60 See Chulsu Kim, "Towards an East Asia Free Trade Agreement," delivered at the symposium on "FTAs: JSEPA and Beyond," Singapore, March 7, 2003.

61 The Straits Times, "Asia gets onto bandwagon of regionalism," January 28, 2003, p.16.

and Latin American levels of around 10 percent.[62] These differences in their trade policy regimes and in their levels of development could certainly provide enormous challenges for the East Asian countries to form together as a regional economic grouping. In addition, there are some political and bilateral disputes which have to be settled like the historical hostility between Japan and South Korea, disputes among countries of the ASEAN, and the political implications of the Taiwan issue.[63] While Malaysia has been supportive of an East Asian bloc,[64] other ASEAN countries view it differently. Singapore's position, for example, is that it will be more advantageous for ASEAN to maintain separate trade deals each with China, Japan and South Korea, instead of a joint agreement with them.[65] The main reason is that ASEAN might be overwhelmed by the combined power of the three giant economies and this may lead to the marginalization of the ASEAN economies particularly the smaller and poorer new members (Vietnam, Cambodia, Laos and Myanmar).

CONCLUSION

The regional integration process in ASEAN has evolved gradually during the past four decades. To move towards closer economic integration, ASEAN has undertaken both widening and deepening economic activities. While the enlargement process from five to ten members has resulted in a two-tier grouping, the development gaps between the higher and lower income countries can be narrowed down through several mechanisms including the provision of financial and technical assistance to the lower income countries and by encouraging more trade and investments in them.

ASEAN has also followed trade and investment liberalization measures aimed at improving the competitiveness of their economies and increasing the pace of regional integration. On the trade front, these measures, which include PTAs and CEPT, have been implemented towards achieving AFTA. While the PTAs proved to be ineffective because of the low utilization rate, the CEPT has enabled ASEAN to move towards a higher plane with the reduction of tariffs to 0-5 percent for ASEAN-6 on at least 90 percent of its tariff lines in the inclusion list. However, intra-ASEAN trade has remained low at 20-25 percent of its global trade, with much of this being accounted for by trade between Singapore, Malaysia and Indonesia. This fact is attributed to various factors including the favorable treatment given to imports of capital goods from developed countries, the different pace of industrialization among ASEAN countries, and the greater significance of extra-ASEAN economic ties particularly with Japan, the US and the EU.

On the investment front, ASEAN has undertaken measures to promote and encourage FDI including regional initiatives like the ASEAN Investment Area (AIA) and the ASEAN

62 The Straits Times, "Asia gets," p.16.

63 The Korea Herald, "Toward an East Asian economic community," February 27, 2003.

64 Having advocated the idea of an East Asia economic grouping long time ago, Malaysia's PM Mahathir Mohamad resurrected it further during the 1997/98 economic crisis when he suggested the formation of an Asian monetary system towards a stable Asian currency. He brought up the idea again in Brunei in September 2001. See The Straits Times, "ASEAN may become an East Asia grouping," Oct 12, 2002, p.28.

65 The Straits Times, "ASEAN may become...," p.28.

Industrial Cooperation (AICO) and sub-regional schemes like growth areas. Past regional schemes like AIP, AIC and AIJV had proved to be less successful.

Thus, despite regional and sub-regional initiatives, ASEAN economic integration has proceeded at a snail pace because of some factors which include, among others, a weak organizational structure, the consensus decision-making approach, lack of political commitment, the ineffectiveness of regional economic initiatives, the dominance of national over regional economic interests, and the significance of outside linkages.

With extra-regional being more significant than intra-regional economic linkages, ASEAN has implemented various multilateral and regional strategies to support the principles and objectives of the WTO, APEC and ASEM. However, with the growing importance of bilateral FTAs, some countries in ASEAN, led by Singapore, have completed or are planning to form FTAs with countries outside the grouping. As a free trader and a vocal champion of free trade, Singapore has supported and will continue to support the promotion of free and open trade at the multilateral level through the WTO and at the regional level through ASEAN, APEC and ASEM.

However, the failure of the WTO Ministerial Meeting in Seattle, the delays in the implementation of tariff cuts among ASEAN countries, and the slow progress of APEC's initiatives have encouraged Singapore to forge FTAs with both developed and developing countries outside the ASEAN grouping. Moreover, Singapore has weighed the likely negative consequences of the proliferation of FTAs and further regional integration efforts that are taking place in Europe and America which could provide a global imbalance in favor of the trans-atlantic regions of the world. Singapore, ASEAN, Asia, and the Asia-Pacific could be left behind if nothing is done from the Asian side. Singapore has courageously taken the initiative of negotiating FTAs.

Having been viewed as parallel and complementary to the global and regional initiatives, FTAs has economic and strategic rationale for Singapore. FTAs can generate substantial foreign exchange savings for Singapore's exporters, guarantee Singapore companies access to the goods and services markets of the partner countries, help to anchor Singapore in the radar of its partner countries like New Zealand, EFTA, Japan, Australia, United States, Canada, Mexico, India and Korea, and build bridges to the regions to which these countries represent including Asia, Oceania, America and Europe.

Singapore's FTA policy, however, has been met with criticisms particularly during its early phase. It was viewed as against the ASEAN spirit, and could provide a backdoor for goods from her partner countries to enter ASEAN duty-free. From Singapore's point of view, FTAs could serve as a trailblazer which other ASEAN countries could join. Indeed, over a period of two years since her first FTA was concluded with Japan, the criticisms against Singapore's FTAs have subsided. In fact, other ASEAN countries, and even the ASEAN grouping itself, have expressed keen interest in establishing FTAs with other countries like China, the United States, Japan and India. Aimed at promoting trade and investments between the bilateral partners, these FTAs are and must be consistent with the WTO, can be WTO-plus and pursue open regionalism to achieve open and free trade and investment in the future.

QUESTIONS FOR DISCUSSION

1. Some countries in the world form regional economic groupings such as the Association of Southeast Asian Nations (ASEAN), the North American Free Trade Agreement (NAFTA), the European Union (EU), the Australia-New Zealand Closer Economic Relations (CER) and the Southern Common Market (MERCOSUR), to name a few. Why do countries form regional groups?
2. The EU is expanding further to include some central and eastern European countries. By the year 2005, the Free Trade Area of the Americas (FTAAs) will be formed to include northern, central and southern American countries. It is also predicted that regional trading agreements could reach up to 300 by the year 2005. Discuss the consequences and implications of this trend in the ASEAN context.
3. ASEAN was formed in 1967 by five founding members, namely, Indonesia, Malaysia, the Philippines, Singapore and Thailand. Brunei joined in 1984. Other new members were admitted such as Vietnam (1995), Laos and Myanmar (1997) and Cambodia (1999). Discuss the benefits and costs of ASEAN enlargement to old and new members.
4. Despite its formation in 1967, the ASEAN regional economic integration has proceeded at a very slow pace. Why?
5. Explain clearly whether you agree or disagree with the following statement: "It is in the interest of all Asian states to conclude bilateral trade deals because multilateral talks at the WTO are moving slowly."

SUGGESTED MATERIALS FOR CASE STUDIES

Blackhurst, Richard, 1997, "The WTO and the Global Economy," *The World Economy,* Vol.20, No.5, pp. 527-544.

Ong, Eng Chuan, 2003, "Anchor East Asian Free Trade in ASEAN," *The Washington Quarterly,* Vol.26, No.2, pp.57-72.

REFERENCES FOR CHAPTER 8

Ariff, Mohamed, 1998, "Economic Regionalism versus Multilateralism: Dilemmas for Southeast Asia?" *Paper presented at ISEAS 30th anniversary conference on Southeast Asia in the 21st Century:* Challenges of Globalization, Singapore.

Asian Economic News, 2001, "Singapore Free Trade Pact Worrisome, Mahathir says," March 5.

Daquila, Teofilo C. 1999, "The ASEAN Experience of Economic Cooperation," *Paper presented at "The East African Forum on the East African Community: Economic Aspects of Integration,"* organized by Friedrich Ebert Foundation, 27-29 September, Kampala, Uganda.

Daquila, Teofilo C. 2001, "Towards Strengthening ASEAN Integration: Challenges, Strategies and Prospects," in Apirat Petchsiri, Alfred Kellerman, Charit Tingsabadh and Pornsan Watananguhn (eds.), *Strengthening ASEAN Integration: Lessons from the EU's*

Rule of Law, Thailand: Chulalongkorn University's Interdisciplinary Department of European Studies, the Center for European Studies, and TMC Asser Institute of the Netherlands, pp.77-87.

Daquila, Teofilo C. 2002, "ASEAN Economic Performance: Revisiting the Past, Looking to the Future," *Harvard Asia Quarterly,* Mass.: Harvard University, Vol. 6, No.3, pp.9-14, online exclusive.

Daquila, Teofilo C. and Le Huu Huy, 2003, "Singapore and ASEAN in the Global Economy: Case of Free Trade Agreements," *Asian Survey* (USA: University of California, Berkeley), Vol.XLIII, No.6, pp.908-928.

Davidson, Paul, 2002, *ASEAN: The Evolving Legal Framework for Economic Cooperation*, Singapore: Times Academic Press, pp.14-50.

Hatakeyama, Noboru, 2003, "EAFTA not a dream, but a reality," *Presented at the symposium on "FTAs; JSEPA and Beyond,"* Singapore, March 7.

Kim, Chulsu, 2003, "Towards an East Asia Free Trade Agreement," *Paper delivered at the symposium on "FTAs: JSEPA and Beyond,"* Singapore, March 7.

Langhammer, Rolf, 1992, "Regionalism in Place of or Together with Multilateralism" delivered before the *Economic Society of Singapore*, July 9.

Park, Sung-Hoon, 2002, "East Asian Economic Integration – Finding a Balance between Regionalism and Multilateralism," *EIAS Briefing Paper*, Brussels: European Institute for Asian Studies.

Philippine Star, "Arroyo Pushes Free Trade with Japan," December 4, 2002.

Stubbs, Richard, 2002, "ASEAN Plus Three: Emerging East Asian Regionalism?" *Asian Survey,* Vol.42, No.3, pp. 440 – 455.

The Business Times (BT)

- "Bilateral pacts could have catalytic effects: BG Yeo," January 18, 2000.
- "Singapore won't be back door to AFTA," May 3, 2001.
- "S'pore's trade pacts are not FTAs," October 12, 2001
- "The paradox of Asia's FTAs," December 18, 2002.
- "FTA with India next on S'pore agenda: BG Yeo," January 30, 2003.
- "Singapore, Australia sign free trade agreement," February 17, 2003.
- "Singapore seals FTA deals with Australia," February 18, 2003.
- "EU, ASEAN pledge to boost trade, political ties," February 24, 2003.

The Hindu, "Malaysia Cautions on Trade Pacts," November 23, 2000.

The Korea Herald, "Toward an East Asian Economic Community," February 27, 2003.

The Straits Times (ST)

- "PSA's cargo volume down 8.9% last year", January 19, 2002.
- "Asia gets onto bandwagon of regionalism," January 28, 2002, p.16.
- "FTA 'customs union' to benefit Southeast Asia*,* March 17, 2002.
- "S'pore, India for economic partnership," April 9, 2002, p.1.
-"Denmark backs Singapore-EU free trade pact," April 18, 2002, p.6.
- "ASEAN 'slow' on free-trade links," May 3, 2002, p.1.
- "ASEAN must latch on to China's growth," May 7, 2002, p.A6.
- "ASEAN may become an East Asia grouping," Oct 12, 2002, p.28.
- "Singapore, NZ and Chile go for 3-way trade talks," October 28, 2002.
- "Spore-Seoul free trade talks to begin next year," November 15, 2002
- "China's rise has not been at ASEAN's expense," November 19, 2002, p.A16.

- "How the FTA was won," November 23, 2002, p.28.
- "Chinese tourists heading for Southeast Asia," December 14, 2002, p.A2),
- "Malaysia aims for first free-trade deal with Japan," December 13, 2002, p.A22.
- "Asia gets onto bandwagon of regionalism," January 28, 2003, p.16.
- "EU and ASEAN ministers pledge closer trade and intelligence ties," January 29, 2003, p.A6.
- "Bush gives go-ahead for FTA pact with S'pore," February 1, 2003, p.A12.
- "S'pore and India plan talks on free-trade pact," February 4, 2003.
- "S'pore values both WTO deals, FTAs", February 21, 2003, p.A18.

Tsugami, Toshiya, 2003, "On ASEAN-China Free Trade Agreement – a personal view from Japan," Presented at a symposium on "FTAs: JSEPA and Beyond", organized by the Japan Economic Foundation and Singapore Institute of International Affairs, Singapore, March 7.

Wu, Friedrich and Kok Keong Puah, 2003, "Foreign Direct Investment in China and Southeast Asia: Has ASEAN been losing out?" *Journal of Asian Business,* Vol.19, No.1.

Internet Sources

Kaur, Hardev, 2003, "Amid globalization trend, Pacific Rim sees a bellweather on bilateral trade," *The WorldPaper,* [accessed 21 April] < *http://www.worldpaper.com/2001/may01/tradeblocs4.html* >

Philippine Star, December 4, 2002: <*http://www.philstar.com/philstar/print.asp?article=103628*>

Singapore's MTI website: [accessed January 14, 2003] < *http://www.mti.gov.sg/public/FTA/frm_FTA_Default.asp?sid=37&cid=1183* >

WTO website: http*://www.wto.org.*

WTO, 1995, *Regionalism and the World Trading System*, Geneva: World Trading Organization.

WTO website: *http://www.wto.org/wto/develop/regional.htm* – Regional Integration and the Multilateral Trading System, printed on 01 October 1, 1999.

PART IV:
THE 1997/98 ECONOMIC CRISIS IN SOUTHEAST ASIA

Chapter 9

CAUSES AND CONSEQUENCES OF THE CRISIS[1]

ABSTRACT

The 1997/98 economic crisis faced by the Southeast Asian economies was linked to the interactions between the households, corporate and government sectors in the pursuit of their three main activities such as production, demand and income. The first section of this chapter investigates the various conditions which existed before the crisis and which contributed to the crisis. These include rising income expectations, worsening current account deficits, rising external indebtedness, and rapid expansion of domestic credit. The second section analyzes the impacts of the crisis on the four sectors such as the external (trade and financial capital flows), production, labor and financial sectors.

INTRODUCTION

As discussed in the first chapter, the economies of Southeast Asia (such as Indonesia, Malaysia, the Philippines, Singapore and Thailand) had achieved a remarkable economic growth for an average of about 7.0 per cent during the 1960-96 period. However, the region was hit by the financial crisis in 1997 which began in Thailand and had spread to the rest of the region. The crisis came as a total shock. It was not predicted even by the IMF. As Vassily Mikheev, a Russian economist stated,

> As the IMF annual edition "*World Economic Outlook*" suggests, in May 1997, the Fund was still being pretty optimistic about the development prospects in Asian states that were shortly to find themselves neck-deep in crisis. The IMF forecast a 6.8% GDP growth in Thailand in 1997, further increasing to 7% in 1998; Indonesia was supposed to hit the 8.5% growth rate within 1997-98; Malaysia, 6.4%; and the Philippines, 3.6%, likewise within a two-year period.[2]

---

1 Earlier versions of this chapter include guest lectures and seminar presentations at the following institutions: El Colegio de Mexico (1998), Nordic Institute of Asian Studies (Copenhagen, 1999), Ludwig-Maximilians Universitaet Muenchen (Munich, 1999), University of Sweden's Center for Pacific and Asian Studies and Stockholm School of Economics (1999), and the University of Paris Sciences-Po Asia-Europe Program (1999); and invited conference papers presented at Chulalongkorn University (1999) and the Center for the Study of International Institutions (Austria, 2003).

2 Vassily Mikheev, "The Financial Crisis in Asia and Its Economic and Political Consequences," *Far Eastern Affairs,* No.2, 1998, p.53.

There were others who argued that even the international credit rating agencies should be blamed because their ratings did not give the correct signals to the international lenders. Examples of these agencies are Standard and Poor's and Moody's whose ratings did not accurately reflect the true ability to repay debts as in the case of Korea whose credit ratings were AA- until October 24, 1997.[3] Even Radelet and Sachs also pointed out that the credit ratings for all the would-be crisis economies were actually improving from 1995 until the eve of the crisis.[4]

On July 2, 1997, the Bank of Thailand announced the floating of the baht after its intervention in the foreign exchange market to keep the exchange rate failed. What began as a currency crisis resulted in a banking crisis and eventually generated a contagion effect to other neighboring countries including Indonesia, Malaysia, the Philippines and Singapore.[5] However, it was not contagion from Thailand that made the countries vulnerable to a financial crisis but because of the home-grown economic problems which include a growing current account deficit, excessive short-term foreign borrowings, a banking sector weighed down by speculative property loans and, corrupt government and business practices.[6] The disturbances, however, were not limited to the Southeast Asian region, but the rest of the Asian region. As Krugman predicted:

> Almost every economy in Asia will feel the ripples from this summer's [1997] wave of devaluations: higher interest costs because the international markets fear further devaluations, lower export prices because the devaluations will intensify competition, reduced capital inflows because once ebullient foreign investors have become suddenly wary, and maybe a growth slowdown.[7]

Wade even extended the impact of the crisis to the rest of the world as follows:

> The devaluation of the Thai bath in July 1997 precipitated a wave of currency crises or financial instability from Thailand, to the rest of Southeast Asia, to Taiwan, to Hong Kong, to Korea, to the Philippines, to Russia, to Brazil, to Estonia, to Australia and New Zealand.[8]

Adelman and Yeldan also spoke about the global impact of the crisis:

---

3 See, for example, Youn-Suk Kim and Hyeng Keun Koo, "Asia's Contagious Financial Crisis and its Impact on Korea," *Journal of Asian Economics,* Vol.10, 1999, p.115.

4 Steven Radelet and Jeffrey Sachs, "The East Asian Financial Crisis: Diagnosis, Remedies and Prospects," *Brookings Paper on Economic Activity,* 1998, Vol.1, pp.1-90, as cited in Ha-Joon Chang, "The Hazard of Moral Hazard: Untangling the Asian Crisis," *World Development,* Vol.28, No.4, 2000, p.784.

5 The crisis even spread outside the region hitting Asia's third largest economy, South Korea in November 1997 with the won falling sharply by 10 percent per day, the limit of its trading band. Moreover, several major firms became insolvent, and by mid-December smaller companies collapsed at the rate of fifty per day. Korea's short-term interest rates increased to 30 percent and above. For more discussion, see James Dean, "Asia's Financial Crisis in Historical Perspective," *Journal of the Asia Pacific Economy,* Vol.3, No.3, 1998, pp.267-283. For excellent discussion on the nature of the Korean crisis, see Ha-Joon Chang, "Korea: The Misunderstood Crisis," *World Development,* Vol.26, No.8, 1998, pp.1555-1561.

6 Anna Schwartz, "International Financial Crises: Myths and Realities," *The Cato Journal*, Vol.17, No.3. 1998. [http://www.cato.org/pubs/journal/cj17n3-3.html].

7 Paul Krugman, "What Ever Happened to the Asian Miracle?" *Fortune,* August 18, 1997, p.12

8 Robert Wade, "The Asian Debt-and-Development Crisis of 1997-?: Causes and Consequences," *World Development,* Vol.26, No.8, 1998, p.1535.

The Asian financial crisis has had a profound impact on the global economy. Global growth has been slower; risks have been higher; and the international flows of capital have been severely disrupted.[9]

PRE-CRISIS CONDITIONS

The economic crisis facing the Southeast Asian region can be linked to the interactions between the households, corporate and government sectors in the pursuit of their three main economic activities; namely, production, demand and income. There are various economic conditions which existed prior to the crisis and which contributed to the crisis. These include rising income expectations, worsening current account deficits, rising external indebtedness, and rapid expansion of domestic credit. An investigation of these conditions is necessary following the breakdown of the orthodox economists' explanation of the East Asian miracle in the context of a set of policies known as the "Washington consensus" which includes "financial sector liberalization, privatization of state-owned enterprises, fiscal discipline and trade, exchange rate and foreign investment deregulation."[10] The crisis has called for a reconsideration of the so-called "East Asian miracle." Even Jeffrey Sachs pointed out that "[o]f course, all is not well in Asia's economic management." He further stated that:

> East Asia's currencies remained peg to the U.S. dollar too long after the dollar strengthened sharply against the Japanese yen and the German mark. The result was that Asia's economies lost export competitiveness vis-à-vis Europe and Japan. They also lost competitiveness to China which devalued the yuan against the dollar in 1994, which helped spur sharply higher exports. Some of that increase in Chinese shipments marked a shift in business away from other countries of East Asia. If the East Asian currencies had been floating in the market place, they would have declined gradually against the dollar from 1995 onward. As it turned out, they came down with a thud this past summer.
>
> In addition to short-term currency mismanagement, the region also played with fire by encouraging large inflows of short-term capital from abroad. In many countries in the region, capital markets were liberalized in the 1990s, while supervision of banks and other financial institutions was lax. Many of the short-term loans from abroad found their way into real estate ventures and other speculative investments, in some cases controlled by cronies of government officials. Following the currency devaluations and tightening of credit, many of these projects will now go into default, and may even lead to bank closures in the region. Even as exports pick up in 1998, the construction sector is likely to remain depressed in parts of Southeast Asia.[11]

Rising Income Expectations

Economic agents in Southeast Asia had been used to and had lived with high level of growth over the past 35 years. Consequently, they had expected that the "economic miracle" would continue and had made their economic decisions based on rising income expectations

---

9 Irma Adelman. and Erinc Yeldan, "The Minimal Conditions for a Financial Crisis: a Multiregional Intertemporal CGE Model of the Asian Crisis," *World Development,* Vol.28, No.6, 2000, p.1087.

10 Kanishka Jayasuriya and Andrew Rosser, "Economic Orthodoxy and the East Asian Crisis," *Third World Quarterly,* Vol.22, No.3, 2001, pp.381.

11 Jeffrey Sachs, "Asia's Miracle is Alive and Well," *Time,* September 29, 1997.

particularly on decisions affecting their consumption and investments including investments in property and capital markets. The so-called 'East Asian economic miracle' had dulled the willingness to take risks of people acting on capital markets, and that these people had been moved to "irrational exuberance," as Alan Greenspan put it, or what Garnaut referred to as the "psychology of a long boom."[12] Even Krugman pointed out that "... too many investors, domestic and foreign, took it as an excuse to believe that the good times could just keep on rolling – in particular that the overheated Southeast Asian boom of the mid-'90s ... could continue without limit."[13] The idea that high growth could go on forever seems to have become firmly implanted.[14]

As the Southeast Asian economies grow and continue to grow, incomes per capita and hence savings increase. With high growth and rising incomes, economic agents tend to increase their demand for goods and services. Demand tends to rise further if agents expect their economy to continue to grow. Prior to the crisis, evidence shows that broadly, all demand indicators expanded markedly. This is shown in Table 9.1. First, private consumption increased in all but Indonesia, with significant expansion in Malaysia and Thailand during the 1990-95 period relative to 1980-90. Second, general government consumption grew in all but Indonesia and Singapore, with marked expansion in Malaysia and the Philippines. Third, domestic investment demand by both private and public sectors rose markedly for all countries – growing by about twice in Singapore, more than double in Indonesia and in the Philippines, and about six-fold in Malaysia. Finally, merchandise imports also increased significantly in all countries. In particular, the import of machinery and transport equipment for ASEAN-5 rose from an average of 30 per cent in 1980 to 44 per cent in 1995.

On the production front, as the economy grows and continues to grow, it experiences a structural transformation away from the traditional agricultural sector towards modern non-agricultural (manufacturing and services) sector and hence indicates a change in the preferences of producers to accommodate the changing tastes and preferences of demanders. Consequently, resources are re-allocated away from agriculture towards manufacturing and services sectors. In 1995 relative to 1970, Indonesia, Thailand and Malaysia experienced a rapid structural transformation with the shares of their agricultural sectors declining from 46 to 17 per cent of GDP, from 32 to 13 per cent, and from 30 to 11 per cent, respectively. On the other hand, the share of the manufacturing sector increased significantly from 11 to 24 per cent of GDP, from 16 to 33 per cent, and from 18 to 29 per cent, respectively.

12 Ross Garnaut, "Economic Lessons," in Ross McLeod and Ross Garnaut, eds., *East Asia in Crisis: From being a Miracle to Needing one?* London: Routledge, 1998, p.354.

13 Paul Krugman, "Wrong, It Never Existed," *Time*, September 29, 1997, p.37.

14 Helmut Hesse and Laura Auria, "The Financial Crisis in Southeast Asia: Causes and Effects on the Global Economy," *Economics,* Vol.57, 1998, p.58.

Table 9.1. Growth Rates of Demand Indicators in Southeast Asia, (in %)

	INDONESIA	MALAYSIA	PHILIPPINES	SINGAPORE	THAILAND
(1) Private Consumption					
1980-90	5.5	3.7	2.6	5.8	5.9
1990-95	4.7	7.2	3.2	6.6	8.1
(2) Private Consumption Per Capita					
1980-90	3.6	1.0	0.2	4.1	3.9
1990-95	3.0	4.7	1.0	4.5	7.1
(3) Central Government Consumption					
1980-90	4.6	2.7	0.6	6.7	4.2
1990-95	3.1	8.8	2.9	6.1	5.0
(4) Gross Domestic Investment					
1980-90	7.0	2.6	-2.1	3.7	9.4
1990-95	16.3	16.0	3.2	6.0	10.2
(5) Merchandise Exports					
1980-90	-0.3	8.6	3.9	9.9	14.0
1990-95	11.7	20.0	16.2	17.6	18.6
(6) Merchandise Imports					
1980-90	2.6	7.7	2.9	8.0	12.7
1990-95	11.5	20.3	18.0	15.5	15.3

Source: World Bank, *World Development Indicators*, Washington D.C.: World Bank, 1997, pp.179-180 for items (1) to (4) and pp.155-156 for items (5) and (6).

Moreover, as the economy expands, more institutions have been created and supplied to provide a wider variety of goods and services in response to changing demand conditions. In the manufacturing sector, about a third of the manufacturing value-added in Indonesia, Thailand and the Philippines was in food and beverages. In Malaysia and Singapore, the manufacture of machinery and transport equipment increased significantly during the 1980-1995 period from 20 to 36 per cent and from 44 to 58 per cent of the total manufacturing valued added, respectively (see Table 9.2).

In the financial sector, more financial institutions have been established including commercial banks, savings banks, merchant banks, insurance companies and others. Households have been provided with a wider variety of financial instruments ranging from simple deposits, stocks, bonds, unit trusts, foreign currency accounts, etc. Real estate and construction activities increase as households purchased houses, as firms built more factories, and as government built more infrastructure facilities. The prices of stocks and property rose markedly and generated a bubble economy in the Southeast Asian region prior to the crisis. There was an enormous increase in wealth arising from substantial capital gains. Gross domestic investment in Indonesia expanded by 16.3 per cent in 1990-95 period as compared to 7.0 per cent in the 1980-90 period as seen in Table 9.1. For Malaysia, Singapore and Thailand, investment grew by 16 per cent from 2.6 per cent, by 6.0 per cent from 3.7 per cent, and by 10.2 per cent from 9.4 per cent, respectively. In the case of the Philippines, while investment contracted by an average of 2.1 per cent in 1980-90 period, it expanded by 3.2 per cent in the 1990-95 period.

Table 9.2. Structure of Manufacturing in Southeast Asia, (% of value added in manufacturing)

	Value Added (US$ million)	Food & beverage Value Added	Textiles & Clothing Value Added	Machinery &Transport Equipment Value Added	Chemical Value Added	Other Manufac-turing Value Added
Indonesia						
1980	10133	32	14	13	11	30
1994	41186	26	15	12	10	36
Malaysia						
1980	5054	24	7	20	5	43
1994	22387	9	6	36	10	39
Philippines						
1980	8354	30	13	12	14	31
1994	14917	31	11	14	16	28
Singapore						
1980	3415	5	5	44	5	41
1994	18119	4	2	58	9	28
Thailand						
1980	6160	55	8	9	7	21
1994	40791	...	...	...	...	...

Source: World Bank, *World Development Indicators*, Washington D.C.: World Bank, 1997, pp.151-152.

Worsening Current Account Deficits

With higher growth rate and rising expectations that growth will continue, overall demand increases. When total spending (absorption) exceeds income, we have a current account deficit, or equivalently, a national deficit. Thus, a current account deficit arises when (i) both private and public sectors have deficits, (ii) private sector deficit is greater than public sector surplus, or (iii) public sector deficit is greater than private sector surplus. Singapore had the strongest net external financial position as it registered a current account surplus of about 14 per cent of GDP during the 1993-95 period as shown in Table 9.3. Singapore's public and private sectors were both in healthy surplus positions. The other Southeast Asian economies had high levels of current account deficits, with Thailand having the largest deficit at 6.3 per cent of GDP and Indonesia, the smallest deficit at 2.2 per cent of GDP. Since the public sectors in these countries were broadly in surplus positions during the 1993-95 period, the net external deficit were attributed mainly to the private sector deficits in these countries.

The issue is whether to allow the current account deficit to continue or not. If current account deficit continues, this can be financed by depleting foreign exchange reserves. However as reserves are limited, the current account deficits cannot be sustained. Assuming instead that the government intends to correct the deficit, it can undertake (i) expenditure-switching policies via a devaluation of the exchange rate making exports cheaper and imports expensive, and (ii) expenditure-reducing policies via a tight fiscal policy (e.g. reduce government spending or increase taxes) and/or a tight monetary policy (e.g. reduce money supply or increase interest rates) aimed at reducing domestic demand. However, in a model with financial capital mobility, it is possible for the current account to be sustained. The massive influx of foreign capital including foreign direct investments and foreign borrowings can be used to finance the current account deficits. In cases where foreign direct investments are insufficient to cover the deficit, the difference can be financed by foreign borrowings. Moreover, with capital mobility the need to devalue the exchange rate consistent with the market rate, given huge current account deficits, is not at all that urgent and hence results in an overvalued exchange rate.

Table 9.3. Indicators of Net External Financial Position: 1993-95 (% of GDP)

	INDONESIA	MALAYSIA	PHILIPPINES	SINGAPORE	THAILAND
(1) Current account balance	-2.2	-4.7	-4.3	13.9	-6.3
(2) Gross domestic savings	35.6	36.7	16.0	...	36.2
(3) Gross domestic investment	35.1	38.1	23.5	34.9	41.6
(4) Savings-investment gap	0.5	-1.4	-7.5	...	-5.4
(5) Overall fiscal deficit	...	2.1	...	5.3	2.3
(6) Private sector deficit	...	-3.5	...	...	-7.7
(7) Net FDI					
- 1980	0.2	3.8	-0.3	...	0.6
- 1995	2.2	6.8	2.2	...	1.2

Source: World Bank, World Development Indicators, Washington DC: World Bank, 1997, pp.187-188 for items (1), (2), (3) & (5) and pp.233-234 for item (7). Item (4) = (2) – (3) and item (6) = (4) – (5).

Rising External Indebtedness

Why have countries not learned from bad debt experiences? During the early 1980s, the Philippines faced a severe debt crisis arising from a substantial exposure in short-term loans accounted for mainly by the public sector. However, such an experience did not seem to provide meaningful lessons for other countries in the region as other Southeast Asian economies incurred rising levels of foreign debt. Indonesia had the highest level of foreign debt among Southeast Asian countries reaching US$108 billion in 1995, a five-fold increase relative to 1980 as shown in Table 9.4. About 80 per cent of it has long-term maturity. In 1997, about half of Indonesia's debt had a short-term maturity due to the increase in

Indonesia's corporate debt. Malaysia's external debt also rose five times reaching US$34 billion in 1995, of which about a third was in short-term private non-guaranteed debt. Thailand's external debt increased sharply to about US$57 billion, a seven-fold increase relative to 1980. The proportion of private debt rose markedly from 20 percent to 37 percent. In 1997, this share reached 50 per cent. The punishingly high domestic interest rates in Thailand prompted increasing numbers of Thai borrowers to go overseas for cheap capital and this resulted in a flood of cheap foreign money that allowed banks to make foreign currency loans in U.S. dollars at interest rates lower than loans in bath.[15] For example, Thai corporate borrowers discovered that they could borrow at an interest rate of 5-8 percent instead of paying more than 13 percent when borrowing domestically and therefore could earn more money simply by borrowing abroad and depositing the baht in Thailand.[16] Consequently, Thailand's foreign debt in July 1998 stood at US$87 billion, 68 percent of which was private debt. The amount of foreign debt created by the banks and finance companies totalled US$33 billion.[17]

Table 9.4. External Debt in Southeast Asia (% of total debt)

	Total Debt, Mln US$	Long-term debt	Public & publicly guaranteed debt		Private debt	Use of IMF Credit
			Total	IBRD		
Indonesia						
1980	20938	86.7	71.7	7.7	15.0	0
1995	107831	79.3	60.6	12.3	18.7	0
Malaysia						
1980	6611	79.5	60.6	7.6	18.9	0
1995	34351	78.8	46.2	3.1	32.7	0
Philippines						
1980	17417	50.6	36.5	5.5	14.1	6.0
1995	39445	84.8	75.8	13.1	9.0	1.8
Thailand						
1980	8297	68.0	47.5	8.5	20.5	4.2
1995	56789	67.8	30.3	3.4	37.4	0

Source: World Bank, World Development Indicators, Washington D.C.: World Bank, 1997, pp.219-220.

In the case of the Philippines, the proportion of long-term debt increased to 85 percent in 1995, with short-term debt being about 9 percent. This shows an improvement in the Philippine foreign borrowing behavior which presumably reflects that the Philippines has learned from its severe debt problem in the 1980s. The Brady debt deal of 1992 and the

15 Leif Roderick Rosenberger, "Southeast Asia's Currency Crisis: A Diagnosis and Prescription," *Contemporary Southeast Asia,* Vol.19, No.3, 1997, p.229.

16 Laurids Lauridsen, "The Financial Crisis in Thailand: Causes, Conduct and Consequences," *World Development,* Vol.26, No.8, 1998, p.1576.

17 Nidhiprabha Bhanupong, "Economic Crises and the Debt-Deflation Episode in Thailand", *Asean Economic Bulletin,* Vol.15, No.3, 1998, p.309.

sustained growth in exports helped a lot.[18] From a high debt service burden at the height of the 1980s crisis of close to 25 per cent of export earnings, the external debt service ratio fell to 16 per cent of export earnings in 1994 to just below 10 per cent by 1997.

Rising external indebtedness, however, does not necessarily become a burden. This depends on how the proceeds of the foreign borrowings are used. An increase in external debt can be attributed to current account deficits, to increases in foreign exchange reserves, to private capital outflows, minus net outflow of portfolio investments and direct investments or a combination of these proximate sources. In the first case, we may look at a rising gross external debt to finance capital flight, not current account deficits. The government or the central bank borrows abroad or runs down existing foreign exchange reserves and sells foreign exchange to domestic residents so that they can acquire foreign assets. In this first case, there is no change in aggregate net foreign assets. If there is a current account deficit, then it is almost entirely financed by direct investment and portfolio capital inflows or by falling foreign exchange reserves under a fixed exchange rate regime.

In the second case, we may look at an increased external debt reflecting current account deficits and not capital flight. We can probably assume here that direct investments and portfolio investments finance only a part of the current account deficits so that external debt rises by the difference. In practice, the cumulative current account deficits are the more common counterpart of increased external indebtedness, which results in a decline in aggregate net foreign assets (or an increase in aggregate net foreign liabilities). If the increase in external debt is used to finance current account deficits, then net foreign liabilities rise. Moreover, we have to distinguish between the two cases of an increase in external debt: (a) whether to finance consumption, or (b) whether to finance investments. If the increase in foreign debt is used to finance consumption, then we are simply mortgaging our future. If it used to finance investment, we have to distinguish between productive and unproductive investments. With productive and profitable investments, future repayments can be generated and simply we have liquidity problems. But if the proceeds of the loans are invested in non-performing assets and speculative activities, then there will be serious repayment problems. The quality and profitability of investments is what counts.

A common problem of many Asian banks is the weakness in the process of capital allocation as there were too many investments that failed to yield positive rates of return on a risk-adjusted basis.[19] The recent crisis has indeed given us a cause for alarm due to over-investment in unproductive, unprofitable and risky activities in some countries including real estate and construction activities which were financed mostly by short-term foreign capital. Property lending accounted for a quarter of total bank lending in Malaysia and the Philippines, and 20 per cent in Thailand. Thus, an investment bubble of careless lending was created since a substantial part of the loan money was channelled into already inflated assets in the real estate sector.[20]

Based on the incremental-capital-output ratio (ICOR) as a measure of the overall investment efficiency, the ICOR estimates in the Asian region had increased sharply in the

18 Gerardo Sicat, "The Philippine Economy in the Asian Crisis," *ASEAN Economic Bulletin,* 1998, Vol.15, No.3, p.291.

19 Gunter Dufey, " Asian Financial Markets: A Pedagogic Note," *Journal of Asian Business,* Vol.15, No.1, p.66.

20 Laurids Lauridsen, "The Financial Crisis in Thailand ...," 1998, p.1576.

1993-96 period relative to the 1987-1992 period, suggesting that the efficiency of investments was already falling in the four years prior to the 1997 crisis.[21] For example, ICOR estimates for Thailand rose from 3.4 in the period 1987-1992 to 5.1 in the period 1993-1996, and for Malaysia, from 3.7 to 4.8 during the same comparative period. The risk increased as the number of central business district offices in Bangkok rose, where vacancy rates were estimated to reach 15 per cent in 1997 and 20 per cent in 1998-99. In Indonesia, the vacancy rates were estimated to double in 1998-99 from 10 per cent in 1997. Moreover, during the 1992-1996 period, a total of 755,000 housing units were built in Bangkok, which was double the estimate in the national development plan, and this led to an excessive supply of housing units sending the vacancy rates to as high as 14 percent.[22]

The imprudent lending and borrowing by various economic agents were attributed to what is known as the moral hazard factor in which agents believe that they will be bailed out in the event of a crisis. Both international lenders and borrowers believed that a lender of last resort such as the IMF or the host government would bail them out. In this regard, the IMF has been criticized for encouraging moral hazard.[23] However, most accounts argue that the national institutions of the Asian countries to be the main sources of moral hazard that was behind the crisis.[24] The most popular variety of the moral hazard argument is that of crony capitalism where personal connections and political patronage, rather than entrepreneurial abilities, determine who gets access to credit and other resources. Moreover, Indonesia and Malaysia have experienced institutional weaknesses and financial systems that allocate funds based on political connection and government favors rather than the standard credit analysis found in Western countries.[25] The relatives and friends of the former president were in charge of concerns trying to make aircrafts, automobiles and banks. These people could gain access to banks and other financial institutions in order to finance their business enterprises regardless of viability.[26] One example was a US$236 million loan from Peregrine Hong Kong (which went bust in Jan 1998) to a taxi company in Jakarta, which was virtually unsecured but for the fact that one of the daughters of former President Suharto was a partner.[27]

The moral hazard problem in Asia magnified the financial vulnerability of the region during the process of financial markets liberalization in the 1990s, exposing its fragility vis-à-vis the macroeconomic and financial shocks that occurred in the period 1995-1997.[28] In Southeast Asia, domestic banks and financial institutions found it easier to obtain foreign

---

21 Giancarlo Corsetti, Paolo Pesenti and Nouriel Roubini, "What Caused the Asian Currency and Financial Crisis?" *Japan and the World Economy*, Vol.11, 1999, p.317.

22 Laurids Lauridsen, "The Financial Crisis in Thailand …," 1998, p.1576.

23 Ronald McKinnon and H. Pill, "International Overborrowing – A Decomposition of Credit and Currency Risk", *World Development.* Vol.26, No.7, 1998, pp.1267-1282; Jeffrey Frankel, "The Asian Model, the Miracle, the Crisis and the Fund," A speech delivered at the US International Trade Commission, April 16, 1998.

24 Ha-Joon Chang, "The Hazard of Moral Hazard: Untangling the Asian Crisis," *World Development,* Vol.28, No.4, p.775.

25 Werner Baer, William Miles and Allen Moran, "The End of the Asian Myth: Why were the Experts Fooled?" *World Development.* Vol.27, No.10, 1999, p.1735.

26 Graham Bird and A. Milne, "Miracle to Meltdown: A Pathology of the East Asian Crisis," *Third World Quarterly,* Vol.20, No.2, 1999, p. 425.

27 Mohammad Sadli, "The Indonesian Crisis," *ASEAN Economic Bulletin,* Vol.15, No.3, p.273.

28 Giancarlo Corsetti, Paolo Pesenti and Nouriel Roubini, "What Caused the Asian …" 1999, pp.306-307

loans.[29] Moreover, the moral hazard problem is compounded by the inefficiency of the central banks as in the case of the Bank of Thailand which made a mistake when it permitted local financial banks to conduct foreign exchange transactions with offshore banks.[30] In addition, before the floating of the baht, the Bank of Thailand had poured out an enormous amount of 430 billion baht to help shore up the failing financial institutions.[31]

Rapid Expansion of Domestic Credit

Overall domestic credit provided by the banking sector as a proportion of GDP rose significantly in the Southeast Asian countries except Singapore (see Table 9.5). In Malaysia, it expanded by about two times to 132 percent of GDP in 1995 relative to 1990. In Thailand, it grew significantly to 137 percent of GDP. In the Philippines, it rose more than twice to about 63 percent of GDP. In Singapore, domestic credit expansion remained at 76 percent of GDP in 1990 and 1995 which indicates the ability of the Monetary Authority of Singapore to control credit expansion. Credit to the private sector was at extremely high levels in Malaysia and Thailand at 130 per cent and 140 per cent of GDP in 1995 as compared to 50 percent and 42 percent in 1980, respectively. In Singapore, credit to the private sector grew to about 107 percent of GDP in 1995 from 81 percent in 1980. The Philippines registered the lowest level of credit granted to the private sector at 45 percent of GDP in 1995 from 42 percent.

The rapid growth in overall domestic credit granted by the banking sector came from two sources: (i) an increase in domestic savings due to higher economic growth and rising per capita income as well as from massive capital gains due to higher asset prices, and (ii) massive inflows of foreign capital as foreign confidence built up with the expectations that the economy would continue to boom. Domestic credit expands rapidly when there are inadequate supervision and controls and particularly on the inflows of foreign capital. Table 9.6 shows that the net private capital flows and its three components (foreign direct investments, portfolio investments and bank and trade related-financing) expanded significantly in 1995 relative to 1980. The massive influx of foreign capital to the process of financial liberalization of interest rates, foreign exchange controls, portfolio management, and new facilities and institutions during the period from 1988 to 1996.[32]

The problem, however, was that financial market liberalization in Asia occurred before there were appropriate state or collective institutions to monitor and regulate financial institutions or local expertise to manage them and which led to the establishment of a horde of new banks and finance companies, including the more than 200 banks in Indonesia, within a short span of time and with inadequate experience in money management.[33]

29 Helmut Hesse and Laura Auria, "The Financial Crisis in Southeast Asia...," 1998, p.59.

30 The Nation, "Learning from Thailand's Mistakes," *The Nation,* November 17, 1998, p.B1-B2.

31 Ivory Tower, "Mexico 1994 versus Thailand 1997," *TDRI Quarterly Review,* Vol.12, No.3, 1997, p.12.

32 Vichyanond Pakorn, "Thailand's Financial Evolution and the 1997 Crisis," Paper presented for the conference, The Miracle Undone: Asia's Financial Crisis, C.I.D.E. Mexico City, 20 February 1998.

33 Linda Y.C. Lim, "Whose Model Failed? Implications of the Asian Economic Crisis," *The Washington Quarterly*, Vol.21, No.3, 1998, p.28-29.

Table 9.5. Domestic Credit Expansion in Southeast Asia (% of GDP)

	Domestic credit provided by the banking sector (1)		Liquid Deposits (2)		Quasi-liquid Deposits (3)		Credit to the private sector (4)	
	1990	1995	1990	1995	1990	1995	1980	1995
Indonesia	45.5	...	40.4	...	29.1	...	8.8	...
Malaysia	77.9	131.9	66.3	121.7	44.3	91.9	49.9	129.5
Philippines	26.9	62.9	36.8	55.1	28.1	44.9	42.2	45.0
Singapore	76.0	76.2	123.9	115.5	100.9	94.1	81.0	106.7
Thailand	90.7	136.5	74.8	79.5	65.9	70.2	41.7	139.9

Source: World Bank, *World Development Indicators*, Washington D.C.: World Bank, 1997, pp.269-270 for columns (1), (2) and (3), and pp.233-234 for column (4).

The maturity structure of the capital inflows changed from long-term foreign direct investment to short-term portfolio funds and loans and the build up of such investments in the domestic economy can make a country vulnerable to a sudden reversal of flows. The vulnerability and the excessive growth of the domestic credit has certainly contributed to instability in the banking and financial sector "as the allocation of credit was increasingly skewed towards the non-tradable and risky sectors, namely the property and stock markets.[34] And indeed when firms and banks in the Asian region failed to meet their foreign loan obligations, a financial panic took place which resulted in a huge withdrawal of capital from the Asian region. By the end of 1997, the net outflow of foreign bank loans reached US$34 billion.[35]

Table 9.6. Private Capital Flows in Southeast Asia (in US$ million)

	Net Private Capital Flows		Foreign Direct Investment		Portfolio Investments				Bank and trade-Related financing	
					Bonds		Equities			
	1980	1995	1980	1995	1980	1995	1980	1995	1980	1995
INDO	3325	11648	1093	4348	26	2248	312	4873	1804	180
MSIA	1799	11924	2333	5800	-212	2240	293	2299	-614	1585
PHIL	639	4605	530	1478	395	1060	0	1961	-286	449
SPORE	...	...	...	...	...	...	...	...	...	...
THAI	4498	9143	2444	2068	-87	2023	449	2154	1692	2898

Source: World Bank, *World Development Indicators*, Washington D.C.: World Bank, 1997, pp.237-238.

34 Bank Negara Malaysia, *The East Asian Crisis – Causes, Policy Responses, Lessons and Issues.* Group of 15 Working Paper No.4, Switzerland, June 1998, p.6

35 Steven Radelet and Jeffrey Sachs, *The Onset of the East Asian Financial Crisis,* Cambridge: National Bureau of Economic Research, 1998, p.10; see also Steven Radelet and Jeffrey Sachs, *The East Asian Financial Crisis: Diagnosis, Remedies and Prospects,* Cambridge: Harvard Institute for International Development, 1998.

Impact of the Crisis

The economic crisis which hit the Asian region had severely affected the Southeast Asian economies, particularly Thailand, Indonesia and Malaysia, and even Singapore and the Philippines.

External Sector

The external sector refers to the balance of payments which is the sum of the current account balance and the capital account balance. The current account balance is defined as the exports of goods and services less imports of goods and services plus net transfers. The capital account balance consists of short-term, medium-term and long-term capital flows. It is broken down into portfolio investments, direct investments and other investments including foreign loans.

Effect on the Exchange Rates

The most important variable that was attacked furiously is the exchange rate as it affects production, trade and capital flows. The speculative attacks on the regional currencies triggered the currency crisis and the eventual devaluation which led to severe weakening of the ASEAN currencies against the US dollar particularly the Thai baht, the Indonesian rupiah, the Malaysian ringgit and the Philippine peso. The Singapore dollar was also impacted but not as severely as the other currencies. Table 9.7 shows the average exchange rates of ASEAN currencies vis-à-vis the US dollar.

The fall in the rupiah was much more than the Thai bath for a number of reasons. First, the economic fundamentals of Indonesia were, in retrospect, much less stronger than they seemed.[36] In terms of the macroeconomic fundamentals such as the size and the rate of growth of the current account deficits, the level and decline of foreign exchange reserves, the slowing down of exports, the rate of inflation, and large private capital inflows, one could say that Indonesia would hardly be considered inferior to Thailand or that Indonesia's macroeconomy were in much better shape than that of Thailand.[37] Later, it became clear that the fundamental weakness in the Indonesian economy lay within the private sector, which went on an investment spending spree, abetted by an ever increasing volume of foreign loans made available at minimum security and prudence. Second, the negative market response to the ambiguity in the policy stance of former President Soeharto sent mixed signals of the sincerity of his commitment in the early stage of IMF intervention.

---

36 Mohamed Sadli, "The Indonesian Crisis...," 1998, p.273.

37 See Andrew MacIntyre, "Political Institutions and the Economic Crisis in Thailand and Indonesia," *ASEAN Economic Bulletin,* Vol.15, No.3, p.366; Hal Hill, *Southeast Asia's Economic Crisis: Origins, Lessons and the Way Forward*, Singapore: Institute of Southeast Asian Studies, 1998, p.8.

Table 9.7 – Average Exchange Rates of ASEAN Currencies vis-à-vis the US dollar

	1997Q2	1997Q3	1997Q4	1998Q1	1998Q2	1998Q3
Indonesia	2437.2	2791.3	4005.7	9433.4	10460.8	12252.1
Malaysia	2.5081	2.7771	3.4818	3.9960	3.8451	4.0570
Philippines	26.371	29.798	35.384	40.639	39.379	42.865
Singapore	1.4348	1.4880	1.5960	1.6761	1.6449	1.7293
Thailand	25.90	33.034	40.662	47.094	40.331	41.059

Source: IMF, *International Financial Statistics*, Washington D.C.: International Monetary Fund, 1998.

Not only did the currencies weaken but also did the regional domestic interest rates rise as seen in Table 9.8. Indonesia had the largest increase in interest rates from the pre-crisis rate of 18.72 per cent to 34.9 per cent during the third quarter of 1998. The hefty devaluations and increases in interest rates generated severe impact on various sectors of the respective economies; namely, the external, production, labor and financial sectors. This section provides an analysis of the impact of the economic crisis on these sectors.

Table 9.8 – Interest Rates in Southeast Asia (in %)

	1997Q2	1997Q3	1997Q4	1998Q1	1998Q2	1998Q3
Indonesia	18.72	23.38	26.19	26.33	32.16	34.93
Malaysia	9.34	9.60	9.98	11.16	12.21	n.a.
Philippines	13.21	17.42	20.70	20.43	17.06	.n.a.
Singapore	6.26	6.26	6.51	7.77	7.77	7.72
Thailand	12.75	13.92	14.92	15.25	15.25	14.83

Source: IMF, *International Financial Statistics*, Washington D.C.: International Monetary Fund, 1998.

Effect on Exports of Goods and Services

As exchange rate depreciates, exports become cheaper. But exports from the Southeast Asian region had remained stagnant due to weak demand from importing countries and the emergence of more competitive new markets. Table 9.9 shows that Southeast Asian global exports dropped significantly during the period from 1997Q3 to 1998Q3. The lack of international trade finance hindered the import-production-export capabilities of manufacturing firms particularly in Indonesia whose exports have collapsed as banks rejected letters of credit due to the concern about the viability and risks of Indonesian banks.

However, the type of commodity being produced and exported matters as far as the impact of the crisis is concerned. If a country produces a large proportion of its exports in the form of intermediate goods, then the impact of the crisis is much less severe as these goods are essential in the manufacture of other goods. For example, about 81 percent of Singapore's exports to the region are intermediate goods which are needed to manufacture products for exports to developed markets outside the region. However, the all important non-oil exports and even re-exports were affected by the crisis due to the weak import demand. Not only that exports of goods have been affected, even the exports of services from labor-abundant countries of Indonesia, Thailand and the Philippines to labor-scarce countries of Singapore and Malaysia.

Table 9.9 Southeast Asia's Global Exports, (Quarterly Changes, %)

	1997Q3	1997Q4	1998Q1	1998Q2	1998Q3	1998Q4
Indonesia	0.4	-12.1	-42.4	-8.6	2.5	13.1
Malaysia	-5.7	-4.8	-24.0	-0.1	-3.1	4.1
Philippines	3.3	-4.4	-13.9	-8.4	6.4	1.4
Singapore	1.4	-5.3	-17.5	-4.6	-0.2	3.6
Thailand	-7.2	-13.9	-19.4	-2.1	-1.0	10.3

Source: IMF, *International Financial Statistics*, Washington D.C.: International Monetary Fund, 2000.

Effect on Imports of Goods and Services

As exchange rate depreciates, imports become more expensive. This, combined with falling incomes, reduced the demand for imported goods by Southeast Asian countries as shown in Table 9.10 particularly during the first two quarters of 1998. The US trade data showed the substantial state-by-state picture of the value of the Asian marketplace to American exports in which thirty-percent of US exports went to Asia. Among eight states, California, Washington and Oregon exported more than 50 per cent to Asia. US export sales to the hard-hit region fell by 11.5 per cent in the first quarter of 1998.[38] In Europe, Asia's financial crisis started to affect Europe's exports from heavy machinery to telephones inducing further unemployment.[39]

Table 9.10 Southeast Asia's Global Imports, (Quarterly Changes, %)

	1997Q3	1997Q4	1998Q1	1998Q2	1998Q3	1998Q4
Indonesia	4.9	-0.7	-10.0	-1.0	7.1	-1.4
Malaysia	0.9	-1.4	-12.0	-0.9	3.3	5.2
Philippines	12.8	2.6	-4.5	-0.4	11.5	3.2
Singapore	-0.1	-0.7	-8.9	0.2	-2.1	1.7
Thailand	4.0	1.9	-9.7	-1.7	4.4	2.5

Source: IMF, *Direction of Trade Statistics*, Washington D.C.: International Monetary Fund, 2000.

Even the imports of services including educational expenditures overseas of students from the region have dropped. In the case of Malaysia, prior to the crisis, there were about 50,000 Malaysians who were studying in Britain, the US, Australia and the Middle East. In response to the crisis, many universities in Britain had offered assistance to students through reduced tuition fees, reduced accommodation costs, and arranging flexible repayment schemes. Asian students studying abroad were asked to either return home, where educational fees are lower or cut their expenses and look for jobs to supplement their pocket and tuition money. This is particularly so for those Southeast Asian students in Japan where costs are extremely high.

38 The Straits Times, "Billions of $ clients of US States," April 3, 1998, p.8.

39 The Straits Times, January 21, 1999, p.52.

Effect on Trade Balance and Current Account

Despite a lower export growth, some countries in the Southeast Asian region had in fact generated substantial trade surpluses due to cuts in import spending. A trade surplus of US$150 billion was generated jointly by Malaysia, Thailand, Indonesia, the Philippines and South Korea. Thailand's current account went into a substantial surplus throughout 1998, with a cumulated surplus of US$11.7 for the first 10 months. However, it was achieved at a very high cost particularly in terms of a severe economic recession and serious unemployment problems.[40] Malaysia was able to turn around from a current account deficit of RM14 billion in 1997 to about RM20 billion in 1998 as its trade surplus increased from RM11 billion to about RM43 billion.[41] Table 9.11 shows the improvement in the current account balance of Southeast Asian countries during the 1997-98 period.

Effect on Capital Account

The volatility and weakening of the regional currencies affected foreign investors' confidence. As such, there was massive short-term capital outflows and reduced foreign investments in the region including direct investments. This is shown by a sharp and largest reversal of capital flows from a net private capital inflow of US$97 billion in 1996 to a net private capital outflow of US$12 billion in 1997 for Indonesia, Malaysia, the Philippines, Thailand and South Korea. In East Asia, an aggregate of US$100 billion had flown out in the past 18 months since July 1997. This could be explained by what is known as the "reverse free-rider" behavior, which states that "if an individual investor sees other investors pulling out, that alone is an incentive for him to pull out, irrespective of the merits of the investment process itself."[42]

Table 9.11. Current Account Balance (% of GDP)

	1996	1997	1998
Indonesia	-3.3	-3.0	3.4
Malaysia	-4.9	-5.1	15.7
Philippines	-4.7	-5.2	2.0
Singapore	15.9	15.8	20.9
Thailand	-7.9	-1.9	12.2

Source: UNCTAD, *Trade and Development Report*, Switzerland: United Nations Conference on Trade and Development, 1999, p.31.

In the case of Southeast Asia, it was estimated that total FDI inflows during the January-June 1998 period was only half of that during the July-December 1997 period. The Singapore government targeted an FDI level of S$7.8 billion in 1998 which was lower than the S$8.5 billion in 1997. Thus far, about $5.7 billion was approved during the January-September 1998 period, with $1.8 billion in the third quarter. Thailand's FDI was expected to hit around

40 Sussangkarn Chalongphob, "Thailand: Toward Economic Solvency," Paper presented at the 1999 Regional Outlook Forum, organized by the Institute of Southeast Asian Studies (ISEAS), Singapore, January, 1999.

41 Zainal Aznam Yusof, "Malaysian Economic Outlook: Moving Towards a Slow Recovery," Paper presented at the 1999 Regional Outlook Forum, organized by ISEAS, Singapore, January, 1999, p.15.

42 See James Dean, "Asia's Financial Crisis…," p.275.

US$10 billion in 1998 arising mainly from mergers and acquisitions of Thai firms and from investments in insurance and services. So far, Thailand had around US$7 billion in direct investment inflow during the first ten months of 1998. In the case of Indonesia, the value of foreign investments approved by the government from Jan-March 1998 fell by 22 per cent to US$5.1 billion amid concerns about rising inflation and a contracting economy.

While most of the Asian countries have been experiencing slowdown in FDI inflows, China has certainly benefited. As the second highest recipient of FDI in the world in the last four years, China generated an aggregate of US$27 billion from January-August 1998 and expected to hit US$40 billion by the end of 1998. Investments from Europe had increased by 87 percent and from the United States and Canada, by 19 percent. Taiwan's investments also had increased by a hefty 42 percent at US$695 million during the first six months of 1998. Investments from Southeast Asia had dropped: from Singapore, by 42 percent; from Thailand, by 30 percent; and from Indonesia, by 42 percent. Japanese investments also had fallen by 31 percent during the January-June 1998.

Production Sector

Various components of the aggregate demand were influenced severely by the crisis; namely, private consumption, private investment, government spending, exports and imports. Due to the inflationary pressures brought about by the weakening of the regional currencies and because of the shortage of basic commodities, prices increased significantly during the initial phase of the crisis particularly in response to panic-buying activities in some parts of the region. Thailand did not experience as much severe inflationary pressures as other countries as it has been blessed with abundant agricultural produce. With higher prices and declining incomes, private consumption fell. With massive losses combined with the on-going credit crunch and pessimistic business expectations, private investment was also affected severely. Even the government sector implemented some expenditure-cutting measures which include (i) budget cuts in the Malaysian government expenditure programs for the youth from M$1.2 million in 1997 to M$300,000 in 1998[43] and (ii) cancellation by the Thai government of the agreement for its purchase of F-18 from the United States.

With reduced export and import demand, total demand declined. Production and hence output also fell. Consequently, the rates of growth of real GDP contracted and economic projections were revised a number of times. This was true not only in the case of economies in Southeast Asia but also in other parts of the world as shown in Table 9.12. Among ASEAN, Indonesia was the worst hit with a growth contraction of real GDP by 13.7 per cent in 1998. This was followed by Thailand (-7.8 per cent) and Malaysia (-6.7 per cent). Singapore's growth estimate was between 0.5 per cent to 1.0 per cent, but actually grew by a modest 1.5 per cent. Other Asian economies also contracted in 1998; namely, South Korea (-5.6 per cent), Hong Kong (-5.1 per cent) and Japan (-2.8 per cent).

---

[43] The Straits Times, January 20, 1998, p.27.

Table 9.12. Real GDP Growth Rates, in %

	1997	1998 Final Forecast	1998 Actual	1999 Forecast*
Indonesia	4.9	- 13.0	- 13.7	- 1.0 to +1.0
Malaysia	7.7	– 5.0	- 6.7	1.0
Philippines	5.2	- 1.0	- 0.5	2.5
Singapore	7.8	0.5 to 1.0	1.5	-1.0 to +1.0
Thailand	- 0.4	- 8.2	- 7.8	1.0
Japan	2.5	- 2.5	- 2.8	0.5
China	8.8	8.0	7.8	7.0
Hongkong	5.3	- 5.0	- 5.1	0.5
South Korea	5.5	- 7.8	- 5.6	2.0
Taiwan	6.8	5.0	4.8	4.8

Note: * National government forecasts, Source: Straits Times (Various issues), Sussangkarn Chalongphob, "Thailand: Toward Economic Solvency"; Zainal Aznam Yusof, "Malaysian Economic Outlook: Moving Towards a Slow Recovery"; Hadi Soesastro, "The Indonesian Economy under Habibie," Regional Outlook Forum, organized by ISEAS, Singapore, January 1999; and ADB Asian Development Outlook, Manila: Asian Development Bank, 1999.

The Philippine economy posted a much lower contraction of 0.5 per cent and hence was not as severely affected as other Asian economies due to the following factors. First, the Philippine monetary authorities had implemented banking and financial reforms following the severe economic crisis in the early 1980s. Financial reforms commenced in the early 1980s and continued in the 1990s. These reforms include strengthening prudential regulations in relation to minimum capitalization requirements, increasing compliance with with the minimum capital to risk asset ratio, the single borrower limit, the limit on DOSRI loans, stipulations regarding interlocking directorships and management, making provisions for loan losses or doubtful accounts and reviewing the bailout policy for problematic banks, rehabilitation of the Central Bank, increasing bank's capitalization, and unification of the Manila and Makati exchanges and liberalization of foreign investment and foreign exchange transactions[44] Because of these reforms, authorities were in a better position to handle the crisis by lowering interest rates and a moderate rebound of the peso.

Second, the Philippine economy, with a low base growth, did not experience the high-growth phenomenon experienced by other Southeast Asian economies. It expanded only by 2.1 percent during the 1980s and by 2.8 percent during the 1991-96 period while the other economies grew by some 6 to 8 percent during the same period. Third, exports and private consumption remained high and helped offset the fall in private investment Philippine merchandise exports rose by 15-20 percent since much of these exports go to the United States which has had a strong economy.[45] Moreover, in terms of non-merchandise exports, a substantial source of foreign exchange revenues is a record US$6 billion remittance of overseas Filipino workers which have helped the affected families to cope up better with the

---

44 See Ponciano Intal, Jr., Melanie Milo, Celia Reyes and Leilani Basilio, "The Philippines," in *East Asia in Crisis: From Being a Miracle to Needing One*? Ross McLeod and Ross Garnaut (eds), London: Routledge, 1998, p.145-161; Gerardo Sicat, 1998, p.292; Stanley Fischer, "The Asian Crisis: The Beginning of the End?", Speech delivered at the Asia Society, Manila, February 26, 1999, at http://www.asiasociety.org/speeches/fischer.html

45 R. McKee, 'Philippines could be worse," 2000. http://www.megastories.com/seasia/philippi/philippi2.html

crisis. Fourth, the Philippine foreign debt exposure has improved by significantly reducing the proportion of short-term private debt as analyzed earlier. Thus, the Philippine economy has proved to be more robust and resilient than Thailand, Indonesia, and South Korea particularly.

Labor Sector

Many workers were retrenched and some contracts were not been renewed. Unemployment increased. Indonesia has had the largest and fastest growing number of unemployed workers due to bankruptcies, closures, mergers and credit crunch. A case in point was highlighted in a *Far Eastern Economic Review* article depicting the sad plight of Sugiyanto:

> In mid-October (1997), 21 year old Sugiyanto was still swinging a shovel at a Jakarta construction site. Six months earlier he had made a personal pilgrimage by overnight bus to the capital from the village of Banjarjo in central Java. "On TV, it looked so easy to make money in Jakarta." The money, however, has since dried up. Indonesia's financial crisis has brought many construction projects to a halt. With new jobs scarce, Sugiyanto slunk home to Banjarjo in early November – only to find that his father's rice paddies had dried up too. Months of dry weather have turned the fields in to a parched brown expanse. No work, no monsoon, no escape. For Sugiyanto, there's nothing to do all day but slump over a motorcycle, hoping to cadge a few faded bills in return for offering lifts. There are few takers. Villagers would rather spend their money on water.[46]

In Malaysia, a total of 29,188 workers across the country were retrenched between May 1997 and the middle of March 1998. Most of those affected were in the construction and industrial sectors. There were about 1.3 million registered foreign workers and some 300,000 illegal workers in Malaysia. From 2.6 percent in 1997, Malaysia's unemployment rate was forecast by the Ministry of Finance to rise to about 5 percent in 1998.

In Thailand, about 44,753 workers were dismissed in 1997, with about 70 percent being laid off in the second half of 1997. Total unemployment was forecast to reach 2.2 million in 1998 according to the Thai Farmer Bank Research Center as Thailand shifts from a tight labor market to a surplus of low- and medium-skilled workers.[47] The national labor force survey estimated that Thai's unemployment rate would reach about 5 percent in 1998.[48] The social impacts in Thailand while widespread were not as noticeably severe as in some of the other crisis countries partly due to the agricultural sector which has been able to provide some form of safety net. Many migrants in the urban areas have families back on the farm whom they can turn to. As most Thai farmers own their land, they could reap most of the benefits from the increase in the prices of primary commodities, and could help to cushion the effects on relatives who had lost jobs in the cities and who eventually provided additional assistance in terms of manpower and a redundancy payment of six months wages.

---

46 See Margot Cohen, *Far Eastern Economic Review,* December 25, 1997, as cited in World Bank, *East Asia: The Road to Recovery,* Washington D.C.: World Bank, p.1.

47 Chalamwong Yongyuth, "Economic Crisis, International Migration and the Labor Market in Thailand," *TDRI Quarterly Review.* Vol.13, No.1, 1998, p.14.

48 Sussangkarn Chalongphob, "Thailand: Toward Economic Solvency…," 1999.

The economy-wide unemployment rate in the Philippines reached some 13.3 per cent in the first quarter of 1998, higher than the 10.7 per cent rate in the same period a year ago. The unemployment rate in the Manila region alone jumped to around 19 per cent. In the whole Philippines, it was estimated that an additional 1 million jobs would be lost as more than 1,000 companies, mostly manufacturing, were closed and as the nation experienced a 9-month drought. From January 1, 1998 to September 30, 1998, some 2,402 enterprises resorted to closure and retrenchment of workers with the bulk of those affected coming from the National Capital Region of Metro Manila.[49]

Even Singapore workers were not spared. While Singapore experienced full employment of around 2 per cent from 1989 to 1997, the unemployment rate rose to 2.3 per cent in October 1998 and was estimated to reach 4-5 per cent in 1998. It was projected that retrenchment in 1998 would reach about 25,000, but it actually hit the 27,000 mark. The issue of cyclical versus structural unemployment was also discussed. Weak demand results in a cyclical unemployment. But with the intended shift towards a knowledge-based economy, structural unemployment arises as some 600,000 workers, mostly aged above 40, have lower education. The difference between Singapore and other Southeast Asian economies is that the Singaporean government has resources to implement a training and re-training manpower program to ensure that workers' skills be upgraded and continued to be employable. There are much less opportunities for other ASEAN governments to follow Singapore's policy as they have less resources to work with.

What about the plight of foreign workers in Southeast Asia? Thailand, for example, reported that it would deport 300,000 foreign factory workers as part of a plan to repatriate one million illegal migrants (mostly from Myanmar) to make the jobs available for the Thais. Under the plan, employers of illegal workers would be given 45 days to prepare their repatriation, otherwise legal action would be taken against the employers [50] At least 2 million jobs were expected to be lost. In some other countries, a number of workers and expatriates had to return home as their contracts were not renewed or as a result of the restructuring and downsizing activities taking place in many companies. Some decided to look for other jobs or remained in their jobs but at less favorable terms including reduced wages and benefits. In some countries, while prices increased markedly due to hefty devaluation, lowering of nominal wages would lead to a reduction in the purchasing power of workers.

Financial Sector

The crisis has exposed the weaknesses of banking and financial sector as most banks and finance companies had massive amounts of non-performing loans. In Malaysia, the net non-performing loans (NPLs) of the banking system, on the basis of the 6-month criteria, decreased from 8.9 percent as at end-June 1998 to 8.1 percent as at end-September 1998. Based on a 3-month criterion, NPL increased to 12.8 percent. Standard and Poor estimated that it would reach 32 per cent of total loans in 1999. For Thai banks, the ratio of NPLs to

---

49 Mario Lamberte and Josef Yaf, *Scenarios for Economic Recovery: The Philippines,* Discussion Paper No.99-05, Manila: Philippine Institute for Development Studies, 1999.

50 The Straits Times, January 20, 1998, p.23.

total lending rose from 29.4 percent in 1998Q1 to 46 percent in October 1998 while the corresponding ratios for finance companies were 43.8 percent and 63.6 percent, respectively.

In Singapore, the Deputy Prime Minister announced to the Parliament in February 1998 that the regional exposure of domestic banks "was not alarmingly high" and that local banks had made provisions for their regional loans.[51] It was also reported that the six local banking groups exposure to the five worst hit economies reached some 17 per cent or S$5.9 billion of their loans as at August 1998, but was only 2.7 per cent of total loans. While housing loans in Singapore was valued at S$10.4 billion in 1985, it expanded to S$64 billion in March 1998. The total exposure of financial institutions such as the Housing Development Board and the Central Provident Fund reached some S$140 billion, out of which some S$25 billion was granted by the banks to building and construction industry.

As analyzed in the first section, the massive expansion of domestic credit prior to the crisis enabled both individuals and firms to borrow heavily and invest the proceeds of their loans in non-productive and speculative projects including real estate and construction business. The consequent massive losses of banks and finance companies resulted in their closures and mergers. For example, in Thailand, 56 finance companies were closed towards the end of 1997. This was reminiscent of the closure of 24 finance and security companies in 1983 arising from the financial crisis experienced by the Thai economy in the early 1980s due to poor managerial practices accompanied by inadequate regulations and supervision of financial institutions.[52] In 1998, four commercial banks were taken over by the state due to bad loan portfolios. The commercial banks need to raise 200 billion baht (S$8.3 billion). However, because of poor credit ratings, it had become difficult for the Thai banks to raise new capital. Thailand's five biggest banks had their credit ratings cut by Moody's Investors. These banks were Bangkok Bank, Krung Thai Bank, Thai Farmers Bank, Siam Commercial Bank, and Bank Ayudhya. The downgrading affected US$4.4 billion of outstanding debt.[53]

The stock markets also bore the brunt of the crisis because of the drastic decline in the stock prices which in turn led to the shrinking of people's wealth. For example, in Malaysia, between July 1997 and mid-January 1998, the all-ordinaries index of the Kuala Lumpur Stock Exchange fell by over 65 percent, whipping off almost US$225 billion of share values, the biggest stock market plunge among the crisis countries.[54] In the case of Singapore, the stock market price index, which rose by some 145 percent during 1990-96, had fallen by more than 60 percent off its peak by the third quarter of 1998, reflecting a serious erosion of investor confidence.[55]

Moreover, the massive losses of international banks with large exposure in the region have contributed to the shortage of foreign loans in the region. For example, Japanese banks were the biggest losers in the Asia-Oceania region for a combined net loss of US$36.8 billion

---

51 Business Times, February 20, 1998.

52 Barry Johnston, "Distressed Financial Institutions in Thailand: Structural Weaknesses, Support Operations and Economic Consequences," in Sundararajan V. and Tomas Balino (eds), *Banking and Crisis: Cases and Issues*, Washington DC: IMF, p.234.

53 The Straits Times, April 1, 1998, p.6.

54 Prema-chandra Athukorala, "Swimming against the Tide: Crisis Management in Malaysia," *ASEAN Economic Bulletin,* Vol.15, No.3, 1998, p.282.

55 Siow Yue Chia, "The Asian Financial Crisis: Singapore's Experience and Response," *ASEAN Economic Bulletin,* Vol.15, No.3, 1998, p.302.

from US$2.56 billion a year ago.[56] Bad loans of Japanese banks reached an aggregate of US$600 billion since the 1980s. The substantial exposure of Japanese banks in non-performing loans or bad loans is indeed worrisome and would certainly lead to credit squeeze in the region. The social unrest and political instability in some parts of the region had added to the lack of financial capital.

CONCLUSION

In this chapter, we identified the conditions which existed before the crisis and which contributed to the crisis. These include rising income expectations which had stimulated consumption and investment spending, huge current account deficits largely due to private sector deficits; serious external debt problems arising from higher proportion of short-term commercial loans; and rapid domestic credit creation which was due to massive capital inflows; and higher per capita savings. We also analyzed the severe consequences of the economic crisis including weaker domestic currencies, rising current account surpluses (due to reduced import spending combined with weaker exports), massive short-term capital outflows, reduced foreign direct investments, output contraction, massive unemployment as well as closures and mergers of banks and finance companies. The severity of the impact, however, varies across the crisis-hit countries with Indonesia and Thailand being the most severely affected, and Singapore, the least.

QUESTIONS FOR DISCUSSION

1. What has caused the 1997/98 economic crisis in Southeast Asia?
2. The 1997/98 crisis had devastating consequences on the different sectors of the economy. Some sectors were hit more than others. Discuss.
3. On the one hand, the rapid economic growth experienced by the Southeast Asian economies, particularly during the past three decades and a half prior to the 1997/98 crisis, could have not taken place had they not depended on developed countries particularly Japan, the United States and the EU for trade, investments, loans, technology and aid. On the other hand, it is this dependence on developed countries that contributed significantly to the crisis. Do you agree or disagree with these statements? Explain.

SUGGESTED MATERIALS FOR CASE STUDIES

Asia

Lim, Linda Y.C., 1998, "Whose 'Model' Failed? Implications of the Asian Economic Crisis," *Washington Quarterly,* Vol.21, No.3, pp.25-36.

56 Asiaweek, September 11, 1998, p.83.

Malaysia

Jomo K.S., 1998, "Financial Liberalization, Crises and Malaysian Policy Responses," *World Development,* Vol.26, No.8, pp.1563-1574.

Philippines

Lim, Joseph, 2000, "The Effects of the East Asian Crisis on the Employment of Women and Men: The Philippine Case," *World Development,* Vol.28, No.7, pp.1285-1306.

References for Chapter 9

Adelman, Irma and Yeldan, Erinc, 2000, "The Minimal Conditions for a Financial Crisis: a Multiregional Intertemporal CGE model of the Asian Crisis," *World Development,* Vol.28, No.6, pp.1087-1100.

Asian Development Bank, 1999, *Asian Development Outlook*, New York: Oxford University Press for ADB.

Asian Development Bank, Various Issues, *Key Indicators for Asian and Pacific Developing Countries,* New York: Oxford University Press.

Asiaweek, September 11, 1998, p.3.

Athukorala, Prema-Chandra, 1998, "Swimming against the Tide: Crisis Management in Malaysia," *ASEAN Economic Bulletin,* Vol.15, No.3, pp.281-289.

Baer, Werner; Miles, William and Moran, Allen, 1999, "The End of the Asian Myth: Why were the Experts Fooled?" *World Development,* Vol.27, No.10, pp.1735-1747.

Bank Negara Malaysia, 1998, *The East Asian Crisis – Causes, Policy responses, Lessons and Issues.* Group of 15 Working Paper No.4, Switzerland.

Bhanupong, Nidhiprabha, 1998, "Economic Crises and the Debt-Deflation Episode in Thailand," *Asean Economic Bulletin,* Vol.15, No.3, pp.309-318.

Bird, Graham and A. Milne, 1999, "Miracle to Meltdown: a Pathology of the East Asian Crisis," *Third World Quarterly,* Vol.20, No.2, pp. 421-437.

Chalongphob, Sussangkarn, 1999, "Thailand: Toward Economic Solvency," paper presented at the 1999 Regional Outlook Forum, organized by the Institute of Southeast Asian Studies (ISEAS), Singapore, January.

Chang, Ha-Joon, 2000, "The Hazard of Moral Hazard: Untangling the Asian Crisis," *World Development,* Vol.28, No.4, pp.775-788.

Chia, Siow Yue, 1998, "The Asian Financial Crisis: Singapore's Experience and Response," *ASEAN Economic Bulletin,* Vol.15, No.3, pp.297-308.

Cohen, Margot Cohen, *Far Eastern Economic Review,* December 25, 1997, as cited in World Bank, *East Asia: The Road to Recovery,* Washington D.C.: World Bank, p.1.

Corsetti, Giancarlo, Paolo Pesenti, and Nouriel Roubini, 1999, "What Caused the Asian Currency and Financial Crisis?" *Japan and the World Economy*, Vol.11, No.3, pp.303-373.

Dean, James, 1998, "Asia's Financial Crisis in Historical Perspective," *Journal of the Asia Pacific Economy,* Vol.3, No.3, pp.267-283.

Dufey, Gunter, 1999, " Asian Financial Markets: A Pedagogic Note," *Journal of Asian Business*. Vol.15, No.1, pp.65-71.

Frankel, Jeffrey, 1998, "The Asian Model, the Miracle, the Crisis and the Fund," A speech delivered at the US International Trade Commission, April 16.

Hadi, Soesastro, 1999, "The Indonesian Economy under Habibie," paper presented at the 1999 Regional Outlook Forum, organized by ISEAS, Singapore, January.

Hesse, Helmut and Auria, Laura, 1998, "The Financial Crisis in Southeast Asia: Causes and Effects on the Global Economy," *Economics,* Vol.57.

Hesse, Helmut and Laura Auria, 1998, "The Financial Crisis in Southeast Asia: Causes and Effects on the Global Economy," *Economics*. A Biannual Collection of Recent German Studies, Tübingen: Institut für Wissenschaftliche Zusammearbeit, Vol. 57, pp. 45-70.

Hill, Hal, 1998, "Southeast Asia's Economic Crisis: Origins, Lessons and the Way Forward", Paper presented at the ISEAS 30th anniversary conference: Southeast Asia in the 21st Century, Singapore, July 30- August 1.

Intal, Ponciano Jr, Melanie Milo, Celia Reyes and Leilani Basilio, 1998, "The Philippines," in *East Asia in Crisis: From Being a Miracle to Needing One*? in Ross. H. McLeod and R. Garnaut (eds.), London: Routledge, pp.145-161.

International Monetary Fund, Various Issues, *International Financial Statistics,* Washington DC.: IMF.

Johnston, Barry, 1991, "Distressed Financial Institutions in Thailand: Structural Weaknesses, Support Operations and Economic Consequences," in Sundararajan V. and Balino, T. (eds), *Banking and Crisis: Cases and Issues,* Washington DC: IMF.

Kim, Youn-Suk and Hyeng Keun Koo, 1999, "Asia's Contagious Financial Crisis and its Impact on Korea," *Journal of Asian Economics,* Vol.10, No.1, pp.111-121.

Krugman, Paul, 1994, "The Myth of Asia's Miracle," *Foreign Affairs*, Vol.73, No.6, pp. 62-78.

Krugman, Paul, 1997, "What Ever Happened to the Asian Miracle?" *Fortune,* August 18, p.12

Lamberte, Mario and Josef Yaf, 1999, *Scenarios for Economic Recovery: The Philippines*. Discussion Paper No.99-05. Manila: Philippine Institute for Development Studies.

Lim, Linda Y.C., 1998, "Whose Model Failed? Implications of the Asian Economic Crisis," *The Washington Quarterly*, Vol.21, No.3, pp.25-36.

MacIntryre, Andrew, 1998, "Political Institutions and the Economic Crisis in Thailand and Indonesia," *ASEAN Economic Bulletin,* Vol.15, No.3, pp.362-372.

McKinnon, Ronald and H. Pill, 1998, "International Overborrowing – A Decomposition of Credit and Currency Risk", *World Development.* Vol.26, No.7, pp.1267-1282.

Pakorn, Vichyanond., 1998, "Thailand's Financial Evolution and the 1997 Crisis," Paper presented for the conference, The Miracle Undone: Asia's Financial Crisis, C.I.D.E. Mexico City, February 20.

Radelet, Steven and Jeffrey Sachs, 1998, *The Onset of the East Asian Financial Crisis,* Cambridge: National Bureau of Economic Research.

Radelet, Steven and Jeffrey Sachs, 1998, *The East Asian Financial Crisis: Diagnosis, Remedies and Prospects,* Cambridge: Harvard Institute for International Development.

Rosenberger, Leif Roderick, 1997, "Southeast Asia's Currency Crisis: A Diagnosis and Prescription," *Contemporary Southeast Asia,* Vol.19, No.3, pp.223-251.

Sadli, Mohammad, 1998, "The Indonesian Crisis," *ASEAN Economic Bulletin,* Vol.15, No.3, pp.272-289.

Sicat, Gerardo, 1998, "The Philippine Economy in the Asian Crisis," *ASEAN Economic Bulletin,* Vol.15, No.3, pp.290-296.

The Nation, "Learning from Thailand's Mistakes," November, 17, 1998, p.B1-B2.

The Straits Times, January 20, 1998, p.27 and p.23.

The Straits Times, April 1, 1998, p.6

The Straits Times, "Billions of $ clients of US States," April 3, 1998, p.8.

The Straits Times, January 21, 1999, p.52.

Tower, Ivory, 1997, "Mexico 1994 versus Thailand 1997," *TDRI Quarterly Review,* Vol.12, No.3, pp.9-14.

UNCTAD, 1999, *Trade and Development Report*, Geneva: UNCTAD.

Wade, Robert, 1998, "The Asian Debt-and-Development Crisis of 1997-?: Causes and Consequences," *World Development,* Vol.26, No.8, pp.1535-1553.

World Bank, 1997, *World Development Indicators*, Washington DC: The World Bank.

Yongyuth, Chalamwong, "Economic Crisis, International Migration and the Labor Market in Thailand," *TDRI Quarterly Review.* Vol.13, No.1, pp.12-21.

Zainal A.Y., 1999, "Malaysian Economic Outlook: Moving Towards a Slow Recovery," paper presented at the 1999 Regional Outlook Forum, organized by ISEAS, Singapore, January.

Internet Sources

Fischer, Stanley, 1999, "The Asian Crisis: the Beginning of the End?", speech delivered at the Asia Society, Manila, February 26, at *http://www.asiasociety.org/speeches/fischer.html*

McKee, R. 'Philippines could be worse," 2000. *http://www.megastories.com/seasia/philippi/philippi2.html*

Schwartz, Anna, 1998, "International Financial Crises: Myths and Realities," *The Cato Journal*, Vol.17, No.3. as obtained from [*http://www.cato.org/pubs/journal/cj17n3-3.html*].

Chapter 10

POLICY RESPONSES TO THE CRISIS[1]

ABSTRACT

In response to the crisis, various policies were adopted by the international organizations and by the respective economies in the region. This chapter evaluates each of these policies. The differences in their policy actions are highlighted and explained. This chapter also examines the various strategies aimed at improving the global financial architecture.

INTRODUCTION

In response to the crisis, the respective governments in Southeast Asia have adopted various policy responses which include, among others, reliance on international financial assistance, demand-management policies (fiscal, monetary and exchange rate policies), supply-side policies and capital controls, bank restructuring, and privatization. The differences in their policy responses manifest (i) the extent and nature of the crisis (e.g. Malaysia's relatively smaller foreign debt vs. Indonesia's huge foreign debt), (ii) the pervasiveness and severity of the impact of the crisis (e.g. Singapore's banking and financial sector being less affected than in Thailand and Indonesia), (iii) the governments' priorities, in terms of achieving either a move towards internal balance (less severe impact on unemployment) or a move towards external balance (trade surplus) or both, and (iv) the government leaders' willingness to subscribe to international financial order and its conditionalities (Thailand and Indonesia following the IMF conditions which required painful and immediate reforms versus Malaysia's non-subscription to IMF's conditionalities and instead adopt a 'pragmatic' approach).

---

[1] Earlier versions of this chapter include guest lectures and seminar presentations at the following institutions: El Colegio de Mexico (1998), Nordic Institute of Asian Studies (Copenhagen, 1999), Ludwig-Maximilians Universitaet Muenchen (Munich, 1999), University of Sweden's Center for Pacific and Asian Studies and Stockholm School of Economics (1999), and the University of Paris Sciences-Po Asia-Europe Program (1999); and invited conference papers presented at Chulalongkorn University (1999) and the Center for the Study of International Institutions (Austria, 2003).

POLICY RESPONSES

International Financial Assistance

Thailand and Indonesia availed of the international financial assistance organized by the IMF and the World Bank with funds coming from them and various countries led by the US, Japan and the European Union (EU). In August 1997, the Thai government accepted an international financial package which consisted of a medium-term loan of US$17.2 billion to shore up Thai's foreign exchange reserves.[2] It also obtained US$1 billion trade assistance from the Asian Development Bank (ADB) to help Thai exporters. This came in the form of ADB-guaranteed export-financing facility involving 9-10 commercial banks from the US, Japan and EU. The ADB's move followed the IMF's relaxation of the budget surplus requirement from a target of 1 percent of the country's GDP to a modest deficit in the region of 1-2 percent due to the changed circumstances including slowing down of Thailand's economic growth.[3]

On October 8, 1997, Indonesia sought IMF assistance and on November 5, 1997, the IMF announced a US$43 billion financial package for Indonesia. This package consisted of a combined loan of US$18 billion from the IMF, World Bank and Asian Development Bank (ADB); US$20 billion from bilateral donor countries; and, US$5 billion from Indonesia's own reserves.[4] The bilateral donor countries include Singapore, Malaysia, Japan and Australia which had offered an additional US$11 billion financial rescue package to Jakarta since these countries have traded heavily with Indonesia and have long-term investments that they understandably want protected.[5]

However, the size of the total international package was exaggerated for two reasons.[6] First, some of the loans from the ADB, World Bank and other governments which contributed to the package would have been provided under the normal lending programs to Indonesia. Second, the US$5 billion of Indonesia's own foreign assets, which had not previously been counted as part of its official foreign exchange reserves, was also included. It is to be noted that Indonesia's call for the IMF support was rather slow in contrast to Thailand due to two factors. First is the optimistic assessment of Indonesia's growth fundamentals and economic prospects provided by the IMF and World Bank. Moreover, on May 30, 1996, the World Economic Forum ranked Indonesia 15th in terms of its economic competitiveness, an

---

2 Key elements of the financial package included financial restructuring measures (such as closure of insolvent financial institutions); fiscal adjustment measures equivalent to some 3 percent of GDP to bring the fiscal balance back into surplus and contribute to shrinking the current account deficit; and control of domestic credit. For full discussion, see Timothy Lane and Marianne Schulze-Ghattas, *IMF-Supported Programs in Indonesia, Korea and Thailand: A Preliminary Assessment,* Occasional Paper No.178, Washington D.C.: International Monetary Fund, 1999, p.2.

3 The Straits Times, "Thailand gets reprieve with fresh financing plan from ADB," February 14, 1998, p.53.

4 Soedradjad Djiwandono, "Bank Indonesia and the Recent Crisis," *Bulletin of Indonesian Economic Studies,* Vol.36, No.1, 2000, p.56.

5 Leif Roderick Rosenberger, "Southeast Asia's Currency Crisis: A Diagnosis and Prescription," *Contemporary Southeast Asia,* Vol.19, No.3, p.244.

6 George Fane, "Indonesian Economic Policies and Performance," *The World Economy*, Vol.22, No.5, July 1999, p.661.

improvement from its 30th rank a year ago.[7] Second, former President Suharto was reluctant to adhere to the stringent IMF conditions as it could significantly erode his power and strength. In February 1998, the Suharto government even proposed the establishment of a currency board but gave up the idea due to strong pressures from various sectors, compounded with political uncertainties and civil unrest. On May 21, 1998, President Suharto resigned amidst Indonesia's economic, political and social problems.

The IMF-arranged financial assistance to Indonesia was subject to various stringent conditions and reforms. These include (a) a revision of the 1998/99 budget to start in April 1998 with the following targets – zero economic growth, 20 percent inflation, rupiah pegged at 5000 to US$ and budget deficit of 1 percent of GDP, (b) a gradual phasing out of government subsidies for domestic fuels and electricity, (c) giving autonomy to Bank Indonesia to set interest rates, and (d) encouraging banks to merge and adhere to requirements and rules. One of the additional reforms would have been the dismantling of the National Logistics Agency (Bulog) as it was accused of monopolizing the commodity markets to the detriment of the consumers and the protectors. However, a United Nations report stated that Bulog is what stands in the way of mass starvation for millions in the remote parts of Indonesia due to its price-stabilizing role. The report projected that there will be a shortage of 3.5 million tons of rice in 1998 and hence called on the international community to donate 2 million tons either in kind, cash or credit.[8]

Malaysia succumbed to the crisis with only a little foreign debt exposure and this had enabled Malaysia to muddle through without an IMF-sponsored rescue package.[9] Moreover, former PM Mahathir did not want to follow a "high-interest rate and reduced-spending" strategy imposed by the IMF. While high interest rates could lead to exchange rate stability in the short-run, it would certainly be detrimental to banking and industries in the medium to long run. Certainly, the Malaysian government had placed a stronger preference for a 'low interest rate and increased spending policy' as it would generate less severe impact on the larger proportion of its population. The Philippines, which was supposed to exit from over three decades of economic stewardship by the IMF, was given extension to do so provided that the government passed a new oil deregulation law and boost government revenues. It entered into a precautionary arrangement which was has less stringent conditions than the full-fledged standby arrangement that Indonesia and Thailand entered into with the IMF.[10] The IMF agreed to extend the US$1.3 billion aid package to the Philippines and effectively put an end to the planned graduation from the IMF program in the meantime.[11] Singapore did not need to resort to IMF funding because of its healthy financial position. Singapore was in a position to lend a helping hand instead as illustrated by its assistance to Indonesia, Thailand and Malaysia.

As for international financial assistance, there are a number of relevant issues. First, has the IMF done its role properly? There has been a growing debate on whether the IMF has

---

7 Mohammad Sadli, "The Indonesian Crisis," ASEAN Economic Bulletin, Vol.15, No.3, 1998, pp.272-289.

8 The Straits Times, "Jakarta agency wards off starvation," April 21, 1998, p.20.

9 Prema-chandra Athukorala, "Swimming against the Tide: Crisis Management in Malaysia," *ASEAN Economic Bulletin,* Vol.15, No.3, 1998, pp.281-289.

10 Soedradjad Djiwandono, "Bank Indonesia...," 2000, p.52.

11 Gerardo Sicat, "The Philippine Economy in the Asian Crisis," *ASEAN Economic Bulletin,* Vol.15, No.3, 1998, p.292.

prescribed the correct policies or not. Based on its practice, the IMF has imposed its orthodox policies of restrictive fiscal and monetary policies (cutbacks in government spending and high interest rates) and closures of companies and financial institutions deemed insolvent. However, it has been perceived by many that these tight macroeconomic conditions set by the IMF were "highly controversial" and "dead wrong" because despite these policies the crisis-hit Asian economies continued to deteriorate including the failure of the high interest rates to attract capital inflows and prevent capital outflows, and the resultant rising level of debt service obligations.[12] Jeffrey Sachs, one of the well-known critics, argued that:

> The region does not need wanton budget cutting, credit tightening and emergency bank closures. It needs stable or even expansionary monetary and fiscal policies to counterbalance the decline in foreign loans.[13]

Even then World Bank's former chief economist Joseph Stiglitz critically stated that "[o]ne ought to focus on things that caused the crisis, not on things that make it more difficult to deal with."[14] The IMF's Policy Division Director Jack Boorman also admitted that "mistakes were probably made when it [the IMF] recommended the 16 bank closures without giving investors adequate guarantees" and "that the policy regarding depositor guarantees now appears to have been ill-advised."[15] In another occasion, Mr. Hubert Neiss, then IMF's top representative to Asia, added that "[h]ad we known the depth of the recession, we would not have recommended such a tightening of fiscal policy, instead of a loosening of policy."[16]

Expansionist, instead of restrictive, policies should have been implemented immediately to counteract the contractionary impact of the crisis. As Corden put it,

> The IMF is not straightforwardly right or wrong. It is probably now mostly right with its prescriptions and conditions for the countries affected by the Asian financial and currency crisis. But it went off the rails at the beginning in 1997, though it has gone gradually back on again, being flexible.[17]

However, there has been a chorus of disapproval as far as the role of the IMF is concerned, that is, whether the IMF had ameliorated or exacerbated the crisis situation. As a consequence, it has been suggested that there is a fundamental need to strengthen the international financial architecture including the need to reform the IMF. Among the proposals, the French suggested a need to boost the role of a 24-member IMF advisory group that includes 10 representatives from emerging markets and give them a louder voice in IMF decisions. It has been perceived that the IMF policies reflect too much the views of the United

---

12 For more discussion, see James Dean, "Asia's Financial Crisis in Historical Perspective," *Journal of the Asia Pacific Economy,* Vol.3, No.3, 1998, pp.267-268.

13 Jeffrey Sachs, "IMF Orthodoxy isn't what Southeast Asia needs," *International Herald Tribune,* November 4, 1997, p.8, as cited in Richard Robison and Andrew Rosser, "Contesting Reform: Indonesia's New Order and the IMF," *World Development,* Vol.26, No.8, 1998, pp.1594.

14 *The International Herald Tribune,* January 16, 1998, p.11, as cited in James Dean, "Asia's Financial Crisis...," p.268.

15 The Straits Times, "We badly misgauged Asian crisis," January 20, 1999, p.1.

16 The Straits Times, "IMF to review bail-out conditions," January 29, 1999, p.93.

17 Max Corden, "*The Asian Crisis: Is there a Way Out?*" Public lecture delivered in Singapore as a Distinguished Fellow in International Economics and Finance, ISEAS, Singapore, 1998, p.2.

States. However, the French proposal was opposed by the US.[18] The British proposed to merge parts of the Fund with the World Bank and the former US Secretary of State George Shultz proposed to scrap the IMF.

On the other hand, there are others who view that the IMF should continue to exist and what is needed is to inject additional resources to the IMF to provide temporary assistance to afflicted economies. As Corden further declared,

> The IMF is needed, desperately needed, in situations like the Asian crisis, that there is no need to establish a new organization, and that it would be foolish – as some US rightwingers propose - to abolish it. The IMF should be provided with adequate resources to cope with major crises and these resources should not be used primarily to rescue international banks and other financial institutions – nor the owners and managers of domestic institutions in crisis countries – but to provide temporary relief to allow for necessary adjustments without major recessions or adverse effects on the mass of the population, and especially the poorest.[19]

Second, was there immediate action on the part of the IMF, the United States and the European Union? The answer is NO. The lack of immediate financial support from the international community contributed to the worsening of the crisis. The IMF admitted on January 19, 1999 that it had "badly misgauged" the severity of the Asian economic crisis. A long delay in the US Congress' approval of the increased funding for the IMF certainly proved to be a very costly exercise for the crisis-hit economies. The European Union's assistance came indirectly – that is, through its contribution to the IMF. Moreover, the Southeast Asian region is considered to be a much lower priority for the EU as compared to the Central and Eastern European countries including Russia where an enormous amount of financial assistance was given by the EU.

Third, why were Asian-based initiatives not supported? During the early phase of the crisis, Japan proposed the establishment of an Asian Monetary Fund to be capitalized at US$100 billion in order to provide the immediate financial assistance to the crisis-hit economies. Japan had good reasons for putting its money on the table as its banks were heavily exposed in Thailand, South Korea and Indonesia and it is in their interests to stabilize the volatile currency markets.[20] Moreover the Japanese economy is deeply integrated with its neighbors so that any slowdown or collapse would affect Japan immediately. The United States simply dismissed Japan's proposal as it would diminish the effectiveness of the IMF and its policies. Moreover, the US and the IMF feared that they would lose their influence in the Asian region. On its own initiative, Singapore also proposed the establishment of a multilateral fund to provide financial guarantees that would assist Indonesian's traders, but it did not receive much support from developed countries.

Fourth, should there be a bailout mechanism by the IMF? Who actually benefits from this bailout? It is argued that no firm or company should be shielded from bankruptcy by the IMF nor should there be any official bailout nor should foreign lenders be bailed out, knowing that 'it was misguided allocation of credit that got Asian countries into difficulty."[21] It is also

---

18 The Straits Times, "Camdessus supports plan," October 8, 1998, p.42.

19 Max Corden, "The Asian Crisis ...," 1998, p.61.

20 Nicola Bullard, Walden Bello and Kamal Mallhotra, "Taming the Tigers: the IMF and the Asian Crisis," *Third World Quarterly*, Vol.19, No.3, 1998, pp.505-555.

21 See James Dean, "Asia's Financial Crisis...," p.268.

viewed that this bailout mechanism has actually benefited, not the poor population, but a rather limited number of people including investors and lenders at the expense of the larger majority of the population. In the Mexican case, it was the bailout that punished 100 million people and in the Thai case, the rescue package, rather than benefiting the 60 million people, can end up in the hands of politically connected speculators who will bail out their money-losing ventures.[22] Johnson also stated that the IMF's money which went to Thailand, Indonesia and South Korea did not go the people of those countries as it went to the foreign banks that made too many shaky and imprudent loans to Thai, Indonesian and South Korean banks and businesses in the first place.[23] Thus, Corden proposed that in the restructuring of the financial architecture, both the creditors and investors should also be made accountable and share the consequences should a crisis occur.[24]

Demand-Management Policies

These are the orthodox policies aimed at affecting the various components of aggregate demand; namely, private consumption, private investment, government spending, exports and imports. These policies come in the form of (i) fiscal policy through changes in government spending and/or taxes, (ii) monetary policy through changes in money supply or interest rates, and (iii) exchange rate policy through intervention in the foreign exchange market to keep the exchange rate fixed or allowing the exchange rate to float but the Central Bank engages in some form of market intervention.

Fiscal and Monetary Policies

During the early phase of the crisis, Thailand and then Indonesia after some time, followed some expenditure-reducing policies through restrictive fiscal and monetary policies, following the IMF's prescribed policies. As Lane and Schulze-Ghattas stated:

> Macroeconomic policy adjustment was an essential element of the [IMF-supported] programs: monetary policy was aimed mainly at preventing a spiral of depreciation and inflation from emerging, while fiscal policy was initially intended mainly to provide some modest support for external adjustment and make room for the non-inflationary financing of the carrying costs of the needed bank restructuring.[25]

The Thai and Indonesian governments undertook austerity measures and reduced the expansion of domestic credit. With credit squeeze, private consumption, particularly of consumer durables, declined. Moreover, given the lack of animal spirits, a tight credit market and high interest rates, private investment also fell markedly. Singapore, Malaysia and the Philippines also adopted IMF-like austerity measures in some areas particularly on current government operations. Singapore, however, has continued to increase its expenditure on

---

22 Anna Schwartz, "International Financial Crises: Myths and Realities," *The Cato Journal*, Vol.17, No.3, 1998, p.4. as obtained from [http://www.cato.org/pubs/journal/cj17n3-3.html].

23 Chalmers Johnson, "Economic Crisis in East Asia: The Clash of Capitalisms," *Cambridge Journal of Economics,* Vol.22, 1998, pp.653-661.

24 Max Corden, "The Asian Crisis…," 1998, p.61.

25 See Timothy Lane and Marianne Schulze-Ghattas, *IMF-Supported Programs…, p.1.*

areas which could increase its productivity including investments on infrastructure and education.

The problem with the IMF's restrictive measures is that given an economic slowdown, any further tight fiscal and/or monetary policies would certainly aggravate the recessionary conditions faced by Southeast Asian economies. In the case of Singapore, it continued to implement infrastructure development projects to counteract the slowing down of its economy. With the turn of events in Malaysia, monetary policy had become expansionist with massive injection of domestic liquidity and the consequent lowering of interest rates. Benchmark interest rates fell from 11 percent to 8 percent on September 7, 1998. Moreover, statutory reserve requirements were reduced from 14.5 percent in March 1989 to 4 percent in September 1998. The lowering of interest rates was expected to boost domestic spending particularly private investment. Despite cuts in some sectors, overall government spending would be increased by 20 percent with increased spending in investments in physical and social infrastructure projects.

The effect of an expansionist fiscal and/or monetary policy is smaller in Singapore than in Malaysia given that the former is more highly open economy than the latter. Equivalently, the expenditure multiplier and hence the impact on GDP and employment will be much smaller in Singapore than in Malaysia.[26]

Exchange Rate Policies

As the Thai baht, Indonesian rupiah, Malaysian ringgit, Philippine pesos and Singapore dollar faced mounting attacks during the initial phase of the crisis, the respective central banks in Southeast Asia defended their currencies by intervening in the foreign exchange market, that is, selling US dollars in exchange for domestic currencies. Is it simply the Southeast Asian people doing the selling? Definitely not. It would certainly take an incredibly huge magnitude of currency sale to effect large fluctuations of the exchange rate and that substantial part of these transactions had taken place outside the Southeast Asian region.

It was argued that the hedge funds had contributed significantly to the massive exchange rate changes as they specialize in high risk financial instruments which involve currency and stock movements. Since 1992, the number of hedge funds had expanded more than three times to around 1500 funds. These hedge funds had managed assets worth more than US$200 billion including the large investments of some giant international banks.[27] However, some of these banks incurred huge losses from these investments in hedge funds. For example, Citigroup's Salomon Smith Barney unit lost US$1.33 billion in trading during the third quarter of 1998. Another example is UBS Warburg Dillon Read unit which lost money in 1998 and the near collapse of the hedge fund LTCM cost the bank 790 million francs. Bank America lost about US$573 million on loans to D.E. Shaw & Co., a hedge fund and securities firm.

Given the hefty depreciations of their respective currencies in the July-December 1997 period, could the central banks then continue to fight and defend their own currencies? The answer is NO as their holdings of foreign exchange reserves are limited. They would simply deplete their stocks should they continue to do so. Instead, they should allow their exchange

---

26 See Figure 10.1 in Appendix 1 for graphical analysis of demand-management and supply-side policy responses to the 1997/98 economic crsisis.

27 The Straits Times, "Banking giants beat hasty retreat after hedge fund losses," January 27, 1999, p.47.

rates to float. The Bank of Thailand had indeed wasted a large proportion of its foreign exchange reserves in order to defend the baht but to no avail. In an interview during the World Economic Forum at Davos in 1999, former Senior Minister Lee Kuan Yew (now Minister Mentor) noted that the Thai mistake was not that they did not know that hedge funds were attacking their currency, but that they tried to defend it – with the result that their reserves were depleted by US$23 billion.[28] This was indeed a very costly mistake which was further made serious by the Bank of Thailand's (through the Financial Institutional Development Fund) extension of financial support to the beleaguered financial institutions in the amount of 1.1 trillion bath (US$29 billion).

In the case of South Korea, its former central bank governor admitted that the Bank of Korea wasted up to US$26 billion between late 1996 and February 1997 in a futile attempt to defend the won.[29] In the Philippines, when speculation against the peso became heavy in July 1997, the authorities used almost one billion US dollars of reserves within few days without any positive results.[30] In Malaysia, Bank Negara Malaysia sold close to US$1.5 billion to prop up the ringgit when it came under heavy speculative attack in mid-May 1997.[31] The intervention in the foreign exchange markets became very costly as it resulted in the depletion of foreign exchange reserves at a time when regional economies were experiencing an export slowdown which adversely affected the inflow of foreign exchange earnings.[32]

Faced with tremendous attacks on their currencies and given the limited amount of international reserves, Thailand and Indonesia could no longer defend their currencies under the fixed exchange rate system. Consequently, the Thai baht and the Indonesian rupiah were floated on the July 2, 1997 and on August 13, 1997, respectively. The Thai bath/US$ rate moved immediately from 25 to 30 and rose drastically to 55 by January 1998.[33] It subsequently moderated to 45 by February 1998. The Indonesian exchange rate reached Rp15,000 per dollar in late January 1998 from Rp2,658 per dollar immediately before the August 1997 devaluation.[34] The Malaysian ringgit, the Philippine peso and the Singapore dollar also experienced significant weakening, but of different magnitudes. The devaluation of their respective currencies has the expenditure-switching effect away from imports (as imports become expensive) towards domestic goods. However, despite deep currency devaluations, the region's exports continued to be very weak. This indicates that devaluation by itself is no guarantee for an export-led recovery. The main problem faced by the Southeast Asian manufacturers was the lack of trade finance as most banks had restrained from extending loans due to fear of losing money.

---

28 The Straits Times, "Europe can differentiate now, says SM," February 3, 1999, p.3.

29 The Straits Times, "Seoul wasted forex reserves in bid to halt meltdown," January 26, 1999, p.15.

30 Gerardo Sicat, "The Philippine Economy…," 1998, p.292.

31 Prema-chandra Athukorala, "Swimming against the Tide…," 1998, p.282.

32 Bank Negara Malaysia, *The East Asian Crisis – Causes, Policy responses, Lessons and Issues.* Group of 15 Working Paper No.4, Switzerland, June 1998, p.6.

33 Peter Warr, "What Happened to Thailand?" *The World Economy,* Vol.22, No.5, 1999, p.645.

34 George Fane, "Indonesian Economic Policies…," 1999, p.662

Supply-Side Policies

Supply-side policies include those which affect capital, labor, technology and other factors of production – policies which affect the costs of doing business. Short-run policies include those which the government can directly influence such as cuts in both labor and non-labor costs including office and industrial rents, utility charges, statutory charges and port tariffs.

As Singapore is a very open economy, reliance on expansionist demand-management policies would indeed generate a very limited expansion of GDP and employment. As such, Singapore has depended heavily on supply-side policies aimed at reducing the costs of doing business in Singapore. These policies consisted of a S$10.5 billion cost-cutting measures.[35] This package consisted of a 10-percent rebate in corporate taxes, property tax rebates, cuts in industrial land rentals of up to 40 percent, lower transport charges through cuts in customs and excise duties for cars and petrols, and lower utility and telecommunication rates. Even in the case of the 1985/86 recession, Singapore also implemented cost-cutting measures to restore competitiveness including a reduction in compulsory employers' contribution to the Central Provident Fund (CPF) from 25 percent of wages to 10 percent, a reduction in corporate taxes, and accelerated depreciation.[36]

A large component of the production costs is labor cost. Thus, the Singapore government has depended on wage guidelines including wage cuts, restraint in wage increases, and even cuts in the contribution rates to the CPF, a compulsory savings scheme in Singapore in which both employers and employees each contribute 20 percent of the employees' salary to this fund. As part of the cost-cutting package cited above, the government reduced the annual variable component for civil servants in 1998 to ¾ month, down from the two months given last year. High salary officers and civil servants also received wage cuts from 1 to 5 percent. Even ministerial pay was cut by 10 percent. A significant component of the package is a 10-percentage point CPF cut in the employer's contribution rate from January 1999 for up to two years.

However, in high-inflation countries (due to hefty devaluation of their currencies), like Indonesia and the Philippines, cuts in nominal wages will lead to reduction in real wages. Singapore had experienced falling consumer prices as a result of the crisis. Had Singapore allowed its currency to depreciate according to market forces, this would result in higher domestic prices. Consequently, a cut in (or even freezing of) nominal wages would lead to erosion of real wages. For example, in Indonesia, the minimum wages in 1998 were frozen at 1997's level, but given high rates of inflation to hit 50 percent in 1998, Indonesia's real incomes were halved.[37]

Long-run policies include training and re-training programs for workers and more research and development activities for innovations and improvement in technology aimed at improving productivity. In Singapore, there are more than 600,000 workers with less than secondary education. As such, it is extremely important that these workers upgrade their skills and learn new tasks to be more productive and to be more employable in the future. There are

---

35 The Straits Times, "Government decides on $10.5 billion cut," November 25, 1998, p.1.

36 Max Corden, *Pragmatic Orthodoxy: Macroeconomic Policies in Seven East Asian Economies.* Occasional Papers No.61. New York: International Center for Economic Growth, 1996, p.36.

37 The Straits Times, "Indonesia's urban poor: wage freeze set to halve real incomes," April 1, 1999, p.4.

also other schemes such as the job re-design programs implemented by the Singapore Productivity and Standards Board which involves changing both job content and arrangement to encourage workers to become more productive.

Supply-side policies also include those policies which will stimulate an increase in capital formation. These include incentives to save and invest including cuts in corporate taxes and liberalization of some investment rules particularly on foreign direct investments as it contributes to capital formation. Given the crisis, it is indeed difficult to woo foreign investors without generous incentives including loosening the rules on foreign ownership. In Thailand, George Soros decided to invest in Thai steel mills and Thai companies dealing with electronics components. Singapore's DBS Bank bought Thai Sri Danu, Thailand's 12th largest bank, and ABN Amro of the Netherlands took a 75 percent stake in the Bank of Asia. Bangkok Bank and Thai Farmers Bank are among the many other banks seeking foreign capital.[38] Thus, the crisis had effectively forced the region's governments and firms to make deals with foreigners - with US and European investors rushing to acquire companies at bargain prices. The region's companies needed capital to recover. It is foreign capital which can provide the financing gap as domestic savings fall with erosion of per capita incomes in the region.

Capital Controls

Malaysia was also hit by the crisis as manifested in the loss of investors' confidence, significant capital outflows, depletion of foreign exchange reserves, severe impact on the stock markets, and marked depreciations of the ringgit. With Anwar Ibrahim as then finance minister, Malaysia followed IMF-like policies including tight monetary and fiscal policies (essentially, a combination of high-interest rate and reduced government spending policy) together with financial reforms. However, with the sacking of Anwar Ibrahim in August 1998, former PM Mahathir rejected the IMF-like policies. Instead, taking over from Anwar Ibrahim as finance manager, PM Mahathir tried to rescue the Malaysian economy through a combination of easier fiscal and monetary policies (i.e. higher government spending and lower interest rates, respectively) and imposition of capital controls.

Former PM Mahathir argued strongly that the speculators were mainly responsible for the crisis and suggested that international monetary authorities led by the IMF should be able to impose measures that would contain the flows of international financial capital particularly short term. While Malaysia continued to experience massive pressures on its ringgit and while no concrete measures were done to curtail short-term capital movements, Malaysia unilaterally imposed currency and capital controls on September 1, 1998. The controls which cover external accounts, authorized deposit institutions, trade settlement and currency held by travelers, were expected to contain the speculation on the ringgit and to minimize the impact of the short-term capital flows on the domestic economy.[39] The ringgit was also fixed to the US dollar at RM3.80. Malaysia was not the first, or only country in the world that imposed

---

[38] The Washington Post, "US, European firms finding Asian companies willing to deal," May 24, 1998, p.H4.

[39] Zainal Aznam Yusof, "Malaysian Economic Outlook: Moving Towards a Slow Recovery," Paper presented at the 1999 Regional Outlook Forum, organized by ISEAS, Singapore, January 1999, p.5.

capital controls. As at 1997, the IMF reported that 128 countries have still regulated their international financial transactions in some ways.[40]

These controls were largely aimed at the substantial offshore ringgit market in Singapore which constrained the ability of Malaysia's authorities to lower domestic interest rates. Consequently, all offshore ringgit had to be brought on shore by the end of September 1999. Moreover, the government restricted capital outflows by imposing a one-year holding period for repatriation of portfolio capital inflows. As Singapore's economy has been too closely linked with that of Malaysia, the Singapore government decided to stop trading on its Central Limit Order Book (CLOB) over-the-counter market, which was dominated by Malaysian stocks. This act resulted in a temporary freezing of over US$10 billion worth of Malaysian assets held in Singapore.

Certainly, Malaysia's imposition of capital controls met with strong criticisms from many countries as such policy has been viewed to derail the on-going financial liberalization activities. The long-term effects would be harmful due to lack of investors' confidence as could be gauged from a ranking by Euromoney. Malaysia was ranked 51st with a score of 41.89, which was 21 places down from its ranking in 1997. Singapore ranked 21st with a score of 89.17, the top in the league of Asian nations. All 180 countries involved were assessed on nine criteria ranging from economic performance and political risk, to debt indicators and access to long- and short-term financing, and other criteria.[41]

The imposition of capital controls is indeed costly and ineffective arising from administrative problems and rampant evasion. However, it was argued that short-term effects would be favorable to Malaysia. In fact, Malaysia reported that its current account balance had improved and that its foreign exchange reserves had increased. With capital controls, the Malaysian government was able to inject domestic liquidity into the economy aimed at boosting domestic demand particularly domestic investment and has allowed the economy to pick up. In May 1999, the former IMF managing director Michel Camdessus noted Malaysia's ability to recover from the crisis through its adoption of "soft system of control" together with structural reforms.[42] Thus, as Tomoika stated, "Malaysia subsequently proved that the negative opinions *[about its capital controls]* were not necessarily prophetic, as the economy has shown a relatively health recovery."[43]

The question most people asked then was "How long would Malaysia keep its capital controls?" In an interview at the World Economic Forum in Davos in 1999, former PM Mahathir stated that the controls would not be permanent, but would remain in place "until the international community devises a new financial regime that curbs currency traders."[44] However, the Malaysian government looked into the possibility of adjusting the 12-month holding period for portfolio investors, considering two of the possible options – exit tax and a most-favored investor status which gives exemptions to long-standing investors from exit taxes under certain conditions. About a fifth of the total KLSE re-capitalization of RM300 billion (end-November 1998) is owned by foreign interests. It was expected that after

[40] The Straits Times, "Malaysia's real problem," October 7, 1998, p.37.

[41] The Straits Times, "Singapore still least risky Asian nation," October 11, 1998, p.32.

[42] Business Times, May 18, 1999, p.9.

[43] Noriyuki Tomioka, "Causes of the Asian Crisis, Asian-style Capitalism and Transparency," *Asia-Pacific Review,* Vol.8, No.2, 2001, pp.47-65.

[44] The Straits Times, "Start of KL's exit tax 'weeks away," January 31, 1999, p.2.

September 1, 1999 around RM5 billion to RM20 billion of funds would be repatriated.[45] In February 1999, the one-year holding period was replaced with a system of graduated exit levies, and was further relaxed in September 1999. As Haggard stated, capital controls *[in Malaysia]* were carefully crafted to assure foreign direct investors and by mid-2001, they had been dismantled.[46]

Bank Restructuring

The first set of policies involves comprehensive measures and restructuring in the banking sector including the closure of insolvent banks and finance companies, as well as recapitalization and mergers of weak but viable financial institutions. In Indonesia, sixteen banks were closed in November 1997 and four state banks were merged into a single institution. The government established the Indonesian Banking Restructuring Agency (IBRA) to supervise and manage the restructuring of banks in poor financial condition and to manage the assets acquired during the restructuring process. Immediately, IBRA acquired 54 banks which accounted for 40 percent of the banking assets. In August 1998, it further took over seven major banks and the activities of seven other banks were frozen. It was estimated that the restructuring of the banking system will require a huge amount of over 400 trillion rupiahs, which is equivalent to more than half of the country's GDP.[47]

In Thailand, the Financial Institution Development (FIDF) has been created to repair the banking system including the screening of the rehabilitation plans submitted by the 58 suspended financial companies in order to determine their status. This led to the closure of the 56 financial companies. In the first half of 1998, it was reported that borrowings by FIDP to finance its bail-out of weaker financial institutions has reached over 700 billion baht in May 1998. To lessen its dependence on the costly repurchase securities market, the Thai government passed a new law in May 1998 which enabled it to issue government bonds of up to 500 billion baht to pay for the debt of the FIDF.[48] Moreover, with seed money of 1 billion baht, the Thai government established the Asset Management Corporation to manage the disposal of the assets which belonged to the closed finance companies.

In Malaysia, the Asset Management Company (AMC) called Danaharta was created to repair the banking sector. It intended to acquire 18 banks under Phase I (weaker banks that require recapitalization by Danamodal). As at end-December 1998, Danaharta had signed agreements with 13 banks and expected to acquire the remaining banks by the first quarter of 1999.[49] A significant step undertaken by the Malaysian government was the merger of 58

---

45 Zainal Aznam Yusof, "Malaysian Economic Outlook…," 1999, p.8.

46 Stephen Haggard, "Politics, Institutions and Globalization: The Aftermath of the Asian Financial Crisis," *American Asian Review,* Vol.19, No.2, 2001, pp.71-98.

47 Hadi Soesastro, "The Indonesian Economy under Habibie," Paper presented at the 1999 Regional Outlook Forum, organized by ISEAS, Singapore, January 1999, p.14.

48 Sussangkarn Chalongphob, "Thailand: Toward Economic Solvency," Paper presented at the 1999 Regional Economic Outlook, organized by the Institute of Southeast Asian Studies (ISEAS), Singapore, January 1999, p.3.

49 Zainal Aznam Yusof, "Malaysian Economic Outlook…," 1999, p.10.

financial institutions into six large banking groups which were expected to provide competition with foreign banks.[50]

The second set of policies involves restructuring of the external debt including rolling over and rescheduling the settlement of external debt particularly short-term debt. By the end of March 1998, Indonesia's private sector debt was estimated at about US$72.5 billion of which about half was to be repaid within one year. It was found that Indonesia's private sector debt is very difficult to manage as it is spread among hundreds of corporations with issued paper of widely differing quality. Various activities have been undertaken to help manage Indonesia's private debt including the creation of the Indonesian Debt Restructuring Agency (INDRA) whose operation involves a conversion of the foreign exchange loans of participating domestic debtors into rupiah denomination and their repayment switched to INDRA, which will make the repayments in foreign exchange to international creditors. Another instrument, called the Jakarta Initiative, was created to help companies restructure their debt and facilitate out of court settlement. However, both INDRA and the Jakarta Initiative have no takers.[51] In the case of Thailand, it was reported that at the start of 1998, it had about US$35 billion in short-term debt. The risks were not over yet as there was still about US$25 billion of short-term debt remaining which needed to be restructured including debt-equity conversion.[52] In the case of Malaysia, a "club loan" was formed by a group of 12 foreign banks incorporated in Malaysia and extended a loan of RM5.13 billion (US$1.35 billion) to the Malaysian government to help restructure banks.[53]

Privatization

Southeast Asian economies have adopted privatization activities that have provided additional financial resources and more competition. Privatization aims to eliminate the weak and inefficient producers particularly those which have received massive government protection. In Indonesia, the government planned to sell 12 state-owned enterprises (SOEs) to raise revenues estimated at Rp15 trillion, as part of an agreement with the IMF. However, the first privatization exercise (the selling of PT Semen Gresik, a group of cement companies) was not successful due to the protests of the people in West Sumatra against privatization. In the end, the Cemex from Mexico was only a minority shareholder as it was allowed only to buy a 20 percent share.[54] An estimated target of Rp13.0 trillion was set for the fiscal year 1999-2000, but only half of it was realized due to some problems including its unpopularity among the Indonesian people because of their belief that some public enterprises should remain government-owned and because of the threat felt by them due to loss of privileges or due to unemployment arising from privatization.[55]

In the case of Malaysia, its privatization programme involves the sale, in full or part, of government companies; contracts for private companies to invest and run services such as

50 M. Shanmugam, "Merger by Decree," *Malaysian Business,* October 16, 1999, p.11.

51 Hadi Soesastro, "The Indonesian Economy...," 1999, p.14.

52 Sussangkarn Chalongphob, "Thailand ...," 1999, p.2.

53 Zainal Aznam Yusof, "Malaysian Economic Outlook...," 1999, p.9

54 Hadi Soesastro, "The Indonesian Economy...," 1999, p.7.

55 George Fane, "Survey of Recent Developments," *Bulletin of Indonesian Economic Studies,* Vol.36, No.1, April 2000, p.28.

hospital maintenance and concessions to invest and operate attractive projects such as the national sewerage system. Malaysia's privatization was, however, not directly in response to the crisis as it began as early as 1984. It was reported that privatization in Malaysia has helped the government save about RM7 billion (S$2.8 billion) annually in operating expenditure and RM73 billion in development spending. The sale of government-owned shares and assets had generated more than RM20 billion. Since the early 1990s, however, problems have cropped up as many investors saw privatization as a way to get rich and nothing else. Government's contracts are given to those with a track record and not overnight wealth-seekers.[56]

In the case of Thailand, privatization includes government-owned enterprises in transport, utilities, energy and communications. It is expected that the privatization of a large number of government-owned enterprises including the Rathachaburi project, the Airport Authorities and the Thai Airways, would be completed before the end of the year 2000.[57]

Improving the Global Financial Architecture

The globalization of financial markets has taken place at a much more rapid pace than the globalization of commodities and labor because of the tremendous developments in the information and communications technologies that have made financial transactions easier, faster and cheaper. However, the only constraints to financial transactions are national regulations which have been liberalized at a fast pace. As Tobin stated, "most observers, West and East, public and private, in governments and international institutions, in banks and businesses, in big countries and small, now agree that *financial globalization went too far too fast*."[58] He further stated that:

> As these *[national regulations]* have been liberalized in country after country, international financial flows have flooded national securities markets and inundated banking systems all over the world. These flows could be the vehicles by which savings in the advanced capitalist democracies are channelled into productive capital investments in the developing countries of Asia, Africa, and Latin America. Or they could be causes of currency crises, recessions and depressions, unemployment and deprivation in those countries. Or both.[59]

In East Asia, there have been 80-100 crises over the past quarter century.[60] Crises have become more frequent and more severe indicating a fundamental weakness in global economic arrangements. In the case of the 1997/98 economic crisis, the impact was so devastating that even the ADB characterized the economic hardship during the crisis as

56 The Straits Times, "KL's privatization policy draws flak," April 21, 1998, p.24.

57 Dredner Kleinwort Benson, "Privatization in Thailand 2000," *Asiamoney,* May 2000, p.17-18.

58 James Tobin, "Financial Globalization," *World Development,* Vol.28, No.6, 2000, p.1102.

59 James Tobin, "Financial Globalization," ... p.1101.

60 Carl-Johan Lindgren, Gillian Garcia, and Matthew I. Saal, *Banking Soundness and Macroeconomic Policy,* Washington D.C.: International Monetary Fund, 1996, p.20, as cited in Joseph Stiglitz, "Capital Market Liberalization, Economic Growth, and Instability," *World Development,* Vol.28, No.6, 2000, p.1075.

similar to that suffered during the Great Depression.[61] The severity of the crisis, the speed of its transmission, and the weak international response have all contributed to wide-ranging deliberations on the governance of international finance. The resultant issues discussed have focused on the need to improve the global financial architecture to prevent future crisis, and to manage it more effectively should it occur. The 1999 issue of the *Asian Development Outlook* published by the ADB provides an excellent analysis of the proposals aimed at strengthening the international financial architecture, namely, (a) controlling capital flows, (b) improving regulatory standards, (c) rethinking exchange rate regimes, (d) creating an international lender of last resort, and (e) bailing in the private sector. Each of these proposals will be briefly discussed below.[62]

Capital Controls

The Asian crisis showed that ill-planned liberalization of capital flows could lead to financial instabilities. As Jeffrey Sachs has argued, "It was financial market reform that allowed the Thai and South Korean banks to tap into short-term international loans in the early 1990s, thereby bringing together these banks with excited young investors who were happy to be in Bangkok and Seoul for the first time."[63] When countries free up their capital accounts, they become more susceptible to crisis because of the weaknesses in the domestic financial system arising from the lack of adequate and stringent supervision and regulation of financial institutions. As pointed by Ha-Joon Chang, the Korean crisis is a crisis from under-regulation rather than from over-regulation.[64] In Thailand's case, Dr. Olarn Chaipravat, the president of Siam Commercial Bank, admitted that Thailand committed two mistakes involving its financial and foreign exchange market regulations:

> The first mistake lay in the Bank of Thailand's lax regulations, which allowed the inexperienced local commercial banks to directly conduct foreign exchange transactions with offshore banks. The Bank of Thailand also had no experience in dealing with direct US dollar/baht transactions with offshore banks, except with the International Monetary Fund.... *[The second mistake]* involves the lax finance and banking regulations in supervising the offshore baht denominated debt market. During the early 1990s, at the height of the financial bubble, Thai companies avoided high interest rates at home to fight inflation by floating commercial paper in the offshore market as a means to raise cheap money.[65]

Even Joseph Stiglitz used an analogy by comparing capital account liberalization to putting a race car engine into an old car and setting off without checking the tires or training the driver. He further stated that:

---

61 See Asian Development Bank, *Asian Development Outlook 1999,* New York: Oxford University Press, p.21.

62 For a complete discussion, see Asian Development Bank, *Asian Development Outlook 1999,* pp.38-45.

63 Jeffrey Sachs, "Global Capitalism: Making it Work," *The Economist*, September 12, 1998, p.24, as cited in Kanishka Jayasuriya and Andrew Rosser, "Economic Orthodoxy ...," p.386.

64 See Ha-Joon Chang, "Korea: The Misunderstood Crisis," *World Development,* Vol.26, No.8, 1998, pp.1555-1561.

65 *The Nation,* "Learning from Thailand's Mistakes," November 17, 1998, p.B1.

> Perhaps with appropriate tires and training, the car might perform better; but without such equipment and training, it is almost inevitable that an accident will occur. One might actually have done far better with the older, more reliable engine: performance would have been slower, but there would have been less potential for an accident. Similarly, the international economic architecture must be designed to "work" not just in the presence of perfect economic management, but with the kind of fallible governments and public officials that in fact occur in democratic societies.[66]

There are two types of challenges that could result from private capital inflows.[67] First, massive inflows of capital have resulted in economic overheating and the problems associated with the appreciation of the real exchange rate. Second, sharp reversals in capital inflows have proved disruptive and costly. To minimize the risks associated with capital mobility, there are two sets of proposals: first, those measures aimed at slowing down capital inflows, and second, those measures aimed at controlling capital outflows.

To control ***capital inflows***, particularly "hot money," James Tobin proposed the introduction of a "simple small tax on foreign exchange transactions, levied at an agreed common rate by all countries where such transactions originate in significant amount."[68] Another measure is to tax foreign borrowings. As in Chile's case, domestic companies borrowing abroad had to place 30 percent of the proceeds at the Chilean central bank for a period of one year. Also another way is to set limits on open foreign currency positions of *both* domestic banks and companies since a regulation that focuses only on local banks will shift the foreign borrowings to local companies.

The policy of controlling ***capital outflows*** will enable the central bank authorities to lower the domestic interest rates in order to stimulate the domestic economy. However, this policy is viewed to be risky as it can unsettle the domestic markets and possibly generate negative impacts for the market access of other developing economies. Moreover, the imposition of controls on capital outflows can create incentives for corruption and hence weakens the political support towards unpopular structural policy reforms.

Improving Regulatory Standards

There are several proposals which came from the Group of 22 (G22) working reports aimed at improving the international standards of financial regulation and supervision. One set of proposals is concerned with transparency and accountability like requiring private companies to follow national accounting standards and requiring financial institutions and companies to compile and publish data and other related information on their international transactions. Another set of proposals, which is concerned with strengthening the financial systems, identifies the weaknesses and problems of many domestic financial sectors like

---

66 Joseph Stiglitz, "Capital Market Liberalization, Economic Growth, and Instability," *World Development,* Vol.28, No.6, 2000, p.1075.

67 Pradumna Rana, "Private Capital Flows to Asian Developing Countries: Past Trends and Future Prospects," *Asian Economic Crisis: Causes, Consequences and Policy Lessons,* Development Papers No.20, Bangkok: United Nations Economic and Social Commission for Asia and the Pacific, 1999, p.91.

68 According to Tobin, a tax of 0.1 or 0.2 percent means nothing for a round trip of a year or more from one currency to another and back. But for one-week round trips, it would be equivalent to a difference between interest rates in the two markets of 10 or 20 percent per year. See James Tobin, "Financial Globalization," ... p.1104.

inadequate risk management, defective deposit insurance schemes, and the mismatched assets and liabilities. The proposal is to encourage both industrial and developing countries to adopt the international supervisory standards prescribed in the Basle Capital Accords including requiring banks to adhere to the minimum capital adequacy standards. To improve the existing regulatory standards, several proposals include the need to tighten the rules on foreign borrowing in developing countries and the need to update the Basle capital adequacy standards (as the risk weightings for short-term loans are much lower than for the long-term loans and hence induces banks to provide more short-term rather than long-term loans). A more radical proposal to improve regulatory and supervisory standards is to create an international financial authority for financial institutions and a board of overseers of global financial markets. Although the creation of a global financial authority is viewed as unrealistic, the G7 has created a "Financial Stability Forum" which brings together central bank officials, finance ministers, financial regulators and representatives of multilateral organizations. The Forum aims to identify and evaluate the issues and uncertainties affecting the international financial system, and to determine the policy actions needed to respond to these uncertainties.

Rethinking Exchange Rate Regimes

The experiences of some Asian countries during the July 1997/98 crisis showed that fixed, but adjustable, exchange rate system could not be sustained given an increasingly mobile global capital. With speculative attacks on their currencies, the monetary authorities had to impose tight monetary and fiscal policies, that is, high interest rates and budget cuts. Moreover, the fixed exchange rate system had encouraged domestic financial institutions and companies to engage in heavy foreign borrowings without hedging.

The general consensus now is for countries to link their currencies to another by adopting a currency board system or by forging a currency union, or by allowing their currency to float. A flexible exchange rate system has several advantages. First, countries with fixed exchange rates have to defend their currencies in times of speculative attacks by depleting their limited foreign reserves and hence suffer crisis of investor confidence. With a flexible exchange rate system, countries are less likely to face this crisis of investor confidence. Second, countries with a fixed exchange rate system cannot inject domestic liquidity to the financial system given the limited stock of foreign reserves. In a flexible exchange rate system, the exchange rate adjusts and hence gives monetary authorities the freedom to provide domestic liquidity to the system.

Creating an International Lender of Last Resort

While central banks act as the lender of last resort in national economies, it has been proposed that an international body be created to perform the similar function in an international environment with highly integrated capital markets. It has been suggested that the International Monetary Fund should be given this role since it has generally been performing this function. It has injected liquidity in some countries with balance of payments crises.

Several conceptual and practical problems, however, exist regarding this lender of last resort role. For example, the lender of last resort should be able to provide indefinite amount of liquidity if a country suffers from liquidity crisis, and it should demand restructuring and adjustment if a country suffers from insolvency crisis. However, the experience of the 1997/98 Asian crisis showed that it is difficult to distinguish between illiquidity and insolvency. Another problem arises from the fact that while central banks have the power to close or merge insolvent banks and financial institutions, the same does not apply to an international lender of last resort, that is, it has no power to close down national central banks, much more an erring government. The third problem refers to the inability or the lack of capacity of the international lender of last resort to print more money in order to provide an unlimited amount of liquidity. This problem arises because of the limited amount of resources of this lender of last resort.

An interesting proposal put forward by Japan is the establishment of regional currency support mechanisms, for example, in Asia, Western Hemisphere and Eastern Europe, with the objective of complementing the role and function of the IMF. Countries that are economically interdependent through trade and investments could pool their financial resources together to provide for this regional currency support mechanism. An example of this mechanism is the proposal by Japan to form an Asian Monetary Fund (AMF) in September 1997. While the ADB complements the World Bank, the proposed AMF could also complement the IMF. The AMF could provide early warning signals of impending financial crisis most effectively at the regional level given its familiarity with the regional conditions (informational advantage) and regional location. The proposed initial funding was set at US$100 billion half of which would come from Japan and the balance from China, Hong Kong, Singapore and Taiwan. From these funds, the AMF could provide immediate financial support to the crisis-hit countries instead of waiting for a much delayed response from the IMF and other international agencies. The immediate injection of the much needed liquidity into the financial system could prevent the sharp weakening of the regional currencies as experienced in the 1997/98 crisis. Because of the resistance by the IMF and the US due to its potential conflict, the AMF proposal did not push through despite Malaysia's strong support. Alternatively, Japan came up with a US$30 billion Miyazawa initiative for the Asian region, half of which would be used to finance short-term trade, and the other half was to finance medium- and long-term projects for economic recovery of the region.

"Bailing in" the Private Sector

At the center of this proposal is the need to minimize moral hazard. "Bailing in" the private sector will enable some of the burden of the financial crisis to be borne by the private investors and banks. One of the proposals is to encourage the IMF to "lend into arrears" whereby the IMF would lend to countries that are in default to private creditors, as long as the countries involved pursue policy adjustments and the private creditors negotiate for debt restructuring. A more radical proposal is the creation of an international bankruptcy court that will be responsible for restructuring the countries' debt. However, this proposal is not feasible because it would involve nations to give up their sovereignty and because of the differences in the national bankruptcy codes that would make it impossible for countries to reach a single international bankruptcy code.

CONCLUSION

In this chapter, we analyzed the various policy responses which the crisis-hit countries have adopted. Southeast Asian governments responded differently to the crisis including financial assistance, demand-management policies, supply-side policies, capital controls and others. Those differences are reflective of the following circumstances. First is in terms of the willingness of the political leadership to subscribe to the IMF and its conditionalities including implementation of restrictive fiscal and monetary policies, in exchange for its financial rescue package. Thailand followed the IMF's prescription and was awarded its efforts with a US$17 billion package. Indonesia, on the other hand, brought up the idea of setting up a currency board system but was unsuccessful and had to succumb to IMF's loan package and its conditionalities. Malaysia, on the other hand, strongly resisted the IMF's rule and money as former PM Mahathir did not want to follow a high-interest rate and reduced spending strategy imposed by the IMF. As such Malaysia pursued an expansionary fiscal and monetary policy. Such a policy would help the Malaysian economy to recover. Second is in terms of the relative effectiveness of expansionary demand-management in the case of Malaysia and supply-side policies in the case of Singapore. In the case of a very open economy like Singapore, demand-management policies would be less effective. Thus, in addition to increased fiscal spending on infrastructures, Singapore has relied on supply-side measures. Short-run measures include wage cuts, cuts in CPF contribution and cuts in non-wage costs. Long-run measures include training and retraining programs. Third is in terms of the lack of concrete measures to control the outflows of short-term capital which prompted the Malaysian government to impose capital and currency controls.

APPENDIX 1

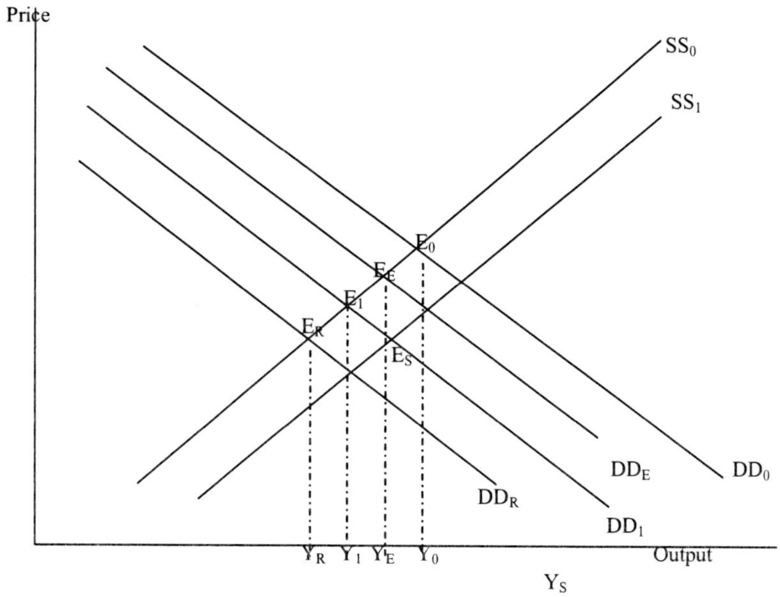

Figure 10.1. Demand-management and Supply-side Policy Responses to the Crisis

From an initial equilibrium position at E_0, the reduction in overall demand shifts the demand curve from DD_0 to DD_1. Income falls from Y_0 to Y_1 creating unemployment problem. A restrictive demand policy shifts the demand curve to DD_R. Income falls further to Y_R and unemployment worsens. During the initial phase of the crisis, the Malaysian government adopted a restrictive policy with the expected contractionary outcome on output and employment. However, it changed its stance to an expansionist one with increased government spending which shifts the demand curve to DD_E and income rises to Y_E. In the case of a very open economy like Singapore, the relative ineffectiveness of demand-management policy has prompted the government to rely heavily on supply-side policies which shifts the supply curve from SS_0 to SS_1. Output is expected to increase from Y_1 to Y_S.

Questions For Discussion

1. In response to the 1997/98 economic crisis, there were two sets of policy responses. First, each of the affected economies in Southeast Asia responded independently by adopting their own economic policies. Second, these economies joined together to pursue a regional approach to the crisis. Discuss how you would reconcile these two sets of policy responses.
2. Discuss what factors account for the differences in the policy responses by Southeast Asian governments.
3. Discuss clearly the lessons that can be derived from the 1997/98 economic crisis in Southeast Asia.

Suggested Materials for Case Studies

Fane, George, 1999, "Indonesian Economic Policies and Performance," *The World Economy*, Vol.22, No.5, pp. 651-668.

Haggard, Stephen, 2001, "Politics, Institutions and Globalization: The Aftermath of the Asian Financial Crisis," *American Asian Review,* Vol.19, No.2, pp.71-98.

References for Chapter 10

Asian Development Bank, 1999, *Asian Development Outlook 1999,* New York: Oxford University Press.

Athukorala, Prema-chandra, 1998, "Swimming against the Tide: Crisis Management in Malaysia," *ASEAN Economic Bulletin,* Vol.15, No.3, pp.281-289.

Bank Negara Malaysia, 1998, *The East Asian Crisis – Causes, Policy responses, Lessons and Issues.* Group of 15 Working Paper No.4, Switzerland.

Benson, Dredner Kleinwort, 2000, "Privatization in Thailand 2000," *Asiamoney,* May.

Bloomberg News, "Banking giants beat hasty retreat after hedge fund losses," *The Straits Times,* January 27, 1999, p.47.

Bullard, Nicola, Walden Bello and Kamal Mallhotra, 1998, "Taming the Tigers: the IMF and the Asian Crisis," *Third World Quarterly*, Vol.19, No.3, pp.505-555.

Chalongphob, Sussangkarn, 1999, "Thailand: Toward Economic Solvency", paper presented at the 1999 Regional Economic Outlook, organized by the Institute of Southeast Asian Studies (ISEAS), Singapore.

Chang, Ha-Joon, 1998, "Korea: The Misunderstood Crisis," *World Development,*Vol.26, No.8, pp.1555-1561.

Corden, Max, 1998, "*The Asian Crisis: Is there a Way Out?*" Public lecture delivered in Singapore as a Distinguished Fellow in International Economics and Finance, ISEAS, Singapore.

Corden, Max, 1996, *Pragmatic Orthodoxy: Macroeconomic Policies in Seven East Asian Economies,* Occasional Papers No.61. New York: International Center for Economic Growth.

Dean, James, 1998, "Asia's Financial Crisis in Historical Perspective," *Journal of the Asia Pacific Economy,* Vol.3, No.3.

Djiwandono, Soedradjad, 2000, "Bank Indonesia and the Recent Crisis," *Bulletin of Indonesian Economic Studies,* Vol.36, No.1, pp.47-72.

Fane, George, 1999, "Indonesian Economic Policies and Performance," *The World Economy*, Vol.22, No.5, pp. 651-668.

Fane, George, 2000, "Survey of Recent Developments," *Bulletin of Indonesian Economic Studies,* Vol.36, No.1, pp.13-45.

Haggard, Stephen, 2001, "Politics, Institutions and Globalization: The Aftermath of the Asian Financial Crisis," *American Asian Review,* Vol.19, No.2, pp.71-98.

Johnson, Chalmers, 1998, "Economic Crisis in East Asia: The Clash of Capitalisms," *Cambridge Journal of Economics,* Vol.22, No.6, pp.653-661.

Lane, Timothy and Marianne Schulze-Ghattas, 1999, *IMF-Supported Programs in Indonesia, Korea and Thailand: A Preliminary Assessment,* Occasional Paper No.178, Washington D.C.: International Monetary Fund.

Lindgren, C., G. Garcia and M.Saal, 1996, *Banking Soundness and Macroeconomic Policy,* Washington D.C.: International Monetary Fund, p.20, as cited in Joseph Stiglitz, 2000, "Capital Market Liberalization, Economic Growth, and Instability," *World Development,* Vol.28, No.6.

Rana, Pradumna, 1999, "Private Capital Flows to Asian Developing Countries: Past Trends and Future Prospects," *Asian Economic Crisis: Causes, Consequences and Policy Lessons,* Development Papers No.20, Bangkok: United Nations Economic and Social Commission for Asia and the Pacific.

Rosenberger, Leif Roderick, 1998, "Southeast Asia's Currency Crisis: A Diagnosis and Prescription," *Contemporary Southeast Asia,* Vol.19, No.3, pp.223-252.

Sachs, Jeffrey, 1997, "IMF Orthodoxy isn't what Southeast Asia needs," *International Herald Tribune,* November 4, p.8, as cited in Robison, Richard and Andrew Rosser, 1998, "Contesting Reform: Indonesia's New Order and the IMF," *World Development,* Vol.26, No.8, pp.1594.

Sachs, Jeffrey, 1998, "Global capitalism: making it work," *The Economist*, September 12, p.24, as cited in Kanishka Jayasuriya and Andrew Rosser, "Economic Orthodoxy and the Asian Economic Crisis," *Third World Quarterly*, Vol.22, No.3, pp.381-396.

Sadli, Mohammad, 1998, "The Indonesian Crisis," *ASEAN Economic Bulletin,* Vol.15, No.3, 1998, pp.272-289.

Schwartz, Anna, 1998, "International Financial Crises: Myths and Realities," *The Cato Journal*, Vol.17, No.3, 1998, p.4. [see http://www.cato.org/pubs/journal/cj17n3-3.html].

Shanmugam, M., 1999, "Merger by Decree," *Malaysian Business,* October 16, p.11.

Sicat, Gerardo, 1998, "The Philippine Economy in the Asian Crisis," *ASEAN Economic Bulletin,* Vol.15, No.3, pp.281-289.

Stiglitz, Joseph, 2000, "Capital Market Liberalization, Economic Growth, and Instability," *World Development,* Vol.28, No.6, pp. 1075-1086.

Soesastro, Hadi, 1999, "The Indonesian Economy under Habibie," *Paper presented at the 1999 Regional Outlook Forum*, organized by ISEAS, Singapore.

The International Herald Tribune, January 16, 1998, p.11, as cited in James Dean, 1998, "Asia's Financial Crisis in Historical Perspective," *Journal of the Asia Pacific Economy,* Vol.3, No.3, p.268.

The Nation, "Learning from Thailand's Mistakes," November 17, 1998, p.B1.

The Straits Times,

---, "Thailand gets reprieve with fresh financing plan from ADB," Feb 14, 1998, p.53.

---, "Jakarta agency wards off starvation," April 21, 1998, p.20.

---, "KL's privatization policy draws flak," April 21, 1998, p.24.

---, "Malaysia's real problem," October 7, 1998, p.37.

---, "Camdessus supports plan," October 8, 1998, p.42.

---, "Singapore still least risky Asian nation," October 11, 1998, p.32.

---, "Government decides on $10.5 billion cut," November 25, 1998, p.1.

---, "We badly misgauged Asian crisis," January 20, 1999, p.1.

---, "Seoul wasted forex reserves in bid to halt meltdown," January 26, 1999, p.15.

---, "IMF to review bail-out conditions," January 29, 1999, p.93.

---, "Start of KL's exit tax 'weeks away," Jan 31, 1999, p.2.

---, "Europe can differentiate now, says SM," February 3, 1999, p.3.

---, "Indonesia's urban poor: wage freeze set to halve real incomes," April 1, 1999, p.4.

The Washington Post, "US, European firms finding Asian companies willing to deal," May 24, 1998, p.H4.

Tobin, James, 2000, "Financial Globalization," *World Development,* Vol.28, No.6, pp. 1101-1104

Tomoika, Noriyuki, 2001, "Causes of the Asian Crisis, Asian-style Capitalism and Transparency," *Asia-Pacific Review,* Vol.8, No.2, pp.47-65.

Warr, Peter, 1999, "What Happened to Thailand?" *The World Economy,* Vol.22, No.5, pp.631-50.

Zainal Aznam Yusof, 1999, "Malaysian Economic Outlook: Moving Towards a Slow Recovery," *Paper presented at the 1999 Regional Outlook Forum*, organized by ISEAS, Singapore.

Chapter 11

SOUTHEAST ASIA'S ECONOMIC PERFORMANCE: REVIEWING THE PAST, LOOKING TO THE FUTURE[1]

ABSTRACT

This chapter provides a retrospective and prospective assessment of Southeast Asia's robust economic performance. It is divided into three sections. The first section presents an overview of the region's economic performance, by focusing on the economic trends and patterns during the past four decades and their major determinants: trade expansion, massive investment inflows, and political and regional stability. The second section assesses the national, regional and multilateral initiatives and strategies that Southeast Asian economies have followed, particularly in the areas of trade and investment. The final section examines the future of Southeast Asia including the domestic and external issues and challenges facing Southeast Asia.

INTRODUCTION

Over the past four decades, the Southeast Asian region has been transformed from a region with enormous economic and political problems to one blessed with relative peace and prosperity. However, the economic strength of the region relies heavily on the economic and political stability of the individual economies and the region as a whole. Further, in light of the limited significance of regional schemes in influencing national economic policies prior to 1992, national strategies have played a significant role in Southeast Asia's economic performance. However, following the signing of the Singapore Declaration in 1992, intra-ASEAN economic cooperation has moved to a higher level. This change is the result of the institutionalization of the ASEAN summit meetings once every three years, the holding of informal summits, and the adoption of trade and investment liberalization measures towards

---

1 Earlier versions of this chapter include guest lectures and seminar presentations at the following institutions: El Colegio de Mexico (1998), Nordic Institute of Asian Studies (1999), Ludwig-Maximilians Universitäet München (1999), Stiftung Wissenschaft und Politik (1999), and the International Institute for Asian Studies (1999); a journal article published online in the Harvard Asia Quarterly, Vol.6, No.3, 2002, pp.9-14; and a conference paper at the 1st ASEAN-India Roundtable Conference (2004).

the achievement of the ASEAN Free Trade Area (AFTA). I argue that as regional economic cooperation increases towards further economic integration with the global economy, both regional and multilateral initiatives will contribute significantly to Southeast Asia's economic performance.

WHAT HAS BEEN ACHIEVED?

Economic Boom

The Southeast Asian region grew strongly in the 1960s with an average growth rate of about 6 percent per annum. This buoyant economic performance continued in the 1970s with an average growth rate of 7.3 percent per annum as regional economies benefited from the massive inflows of foreign exchange receipts, due to the sharp increase in the world price of primary commodities. Growth during the 1970s would have been even higher if not for the oil shocks that negatively impacted the economies of oil importers such as Singapore, Thailand, and the Philippines.

During the 1980s, the region slowed down to an average growth rate of 6 percent. Regional economies experienced recessionary conditions due to the high interest rate policy of the US Federal Reserve Bank, the consequent debt crisis in the region, the recession in Southeast Asia's major trading and investment partners, and the fall in the world prices of primary commodities. However, the 1980s also saw some positive developments with the significant influx of export-oriented foreign direct investment (FDI) from Japan and then from the new industrialized economies (NIEs) like Taiwan, South Korea and Hong Kong.

The recovery from 1991 to 1996 was followed by an economic contraction in 1997-98, due to the economic crisis which began in Thailand in July 1997 and spread to other parts of the region. The crisis led to the weakening of regional currencies, low exports and imports, and massive capital outflows. The region experienced its largest reversal of net private capital flows from a net inflow of US$97 billion in 1996 to a net outflow of US$12 billion in 1997. The crisis also resulted in severe output contraction, massive unemployment (particularly in the manufacturing and financial sectors), closures and mergers of banks and finance companies, and a drastic reduction of people's wealth due to losses in the financial markets.

In 1999-2000, the region showed some signs of economic recovery but was interrupted by poor export performance and low FDI inflows. The September 11 incident further worsened the economic conditions in the region, by causing the economic slowdowns in Southeast Asia's major trading and investment partners – the US, Japan and the EU. From the late 2001 until 2002, the prices of agricultural products rose significantly so that the year 2002 posted a modest recovery for all economies with Thailand and Malaysia recording the largest gains. The year 2003, however, Southeast Asian economies showed a lackluster performance due to the impact of SARS, the Iraq crisis and terrorist-related attacks, the slump in the electronics sector and the collapse of the WTO talks in Cancun.

Over the past four decades, the region has experienced a significant increase in its per capita income. However, there is considerable variation in the per capita incomes between regional economies, which reflects the disparities in economic development and living standards within ASEAN. The region has also experienced a rapid structural change in output, which is evidenced by the decline of agriculture coupled with the rise of the non-agricultural sector (manufacturing and services), and by the rapid expansion of exports and shift away from primary products into manufactured goods. There have been significant inflows of FDI, particularly in export-oriented industries. Moreover, the region has achieved a higher level of social development, as evidenced by higher education levels, lower infant mortality rates, longer life expectancies, reduced fertility rates, and better access to health care.

ASEAN is the world's third largest trading group after NAFTA and the EU. However, unlike the latter two, Southeast Asia has only a limited degree of intra-regional trade. Levels hovered between 20-25 percent of the region's global trade during the 1990s. A significant proportion of this trade came from the bilateral trade ties between Singapore and Malaysia and between Singapore and Indonesia. Without Singapore, intra-regional trade would range between 2 to 5 percent of ASEAN's global trade. The low intra-regional trade dependence stems from various factors including differences in the tariff structure of Southeast Asian economies, the Western orientation of Southeast Asia's trade, and the ineffectiveness of and lack of support for various regional preferential trading schemes. The launching of the Common Effective Preferential Tariff (CEPT) scheme in 1993 has led to a significant increase in absolute terms, but intra-regional trade has remained at around 25 percent of Southeast Asia's global trade.

Massive Investment Inflows

The Southeast Asian region has been a major recipient of FDI (about 2 to 5 percent of global investment in the 1990s), following the EU (40 to 50 percent) and the NAFTA regions (20 to 25 percent). While intra-regional investment in the EU and NAFTA has been historically high, that in Southeast Asia has been very low. The bulk of Southeast Asia's FDI has come from Japan, the United States and the EU, which accounted for about 50-60 percent of FDI in Southeast Asia during the 1990s.

The Southeast Asian region has received three types of FDI since the 1950s. The first type is in natural resources, given the region's abundance of minerals and fuel, particularly oil and gas. The second type has enabled foreign investors to access the Southeast Asian regional market, by setting up domestic manufacturing industries to produce cheap consumer goods for the domestic Southeast Asian market. The third type is trade-oriented FDI in which foreign investors have used the Southeast Asian region as a production and export base of manufactured goods for intra-regional and extra-regional distribution.

The attractiveness of the Southeast Asian region as an investment destination is based on its strategic geographical position, ownership advantages, and returns to investment. Geographical advantages including an abundance of raw materials, low production costs, generous investment incentives, a skilled and hardworking labor force, improved infrastructure, and a politically stable regional environment. In terms of foreign ownership, investors often have stronger control over their products, patents, technologies, production processes, marketing and management techniques than in their home countries. Foreign investors have also benefited from high rates of return on their equity investments in the region.

The Southeast Asian region is not only a recipient of FDI, but is itself an investor. Relatively tight labor conditions and the rising levels of wealth in the 1990s prompted

Singaporean and Malaysian businessmen to venture beyond their borders to the rest of Southeast Asia and to other Asian countries like China and India for new investment opportunities. The region is an increasingly important source of portfolio investments as savings rates rise with the increasing per capita income of the Southeast Asian population. Prior to the July 1997 economic crisis, the Southeast Asian region had also received an enormous amount of foreign portfolio investments due to foreign investors' confidence in the region's rapid economic growth.

Regional Stability

Regional stability is another determinant of Southeast Asia's economic performance. Although it is true that there have been certain instances of instabilities in the Southeast Asian region over the last 40 years,[2] overall there has been broad regional stability and peace. The formation of ASEAN in 1967 – along with the strong and capable leadership of the various heads of government within ASEAN – promoted regional security and political cooperation. The region's impressive economic performance and prosperity has given ASEAN countries a common interest in working together towards promoting and maintaining regional stability. Furthermore, the ASEAN region has consistently followed what is known as the "ASEAN way" of doing things, that is, by consensus. The display of solidarity and the resulting regional stability enhance the group's dealings with other countries by encouraging foreign investment. A survey by the Japanese External Trade Organization (JETRO) revealed that the relatively stable political climate in the ASEAN region was the most important determinant of Japanese direct investments in the region.

Initiatives and Strategies

National Level

The Southeast Asian economies have implemented various national strategies to promote economic growth and development. Until the 1997 crisis, these economies had a stable macroeconomic environment given their fiscal, monetary and exchange rate policies. In terms of fiscal policy, the Southeast Asian governments exercised prudence as reflected in the significant improvement of their budget balances. Regarding monetary policy, the Southeast Asian central banks were successful in reducing inflation from the high levels in the 1970s to lower levels since the 1980s. Except for Singapore, the Southeast Asian economies have relied on the use of conventional instruments like open market purchases and sales of government securities, changes in the discount rate, and changes in the reserve requirements. With respect to exchange rate policy, the Southeast Asian central banks have relied on the

2 These include the Vietnam war from 1962-73, the Vietnamese invasion of Cambodia in 1978, the confrontation between Indonesia, Malaysia and Singapore from 1963-65, the territorial disputes between Malaysia and the Philippines and between Singapore and Malaysia, communist insurgencies and kidnappings in various parts of ASEAN. There were also political instabilities which led to the overthrow of former Philippine Presidents Marcos in 1986 and Estrada in 2000 and former Indonesia's President Suharto in 1998.

devaluation of their domestic currencies vis-à-vis foreign currencies in order to improve the competitiveness of their export commodities. Prior to the 1997 crisis, the Singapore dollar, Malaysian ringgit and the Thai baht were the more stable currencies in Southeast Asia while the Indonesian rupiah and the Philippine peso experienced relatively greater fluctuations. The 1997/98 crisis, however, resulted in a significant weakening of the regional domestic currencies – in particular, the Thai baht, the Indonesian rupiah, and the Philippine peso.

In response to the 1997 crisis, the Southeast Asian governments implemented different policy measures. Thailand and Indonesia adopted restrictive policies: as a result of IMF loan conditions, they closed and merged banks and financial companies. Malaysia, on the other hand, implemented expansionary demand-management policies and capital controls. Singapore relied more on supply-side policy measures such as wage restraints, workers' training and re-training programs. The differences in their policies were due to national variations in (i) the extent and nature of the crisis (e.g. Malaysia's relatively smaller foreign debt compared to Indonesia's huge foreign debt), (ii) the pervasiveness and severity of the impact of the crisis (e.g. Singapore's banking and financial sector being less affected than in Thailand and Indonesia), (iii) the governments' priorities, in terms of achieving either more internal balance (less severe impact on unemployment) or more external balance (trade surplus) or both, and (iv) the governments' willingness to subscribe to the international financial order and its conditions (Thailand and Indonesia following the IMF conditions which required painful and immediate reforms, versus Malaysia's non-subscription to IMF's conditions and instead adopting a "pragmatic" approach).[3]

The Southeast Asian economies have also switched from import-substitution industrialization (ISI) to export-oriented industrialization (EOI). ISI policy, adopted in the 1950s, refers to a process of restricting imports that compete with domestic products such as simple consumer goods, and the subsidization of domestic industries. The Philippines had the longest-standing ISI policy, which led to the developing of an inward-looking manufacturing sector and an urban-biased development policy. On the other hand, Singapore had the shortest ISI policy experience due to the limited economies of scale arising from its small domestic market.

During the late 1960s, Singapore switched to EOI which relied heavily on FDI, particularly in labor-intensive industries. Government intervention in the domestic economy was pervasive and extensive, and took the forms of building infrastructure and establishing wholly-owned or partly-owned industrial and commercial ventures. Since 1979, however, Singapore's EOI policy has shifted away from labor-intensive manufacturing towards more skill-oriented, high-technology and high-value-added industries. The shift in emphasis stemmed from tight labor market conditions and rising domestic costs of production which hurt the competitiveness of domestically-produced goods.

---

[3] Following the onset of the crisis, Malaysia experienced loss of investors' confidence, significant capital outflows, depletion of foreign exchange reserves, severe impact on the stock markets, and marked depreciations of the ringgit. Former PM Mahathir was able to rescue the Malaysian economy through a combination of easier fiscal and monetary policies (ie. higher government spending and lower interest rates) and imposition of currency and capital controls. Moreover, statutory reserve requirements were reduced from 14.5 percent in March 1989 to 4 percent in September 1998. Mahathir's policies proved to be effective as the Malaysian economy staged an economic recovery and capital outflows were contained. As cited in *The Business Times*, May 18, 1999, p.9, the former IMF managing director Michel Camdessus noted Malaysia's ability to recover from the crisis through its adoption of a 'soft system of control'.

During the 1970s and the 1980s, other Southeast Asian economies relied less on ISI policy and began to follow Singapore's EOI policy with FDI. This policy has continued to be implemented. Some factors which accounted for this change in industrialization policy include the limited success of ISI, declining and fluctuating prices of primary commodities, and the consequent pursuit of export-diversification. The need to diversify is reflected in the changing structure of trade - away from primary goods toward manufactured goods on the export side, and the rising proportion of manufactured goods on the import side.

The Southeast Asian economies have embraced free trade, but with varying degrees of openness as reflected by the differences in their tariff structures, extent of protectionism and trade liberalization measures. Being a highly open export-oriented economy, Singapore has the lowest tariffs. Thailand has the highest tariffs, due to its ISI policy which protects domestic manufacturing industries. Indonesia, Malaysia and the Philippines have tariff structures somewhere between Singapore and Thailand. More open economies like Singapore have preferred a faster pace of tariff cuts than the more closed economies like Indonesia and Thailand. However, since most Southeast Asian countries rely on tariffs as a major source of government revenues, tariff reductions have proceeded slowly.

The Southeast Asian governments have opened their economies to FDI to various degrees. With no natural resources and a limited domestic market, Singapore is the most reliant upon FDI. The Philippines, Indonesia, Malaysia and Thailand have natural resources and much larger domestic markets, and therefore could afford to be less dependent upon FDI. Indonesia and Malaysia are oil and gas producers and have benefited substantially from the oil price hikes in the 1970s. However, declining oil prices combined with the fact that oil is a non-renewable resource had convinced both Indonesia and Malaysia to diversify their economies and increase their dependence on FDI. Over the years, the Southeast Asian governments have followed Singapore's policies by relaxing regulations on investments and foreign equity ownership for export firms. Most Southeast Asian governments now allow 100 percent foreign ownership as long as the business produces mainly for exports.

Lastly, the Southeast Asian governments have liberalized their banking and financial sectors. The financial structure has deepened as more banks and non-bank financial institutions have been set up, and as more diverse financial instruments (such as interest-bearing instruments) have been created. Singapore and Malaysia had fairly well-developed financial systems in the 1960s and 1970s, while financial liberalization did not occur in Indonesia, Thailand, and the Philippines until the 1980s. Changes such as interest rate reforms, the entry of foreign banks, and modifications of foreign equity rules have increased trade and investment between Southeast Asian economies and their major trading partners.

Intra- Regional Level

The expansion of ASEAN membership from five nations in 1967 to ten members in 1999, with the addition of Brunei (1984), Vietnam (1995), Laos (1997), Myanmar (1997), and Cambodia (1999), and the rising per capita income, have increased the opportunities for intra-regional trade and investment. Several intra-regional trade liberalization measures aimed at reducing or eliminating tariffs and other trade barriers are in effect: the Preferential Trading Arrangements (PTA), the Common Effective Preferential Tariff (CEPT), and the ASEAN Free Trade Area (AFTA).

Recent figures indicate that intra-ASEAN trade has increased to around 25 percent of total ASEAN trade since CEPT was adopted in 1993. During its 15th meeting, the AFTA Council announced that each of the older six members (Indonesia, Malaysia, the Philippines, Singapore, Thailand and Brunei) had reduced tariffs to 0-5 percent on at least 90 percent of its tariff lines in the inclusion list. The newer ASEAN members are given a longer period to achieve this reduction in light of their current level of economic development. Each member of ASEAN has a 10-year time frame of tariff reduction program under AFTA. Vietnam is targeted to fully implement the AFTA in 2006, while the target year for Laos and Myanmar is 2008, and 2010 for Cambodia.

The ASEAN region has also undertaken measures to liberalize trade in services. The services sector in ASEAN has grown significantly, as reflected in its share of total output. As the region grows and per capita income increases, the ASEAN people demand more goods and services. More services and institutions have been created to meet this rising demand, which is reflected in the growing importance of the services sector, particularly, in financial services, transportation and communications. The ASEAN Framework Agreement on Services was signed by the ASEAN Trade and Industry ministers in December 1995 to liberalize trade in services in seven sectors: air transport, business services, construction, financial services, maritime transport, telecommunications and tourism. During the 4th ASEAN informal summit meeting in Singapore in November 2000, the leaders signed the e-ASEAN Framework Agreement which provides for the liberalization of intra-regional trade in information and communications technology (ICT) products and services by eliminating duties and non-tariff barriers in three stages: 2003, 2004 and 2005, for the original members. For Cambodia, Laos, Myanmar and Vietnam, the three stages will take effect in 2008, 2009 and 2010.

Intra-regional investment liberalization measures have also been adopted. First is the ASEAN Investment Area (AIA) scheme which will encourage a greater private sector participation in welcoming foreign investors. The second initiative is known as the ASEAN Industrial Cooperation (AICO) scheme which allows joint ventures between ASEAN nationals and foreign investors whose products or services will be given tariff preferences. Third is a type of Growth Triangle sub-regional cooperation scheme like the **Si**ngapore-**Jo**hor (Malaysia)-**Ri**au (Indonesia) growth triangle, popularly known as SIJORI. This scheme exemplifies the positive synergy of factor endowments and comparative advantage, whereby Singapore provides excellent infrastructure and skilled labor, while Johor and Riau provide land and lower-cost labor. The success of the SIJORI growth triangle has led to its expansion to include other parts of Indonesia and Malaysia, which is an indication of its positive spill-over effects. This concept has been replicated in other parts of the ASEAN region. including (i) the East ASEAN Growth Area (EAGA) scheme which involves Brunei, Indonesia, Malaysia and the southern Philippines, and (ii) the inter-state areas along the West-East Corridor (WEC) of the Mekong Basin in Vietnam, Laos, Cambodia and North-eastern Thailand under the ASEAN Mekong Basin Development Cooperation scheme.

The recent economic crisis has provided lessons for ASEAN in terms of the need to strengthen financial co-operation. Some of the proposed strategies include the use of domestic currencies in trade settlements and the setting up of the Asian Monetary Fund (AMF) by Japan. The proposed establishment of AMF, to be capitalized at US$100 billion, aims to provide immediate financial assistance to crisis-hit countries in the future. However, the United States dismissed the proposal, fearing that it would diminish the effectiveness of the

IMF and its policies in Asia, and the AMF proposal was rejected in the fifth APEC meeting in Manila. However, PM Mahathir brought up the AMF idea again during the World Economic Forum in Singapore in 1999 and a modified version of the AMF proposal was discussed in the informal summit meeting of the ASEAN Finance Ministers in Manila in 1999. More recently, a network of bilateral swap arrangements among ASEAN countries, China, Japan and the Republic of Korea has been negotiated to assist ASEAN members in times of temporary balance-of-payments crises. Following the agreement on the Chiang Mai Initiatives (CMI), ASEAN agreed to enlarge the size of the ASEAN Swap Agreement to US$1 billion effective in November 2000. Substantial agreements on the bilateral swap arrangements have been reached between Korea and Japan, Malaysia and Japan, and Thailand and Japan.

Extra-Regional Level

ASEAN's involvement in extra-regional forums such as the Asia Pacific Economic Cooperation Forum (APEC) and Asia-Europe Summit Meeting (ASEM) further expands its economic horizons. In APEC, ASEAN has been considered as the cornerstone for an open-regionalism strategy paving the way for the goals of Bogor Declaration (to free trade and investments in the region by 2010 for developed countries and 2020 for developing countries).

There are also new linkages between ASEAN and its third major trading and investment partner, the European Union. The first meeting of ASEM, a trans-atlantic and trans-pacific regional forum,[4] brought together leaders of the ASEAN, EU-15, China, Japan and Korea in its first meeting held in March 1996. This was an important step towards a more meaningful and enhanced relationship between Asia and Europe in establishing political dialogue, economic cooperation, and social and cultural development. There are signs that ASEAN is taking the initiative in establishing these extra-regional connections. A recent ASEAN trade and investment mission to Europe was aimed at attracting more European investments and getting more access to European markets for ASEAN products.

ASEAN's link with the global economy is also strengthened through multilateral organizations like the World Trade Organization (WTO). The goals of the WTO are as follows: (a) that member countries implement tariff reductions in industrial products, (b) that quotas on imports of textile, apparel, and agricultural products are replaced with less restrictive tariffs, (c) that the Multi-Fibre Agreement will be dismantled, (d) that trade in textiles and clothing will be integrated into normal GATT rules, and (e) that dispute settlement mechanisms be strengthened. These trade liberalization measures will impact the ASEAN region as it will have to compete on a less protectionist basis with other countries in agricultural and textile products.

---

4 Various considerations led to the establishment of ASEM. On the EU side, the Europeans in the 1990s took notice of the impressive economic performance of the East Asian economies which led to the European Commission's publication titled 'Towards a New Asia Strategy'. The Europeans were also awakened with the launching of APEC in 1989 and the holding of the first APEC summit in Seattle in 1993. On the Asian side, ASEM will provide opportunities for Asians to encourage Europeans to invest more in the region and to gain continued and better access for Asian products. See Lay Hwee Yeo, "ASEM: Beyond Economics," *Panorama,* April 1999, pp.5-6.

WHAT LIES AHEAD FOR SOUTHEAST ASIA?

The Southeast Asian region has been one of the most dynamic regions in the world. However, following the 1997-98 economic crisis and the September 11 tragic incident, what lies ahead for Southeast Asia? What are the economic growth prospects for Southeast Asia? What are the issues and challenges facing Southeast Asia? These are the questions which this section intends to analyse.

Economic Growth Prospects

What has happened and what will happen in the near and long term are very much dependent on a set factors which impinge on individual economies of Southeast Asia, and the ASEAN regional grouping. These factors can be classified at two levels: first, the internal-external classification, and second, the national-regional-international classification. The internal factors include national policies, domestic factors and developments which affect the respective economies of Southeast Asia. The external factors include (i) those policies, factors and developments which take place within the Southeast Asian region (through the ASEAN regional grouping), (ii) those which arise from ASEAN's external relations with the United States, Japan, the European Union, Australia, China, India, ASEM, APEC and others, and (iii) those which take place at the multilateral level (e.g. WTO, IMF, World Bank) and other international disturbances.

This section does not intend to provide quantitative econometric projections. Instead a synthesis of the existing estimates for the year 2003 and forecasts for the year 2004 will be provided. These estimates and forecasts were prepared by various institutions, both private and government, at the national, regional and international levels. These include the Institute of Southeast Asian Studies (ISEAS), the Asian Development Bank (ADB), the World Bank (WB), the International Monetary Fund (IMF), and the Economic Intelligence Unit (EIU). The general scenarios predicted by these institutions are as follows.

ISEAS: "Regional Outlook": Southeast Asia, 2003-2004

This publication is essentially divided into two components, a political outlook and an economic outlook, which were written by scholars from the region and beyond. The economic outlook section included a summary of the regional economic trends which stated that "the economic outlook for Southeast Asia in 2003 and 2004 is cautiously positive" based on the following conditions/risks:

i. national factors such as the continued dependence on private consumption as the main driver of domestic demand, and the limited growth prospects if excess capacity and weak bank-lending continue to persist, and if progress in corporate restructuring remains sluggish, and

ii. external factors such as the extremely fragile economic revival in the region due to the risks associated with the performance of the U.S. economy, the escalation of oil crisis arising from the Middle East crisis, the lingering effects of the Bali bombing in October 2002, the threat of global deflation, the uncertain outlook for the information technology (IT) sector due to the poor corporate performance by leading companies in this sector, the strengthening of economic relations between ASEAN economies and other countries including China, India, Japan and the United States, and the rapid rise of China.[5]

The Report also stated that regional economies should moderately rebound in 2003 and 2004 provided external developments remain favorable. However, due to uncertainties on the external front, the Report cited that Southeast Asian governments have re-examined their economic development strategies which were largely driven by foreign direct investments (FDI). New sources of growth which are more domestic-based are being considered. These include the development of domestic small and medium enterprises (SMEs) which were neglected during the outward-oriented period of rapid economic growth. However, the medium and long-term prospects depend very much on the success of their economic restructuring activities and on their ability to face the competitive challenges in the future.

ADB: Asian Development Outlook 2003

The ADO 2003 stated that "the Asia-Pacific region will remain a bright spot on the world economic map."[6] It predicted a robust economic growth for East Asian countries in 2003-2004.

April 2003: Overall growth for the Southeast Asian region was estimated at 4.0 percent for the year 2003, which was less than previously expected due to the impact of SARS. Vietnam was expected to be the strongest performer with 6.9 percent for 2003. Singapore, another economy hard hit by SARS, was estimated to post a growth rate of 2.3 percent. Economic growth for Southeast Asia will likely accelerate to 4.8 percent in 2004 due to internal factors such as the continued economic liberalization, an increasingly vibrant private sector, and rising productivity.

September 2003: The ADO 2003 Update stated that a buoyant recovery is projected in Southeast Asia's external markets in the second half of 2003 and in 2004, and domestic consumption is expected to remain strong. However, the Update cited that the slow pace of financial restructuring and an uncertain global economy are expected to cast a shadow on Southeast Asia. In order to ensure long-run economic growth and to avoid short-term macroeconomic volatility, the Southeast Asian governments should address a series of policy issues including financial restructuring and reforms.

World Bank: Global Economic Prospects and Developing Countries 2003

The Report predicted a regional GDP growth of 6.1 percent in 2003 and 6.4 percent in 2004 for East Asia. Growth in the region, excluding China, was expected to reach 3.8 and 4.3 percent in 2003 and 2004, respectively. This highlights the crucial role of China in the East Asian region. The question raised by the Report is: How well are the East Asian countries able to ride out new external and internal disturbances that may arise? The report said that:

> On balance, countries in the East Asian region appear comparatively well placed to weather the present high levels of external risks, especially if they can build on recent successes and continue to advance reforms that further reduce their vulnerability to external shocks and foster sources of domestic productivity growth. Improvements in macroeconomic conditions

5 See Institute of Southeast Asian Studies, *Regional Outlook: Southeast Asia, 2003-2004,* Singapore: ISEAS, pp.44-46.

6 See Asian Development Bank, *Asian Development Outlook 2003*, Manila: ADB, 2003, p.14.

> have been key to cushioning the impact of external shocks and volatility in international capital markets on East Asian countries over the last three years... The adoption of more flexible exchange rate regimes has allowed countries to adapt to external shocks more smoothly.[7]

The Report, however, has some near-term concerns which include (a) a higher level of public sector debt accumulated after the 1997 financial crisis, particularly in Indonesia and the Philippines, (b) weak private investment in the crisis-affected countries, and (c) the October terrorist attack in Bali [and other terrorist-related activities] which affect tourism in Indonesia and Southeast Asia generally, and which also impact on consumer and business confidence.

IMF: World Economic Outlook, Sept 2003

In spite of a slowdown since early 2003, the IMF predicted that Asia-Pacific countries would again be the world's faster growing region in 2003 and that growth is expected to pick up further in 2004. A notable feature of recent performance has been the support to output growth provided by net exports. While domestic demand is clearly playing a greater role in the region than in the period immediately following the crisis, the global cycle remains a key determinant of cyclical developments in the region. However, with the U.S. dollar's decline necessitating a rebalancing of global demand, the Report argued that the need to boost the domestic component of growth in Asia is even more pressing.[8] In its latest forecasts, the IMF revised its September 2003 estimates for this year's growth of the global economy to 4.1 percent from an estimated growth of 3.2 percent last year.[9]

Southeast Asia and ASEAN: Issues and Challenges

National versus Regional Policies

As in chapter 2, it is argued here that the impressive performance of the Southeast Asian economies, particularly Indonesia, Malaysia, Philippines, Singapore and Thailand, during the past four decades was due more to the impact of each member's policies, factors and developments affecting the individual economies rather than that of any regional economic arrangements. Will Southeast Asian economies continue to rely heavily on national economic policies to shape Southeast Asia's future? Will the increasing trend towards regionalism continue? How important is regionalism for ASEAN and Southeast Asia's future? Is there a need to strengthen ASEAN economic relations with countries and regions outside ASEAN? Should Singapore's FTA policy be replicated by other ASEAN members and the ASEAN itself? Should ASEAN integrate deeper towards an ASEAN Economic Community, or towards a wider East Asian Economic Community? These are some of the challenges and issues that ASEAN is facing in the future.

---

7 World Bank, *Global Economic Prospects and Developing Countries 2003,* Washington DC: World Bank, 2003, p.152.

8 See International Monetary Fund, *World Economic Outlook*, Washington DC: IMF, Sept 2003, p.34.

9 The Straits Times, "IMF expects to raise this year's growth forecast," Feb 3, 2004, p.A9.

Domestic Policy Issues and Challenges

On the domestic front, the growth prospects are very much dependent on the ability of the governments of Southeast Asian economies to provide economic, political and social stability, implement economic reforms, diversify their economies, and contain the effects of disturbances like SARS, bird flu and the like. Thus, the Southeast Asian policy makers are tasked with the following challenges:

i. To provide a sound macroeconomic environment

This is characterized with prudent fiscal policy, low inflation rates, stable exchange rates, and manageable levels of external debt and current account balance. Following the 1997/98 economic crisis, the government budget deficits relative to GDP have broadly increased and this raised a serious concern for Southeast Asian governments particularly for Malaysia and the Philippines. Price instability has become a serious concern for Indonesia and the Philippines. While other currencies have remained broadly stable, the Philippine peso and the Indonesian rupiah have been depreciating. The Philippine peso has plunged to record lows reaching 56.16 per US$ on February 4, 2004 and 56.38 per US$ on March 19, 2004. It is expected to continue in its downward direction because of the uncertainties created by the May 2004 presidential elections (see Figure 11.1). Moreover, the rising levels of foreign debt in the Philippines and Indonesia would create additional uncertainties. The Philippine foreign debt reached US$56 billion in February 2004.

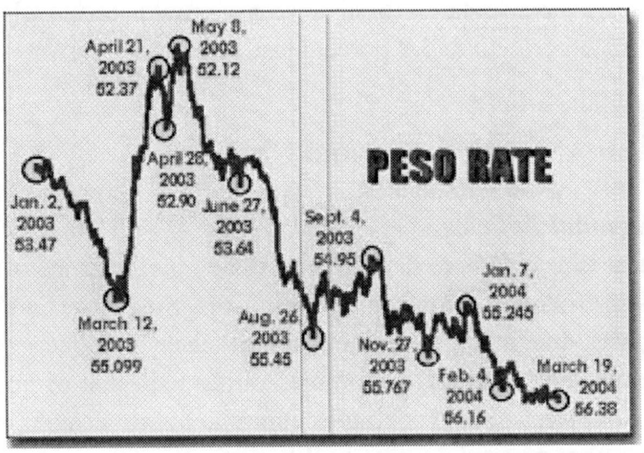

Figure 11.1. – Peso-US Dollar Rate, (Jan 2, 2003 to Mar 19,2004). Source: Malaya, "Peso skids to P56.38:1$," Mar 20, 2004. http://www.malaya.com.ph/mar20/index.htm

ii. To provide a stable political and business environment.

Political stability is essential to promote economic growth as it encourages domestic and foreign investments. It was considered as the most significant determinant of Japanese investments in ASEAN in a survey of Japanese firms which was conducted by JETRO in 1997. The political environment in some countries has been affected by military uprisings, kidnappings, bombings and other terrorist-related activities, people's demonstrations, and elections.

iii. To provide social harmony

This is done by preventing tensions between racial groups (between Chinese and the pribumis in Indonesia in the 1960s and again in 1998, between the Chinese and the bumiputras in Malaysia in the 1960s), religious groups (between Muslims and Christians in the Southern Philippines) and between the poor and rich groups in most countries particularly in the Philippines and Indonesia. However, inspite of all the policies and resources spent on alleviating poverty and reducing income inequality, the world remains one in which unemployment, poverty and income inequality are still the major policy concerns of many governments and institutions worldwide. Chulalongkorn University's well-known political economist, Professor Pasuk Pongpaijit argued that Thailand's income gap between the rich and the poor was the widest in the world.[10] The World Bank (1996) report stated that the Philippines was not able to sustain the required growth long enough to reduce the poverty incidence to the levels of neighboring Southeast Asian countries. The WB report indicates that structural distortions, especially high inequality, in the economy that have prevented trickle down of benefits of economic growth to the level of poor.

So, is there still hope for the millions of poor in the world particularly in Southeast Asia? Can social harmony be achieved? Yes, as long as the political and economic leadership work hand-in-hand to enhance the economic and social standards of living of the poorer population. It requires strong and committed political and economic leaders, strong support from and participation by the private sector, and people's support of government policies. People must strongly believe that their government leaders have the strong will and commitment to implement policies and reforms for their betterment. Credibility bonus is essential. However, it is easier said than done. In reality, it is very difficult to reduce poverty and narrow the income gap given the interplay of politics, economics and industry, and the conflicting goals of the various interest groups in the economy such as businesses, religious groups, the elite, farmers, small and medium entrepreneurs, etc.

As the saying goes, "the rich get richer and the poor become poorer." The income gap between the rich and poor nations and between the rich and poor peoples will continue to increase should the superior group do nothing about the conditions of the inferior group. In this regard, the study by Clark and Sison revealed, among others, that majority of the respondents suggested that some elite people cared while others did not; and those who did care did too little or acted primarily out of self-interest.[11] In fact, there are some people in the superior group like the elite who wish the poor to remain poor because of the benefits that can be derived from poverty. For instance, politicians often depend on the poor at election time for support that propels them to political office.

iv. To continue implementing economic reforms.

This is particularly true for the CLMV countries as they undergo transition from central planning to market-oriented economies, and for the crisis-hit countries (e.g. financial restructuring). In the case of Indonesia, some have argued that there was a lack of seriousness on the part of the Indonesian political leadership to undertake economic reforms.[12] Many

---

10 Bangkok Post, August 25, 2003.

11 Gerard Clark and Marites Sison, "Do the well-off really care about the plight of the poor?", *Development and Change,* Vol.34, No.2, 2003, pp.215-242.

12 CSIS, "IMF Strategy," CSIS website (www.csis.or.id).

policies stated in the Letters of Intent were not performed and as such the IMF delayed its loan disbursement for a year. For example, there were delays in the removal of tariff control hiding behind protectionist barriers and in the privatization of state assets and enterprises, so that the process of reforms is being reverted to protectionism.[13] Thus, the lack of commitment on the part of the Indonesian government combined with the delay in the IMF's financial assistance resulted in the ineffectiveness of Indonesia's recovery program.

In Aug 1997, the Thai government reached an agreement with the IMF on a 3-year economic adjustment program as a condition for the financial package amounting to more than US$17 billion. The Thai government implemented tight macroeconomic policies (fiscal and monetary policy) to support external adjustment. The program focuses on a comprehensive restructuring of the financial sector. Other policies aimed at supporting external current account adjustment includes wage restraint, and structural reforms particularly privatization and civil service reform. The program also includes provisions for those affected by the crisis particularly the poor. On June 20, 2000, Thailand completed its 34-month Stand-By Arrangement from the IMF which formed part of an international financial package worth US$17.2 billion from multilateral and bilateral lenders mentioned above. A total of US$14.3 billion was drawn including the US$3.4 billion from the IMF. Scheduled repayments commenced in late 2000. Outstanding obligations at end-June 2002 amounted to US$6.4 billion and repayment was finally completed on July 31, 2003, some two years ahead of schedule – a significant achievement on the part of the Thai government.

v. To continue diversifying their domestic economies

The production structure of Southeast Asian economies has changed: falling agricultural shares to GDP, rising shares of industrial (particularly manufacturing) and services sectors. Following the decline in the world price of crude oil in the 1980s, Brunei and Indonesia have begun to diversify their economies from oil towards non-oil products and services (finance, tourism). Because of the high costs of production (e.g. high labor costs), Singapore's economy has emphasized the significant contribution of the services sector (IT, education, tourism, finance). Services sector has accounted for about 60-70 percent of Singapore's GDP. Moreover, to improve the competitiveness of Singapore's manufactured products and services, several cost-cutting measures have been implemented, namely, cuts in CPF contribution rates, reduction in corporate taxes, and reduction in utility charges. Long-run policies include training and re-training programmes for workers and more research and development activities for innovations and improvement in technology aimed at improving productivity.

vi. To contain the effects of domestic disturbances

These disturbances include SARS epidemic and the bird flu. These cases have proved to be very detrimental to the Southeast Asian economies particularly tourism. On the other hand, the health care and pharmaceutical industries have reaped the benefits because of strong demand and higher prices of their products and services. In the case of the current deadly avian flu virus, at least 10 people were killed and millions of birds in 10 Asian countries were

---

13 CSIS, "Speed up reform, avoid return to protectionism," opinion-editorial in the Jakarta Post, Dec 27, 2002, CSIS website.

culled. The multi-billion dollar poultry industry suffered a devastating blow.[14] Even the Thai stocks were hit when the Stock Exchange of Thailand index plunged by 7.36 percent during the last week of January 2004. The death of a brother and two sisters in Vietnam was reported as possibly the first cases of human-to-human transmission in the current outbreak.[15] However, WHO experts quelled epidemic fears based on the 1997 Hong Kong outbreak in which the virus was passed from infected people to health workers but soon failed to spread further. In containing the effects and spread of SARS, Singapore has been very successful and as such, other countries could learn from her experiences. The problem, however, is with regard to the lack of financial resources in other countries which will certainly limit their ability to prevent and control the spread of SARS and other types of viruses like the current bird flu.

External Issues and Challenges

On the external front, the future of Southeast Asian economies, depend very much on:

i. The economic performance of their trading and investment partners

The US, Japan and the EU are Southeast Asia's major trading and investment partners. The shares of Japan, US and EU fell in 2001 relative to 1993, while the shares of ASEAN, China, Korea and Australia increased. Thus, continuing dependence on the US, Japan and the EU has become a problem because of the weak performance of their economies. According to Tatsuya Torikoshi, senior economist at the Daiwa Institute of Research, consumption is still weak and hence the Japanese economy most likely will not fully recover. In the case of the US, consumer spending, which accounts for 70 percent of the economy, expanded by only 2.6 percent annual pace in the fourth quarter of the year 2003, which was less than the earlier forecast of 3 percent, hence the economy grows less than expected.[16]

Even, the FDI approvals have shown a broadly declining trend. Among Southeast Asia, Singapore and Malaysia have depended heavily on trade and FDI as they are the most open economies. Because of the uncertainties stemming from heavy dependence on trade and FDI, some countries have re-examined their outward-oriented policies in favor of domestic-oriented policies such as promoting domestic SMEs and agricultural activities.

ii. Competitiveness of Southeast Asian economies.

How competitive are Southeast Asian economies with other economies such as China and India? The emerging economies of China and India offer both threats and opportunities to Southeast Asia. On the positive side, with rising incomes per capita, China and India provide bigger markets for ASEAN exports of goods and services. Thus, ASEAN, China and India should work out ways to strengthen their economic relations for their mutual benefit particularly in the areas of education, tourism and information technology. On the negative front, there is the potential of trade and investment diversion away from ASEAN and towards India and China.

---

14 The Straits Times, "Bird flu to hit Thai stocks further," February 2, 2004, p.A10.

15 The Straits Times, - Vietnam may have spread bird flu to sisters, February 3, 2004, p.A3.

16 The Straits Times, "US economy grows 4%- less than expected," January 31, 2004, p.A16.

iii. External disturbances

As shown in Fig.11.2, these disturbances include the oil price increase in the 1970s, external debt crisis in the 1980s, the collapse of commodity prices in the early 1980s, the financial crisis in 1997/98, the SARS crisis in 2003, and most recently, the bird flu virus. Should these disturbances recur, are Southeast Asian governments ready to cope with them? Can the governments handle another crisis like the 1997/98 disturbance? Most Southeast Asian governments are not in a position to do so. The same problems such as the lack of immediate financial support from the US and the EU will be there. ASEAN has no emergency loans except the limited funds which are made available through the swap arrangements signed among ASEAN countries, Japan, China and Korea as part of the Chiangmai initiatives. ASEAN together with Northeast Asia and even South Asian countries should strongly work together towards the setting up of an Asian Monetary Fund which was earlier proposed by Japan during the 1997/98 crisis.

iv. Rising trends towards regionalism

Multilateral trade liberalization, through the GATT since 1947 and the WTO since 1995, has been paralleled by a process of integration through regional trade agreements (RTAs) which is a departure from the guiding principle of non-discrimination among member countries. As shown in Fig. 11.3, the number of RTAs has continued to increase reaching some 250 up to December 2002 and could reach up to 300 by the end of 2005. In the case of Southeast Asia, regionalism has been taking place both within the region through enlargement and deepening activities in the ASEAN regional grouping, and outside the region through the forging of free trade agreements by Singapore and other ASEAN countries with non-ASEAN countries.

a. ASEAN: Towards further Regional Integration

The main challenge for ASEAN is to continue to improve upon various aspects of regional integration including the institutional machinery, political commitment, decision making, and regional integration schemes. Another challenge is related to the enlargement of the grouping into ASEAN-10.

i. Strengthen institutional machinery

The ASEAN Economic Ministerial Meetings has been the decision-making organ for economic matters. Since 1976, the supreme decision-making authority is the ASEAN Heads of Government (HOG) Meeting, also known as the ASEAN Summits, which were held as and when necessary. However, following the Singapore Declaration of 1992, the ASEAN HOG meeting has been institutionalized to be held once every 3 years, with informal meetings in between.

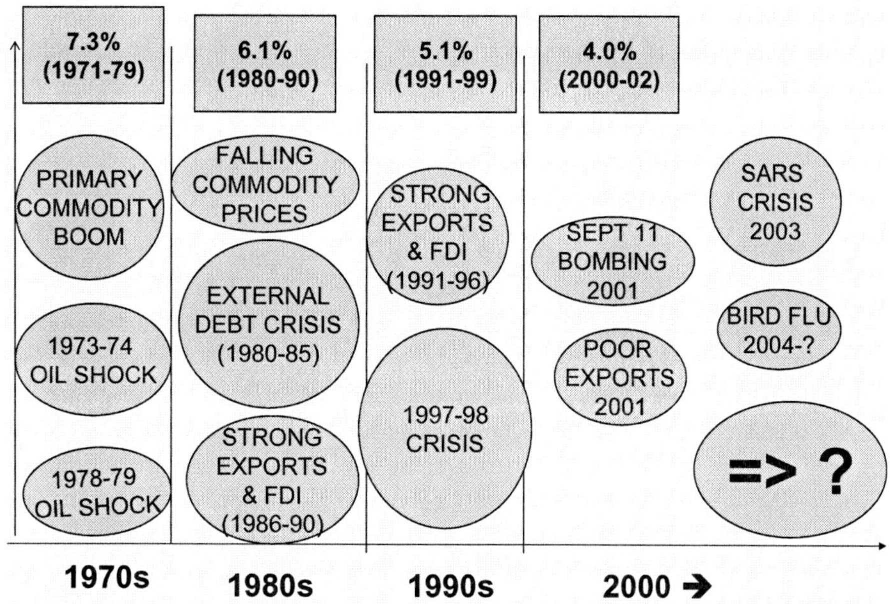

Fig.11.2. – Disturbances in Southeast Asia. Source: Daquila, 2004

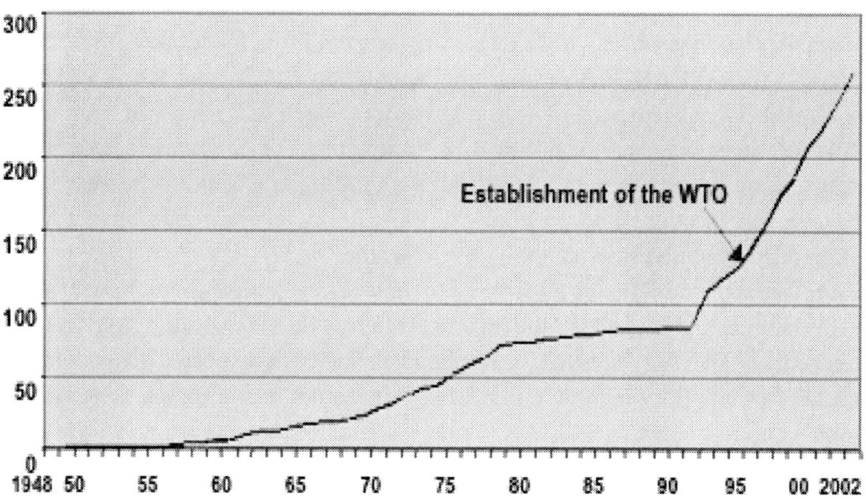

Fig 11.3. Evolution of Regional Trade Agreements (RTAs) in the world, 1948-2002. Source: WTO Secretariat (*http://www.wto.org*)

ii. Improve decision-making

The consensus approach is viewed as a weak point of ASEAN as decision-making has been delayed due to the differences in attitudes and views of member countries, and differences in their levels of development and economic structures. However, some have argued that the consensus approach brings the ASEAN member countries closer and that direct conflicts have been avoided. In light of the impact of the Asian financial crisis in 1997/98, former ASEAN Secretary-General Rodolfo Severino had suggested that ASEAN needs to move away from a 'relationship-based' way of doing things and creating wealth to one that was more rules-based and market-driven. Within ASEAN, a rationalization of the framework for economic cooperation and the development of rules to set the guidelines within which this cooperation can take place is occurring.

iii. More political commitment.

During the 1967-1992 period, there were only four irregular summit meetings which took place in Bali (1976)), Kuala Lumpur (1977), Manila (1987) and Singapore (1992). The holding of only four and irregular summits within 25 years was an indication of the lack of political commitment. Having learned from this shortcoming, the summit meeting has been institutionalized since 1992 to take place once every three years with informal meetings in between. Former ASEAN secretary-general Rodolfo Severino has called for more political commitment within ASEAN in order to achieve greater economic integration. He said that ASEAN "seems to have stuck in framework agreements, work programs and master plans."

iv. Improving regional integration schemes

Trade cooperation: During its 15th meeting, the AFTA Council announced that each of the original six members (Indonesia, Malaysia, the Philippines, Singapore and Thailand) had reduced tariffs to 0-5 percent on at least 90 percent of its tariff lines in the inclusion list. The newer ASEAN members are given a longer period to achieve this reduction in light of their current level of economic development. Vietnam is targeted to fully implement AFTA in 2006, while the target year for Laos and Myanmar is 2008, and 2010 for Cambodia.

On *industrial cooperation*, ASEAN's early schemes included the ASEAN Industrial Projects (AIP), the ASEAN Industrial Complementation (AIC), and the ASEAN Industrial Joint Venture (AIJV) schemes. AIP was relatively ineffective because of lack of feasibility studies, lack of financing, lack of political commitment, lack of private sector participation, and rigidity in equity requirements. With these shortcomings, other schemes like AIC and AIJV had evolved through time providing for flexibility in the requirements allowing the participation of foreign investors and the private sector.

ASEAN has also undertaken measures to *liberalize foreign investments* including the ASEAN Investment Area (AIA), the ASEAN Industrial Cooperation (AICO), and sub-regional schemes. The AIA scheme, formulated in 1998, is expected to encourage greater private sector participation in welcoming foreign investors in the region. The AICO scheme allows joint ventures between ASEAN nationals and foreign investors whose products or services will be given tariff preferences immediately.

On *financial cooperation*, a network of bilateral swap arrangements among ASEAN countries, China, Japan and the Republic of Korea has been negotiated to assist ASEAN members in times of temporary balance-of-payments crises. Following the agreement on the Chiang Mai Initiatives (CMI), ASEAN agreed to enlarge the size of the ASEAN Swap Agreement to US$1 billion effective November 2000. Substantial agreements on the bilateral swap arrangements have been reached between Korea and Japan, Malaysia and Japan, and Thailand and Japan.

v. Enlargement

On a positive note, the ASEAN-10 region brings together some 550 million people and a regional income of about US$550 billion. The huge regional market and the rising per capita income of the ASEAN people offer tremendous trade and investment opportunities for the region and the rest of the world. However, the large gaps in their per capita incomes have resulted in a two-tier regional grouping with Singapore, Brunei, Thailand, Malaysia, the Philippines and Indonesia forming the richer group and Cambodia, Laos, Myanmar and Vietnam (CLMV) comprising the poorer group. To reduce the gap, the richer group should be able to assist the poorer group through trade, investments, technical and financial assistance, loans, and other means. Also, ideally ASEAN should be able to provide some financial assistance to the CLMV group. However, unlike the EU, the ASEAN regional grouping has a very limited budget

b. Strengthening Extra-ASEAN Economic Relations

i. Forging Free Trade Agreements (FTAs)

Given the different stages of policy developments among ASEAN countries, the convergence towards full trade liberalization could be a long way to go unless ASEAN countries, either individually or jointly, do something. Aimed at complementing her regional and global trade liberalization policies, Singapore has concluded five FTAs each with New Zealand, Japan, the European Free Trade Area (EFTA), Australia and the United States. Singapore also has on-going trade negotiations with Canada, Mexico, South Korea, India, and Jordan.

With the passage of time, it is interesting to observe that other ASEAN countries are also keen in forging FTAs. Even Malaysia is now keen to form a bilateral FTA with Japan. Philippine President Gloria Arroyo officially proposed the establishment of a FTA with Japan, during her third visit to Japan on December 4, 2002.[17] The United States has also proposed bilateral FTAs each with Thailand and the Philippines. Australia is also working towards commencing negotiations for an FTA with Thailand. ASEAN itself is keen in establishing FTAs with countries outside the regional grouping such as China, US, Japan and India. Singapore, New Zealand and Chile have even moved on to a higher plane by jointly announcing a new trilateral FTA initiative during the APEC summit held in Los Cabos, Mexico in October 2002.

ii. Towards ASEAN or East Asian Economic Community?

In the future, there are two possible directions that the ASEAN regional grouping could proceed. First is the formation of a common market to be known as *ASEAN Economic Community (AEC)*. During the ASEAN Leaders summit in October 2003, the Declaration of ASEAN Concord II (also referred to as Bali Concord) was adopted in which the AEC is considered as one of the three pillars of an ASEAN Community. Second, the ASEAN+3 countries comprising 10 ASEAN countries, Japan, China and South Korea, could form an

---

17 It is expected that the proposed Japan-Philippines FTA could be beyond the usual FTA to maximize the many areas of complementarity between them. President Arroyo cited examples that Japan can utilize Filipino health care workers given Japan's aging population and Japanese high tech firms can hire skilled young Filipino workers. See *Philippine Star*, "Arroyo pushes free trade with Japan," December 4, 2002.

East Asian Economic Community (EAEC).[18] They can move away from being merely dialogue partners towards becoming more economically integrated. How would East Asian countries benefit from the EAEC? First, the integration of Southeast Asia with Northeast Asia could become one of the driving forces in the global economy as it provides a market of more than 2 billion people (a third of the world's population) and a fifth of global trade. Second, with China being ASEAN's fifth largest trading partner and emerging giant, economic ties with ASEAN for Japan and South Korea could be a means to counteract China's growing economic power. However, the ASEAN regional grouping could be losing its attractiveness to foreign investors in light of China's rising economic might.

CONCLUSION

The ASEAN region has been one of the most dynamic regions in the world. However, following the 1997-98 economic crisis and September 11, what lies ahead for ASEAN? Its future will certainly depend on the implementation of various strategies and initiatives discussed earlier at the national, regional and multilateral levels. The strength and stability of the ASEAN economies individually and the region as a whole are dependent on the national strategies to a large extent, and to regional and multilateral strategies to a lesser extent. However, in the long-run, as ASEAN further integrates with the Asia-Pacific region through APEC, with Europe through ASEM and with the global economy through the WTO, ASEAN will increasingly rely on both regional and multilateral initiatives.

National governments should implement a stable macroeconomic environment through prudent fiscal, monetary and exchange rate policies; the continuation of an export-oriented industrialization strategy centered around the attraction of FDI; and to further reform an develop the banking and financial sectors. From the regional perspective, ASEAN needs to implement trade, investment and financial liberalization measures to achieve a higher degree of integration. On the global level, ASEAN needs to strengthen its linkages with Japan and the US through APEC, and with the EU through ASEM. It also needs to actively participate in future WTO negotiations, as well as in the future re-designing of the global financial architecture.

While the above strategies are desirable, ASEAN's future would also depend on whether economic or political disturbances take place at either national, regional, or international level. Due to their small size, ASEAN economies will continue to be vulnerable to various forms of external influences like hikes in oil prices and interest rates, liquidity crunches, capital account crisis, and poor export performance.

Another issue faced by ASEAN as a regional institution is its continued existence. Delay in the implementation of some intra-regional trade and investment liberalization measures such as tariff cuts on automotive products until 2005, has affected the move towards a more closely knit regional economic grouping. Some countries have instead engaged in the formation and negotiations of bilateral free trade agreements (FTAs). According to the Straits Times (Jan 31, 2001), former Senior Minister Lee Kuan Yew stated that "it is in the interest

---

[18] China, Japan and South Korea are currently ASEAN's dialogue partners under the ASEAN+3 framework. For an excellent discussion of this framework, including its origins, evolution and

of all Asian states to conclude bilateral trade deals because multilateral talks at the WTO are moving slowly."

Thus, to a large extent, ASEAN's future economic performance will continue to be affected by their national strategies and developments taking place within their respective economies. In the long run, however, both regional and global strategies will exert significant influence on the ASEAN region.

QUESTIONS FOR DISCUSSION

1. In our understanding of the Southeast Asian economies, we have observed that some countries have been more successful than others in their transformation away from agricultural towards non-agricultural societies, and from low-income to middle- and high-income countries. Discuss what accounts for the differences.
2. Over the past four decades, the Southeast Asian economies and the ASEAN regional grouping have been faced with internal and external problems and challenges. What are these? How have the Southeast Asian economies and the ASEAN grouping responded to them? Discuss.
3. Some have argued that, unlike the European Union and the North American Free Trade Agreement, the ASEAN regional grouping will cease to exist. Do you agree or disagree? Discuss.
4. The Southeast Asian economies and the region as a whole have been linked to the global economy through trade, foreign investments, loans, technology and foreign aid. To what extent have these linkages been affected by the 1997/98 economic crisis? Will these linkages continue in the future? Discuss.

REFERENCES FOR CHAPTER 11

Asian Economic News, "Singapore Free Trade Pact Worrisome, Mahathir says," March 5, 2001.

Asia Times, "Indonesia faces up to Post-IMF Reality," August 15, 2003.

Asian Development Bank, 2003, *Asian Development Outlook 2003*, Manila: ADB.

Bangkok Post, Aug 25, 2003.

Centre for Strategic and International Studies (CSIS), "IMF," *Opinion and editorial*, March 7, 2003.

Clark, Gerald and Marites Sison, 2003, "Do the Well-off Really Care about the Plight of the Poor?" *Development and Change,* Vol 34, No.2, pp.215-242.

CSIS, "Speed up reform, avoid return to protectionism," opinion-editorial in the *Jakarta Post*, December 27, 2002.

Daquila, Teofilo C., 1999, "The ASEAN Experience of Economic Cooperation," Paper presented at "*The East African Forum on the East African Community: Economic Aspects*

potentials, see Richard Stubbs, "ASEAN Plus Three: Emerging East Asian Regionalism?" *Asian Survey,* Vol.42, No.3, 2002, pp.440 – 455.

of Integration," organized by Friedrich Ebert Foundation, September 27-29, Kampala, Uganda.

Daquila, Teofilo C., 1999, "Growth, Development and Crisis in Southeast Asia," Guest lecture delivered at the *Nordic Institute of Asian Studies* (Copenhagen), Ludwig-Maximilians Universitaet Muenchen (Germany), Stiftung Wissenschaft und Politik (Ebenhausen, Germany), and the International Institute for Asian Studies, Leiden University (Netherlands). June-July.

Daquila, Teofilo C., 2002, "ASEAN Economic Performance: Reviewing the Past, Looking to the Future," *Harvard Asia Quarterly*, (USA: Harvard University), Volume VI, No.3, pp.9-14 (online exclusive).

Daquila, Teofilo C. and Le Huu Huy, 2003, "Singapore and ASEAN in the Global Economy: The Case of Free Trade Agreements," *Asian Survey* (USA: University of California, Berkeley), Vol. XLIII, No.6, pp.908-928.

Daquila, Teofilo C., 2004, "Southeast Asia and ASEAN: Economic Growth Prospects and Challenges," Invited paper presented at the 1st ASEAN-India Roundtable Conference, organized by the Institute of Southeast Asian Studies, Singapore, Feb 9-10.

Davidson, Paul, 2002, *ASEAN: The Evolving Legal Framework for Economic Cooperation,* Singapore: Times Academic Press.

Garnaut, Ross (ed.), 1980, *ASEAN in a Changing Pacific and World Economy,* Canberra: Australian National University Press.

Institute of Southeast Asian Studies, 2003, *Regional Outlook: Southeast Asia, 2003-2004*, Singapore: ISEAS.

Low, Linda, 2001, "Changing Modalities in International Trade," *Panorama,* Vol.2, pp. 63-93.

Naya, Seiji, 1987, "Economic Performance and Growth Factors of the ASEAN Countries," in Linda G. Martin (ed.), *The ASEAN Success Story: Social, Economic and Political Dimensions,* Hawaii: East-West Center, pp.47-87

Noboru Hatakeyama, 2003, "EAFTA not a dream, but a reality," Presented at the symposium on "FTAs; JSEPA and Beyond," Singapore, March 7.

Page, John, 1994, "The East Asian Miracle: Four Lessons for Development Policy," in Stanley Fischer and Julio Rotemberg (eds.), *NBER Macroeconomics Annual*: Vol. 9, 1994, Cambridge: MIT Press, pp.219-269.

Philippine Star, "Arroyo Pushes Free Trade with Japan," December 4, 2002:

Stubbs, Richard, 2002, "ASEAN Plus Three: Emerging East Asian Regionalism?" *Asian Survey,* Vol.42, No.3, pp. 440 – 455.

The Business Times, "Singapore Won't be Back Door to AFTA," May 3, 2001.

The Hindu, "Malaysia Cautions on Trade Pacts," November 23, 2000.

The Straits Times, Various issues

- FTAs: a way to reach out to the world, Jan 31, 2001, p.9.
- ASEAN must deepen economic ties with partners, May 9, 2001, page A7.
- Mega pressured to cut IMF ties, Aug 9, 2002, p.A6.
- ASEAN may become an East Asia grouping, Oct 12, 2002, p.2
- Singapore, NZ and Chile go for 3-way trade talks, Oct 28, 2002.
- China's rise has not been at ASEAN's expense, November 19,2002, p.A16.
- Chinese tourists heading for Southeast Asia, December 14, 2002, p.A2.
- Asia gets onto bandwagon of regionalism, January 28, 2003, p.16.

- S'pore values both WTO deals, FTAs, February 21, 2003, p.A18.
- Two way trade: India urged to change tack towards ASEAN, Nov 26, 2003, p.A4.
- More jobs in Japan but spending stays weak, Jan 31, 2004, p.A17.
- US economy grows 4%- less than expected, Jan 31, 2004, p.A16.
- Corporate travel to India takes off, Feb 4, 2004, p.A14.
- Bird flu to hit Thai stocks further, Feb 2, 2004, p.A10.
- World poultry market jolted, Feb 2, 2004, p.A2.
- Vietnam may have spread bird flu to sisters, Feb 3, 2004, p.A3.
- IMF expects to raise this year's growth forecast, Feb 3, 2004, p.A9.

Tsugami, Toshiya, 2003, "On ASEAN-China Free Trade Agreement – A Personal View from Japan," Presented at a symposium on "*FTAs: JSEPA and Beyond*," organized by the Japan Economic Foundation and Singapore Institute of International Affairs, Singapore, March 7.

World Bank, 2003, *Global Economic Prospects 2003*, Washington DC: World Bank.

World Bank, 1993, The *East Asian Miracle: Economic Growth and Public Policy*, Washington DC: World Bank.

Wu, Friedrich and Kok Keong Puah, 2003, "Foreign Direct Investment in China and Southeast Asia: Has ASEAN been Losing Out?" *Journal of Asian Business,* Vol.19, No.1.

Internet Sources

ASEAN Secretariat, ASEAN Statistical Indicators, updated 30 Sept 2003. <http://*www.aseansec.org*>

CSIS, "IMF Strategy," CSIS website, *<http://www.csis.org.id>*

Economic Intelligence Unit (EIU), Country Reports, May 2003 and July 2003. *<http://www.eiu.com>*

Ministry of Trade and Industry website < *http://www.mti.gov.sg/public/FTA/frm_FTA_Default.asp?sid=37&cid=1183* >

The World Paper, "Amid globalization trend, Pacific Rim sees a bellwether on bilateral trade," *<http://www.worldpaper.com/2001/may01/kaur.html>.*

WTO website: <http://*www.wto.org/wto/develop/regional.htm*> – Regional Integration and the Multilateral Trading System.

REFERENCES

A

ADB, Various Issues, Key Indicators of Developing Asian and Pacific Countries, Manila: Asian Development Bank.

ADB, 'Foreign Direct Investment: An Explanation," *Asian Development Outlook,* Manila: Asian Development Bank.

Adelman, Irma and Yeldan, Erinc, 2000, "The Minimal Conditions for a Financial Crisis: a Multiregional Intertemporal CGE model of the Asian Crisis," *World Development,* Vol.28, No.6, pp.1087-1100.

Agabin, Meliza, 1993, "The Informal Credit Markets in the Philippines," *Asian Economic Journal,* Vol.7, No.2, 1993, pp.209-247. Ahmad, Jaleel, 1997, Exports and Economic Growth in the ASEAN Countries: Cointegration and Causality Tests, *Rivista Internazionale di Scienze Economiche e Commerciale,* Vol.44, pp.419-430.

Ahmed, Momtaz Uddin, 2001, "Foreign Direct Investment and Technology Flows in Asia and the Pacific Region in the 1990s: An Analysis of Trends, Patterns and Policies," in Behrman, J.R, M.Dutta, S.L. Husted, Sumalee, C. Suthiphand, and P. Wiboonchutikula, *Restructuring Asian Economics for the New Millenium,* JAI – Elsevier Science, pp.643-668.

Akamatsu, Kaname, 1962a, ''A Historical Pattern of Economic Growth in Developing Countries,'' *The Developing Economies*, The Preliminary Issue, No.1, pp.3-25.

Akamatsu, Kaname, 1962b, "A Theory of Unbalanced Growth in the World Economy," *Weltwirtschafliches Archiv*, Heft 86, Band 2, pp.523-544.

Alam, Asad, 1995, "The New Trade Theory and its Relevance to the Trade Policies of Developing Countries," *The World Economy,* Vol.18, No.3, pp.367-385.

Alburo, Florian, Carlos Bautista, and Maria Socorro Gochoco, 1992, "Pacific Direct Investment flows into ASEAN," *ASEAN Economic Bulletin,* Vol.8, No.3, pp.284-308.

Antonio Jr., Emilio, 1997, "Industrial Policies in the Philippines: Growing Reliance on Market Mechanisms," in Seiichi Masuyama, Donna Vandenbrink, and Siow Yue Chia (eds), *Industrial Policies in East Asia*, Japan: Nomura Research Institute and Singapore: Institute of Southeast Asian Studies, pp.233-252.

Ariff, Mohamed, 1989, "Industrial Restructuring and Regional Development in the ASEAN Countries: an Overview," Paper presented at the International Conference on Industrial

Transformation and Regional Development in an age of Global Interdependence, Japan: United Nations Center for Regional Development.

Ariff, Mohamed, 1998, "Economic Regionalism versus Multilateralism: Dilemmas for Southeast Asia?" Paper presented at ISEAS 30th anniversary conference on Southeast Asia in the 21st Century: Challenges of Globalization, Singapore.

Asia Times, "Indonesia faces up to Post-IMF Reality," August 15, 2003.

Asian Development Bank, Various Issues, *Asian Development Outlook,* New York: Oxford University Press.

Asian Development Bank, 1997, *Emerging Asia: Changes and Challenges,* Manila: Asian Development Bank.

Asian Development Bank, Various Issues, *Key Indicators for Asian and Pacific Developing Countries,* New York: Oxford University Press.

Asian Economic News, "Singapore Free Trade Pact Worrisome, Mahathir says," March 5, 2001.

Asiaweek, February 14 and 21, 1997.

Asiaweek, September 11, 1998, p.3.

Aswicahyono, Haryo, 1997, "Transformation and Structural Change in Indonesia's Manufacturing Sector," in Mari Pangestu and Yuri Sato (eds.), *Waves of Change in Indonesia's Manufacturing Industry,* Tokyo: Institute of Developing Economies, pp.1-28.

Athukorala, Prema-Chandra, 1998, "Swimming against the Tide: Crisis Management in Malaysia," *ASEAN Economic Bulletin,* Vol.15, No.3, pp.281-289.

Azarcon, Chulia, 1997, "Comparative Tariff Policies of ASEAN Member Countries," *Journal of Philippine Development,* Number 43, Vol.24, No.1, pp.93-135.

B

Baer, Werner; Miles, William and Moran, Allen, 1999, "The End of the Asian Myth: Why were the Experts Fooled?" *World Development,* Vol.27, No.10, pp.1735-1747.

Bagchi, Amiya Kumar, 1989, "Industrialization," in John Eatwell, Murray Milgate and Peter Newman (eds.), *Economic Development,* London and Basingstoke, UK: The Macmillan Press, pp.160-173.

Bahmani-Oskooee, Mohsen and Alse, Janardhanan, 1993, "Export Growth and Economic Growth: An Application of Cointegration and Error-Correction Modeling," *Journal of Developing Areas,* Vol.27, No.4, pp.535-542.

Balassa, Bela, 1988, "The Lessons of East Asian Development: An Overview". *Economic Development and Cultural Change*, Vol.36, No.3, pp.273-289.

Bangkok Post, Aug 25, 2003.

Bank Negara Malaysia, 1998, *The East Asian Crisis – Causes, Policy responses, Lessons and Issues.* Group of 15 Working Paper No.4, Switzerland.

Bank Negara Malaysia, 1991, "The Accelerated Industrialization Drive," *Bank Negara Annual Report*, pp.53-63.

Bautista, Romeo, John Power and Associates, 1979, *Industrial Promotion Policies in the Philippines*, Manila: Philippine Institute for Development Studies.

Benson, Dredner Kleinwort, 2000, "Privatization in Thailand 2000," *Asiamoney,* May.

Bhanupong, Nidhiprabha, 1998, "Economic Crises and the Debt-Deflation Episode in Thailand," *Asean Economic Bulletin,* Vol.15, No.3, pp.309-318.

Bird, Graham and A. Milne, 1999, "Miracle to Meltdown: a Pathology of the East Asian Crisis," *Third World Quarterly,* Vol.20, No.2, pp. 421-437.

Bleaney, Michael, 1996, "Macroeconomic Stability, Investment and Growth in Developing Countries," *Journal of Development Economics,* Vol.48, No.2, pp.461-477.

Bloomberg News, "Banking giants beat hasty retreat after hedge fund losses," *The Straits Times,* January 27, 1999, p.47.

Boltho, A., 1996, "The Assessment: International Competitiveness," *Oxford Review of Economic Policy,* Vol.12, No.3, pp.1-16.

Booth, Anne, 1992, "An Economic Overview of Southeast Asia," *Southeast Asian Affairs,* Singapore: Institute of Southeast Asian Studies, pp.21-43.

Booth, Anne, 1999, "Initial Conditions and Miraculous Growth: Why is Southeast Asia Different from Taiwan and South Korea?" *World Development,* Vol.27, No.2, pp.301-321.

BOT, 2000, *Supervision Report*, Thailand: Bank of Thailand.

Bullard, Nicola, Walden Bello and Kamal Mallhotra, 1998, "Taming the Tigers: the IMF and the Asian Crisis," *Third World Quarterly*, Vol.19, No.3, pp.505-555.

C

Campos, Jose Edgardo and Hilton Root, 1996, *The Key to the Asian Miracle: Making Shared Growth Credible,* Washington, D.C.: Brookings Institution.

Carroll, C., D. Weil, and Lawrence Summers, 1993, "Savings and Growth: A Re-interpretation," Paper presented at the Carnegie-Rochester Public Policy Conference, Bradley Policy Research Centre, April 23-24.

Centre for Strategic and International Studies (CSIS), "IMF," Opinion and editorial, March 7, 2003.

Center for Strategic and International Studies (CSIS), "Speed up reform, avoid return to protectionism," opinion-editorial in the Jakarta Post, December 27, 2002.

Chalongphob, Sussangkarn, 1999, "Thailand: Toward Economic Solvency," paper presented at the 1999 Regional Economic Outlook, organized by the Institute of Southeast Asian Studies (ISEAS), Singapore, January.

Chang, Ha-Joon, 1998, "Korea: The Misunderstood Crisis," *World Development,*Vol.26, No.8, pp.1555-1561.

Chang, Ha-Joon, 2000, "The Hazard of Moral Hazard: Untangling the Asian Crisis," *World Development,* Vol.28, No.4, pp.775-788.

Chen, Edward, 1997, "The Total Factor Productivity Debate: Determinants of Economic Growth in East Asia," *Asian-Pacific Economic Literature,* Vol.11, No.1, pp.18-38.

Cheng, Siok-Hwa, 1980, "Development of ASEAN Agriculture," in Swee Hock Saw (ed.), *ASEAN Economies in Transition,* Singapore: Singapore University Press, pp.70-100.

Chia, Siow Yue, 1986, "Direct Foreign Investment and Industrialization in Singapore," in Chong-Yah Lim and Peter Lloyd (eds.), *Singapore Resources and Growth,* Singapore: Oxford University Press, pp.79-117.

Chia, Siow Yue, 1996, "The Deepening and Widening of ASEAN," *Journal of Asia Pacific Economy,* Vol.1, pp.59-78.

Chia, Siow Yue, 1998, "The Asian Financial Crisis: Singapore's Experience and Response," *ASEAN Economic Bulletin,* Vol.15, No.3, pp.297-308.

Chia, Siow Yue, 2001, "Singapore: Towards a Knowledge-Based Economy," in Seiichi Masuyama, Donna Vandenbrink and Siow Yue Chia (eds.), *Industrial Restructuring in East Asia*, Japan: Nomura Research Institute and Singapore: Institute of Southeast Asian Studies, pp.170-208.

Chou, Catherine, 1999, "Indonesian Banks: Survival of the Fittest," in *Rising to the Challenge in Asia: A Study of Financial Markets,* (Volume 6 – Indonesia), Manila: Asian Development Bank, pp.36-72.

Chowdry, Anis and Iyanatul Islam, 1993, "Financial Development and Economic Performance," in Anis Chowdry and Iyanatul Islam, *The Newly Industrializing Economies of East Asia*, London: Routledge.

Clark, Gerald and Marites Sison, 2003, "Do the Well-off Really Care about the Plight of the Poor?" *Development and Change,* Vol 34, No.2, pp.215-242.

Cohen, Margot Cohen, *Far Eastern Economic Review,* December 25, 1997, as cited in World Bank, *East Asia: The Road to Recovery,* Washington D.C.: World Bank, p.1.

Collins, Susan and Barry Bosworth, 1997, "Economic Growth in East Asia: Accumulation versus Assimilation," in W. Bainard and G. Perry, eds, *Brookings Papers on Economic Activity,* Washington DC: Brookings Institution, pp.135-203.

Corden, Max, 1996, Pragmatic Orthodoxy: Macroeconomic Policies in Seven East Asian Economies, *Occasional Papers No.61*, California: International Centre for Economic Growth.

Corden, Max, 1998, "The Asian Crisis: Is there a Way Out?" *Public lecture delivered in Singapore as a Distinguished Fellow in International Economics and Finance*, ISEAS, Singapore.

Corsetti, Giancarlo, Paolo Pesenti, and Nouriel Roubini, 1999, "What Caused the Asian Currency and Financial Crisis?" *Japan and the World Economy*, Vol.11, No.3, pp.303-373.

Crafts, Nicholas, 1999, "East Asian Growth Before and After the crisis," *IMF Staff Papers,* Vol. 46, No.2, pp.139-166.

D

Daquila, Grace Pablo, 1997, The Determinants of Intra-ASEAN Exports and Imports, M.A. Thesis, Australia: Deakin University.

Daquila, Teofilo C., 1997, "Obstacles to Closer Trade and Investment Links: An ASEAN Viewpoint," in Chia Siow Yue and Joseph L.H. Tan (eds), *ASEAN and EU: Forging New Linkages and Strategic Alliances*, Singapore: Institute of Southeast Asian Studies, and Paris: OECD, pp.103-134.

Daquila, Teofilo C., 1999, "The ASEAN Experience of Economic Cooperation," Invited paper presented at "The East African Forum on the East African Community: Economic Aspects of Integration," organized by Friedrich Ebert Foundation, 27-29 September, Kampala, Uganda.

Daquila, Teofilo C., 1999, "Growth, Development and Crisis in Southeast Asia," Guest lecture delivered at the Nordic Institute of Asian Studies (Copenhagen), Ludwig-Maximilians Universitaet Muenchen (Germany), Stiftung Wissenschaft und Politik (Ebenhausen, Germany), and the International Institute for Asian Studies, Leiden University (Netherlands). June-July.

Daquila, Teofilo C., 2000, "Japanese Economic Policy in Asia: An Asian Perspective," in Verena Blechinger and Jochen Legewie (eds), *Facing Asia – Japan's Role in the Political and Economic Dynamism of Regional Cooperation,* Munich:Germany, Iudicium Verlag, pp.175-198.

Daquila, Teofilo C., 2001, "Towards Strengthening ASEAN Integration: Challenges, Strategies and Prospects", in Apirat Petchsiri, Alfred Kellerman, Charit Tingsabadh and Pornsan Watananguhn (eds.), *Strengthening ASEAN Integration: Lessons from the EU's Rule of Law*, Thailand: Chulalongkorn University's Interdisciplinary Department of European Studies, the Center for European Studies, and TMC Asser Institute of the Netherlands, pp.77-87.

Daquila, Teofilo C., 2002, "ASEAN Economic Performance: Revisiting the Past, Looking to the Future," *Harvard Asia Quarterly,* Mass.: Harvard University, Vol. 6, No.3, pp.9-14, online exclusive.

Daquila, Teofilo C. and Le Huu Huy, 2003, "Singapore and ASEAN in the Global Economy: Case of Free Trade Agreements," *Asian Survey* (USA: University of California, Berkeley), Vol.XLIII, No.6, pp.908-928.

Daquila, Teofilo C., 2004, "Southeast Asia and ASEAN: Economic Growth Prospects and Challenges," Invited paper presented at the 1st ASEAN-India Roundtable Conference, organized by the Institute of Southeast Asian Studies, Singapore, Feb 9-10.

Davidson, Paul, 2002, *ASEAN: The Evolving Legal Framework for Economic Cooperation*, Singapore: Times Academic Press, pp.14-50.

Dean, James, 1998, "Asia's Financial Crisis in Historical Perspective," *Journal of the Asia Pacific Economy,* Vol.3, No.3, pp.267-283.

Department of Foreign Affairs and Trade (DFAT), 1994, *ASEAN Free Trade Area: Trading Bloc Or Building Block?,* Canberra: Australian Government Publishing Service.

Dixon, Chris, 1991, *Southeast Asia in the World Economy,* Cambridge: Cambridge University Press.

Djiwandono, Soedradjad, 2000, "Bank Indonesia and the Recent Crisis," *Bulletin of Indonesian Economic Studies,* Vol.36, No.1, pp.47-72.

Dodaro, Santo, 1993, "Exports and Growth: A Reconsideration of Causality," *Journal of Developing Areas,* Vol.27, No.2, pp.227-244.

Dollar, David, 1992, "Outward-oriented Developing Economies Really do Grow More Rapidly: Evidence from 95 LDCs, 1976-1985," *Economic Development and Cultural Change,* Vol.40, No.3, pp.523-544.

Dorner, Peter and William Thiesenhusen, 1990, "Selected Land Reforms in East and Southeast Asia: Their Origins and Impacts," *Asian Pacific Economic Literature,* Vol.4, No.1, pp.65-95.

Drysdale, Peter and Huang, Yiping, 1995, "Technological Catch-up and Economic Growth in East Asia and the Pacific," *The Economic Record*, Vol.73, No.222, pp.201-211.

Dufey, Gunter, 1999, " Asian Financial Markets: A Pedagogic Note," *Journal of Asian Business.* Vol.15, No.1, pp.65-71.

Dunning, John, 1981, *International Production and the Multinational Enterprise*, London: Allen & Unwin.

E

ESCAP, 2001, Reducing Disparities: Balanced Development of Urban and Rural Areas and Regions within the Countries of Asia and the Pacific, New York: Economic and Social Commission for Asia and the Pacific.

F

Fagerberg, J., 1996, "Technology and Competitiveness," *Oxford Review of Economic Policy,* Vol.12, No.3, pp.39-51,

Fane, George, 1999, "Indonesian Economic Policies and Performance," *The World Economy*, Vol.22, No.5, pp. 651-668.

Fane, George, 2000, "Survey of Recent Developments," *Bulletin of Indonesian Economic Studies,* Vol.36, No.1, pp.13-45.

Fase, M.M.G. and R.C.N. Abma, 2003, "Financial Environment and Economic Growth in Selected Asian Countries," *Journal of Asian Economics,* Vol.14, pp.11-21.

Food and Agriculture Organization (FAO), *Production Yearbook*, Rome: FAO.

Fischer, Stanley, 1997, "Lessons from East Asia and the Pacific Rim," in W. Bainard and G. Perry (eds.), *Brookings Papers on Economic Activity*, Washington DC: Brookings Institution, pp.345-350.

Flaherty, Mark, Peter Vandergeest and Paul Miller, 1999, "Rice Paddy or Shrimp Pond: Tough Decisions on Rural Thailand," *World Development,* Vol.27, No.12, 2045-2060.

Frankel, Jeffrey, 1998, "The Asian Model, the Miracle, the Crisis and the Fund," A speech delivered at the US International Trade Commission, April 16.

Fry, Maxwell, 1995, "Financial Development in Asia: Some Analytical Issues," *Asian-Pacific Economic Literature*, Vol.9, No.1, pp.40-57.

Fukuda, Shin-ichi and Hideki Toya, 1995, "Conditional Convergence in East Asian Countries: The Role of Exports in Economic Growth," in Takatoshi Ito and Anne O. Krueger (eds), *Growth Theories in Light of the East Asian Experience,* Chicago, USA: The University of Chicago Press, pp.247-265.

Fukushima, Kiyohiko and C.H.Kwan, 1995, "Foreign Direct Investment and Regional Industrial Restructuring in Asia," in NRI and ISEAS (compilers), *Foreign Direct Investment in Asia,* Tokyo: Tokyo Club Foundation for Global Studies and Singapore: Institute of Southeast Asian Studies, pp.3-39.

G

Garnaut, Ross (ed.), 1980, *ASEAN in a Changing Pacific and World Economy*. Canberra: Australian National University Press.

Gerald Meier, 1989, *Leading Issues in Economic Development*, New York: Oxford University Press.

Gochoco-Bautista, Maria Socorro, 1999, "The Past Performance of the Philippine Banking Sector and Challenges in the Post-crisis Period," in *Rising to the Challenge in Asia: A Study of Financial Markets,* (Volume 10 – Philippines), Manila: Asian Development Bank, pp.30-78.

Greenaway, David and Wyn Morgan, 1998, "Trade Orientation and Economic Development: Theory and Evidence," in David Sapsford and John-ren Chen (eds), *Development Economics and Policy,* London, UK: Macmillan Press, pp.113-132.

Greenaway, David, Wyn Morgan and Peter Wright, 1997, "Trade Liberalization and Growth in Developing Countries: Some New Evidence," *World Development,* Vol.25, No.11, pp.1885-1892.

H

Hadi, Soesastro, 1999, "The Indonesian Economy under Habibie," paper presented at the 1999 Regional Outlook Forum, organized by ISEAS, Singapore, January.

Haggard, Stephen and Kim, Euysung, 1996, "The Sources of East Asia's Economic Growth," *Access Asia Review,* Vol.1, No.1, pp.31-63.

Haggard, Stephen, 2001, "Politics, Institutions and Globalization: The Aftermath of the Asian Financial Crisis," *American Asian Review,* Vol.19, No.2, pp.71-98.

Harrison, Ann, 1996, "Openness and Growth: A Time-Series, Cross-Country Analysis for Developing Countries," *Journal of Development Economics,* Vol.48, No.2, pp.419-447.

Hatakeyama, Noboru, 2003, "EAFTA not a Dream, but a Reality," Presented at the symposium on "FTAs; JSEPA and Beyond," Singapore, March 7.

Hesse, Helmut and Auria, Laura, 1998, "The Financial Crisis in Southeast Asia: Causes and Effects on the Global Economy," *Economics,* Vol.57.

Hesse, Helmut and Laura Auria, 1998, "The Financial Crisis in Southeast Asia: Causes and Effects on the Global Economy," *Economics.* A Biannual Collection of Recent German Studies, Tübingen: Institut für Wissenschaftliche Zusammearbeit, Vol. 57, pp. 45-70.

Hill, Hal, 1990, "Foreign Investment and East Asian Economic Development," *Asian-Pacific Economic Literature,* Vol.4, No.2, pp.21-58.

Hill, Hal, 1996, "Indonesia's Industrial Policy and Performance: Orthodoxy Vindicated," *Economic Development and Cultural Change,* Vol.45, No.1, pp.147-174.

Hill, Hal, 1997, *Indonesia's Industrial Transformation,* Singapore: Institute of Southeast Asian Studies.

Hill, Hal, 1998, "Southeast Asia's Economic Crisis: Origins, Lessons and the Way Forward", Paper presented at the ISEAS 30th anniversary conference: Southeast Asia in the 21st Century, Singapore, July 30- August 1.

Hill, Hal, 2000, "Export Success Against the Odds: A Vietnamese Case Study," *World Development,* Vol.28, No.2, pp.283-300. Hogendorn, Jan, 1992, *Economic Development,* New York: Harper-Collins Publishers.

I

Intal, Ponciano Jr, Melanie Milo, Celia Reyes and Leilani Basilio, 1998, "The Philippines," in *East Asia in Crisis: From Being a Miracle to Needing One*? in Ross. H. McLeod and R. Garnaut (eds.), London: Routledge, pp.145-161.

International Monetary Fund (IMF), Various Issues, *International Financial Statistics,* Washington DC.: IMF.

International Monetary Fund (IMF), Various Issues, *Direction of Trade Statistics Yearbook,* Washington D.C.: International Monetary Fund.

International Monetary Fund (IMF), Various Issues, *International Financial Statistics,* Washington DC.: IMF.

International Finance Corporation (IFC), 1997, "Foreign Direct Investments," *Lessons of Experience*, No.5, Washington DC, USA: International Finance Corporation.

Institute of Southeast Asian Studies (ISEAS), 2003, *Regional Outlook: Southeast Asia, 2003-2004*, Singapore: ISEAS.

Ismail Md Salleh, 1995, "Foreign Direct Investment and Technology Transfer in the Malaysian Electronics Industry," in NRI and ISEAS (compilers), *Foreign Direct Investment in Asia,* Tokyo: Tokyo Club Foundation for Global Studies and Singapore: Institute of Southeast Asian Studies, pp.133-159.

J

James, William, 1998, "Trade and Financial Market Reforms in ASEAN," *ASEAN Economic Bulletin,* Vol.14, No.3, pp.224-237.

Jomo, Sundaram, 1990, *Growth and Structural Change in the Malaysian Economy*, London: Macmillan Press.

Jomo, Sundaram, Rajah Rasiah, Rokiah Alavi and Jaya Gopal, 1998, "Industrial Policy and the Emergence of Internationally Competitive Manufacturing Firms in Malaysia," in Kazuo Takahashi (ed.), *Asia's Development Experiences – How Internationally Competitive National Manufacturing Firms Have Developed in Asia*, Tokyo, Japan: Foundation for Advanced Studies on International Development, pp.178-261.

Johnson, Chalmers, 1998, "Economic Crisis in East Asia: The Clash of Capitalisms," *Cambridge Journal of Economics,* Vol.22, No.6, pp.653-661.

Johnston, Barry, 1991, "Distressed Financial Institutions in Thailand: Structural Weaknesses, Support Operations and Economic Consequences," in Sundararajan V. and Balino, T. (eds), *Banking and Crisis: Cases and Issues,* Washington DC: IMF.

K

Kanapathy, Vijayakumari, 2001, "Industrial Restructuring in Malaysia: Policy Shifts and the Promotion of New Sources of Growth," in Seiichi Masuyama, Donna Vandenbrink, and Siow Yue Chia (eds.), *Industrial Restructuring in East Asia,* Japan: Nomura Research Institute and Singapore: Institute of Southeast Asian Studies, pp.139-165.

Karseno, Arief Ramelan, 1997, "Perspectives on Government Policy for Industrial Competitiveness in Indonesia," in Seiichi Masuyama, Donna Vandenbrink, and Siow Yue Chia (eds.), *Industrial Policies in East Asia*, Japan: Nomura Research Institute and Singapore: Institute of Southeast Asian Studies, pp.216-232.

Kawai, Hiroki, 1994, "International Comparison of Economic Growth," in H. Urata, (ed.), *Trade Liberalization and Economic Development*, Tokyo: Institute of Developing Economies.

Kawai, Masahiro and Ken-ichi Takayasu, 1999, "The Economic Crisis and Banking Sector Restructuring in Thailand," in *Rising to the Challenge in Asia: A Study of Financial* Markets (Volume 11- Thailand), Manila: Asian Development Bank, pp.38-103.

Kerdpibule, Udom and Eric Ramsetter, 1987, "Foreign Investment Theories and Policy Issues," in Seiji Naya (ed.), *Direct Foreign Investment and Export in Asia,* Kuala Lumpur: Southeast Asia Central Banks Research and Training Center (SEACEN) and Hawaii: East-West Resource Systems Institute, pp.1-23.

Kim, Chulsu, 2003, "Towards an East Asia Free Trade Agreement," Paper delivered at the symposium on "FTAs: JSEPA and Beyond," Singapore, March 7.

Kim, Jong-Il. and Lawrence Lau, 1994, "The Source of Economic Growth of the East Asian Newly Industrializing Countries," *Journal of the Japanese and International Economies*, Vol.8, No.3, pp.235-271.

Kim, Youn-Suk and Hyeng Keun Koo, 1999, "Asia's Contagious Financial Crisis and its Impact on Korea," *Journal of Asian Economics,* Vol.10, No.1, pp.111-121.

Kirkpatrick, Colin, 1989, "The ASEAN Countries: The Next NICs?" *EIU Regional Reference Series*, pp.5-14.

Kojima, Kiyoshi, 1978, *Direct Foreign Investment: A Japanese Model of Multinational Business Operations*, New York: Praeger.

Kojima, Kiyoshi, 1987, "A Model of Trade-Oriented Foreign Investment," in Seiji Naya (ed.), *Direct Foreign Investment and Export Promotion Policies: Policies and Experiences in Asia,* Kuala Lumpur: Southeast Asia Central Banks Research and Training Center and Hawaii: East-West Resource Systems Institute, pp. 159-183.

Krugman, Paul, 1994, "The Myth of Asia's Miracle," *Foreign Affairs*, Vol.73, No.6, pp. 62-78.

Krugman, Paul, 1994, "Competitiveness: A Dangerous Obsession," *Foreign Affairs,* Vol.73, No.2, pp.28-45.

Krugman, Paul, 1997, "What Ever Happened to the Asian Miracle?" *Fortune,* August 18, p.12

Krugman, Paul, "Wrong, It Never Existed," *Time,* September 29, 1997, p.37.

L

Lall, Sanjaya, 2001, "Competitiveness Indices and Developing Countries: An Economic Evaluation of the Global Competitiveness Report," *World Development,* Vol.29. No.9, pp.1501-1525.

Lamberte, Mario and Josef Yaf, 1999, *Scenarios for Economic Recovery: The Philippines.* Discussion Paper No.99-05. Manila: Philippine Institute for Development Studies.

Lane, Timothy and Marianne Schulze-Ghattas, 1999, *IMF-Supported Programs in Indonesia, Korea and Thailand: A Preliminary Assessment,* Occasional Paper No.178, Washington D.C.: International Monetary Fund.

Langhammer, Rolf, 1992, "Regionalism in Place of or Together with Multilateralism" delivered before the Economic Society of Singapore, July 9.

Le, Quoc-Phuong, Duc-Tho Nguyen, and J.S. Bandara, 1996, "Vietnam's Foreign Trade in the Context of ASEAN and the Asia-Pacific Region," *ASEAN Economic Bulletin,* Vol.13, No.2, pp.185-199.

Lee Tsao Yuan, 1990, "NIC Investments in ASEAN: The Pattern in the Eighties", in Soon Lee Ying (ed.), *Foreign Direct Investment in ASEAN,* Kuala Lumpur: Malaysian Economic Association, pp.112-135.

Lian, Daniel and Tsao Yuan Lee, "Financial Development in ASEAN," in Joseph Tan and Zhaohong Luo (eds.), *ASEAN-China Economic Relations*, Institute of World Economics and Politics, and Singapore: Institute of Southeast Asian Studies.

Lim Chong Yah and Associates, 1988, *Policy Options for the Singapore Economy,* Singapore: McGraw Hill, pp. 301-320.

Lim, Chong Yah, 1991, *Development and Underdevelopment*, Singapore: Longman Publications.

Lim, Chong Yah, 2001, *Southeast Asia: The Long Road Ahead.* Singapore: World Scientific Publishing Co. Ltd.

Lim, David, 1994, "Explaining The Growth Performance of Asian Developing Economies," *Economic Development and Cultural Change,* Vol.42, No.4, pp.829-844.

Lim, Hank, 1980, "Pattern of ASEAN Industrialization," Saw Swee Hock (ed.), *ASEAN Economies in Transition*, Singapore: Singapore University Press, pp.169-242.

Lim, Imran and Helen Nesadurai, 1997, "Managing the Malaysian Industrial Economy" in Seiichi Masuyama, Donna Vandenbrink, and Siow Yue Chia (eds.), *Industrial Policies in East Asia*, Japan: Nomura Research Institute and Singapore: Institute of Southeast Asian Studies, pp.185-215

Lim, Linda Y.C., 1995, "Foreign Investment, the State and Industrial Policy in Singapore," in Howard Stein (ed.), *Asian Industrialization and Africa,* St. Martin's Press, New York, pp.205-238.

Lim, Linda Y.C., 1998, "Whose Model Failed? Implications of the Asian Economic Crisis," *The Washington Quarterly*, Vol.21, No.3, pp.25-36.

Lincoln, Edward J., 1987, *Japan's Economic Role in Northeast Asia.* Asian Agenda Report No. 10. Maryland: University Press of America & the Asia Society, pp.xviii-xi.

Lindgren, Carl-Johan, Gillian Garcia, and Matthew I. Saal, 1996, *Banking Soundness and Macroeconomic Policy,* Washington D.C.: International Monetary Fund, p.20, as cited in Joseph Stiglitz, 2000, "Capital Market Liberalization, Economic Growth, and Instability," *World Development,* Vol.28, No.6.

Little, Ian, Richard Cooper, Max Corden, and Sarath Rajapatirana, 1992, *Boom, Crisis Adjustment: The Macroeconomic Experience of Developing Ccountries,* New York: Oxford University Press for the World Bank.

Lloyd-Sherlock, Peter, 2000, "Old Age and Poverty in Developing Countries: New Policy Challenges," *World Development,* Vol.28, No.12, pp.2157-2168.

Low, Linda, 2001, "Changing Modalities in International Trade," *Panorama,* Vol.2, pp. 63-93.

M

MacIntryre, Andrew, 1998, "Political Institutions and the Economic Crisis in Thailand and Indonesia," *ASEAN Economic Bulletin,* Vol.15, No.3, pp.362-372.

McKinnon, Ronald and H. Pill, 1998, "International Overborrowing – A Decomposition of Credit and Currency Risk," *World Development,* Vol.26, No.7, pp.1267-1282.

Medalla, Erlinda, Gwendolyn Tecson, Romeo Bautista and John Power, 1995, *Catching Up with Asia's Tigers,* Vol.1, Main Report, Manila: Philippine Institute for Development Studies.

Mundle, Sudipto, 1998, "Financing Human Development: Some Lessons from Advanced Asian Countries," *World Development,* Vol.26, No.4, 1998, pp.659-672.

Myrdal, Gunnar, 1956, *An International Economy*, New York: Harper & Bros.

N

Naidu, G., 1994, "Johor-Singapore-Riau Growth Triangle: Progress and Prospects," in Myo Thant, Min Tang, and Hiroshi Kakazu (eds.), *Growth Triangles In Asia: A New Approach To Regional Economic Cooperation*, Hong Kong: Oxford University Press, pp.218-242.

Naya, Seiji, 1987, "Economic Performance and Growth Factors of the ASEAN Countries," Martin, L.G. (ed.), *The ASEAN Success Story: Social, Economic and Political Dimensions,* Hawaii: East-West Center, pp. 47-87.

Naya, Seiji and Pearl Imada, 1992, "Economic Success of the NIEs and ASEAN: Some Lessons for Latin America?" *Southeast Asian Affairs,* pp.44-57.

Ng, Edward, 1999, "Central Provident Fund in Singapore: A Capital Market Boost or Drag?" in *Rising to the Challenge in Asia: A Study of Financial Markets,* (Volume – Singapore), Manila: Asian Development Bank, 1999, pp.56-80.

Noboru Hatakeyama, 2003, "EAFTA not a dream, but a reality," Presented at the symposium on "FTAs; JSEPA and Beyond," Singapore, March 7.

O

OECD, 1998, *International Direct Investment Statistics Yearbook,* Paris: OECD.

Oh, Soo-Nam, 1999, "Towards a Sustainable Banking Sector in Malaysia," in *Rising to the Challenge in Asia: A Study of Financial Markets* (Volume 8 – Malaysia), Manila: Asian Development Bank, pp.34-78.

P

Page, John, 1995, "The East Asian Miracle: Four Lessons for Development Policy," in Stanley Fischer and Julio Rotemberg (eds.), *NBER Macroeconomics Annual*, Cambridge: MIT Press, pp.219-269.

Pakorn, Vichyanond., 1998, "Thailand's Financial Evolution and the 1997 Crisis," Paper presented for the conference, The Miracle Undone: Asia's Financial Crisis, C.I.D.E. Mexico City, February 20.

Park, Sung-Hoon, 2002, "East Asian Economic Integration – Finding a Balance between Regionalism and Multilateralism," EIAS Briefing Paper, Brussels: European Institute for Asian Studies.

Parnwell, Michael and Suranart Khamanarong, 1996, "Rural Industrialization in Thailand: Village Industries as a Potential Basis for Rural Development in the North-East," in Michael Parnwell, *Uneven Development in Thailand,* Aldershot, UK: Avebury, pp.161-185.

Patten, Richard, Jay Rosengard and Don Johnston, Jr., 2001, "Microfinance Success amidst Macroeconomic Failure: The Experience of Bank Rakyat Indonesia during the East Asian Crisis," Vol.29, No.6, pp.1057-1069.

Philippine Star, "Arroyo Pushes Free Trade with Japan," December 4, 2002.

Poapongsakorn, Nipon and Belinda Fuller, 1997, "Industrial Location Policy in Thailand: Industrial Decentralization or Industrial Sprawl," in Seiichi Masuyama, Donna Vandenbrink and Siow Yue Chia (eds.), *Industrial Policies in East Asia*, Japan: Nomura Research Institute and Singapore: Institute of Southeast Asian Studies, pp.146-184.

Poapongsakorn, Nipon and Somkiat Tangkitvanich, 2001, "Industrial Restructuring in Thailand: a Critical Assessment", in Seiichi Masuyama, Donna Vandenbrink, and Siow Yue Chia (eds.), *Industrial Restructuring in East Asia*, Japan: Nomura Research Institute and Singapore: Institute of Southeast Asian Studies, pp.109-138.

Porter, Michael, 1990, *The Competitive Advantage of Nations,* New York: The Free Press.

R

Radelet, Steven and Jeffrey Sachs, 1998, *The Onset of the East Asian Financial Crisis,* Cambridge: National Bureau of Economic Research.

Radelet, Steven and Jeffrey Sachs, 1998, *The East Asian Financial Crisis: Diagnosis, Remedies and Prospects,* Cambridge: Harvard Institute for International Development.

Rajan, Ramkishen, 2001, Economic Globalization and Asia: Trade, Finance and Taxation, Discussion Paper No.0108, Centre for International Economic Studies, University of Adelaide.

Ram, Rati and Kevin Honglin Zhang, 2002, "Foreign Direct Investment and Economic Growth: Evidence from Cross-Country Data for the 1990s," *Economic Development and Cultural Change,* Vol.51, No.1, pp.205-215.

Rana, Pradumna, 1987, "Foreign Direct Investment and Economic Growth in the Asian and Pacific Region," *Asian Development Review*, Vol.5, pp.100-115.

Rana, Pradumna, 1999, "Private Capital Flows to Asian Developing Countries: Past Trends and Future Prospects," *Asian Economic Crisis: Causes, Consequences and Policy Lessons,* Development Papers No.20, Bangkok: United Nations Economic and Social Commission for Asia and the Pacific.

Rao, Bhanoji, Teofilo Daquila, and Woo Yuen Pau, 1994, *ASEAN External Debt Perspectives,* Singapore: Times Academic Press.

Rao, Bhanoji and Christopher Lee, 1995, "Sources of Growth in the Singapore Economy and its Manufacturing and Services Sectors," *Singapore Economic Review,* Vol.40, No.1, pp.83-115.

Reinhardt, Nola, 2000, "Back to Basics in Malaysia and Thailand: The Role of Resource-Based Exports in their Export-led Growth," *World Development,* Vol.28, No.1, pp.57-77.

Reynolds, Christopher, 2002, "The Southeast Asian Economic Miracle and International Trade Theory," in *Global Logic: The Challenge of Globalization for Southeast Asian Business,* Singapore: Prentice Hall, pp. 89-118.

Rosenberger, Leif Roderick, 1998, "Southeast Asia's Currency Crisis: A Diagnosis and Prescription," *Contemporary Southeast Asia,* Vol.19, No.3, pp.223-252.

S

Sachs, Jeffrey, "Asia's Miracle is Alive and Well," *Time,* September 29, 1997.

Sachs, Jeffrey, 1997, "IMF Orthodoxy isn't what Southeast Asia needs," *International Herald Tribune,* November 4, p.8, as cited in Robison, Richard and Andrew Rosser, 1998, "Contesting Reform: Indonesia's New Order and the IMF," *World Development,* Vol.26, No.8, pp.1594.

Sachs, Jeffrey, 1998, "Global capitalism: making it work," *The Economist*, September 12, p.24, as cited in Kanishka Jayasuriya and Andrew Rosser, "Economic Orthodoxy and the Asian Economic Crisis," *Third World Quarterly*, Vol.22, No.3, pp.381-396.

Sadli, Mohammad, 1998, "The Indonesian Crisis," *ASEAN Economic Bulletin,* Vol.15, No.3, 1998, pp.272-289.

Sala-I-Martin, Xavier, 2003-2004, "Executive Summary," The Global Competitiveness Report, Switzerland: World Economic Forum, pp.xi-xxiv.

Salvatore, Dominick, 1990, "Trade Restrictions: Tariffs," in *International Economics*, New York: Macmillan Publishing Co., pp.207-286.

Santos-Paulino, Amelia, 2002, "The Effects of Trade Liberalization on Imports in Selected Developing Countries," *World Development,* Vol.30, No.6, pp.959-974.

Saw, Swee Hock (ed.), 1980, *ASEAN Economies in Transition*, Singapore: Singapore University Press, pp.169-242.

Saw, Swee Hock, 1980, "The ASEAN Region in Perspective," in Swee Hock Saw (ed.), *ASEAN Economies in Transition,* Singapore: Singapore University Press, pp.1-42.

Scarlett Epstein, T. and David Jezeph, 2001, "Development – There is Another Way: A Rural-Urban Partnership Development Paradigm," *World Development,* Vol.29, No.8, pp.1443-1454.

Schwartz, Anna, 1998, "International Financial Crises: Myths and Realities," *The Cato Journal*, Vol.17, No.3, 1998, p.4. [see http://www.cato.org/pubs/journal/cj17n3-3.html].

SEACEN, 1995 and 2000 issues, *Financial Statistics Yearbook*, Kuala Lumpur, Malaysia: The Southeast Asian Central Banks for Training and Research (SEACEN).

Shimomoto, Yutaka, 1999, "The Capital Market in Malaysia," in *Rising to the Challenge in Asia: A Study of Financial Markets* (Volume 8 – Malaysia), Manila: Asian Development Bank, pp.80-112.

Sibinruang, Atchaka and Peter Brimble, 1987, in Seiji Naya (ed.), *Direct Foreign Investment Theories and Export Promotion:Policies and Experiences in Asia*, Kuala Lumpur: Southeast Asia Central Bank Research and Training Center, pp. 317-357

Shanmugam, M., 1999, "Merger by Decree," *Malaysian Business,* October 16, p.11.

Sicat, Gerardo, 1998, "The Philippine Economy in the Asian Crisis," *ASEAN Economic Bulletin,* Vol.15, No.3, pp.290-296.

Simon, Jean-Christophe, 1996, "The Thai Manufacturing Sector: New Patterns of Expansion," in Michael Parnwell (ed.), *Uneven Development in Thailand*, Aldershot, UK: Avebury, pp.82-108.

Singaravelu, Ananda and Loh Shen Lee, 1997, "Competitive Advantage: The US and ASEAN," in Tan Teck Meng, Low Aik Meng, John Williams and John Webster (eds), *US-ASEAN Relations: Implications for Business,* Nanyang Business Report Series, Singapore: Prentice Hall, pp.73-97.

Singh, Sukhpal, 2003, "State, Agribusiness Firms and Farmers in Thailand: A Study of the Contract Farming System," Paper presented at the 3rd Asian Studies Foundation Conference, Thailand.

Sinha, Dipendra and Joseph Macri, "Financial Development and Economic Growth: The Case of Eight Asian Countries," *Economia Internazionale*, Vol.55, pp.219-234.

Siroros, Patcharee and Wilaiwan Wannitikul, 1998, "International Competitiveness of Indigenous Firms: Case Studies of the Gems and Jewelry Industry and the Siam Cement Group," in Kazuo Takahashi (ed.), *Asia's Development Experiences – How Internationally Competitive National Manufacturing Firms Have Developed in Asia*, Tokyo, Japan: Foundation for Advanced Studies on International Development, pp.264-310.

Sodersten, Bo, 1980, "The Theory of Comparative Advantage and the Gains from Trade," *International Economics,* New York: St. Martin's Press, pp.11-27.

Soesastro, Hadi, 1996, "Policies Towards Foreign Direct Investment – New Challenges Facing Asian Developing Countries," *The Indonesian Quarterly,* Vol.24, No.2, pp.161-180.

Soesastro, Hadi, 1999, "The Indonesian Economy under Habibie," Paper presented at the 1999 Regional Outlook Forum, organized by ISEAS, Singapore.

Stiglitz, Joseph, 1996, "Some Lessons from the East Asian Miracle," *The World Bank Research Observer,* Vol.11, No.2, pp.151-177.

Stiglitz, Joseph, 2000, "Capital Market Liberalization, Economic Growth, and Instability," *World Development,* Vol.28, No.6, pp.1075-1086.

Stiglitz, Joseph, 2002, *Globalization and its Discontents,* England: The Penguin Press.

Stubbs, Richard, 2002, "ASEAN Plus Three: Emerging East Asian Regionalism?" *Asian Survey,* Vol.42, No.3, pp. 440 – 455.

Suriyamongkol, Marjorie, 1988, *Politics of ASEAN Economic Cooperation,* Singapore: Institute of Southeast Asian Studies, and Oxford University.

T

Tan, Chwee Huat, 1999, *Financial Markets and Institutions in Singapore,* Singapore: Singapore University Press, 1999.

Tan, Gerald, 1996, "Comparative Economic Development," in Gerald Tan, *ASEAN Economic Development and Cooperation*, Singapore: Times Academic Press, pp.26-50.

Tay, Serene, 1993, *Financial and Economic Development in ASEAN*, Singapore: National University of Singapore Department of Economics and Statistics.

Tham, Siew Yean, 1998, "Competition and Cooperation for Foreign Direct Investment: An ASEAN Perspective," *Asia-Pacific Development Journal,* Vol.5, No.1, pp.9-36.

The Business Times (BT)

- "Bilateral pacts could have catalytic effects: BG Yeo," January 18, 2000.
- "Singapore won't be back door to AFTA," May 3, 2001.
- "S'pore's trade pacts are not FTAs," October 12, 2001
- "The paradox of Asia's FTAs," December 18, 2002.
- "FTA with India next on S'pore agenda: BG Yeo," January 30, 2003.
- "Singapore, Australia sign free trade agreement," February 17, 2003.
- "Singapore seals FTA deals with Australia," February 18, 2003.
- "EU, ASEAN pledge to boost trade, political ties," February 24, 2003.

The Hindu, "Malaysia Cautions on Trade Pacts," November 23, 2000.

The International Herald Tribune, January 16, 1998, p.11, as cited in James Dean, 1998, "Asia's Financial Crisis in Historical Perspective," *Journal of the Asia Pacific Economy,* Vol.3, No.3, p.268.

The Korea Herald, "Toward an East Asian Economic Community," February 27, 2003.

The Nation, "Learning from Thailand's Mistakes," November, 17, 1998, p.B1-B2.

The Nation, "Are Anti-Dumping Duties Justified?" Editorial, Feb 21, 2004.

The Straits Times (ST)

---, "Thailand gets reprieve with fresh financing plan from ADB," Feb 14, 1998, p.53.

---"Billions of $ clients of US States," April 3, 1998, p.8.

---, "Jakarta agency wards off starvation," April 21, 1998, p.20.

---, "KL's privatization policy draws flak," April 21, 1998, p.24.

---, "Malaysia's real problem," October 7, 1998, p.37.

---, "Camdessus supports plan," October 8, 1998, p.42.

---, "Singapore still least risky Asian nation," October 11, 1998, p.32.

---, "Government decides on $10.5 billion cut," November 25, 1998, p.1.

---, "We badly misgauged Asian crisis," January 20, 1999, p.1.

---, "Seoul wasted forex reserves in bid to halt meltdown," January 26, 1999, p.15.

---, "IMF to review bail-out conditions," January 29, 1999, p.93.

---, "Start of KL's exit tax 'weeks away," Jan 31, 1999, p.2.

---, "Europe can differentiate now, says SM," February 3, 1999, p.3.

---, "Indonesia's urban poor: wage freeze set to halve real incomes," April 1, 1999, p.4.

---, "FTAs: a way to reach out to the world," January 31, 2001, p.9.

---, "ASEAN must deepen economic ties with partners," May 9, 2001, page A7.

--- "PSA's cargo volume down 8.9% last year", January 19, 2002.

--- "Asia gets onto bandwagon of regionalism," January 28, 2002, p.16.

--- "FTA 'customs union' to benefit Southeast Asia, March 17, 2002.

--- "S'pore, India for economic partnership," April 9, 2002, p.1.

---"Denmark backs Singapore-EU free trade pact," April 18, 2002, p.6.

--- "ASEAN 'slow' on free-trade links," May 3, 2002, p.1.

--- "ASEAN must latch on to China's growth," May 7, 2002, p.A6.

---, "Mega pressured to cut IMF ties," August 9, 2002, p.A6.
--- "ASEAN may become an East Asia grouping," October 12, 2002, p.28.
--- "Will East Asia buy World Bank's economic model?" October 12, 2002, p.28.
--- "Singapore, NZ and Chile go for 3-way trade talks," October 28, 2002.
--- "Spore-Seoul free trade talks to begin next year," November 15, 2002
--- "China's rise has not been at ASEAN's expense," November 19, 2002, p.A16.
--- "How the FTA was won," November 23, 2002, p.28.
---"Chinese tourists heading for Southeast Asia," December 14, 2002, p.A2),
--- "Malaysia aims for first free-trade deal with Japan," December 13, 2002, p.A22.
--- "Asia gets onto bandwagon of regionalism," January 28, 2003, p.16.
--- "EU and ASEAN ministers pledge closer trade and intelligence ties," Jan 29, 2003.
--- "Bush gives go-ahead for FTA pact with S'pore," February 1, 2003, p.A12.
--- "S'pore and India plan talks on free-trade pact," February 4, 2003.
--- "S'pore values both WTO deals, FTAs", February 21, 2003, p.A18.
---, "Two way trade: India urged to change tack towards ASEAN," Nov 26, 2003, p.A4.
---, "More jobs in Japan but spending stays weak," January 31, 2004, p.A17.
---, "US economy grows 4%- less than expected," January 31, 2004, p.A16.
---, "Bird flu to hit Thai stocks further, February 2, 2004, p.A10.
---, "World poultry market jolted," Feb 2, 2004, p.A2.
---, "Vietnam may have spread bird flu to sisters," February 3, 2004, p.A3.
---, "IMF expects to raise this year's growth forecast," February 3, 2004, p.A9.
---, "Corporate travel to India takes off," February 4, 2004, p.A14.
---, "Japan to use Mexico as trade gateway to US, EU," March 15, 2004, p.A15.

The Washington Post, "US, European firms finding Asian companies willing to deal," May 24, 1998, p.H4.

Thomsen, Stephen, 1999, *Southeast Asia: The Role of Foreign Direct Investment Policies in Development,* Working Papers on International Investment, Paris: Organization for Economic Cooperation and Development (OECD).

Tobin, James, 2000, "Financial Globalization," *World Development,* Vol.28, No.6, pp. 1101-1104

Todaro, Michael, 1994, *Economic Development in the Third World,* New York: Longman.

Todaro, Michael, 1994, "Chapter 2 - Diverse Structures and Common Characteristics of Developing Nations", in Michael Todaro, *Economic Development in the Third World,* New York: Longman. pp.27-66.

Todaro, Michael, 1994, "Chapter 10 – Agricultural Transformation and Rural Development," in Michael Todaro, *Economic Development in the Third World,* New York: Longman, pp.285-324.

Tower, Ivory, 1997, "Mexico 1994 versus Thailand 1997," *TDRI Quarterly Review,* Vol.12, No.3, pp.9-14.

Tsao Yuan, 1985, "Growth without Productivity: Singapore Manufacturing in the 1970s," *Journal of Development Economics,* Vol.18, No.1-2, pp.25-38.

Tsugami, Toshiya, 2003, "On ASEAN-China Free Trade Agreement – a personal view from Japan," Presented at a symposium on "FTAs: JSEPA and Beyond", organized by the Japan Economic Foundation and Singapore Institute of International Affairs, Singapore, March 7.

Tomioka, Noriyuki, 2001, "Causes of the Asian Crisis, Asian-style Capitalism and Transparency," *Asia-Pacific Review,* Vol.8, No.2, pp.47-65.

U

United Nations, Various Issues, *Statistical Yearbook for Asia and the Pacific*, Bangkok: UN/ESCAP.

United Nations, 1985, *An Evaluation of Export Processing Zones in Selected Asian Countries,* Bangkok: UN/ESCAP, pp. 21-23.

UNCTAD, 1996, *Investing in Asia's Dynamism,* Switzerland: UNCTAD Division on Transnational Corporations and Investment and Services of the European Commission.

UNCTAD, 1999, *Trade and Development Report*, Geneva: UNCTAD.

V

Vernon, Raymond, 1966, "International Investment and International Trade in the Product Cycle", *Quarterly Journal of Economics,* Vol.80, No.2, pp.190-207.

Vyas, V.S., 1983, "Asian Agriculture: Achievements and Challenges," *Asian Development Review*, Vol.1, No.2, pp.27-44.

W

Wade, Robert, 1998, "The Asian Debt-and-Development Crisis of 1997-?: Causes and Consequences," *World Development,* Vol.26, No.8, pp.1535-1553.

Warr, Peter, 1999, "What Happened to Thailand?" *The World Economy,* Vol.22, No.5, pp.631-50.

Wells, Stephen, 1999, "Moving Toward Transparency: Capital Market in Indonesia," in *Rising to the Challenge in Asia: A Study of Financial Markets* (Volume 6 – Indonesia), Manila: Asian Development Bank, pp.74-111.

Wells, Stephen, 1999, "Solid Crust with Soft Center: A Problem of Enforcement in the Philippine Capital Market," in *Rising to the Challenge in Asia: A Study of Financial Markets* (Volume 10 – Philippines), Manila: Asian Development Bank, pp.80-105.

Werner, Richard, 1999, "Capital Market in Thailand: Issues and Opportunities," in *Rising to the Challenge in Asia: A Study of Financial Markets* (Volume 11 – Thailand), Manila: Asian Development Bank, pp.106-134.

Wong, John, 1979, *ASEAN Economies in Perspective,* Singapore: Macmillan Press.

Wong, John, 1979, "Chapter 4 – Agricultural and Rural Development: Legacy of the Urban Bias," in John Wong, *ASEAN Economies in Perspective*, Singapore: The Macmillan Press Ltd, pp.93-119.

Wong, Poh Kam and Chee Yuen Ng, 1997, "Singapore's Industrial Policy to the year 2000," in Seiichi Masuyama, Donna Vandenbrink and Siow Yue Chia (eds.), *Industrial Policies in East Asia*, Japan: Nomura Research Institute and Singapore: Institute of Southeast Asian Studies, pp. 121-141.

Wong, Poh-Kam, Sock-Yong Phang, Jong-Say Yong and Meng-Kng Chng, 1998, "Development of Internationally Competitive Indigenous Manufacturing Firms in Singapore," in Kazuo Takahashi (ed.), *Asia's Development Experiences – How Internationally Competitive National Manufacturing Firms Have Developed in Asia,* Tokyo, Japan: Foundation for Advanced Studies on International Development, pp. 372-447.

World Bank, 1976, *The Philippines: Priorities and Prospects for Development.* Washington DC: The World Bank.

World Bank, 1983, *The Outlook for Primary Commodities,* Washington D.C.: World Bank.

World Bank, 1991, *World Development Report,* New York: Oxford University Press.

World Bank, 1993, *The East Asian Miracle: Economic Growth and Public Policy,* New York: Oxford University Press.

World Bank, 1997, *World Development Indicators,* New York: Oxford University Press.

World Bank, 2000/01, "Growth, Inequality and Poverty," *World Development Report,* Washington DC: World Bank.

World Bank, 2003, *East Asia Update: Looking Beyond Short-term Shocks - Regional Overview with special focus on East Asia's Urban Transformation,* Washington DC: World Bank.

World Bank, 2003, *Global Economic Prospects 2003*, Washington DC: World Bank.

WTO, 1995, *Regionalism and the World Trading System*, Geneva: World Trading Organization.

Wu, Friedrich and Kok Keong Puah, 2003, "Foreign Direct Investment in China and Southeast Asia: Has ASEAN been losing out?" *Journal of Asian Business,* Vol.19, No.1.

Y

Yongyuth, Chalamwong, "Economic Crisis, International Migration and the Labor Market in Thailand," *TDRI Quarterly Review.* Vol.13, No.1, pp.12-21.

Young, Alwyn, 1995, "Lessons from the East Asian NICS: a contrarian view," *European Economic Review,* Vol.38, No.3-4, pp.964-973.

Young, Alwyn, 1994, "The Tyranny of Numbers: Confronting the Statistical Realities of the East Asian Growth Experience," *Quarterly Journal of Economics,* Vol.110, No.3, pp.641-680.

Z

Zainal Aznam Yusof, 1999, "Malaysian Economic Outlook: Moving Towards a Slow Recovery," Paper presented at the 1999 Regional Economic Outlook, organized by ISEAS, Singapore.

INTERNET SOURCES

ADB, Key Indicators of Developing Asian and Pacific Countries 2002 (*www.adb.org*).

Asia Times, "Vietnamese catfish firm shifts exports from US," Feb 15, 2003 (*http://www.atimes.com/atimes/Southeast_Asia/EB15Ae06.html*)

Asia Times, "Propping up sugar prices a bitter prospect," May 27, 2003. (*http://www.atimes.com/atimes/Southeast_Asia/EE27Ae01.html*)

ASEAN Secretariat (*www.aseansec.org*).

ASEAN Secretariat, 2003, "Joint Media Statement," released during the 17th meeting of the AFTA Council, Phnom Penh, Cambodia, September 1. (see *http://www.aseansec.org /15070.htm*)

Bank of Korea (*www.bok.or.kr*).

Bank of Thailand (*www.bot.or.th*)

Becker, Geoffrey, 1997, Agricultural Exports: Technical Barriers to Trade, CRS Report for Congress, October 21. (see the National Council for Science and the Environment website: *http://www.ncseonline.org/NLE/CRSreports/Agriculture/ag-43.cfm*)

Food and Agriculture Organization of the United Nations – FAOSTAT: *http://apps.fao.org/default.htm*

Fischer, Stanley, 1999, "The Asian Crisis: the Beginning of the End?", speech delivered at the Asia Society, Manila, February 26, at *http://www.asiasociety.org/speeches/fischer.html*

IE Singapore (*www.iesingapore.gov.sg*)

Indonesia's Investment Coordinating Board, Badan Koordinasi Penanaman Modal (BKPM) website, h*ttp://www.bkpm.go.id*

Intellasia, "Vietnam ready to tackle possible US antidumping lawsuit," Jan 1, 2004 (*http://www.intellasia.com/news_today/2004/020104.htm*)

Kaur, Hardev, 2003, "Amid globalization trend, Pacific Rim sees a bellweather on bilateral trade," *The WorldPaper,* [accessed 21 April] < *http://www.worldpaper.com/2001/may0 /tradeblocs4.html* >

LABORSTA, International Labor Office database on labor statistics – *http://laborsta.ilo.org*

McKee, R. 'Philippines could be worse," 2000. h*ttp://www.megastories.com/seasia/philippi/ philippi2.htm*l

Philippine Star, December 4, 2002: *http://www.philstar.com/philstar/print.asp?article= 103628.*

Schwartz, Anna, 1998, "International Financial Crises: Myths and Realities," *The Cato Journal*, Vol.17, No.3. as obtained from [*http://www.cato.org/pubs/journal/cj17n3-3.html*].

Singapore's MTI website < *http://www.mti.gov.sg/public/FTA/frm_FTA_Default.asp?sid= 37&cid=1183* >

Sharma, Krishnan, 2002, The Underlying Constraints on Corporate Bond Market Development in Southeast Asia, United Nations: Development Policy and Analysis Section. [*http://www.combinet.net/wldecnmy/oct2000/KrishnaSharma/constraints.htm*]

Textile World Asia, "EU and Vietnam sign quota agreement," Spring 2003. (See *http://www.textileworldasia.com/News.htm?CD=1846&ID=5025*)

(*unstats.un.org)*

United Nations Population Fund (*http://www.unfpa.org*).

Walden, Bello, 1999, "Asia, Asian Farmers and the WTO," Focus on Trade, No.36, Transnational Institute (TNI). (*http://www.tni.org/archives/bello/asiawto.htm*)

WTO website: http://*www.wto.org*.

WTO website: http://*www.wto.org/wto/develop/regional.htm* – Regional Integration and the Multilateral Trading System.

About the Author

Dr. Teofilo C. Daquila obtained his engineering degree *(cum laude)* in the Philippines funded by a Shell Chemicals scholarship. He was also awarded full scholarships by the University of the Philippines School of Economics (UP) and the *Katholieke Universiteit te Leuven* (KUL, Belgium) which enabled him to complete his MA degree in economics with *Distinction*. Subsequently, he was given a full scholarship by the Australian National University where he obtained his doctorate degree in economics.

Dr. Daquila is a Senior Lecturer in the Southeast Asian Studies Program of the National University of Singapore. His teaching experience includes previous appointments at the Australian National University, the National University of Singapore, Deakin University, the University of Melbourne, George Washington University, and Chulalongkorn University. He has received visiting research fellowships from ANU, El Colegio de Mexico, the Institute of Southeast Asian Studies (ISEAS), Nordic Institute of Asian Studies (Copenhagen), the Ludwig-Maximilians Universität München, the ASEAN University Network, Korea Association of Southeast Asian Studies, and Korea University. For his consulting experience, he has done work for the Friedrich Ebert Foundation (Singapore and Uganda), ISEAS (Singapore), the Institute of Asian Studies (USA), the World Markets Research Centre (London), German Institute of Japanese Studies (Tokyo), and the Vienna Institute for International Economic Studies (Austria). He was a member of the Council of Advisers of the Yuchengco Center based at De La Salle University in the Philippines. He has also been asked as commentator on various economic issues dealing with Southeast Asia and ASEAN by various media including BBC, Reuters, Channelnews Asia, Radio Corporation of Singapore, and Radio Singapore International.

His teaching and research interests focus on (i) the economics of Southeast Asia including growth, development and crisis; economic stabilization policies; money, banking and finance; trade, foreign direct investments and industrialization, migration, and information and communications technology (ICT), (ii) the economic relations of Southeast Asia including intra-ASEAN regional and sub-regional economic integration, extra-ASEAN relations with the European Union, the United States, Japan, China, Korea and Australia, and (iii) regionalism and globalism – economic issues dealing with the WTO, APEC, NAFTA, EU, AFTA and CER.

He has traveled extensively around the world for conferences, public lectures, seminars and workshops. He has published four books such as *The Economies of Southeast Asia: Indonesia, Malaysia, Philippines, Singapore and Thailand* (USA), *Macroeconomic Policy and Its Impact on the Philippine Economy* (USA), *ASEAN External Debt Perspectives* (Singapore), and *National Economic Policy* (Australia). He has also published in refereed journals such as *Asian Survey* (USA), *Harvard Asia Quarterly* (USA), *Journal of Asian Business* (USA), *East Asia: An International Quarterly* (USA), *Cuadernos de Difusion* (Peru), *Asian Economic Journal* (Japan), *ASEAN Economic Bulletin* (Singapore), and *International Journal of Development Banking* (India).

INDEX

A

B

C

D

E

F

G

H

I

J

K

L

M

N

O

P

Q

R

S

T

U

V

W